BLINDED BY THE RIGHT

ALSO BY THE AUTHOR

The Real Anita Hill
The Seduction of Hillary Rodham

BLINDED BY THE RIGHT

THE CONSCIENCE OF AN EX-CONSERVATIVE

DAVID BROCK

Crown Publishers
New York

Published by Crown Publishers, New York, New York.
Member of the Crown Publishing Group, a division of Random House, Inc.
www.randomhouse.com

Crown is a trademark and the Crown colophon is a registered trademark of Random House, Inc.

Printed in the United States of America

Design by Susan Maksuta

Library of Congress Cataloging-in-Publication Data
Brock, David, 1962–
    Blinded by the right: the conscience of an ex-conservative / by David Brock.
    1. Brock, David.   2. Clinton, Bill, 1946—Adversaries.   3. United States—Politics and government—1993–2001.   4. Republican Party (U.S.: 1854–)—Biography.
    5. Journalists—United States—Biography.   6. Conspiracies—United States—History—20th century.   7. Conservatism—United States—History—20th century.   8. Right and left (Political science)—History—20th century.   I. Title.
    E886.2 .B754 2001
    973.929—dc21   2001028853

ISBN 0-8129-3099-1

10 9 8 7 6 5 4 3

First Edition

To the memory of my father, Raymond F. Brock—and for Erin, Kelly, Sean, and Brendan McCracken

ACKNOWLEDGMENTS

I OWE THANKS MANY TIMES OVER to Mark Warren of *Esquire* for conceiving and editing both "Confessions of a Right-Wing Hit Man" and "The Fire This Time: A Letter to the President," two essays on which this book is based.

My agent, Phillippa Brophy, agreed to represent me at a challenging time, and has done so with gusto. The editor who suggested that I write this book, Jonathan Karp of Random House, provided me with crucial early guidance and support. Doug Pepper of Crown took over for Jon at a critical juncture, and did an exemplary edit. I also owe thanks to Camille Smith, the copy chief at Crown, for the care she took with the manuscript.

The folks at *Talk* magazine —especially Tina Brown and Susan Lehman— did me a wonderful favor in serializing this book.

I have many friends to thank, in no particular order, for contributing to this project, in one way or another, whether they realized it or not: Becky Borders, Rusty O'Kelley, Chris Thomson, Joe Conason, Elizabeth Wagley, Barbara Levin, Will Lippincott, Tom Goodwin, Darrin Bodner, Chad Bender, Maer Roshan, Barney Frank and Sergio Pombo, Gretchen Rubin, Stephen Rivers, Sidney Blumenthal, Brian Torres, Aaron Sterling, Michael Dunagan, James Goodwill, Peter Rosenstein, Elizabeth Birch, Christopher McGinness, John Klenert, and Ted Osius.

Neel Lattimore deserves his own sentence. I also owe Lawrence Yanovitch a special debt of gratitude.

Time and again, Ron Haft has gone above and beyond the call of duty as a friend. So, too, has William Grey, without whose love and support I would have never crossed the finish line.

James A. Alefantis makes my life beautiful.

My thanks as well for the love and patience of my family—my mom, Dorothea, my sister, Regina, her husband, Paul McCracken, and their children, Erin, Kelly, Sean, and Brendan.

CONTENTS

PROLOGUE

This is a terrible book. It is about lies told and reputations ruined. It is about what the conservative movement did, and what I did, as we plotted in the shadows, disregarded the law, and abused power to win even greater power.

My story is about those familiar corrupting influences of ambition, greed, and ego. It is about how human weakness, lack of confidence, and emotional discomposure can lead to a susceptibility to manipulation for bad ends. It is also about the dangers of zeal and extremism in a political cause, and about how one can be blinded to the ethics of one's own actions.

I came to Washington in 1986 as a conservative rebel from Berkeley, California, and from that moment through the latter part of the 1990s, as the leading right-wing scandal reporter, I was a witness to, and a participant in, all of the scandals that gripped the capital city—Iran-Contra, the failed nomination of Robert Bork to the Supreme Court, the Thomas-Hill hearings, Troopergate, Paula Jones, Whitewater, and the secret scheming that led to the impeachment of President Clinton. The conservative culture I thrived in was characterized by corrosive partisanship, visceral hatreds, and unfathomable hypocrisy. I worked for leading institutions of the conservative movement—the *Washington Times*, the Heritage Foundation, and the *American Spectator*—where I fought on the wrong side of an ideological and cultural war that divided our country and poisoned our politics.

The process of breaking ranks from a tight-knit political movement has been slow and torturous. The break came not in one decisive moment, but in a series of revelations great and small, about the character and actions of those who were my friends, about my own character and actions, and ultimately about the fanatical cause behind it all. There were times when I was not sure I would live through it to tell this story.

In the 1940s and 1950s, ex-Communist intellectuals created a literary genre documenting their break with Communism. In the 1970s and 1980s, so many liberals became conservatives that a new movement—neoconservatism—was born. Few have traveled in my direction, from conservatism to liberalism, at least publicly. It is the nature of an ideological defection such as mine to be a lone voice, met by denials or silence from my ex-comrades. Only they and I really know what we did and why we did it.

Though I do not know if these wrongs can ever be righted, in this or any other way, I wrote this book as an act of conscience, to correct the public record on events in which I played a central role and to illuminate for others the dangers that I see in an empowered conservative movement. How a man won a Supreme Court seat that I later learned he should never have won, how a lavishly funded campaign of political terrorism and propaganda disabled a presidency—these are events that may seem to perhaps everyone but me as if they happened a lifetime ago. But the wounds on the body politic from this era are still open. In the course of events that I describe in this book, the bad guys often won and justice was not always done. Many of the same forces, and many of the same players, still exert influence—a payback scheme in which old misdeeds are now being rewarded.

Twice as I tried to put this book to press, I was interrupted with official inquiries into the activities of my former associates. Several months ago, Theodore Olson, perhaps the top Republican lawyer in the country and the man who successfully argued the *Bush v. Gore* case for the Bush forces that won Bush the election, was nominated to be solicitor general of the United States. During his Senate confirmation hearing, Olson denied involvement in the *American Spectator*'s Arkansas Project, a $2.4-million dirt-digging operation against the Clintons funded by right-wing billionaire Richard Mellon Scaife. As a four-year veteran of the *Spectator*, I was contacted by the Judiciary committee, and I described what I knew first-hand about Olson's integral role in the project, contradicting his sworn testimony.

While working on *Blinded by the Right* for the past three years, I stayed out of the news and used the time to attempt to find a sense of peace, emotional balance, and personal integrity that had eluded me during my dozen years in the right wing. I had no plan or desire to speak against Olson's nomination; I was simply answering questions. But when I did, failed Supreme Court nominee Robert Bork and former independent counsel Kenneth Starr fanned out in the press to vouch for Olson's character, and the virulent right-wing scandal machine, which my own reporting for the *Spectator* had done much to create back in the early 1990s, went into overdrive to besmirch me. Internet gossip Matt Drudge put up his flashing red sirens and claimed breathlessly that he had obtained a bootlegged copy of this book: "Brock Plans Scorched Earth; Book Outlines Reporter's Rise and Fall in Washington; Threatens Lawsuit Against Drudge." The trouble with Drudge's item was that he didn't have the book.

My last book, a biography of Hillary Rodham Clinton published in 1996, had been widely expected to be as vicious as my first book, my 1993 exposé on Anita Hill, *The Real Anita Hill*. When the Hillary book, *The Seduction of Hillary Rodham*, turned out not to be vicious, the right wing was enraged. Now, prompted by my statements about Olson, Norah Vincent, who had been an editor at the publishing house that brought out *Seduction*, wrote on the *Los Angeles Times* op-ed page, "If the world ended tomorrow and good and evil fought it out for keeps, I imagine that David Brock would be one of the devil's chief recruits." Lucianne Goldberg, the sometime literary agent and chief provocateur of the Monica Lewinsky scandal, called me a "turncoat twinkie" and suggested that the right wing had blackmail photographs of me.

If the senators believed my account, then Olson was seen to have given false and misleading testimony under oath. Despite my own checkered past, forty-seven Democratic senators voted against Olson based primarily on my eyewitness report. He was narrowly confirmed.

Such is the world I live in.

In August 2001, the *Los Angeles Times* called, looking for information on another Bush nominee, Terry Wooten, who had been tapped as a federal district judge. While writing *The Real Anita Hill* in the early 1990s, I searched for the confidential FBI file of Angela Wright, a damaging witness who said she was harassed by Clarence Thomas but never testified, in an effort to smear and discredit her. Wooten, the Republican chief counsel, gave me the file. I gave an interview to the *Times* about Wooten's illegal leaking, and I filed an affidavit with the Judiciary committee swearing to what had happened. When Wooten appeared before the Judiciary committee for his Senate confirmation in August 2001, he flatly denied giving me the FBI file. One of us had committed perjury.

A few weeks later, in late September, I sat across my dining room table from two FBI agents who interviewed me about Wooten and the Wright FBI file. I told them everything I knew about that tawdry episode. The FBI investigation concluded that while I had obtained confidential FBI material, the evidence against Wooten was not definitive, and Wooten was eventually confirmed. Yet regardless of the outcome, I was a witness to these events, and, as in the case of Olson, I believe there is something salutary to be gained simply by speaking and writing about them honestly.

With the security threats to the nation, which were years in the making, now so painfully obvious, a decade's worth of scandal-mongering by the right appears all the more outrageously disgraceful. As the tragedy ushered in a new appreciation of the role of government, the government-hating project of the radical right seemed to suffer a tremendous setback. Yet there was no denying that even in a grave national crisis, some on the hard right did not for a moment suspend their dedication to a zealously intolerant, hate-filled, religious-based ideology.

It was sickening to see conservative commentator Ann Coulter call on America to "invade their countries, kill their leaders, and convert them to Christianity"; or to hear the Reverends Jerry Falwell and Pat Robertson blame the terrorist attacks on people who are pro-choice, gay and lesbian, or members of the American Civil Liberties Union; or to learn that conservative writer Michael Ledeen had pinned the death of Barbara Olson, a conservative pundit who perished, tragically, during the attack on the Pentagon, on the feminist establishment; or to read on the *Wall Street Journal* editorial page an opportunistic recommendation that the Bush administration use the crisis to push through another tax cut and confirm right-wing judges.

The need to shine light on the operations and agenda of the right wing has not abated in the wake of September 11. My intention is that the following political testament, offered in a spirit of both full disclosure and reconciliation, will serve as a cautionary tale of lessons learned the hard way. Even from the depths of depravity and desolation, a conversion of politics, morals, and ultimately of spirit is possible.

Washington, D.C.
November 1, 2001

CHAPTER ONE

THE MAKING OF A CONSERVATIVE

Bobby Kennedy was my first political hero; his legend helped shape my early social conscience. Before heading off to college, I looked forward to serving as an intern at the Robert F. Kennedy Memorial Foundation in Washington, D.C., which was dedicated to continuing RFK's work. The year was 1980, and the country was at an ideological crossroads in the presidential election between Democratic President Jimmy Carter, who had defeated Senator Edward Kennedy in a bitterly contested primary battle, and Carter's conservative challenger, Ronald Reagan, the former governor of California. In Washington, I worked out of a charming old town house with polished pinewood floors for a man named David Hackett, a close friend of Bobby Kennedy's who had worked in the Kennedy Justice Department in the 1960s. A man in his late fifties, with a lean, athletic build and the endearing air of an absentminded professor, Hackett possessed both the brimming idealism of the Kennedy clan and the Kennedy swagger. He zoomed into work each day in a plum-colored Fiat Spider.

Working comfortably with a group of fellow aspiring journalists and liberal public policy advocates from around the country, I was assigned to one of the foundation's projects, the Student Press Service, a youth-run newswire that dispatched reports from the nation's capital on federal policy dealing with young people—financial aid, child welfare, bilingual education, youth employment, national service—to subscribing high school and college newspapers. I had been living in Washington only a few months when I cast my first vote, for Jimmy Carter, who lost his bid for reelection. With the Reagan administration now in power, the mood at the foundation turned grim. Many of the government programs we advocated were in peril;

the Student Press Service reported sympathetically on Democratic efforts to save them. "Budget Plans May Hurt School Desegregation Efforts," read one headline. "Voting Act Extension Causes Controversy," warned another. The cover story for a press service report in late April 1981 was an exposé by me on the Ku Klux Klan Youth Corps—a "segregated Boy Scouts" that was conducting "paramilitary youth camps" throughout the South and West in the early months of the Reagan era. Working the phones and tapping out copy, we were following a liberal political line, which conformed to a view of journalism I had come to in high school, after reading Upton Sinclair's 1906 novel *The Jungle*, a muckraking exposé on the abysmal working conditions in Chicago's meat-packing industry. Journalism was a forum to agitate for social justice.

I took these concerns with me to Berkeley, California, where I enrolled as a freshman in the fall of 1981. I had chosen the University of California at Berkeley specifically because of its long tradition of liberal political activism, beginning with the famed Free Speech Movement of 1964 and culminating in protests against the war in Vietnam in the early 1970s. Yet my first year on the Berkeley campus was not at all what I had anticipated. Rather than a liberal bastion of intellectual tolerance and academic freedom, the campus was—though the phrase hadn't yet been coined—politically correct, sometimes stiflingly so. Many on the faculty, having come of age in the 1960s, adhered to a doctrinaire leftism to which I had never been exposed. Though it is a blunt overgeneralization, the sociology department seemed to me to be filled with socialists, the philosophy department with devotees of Michel Foucault's relativistic deconstructionism. History tended to be taught from the perspective of New Left revisionists, who blamed the Cold War on the United States. In English literature, the Western canon, composed of "dead white European males," was out of fashion.

The politically correct culture was even more ubiquitous in the surrounding left-wing city of Berkeley—some called it Berzerkeley—where many of the sandal-clad 1960s campus activists had settled and were now running fiefdoms like the Rent Control Board. The evils of Reagan's anti-Communist policies in Central America, the campaign to establish a Third World College on campus—these were the subjects of endless rants over lattes at Café Roma. As the arms race with the Soviet Union escalated under Reagan, the nuclear weapons labs run by the university in Livermore and Los Alamos were a rallying point for sometimes-violent student protests. Researchers there were branded "fascists." I decorated my dorm room with postcards portraying the Reagans as victims of a nuclear holocaust, but something felt wrong.

In my sophomore year, as a cub reporter for the *Daily Californian*, the student-run newspaper that was widely read both on the sprawling Berkeley campus and in the city, one of the first assignments that I drew, quite by chance, was to cover a campus speech by Jeane Kirkpatrick, Ronald Reagan's United Nations ambassador and an architect of his hard-line anti-Communist policies in El Salvador and Nicaragua, which countenanced human rights violations throughout the region by our anti-Communist allies. An acerbic, schoolmarmish neoconservative Democrat and former university professor, Kirkpatrick had been invited to deliver the Jefferson Lectures, a distinguished annual series on the history of American political values. As with nearly every campus event in Berkeley, a protest was announced in leaflets that had been stapled onto bulletin boards in the main plaza.

When I arrived at the auditorium at the appointed hour, the expected conga line of sign-holding protesters had not materialized. Berkeley's lecture halls were cavernous, and on this warm day in early fall Dwinelle Hall was filled to capacity. I walked into the hushed room and took a seat up front near the platform. Opening my reporter's notebook, I was set to jot down the details of what I expected to be a rather dry academic address. Kirkpatrick was introduced by the mild-mannered Berkeley law school dean, and she approached the podium with a clutch of papers in a hand that looked more like a bird's claw. No sooner had she begun speaking than several dozen protesters, clad in black sheets with white skeletons painted on them, bolted from their seats, repeatedly shouting, "U.S. Out of El Salvador," and "Forty Thousand Dead," a reference to political assassinations by death squads linked to the U.S.-backed Salvadoran military junta. Kirkpatrick stopped speaking, waiting patiently for the din to die down; but as soon as she uttered another word, the chanting commenced, and it grew louder and louder with each recitation. As an exasperated Kirkpatrick pivoted toward the law school dean for assistance, a protester leaped from his seat just offstage and splashed simulated blood on the podium. After several more attempts to be heard with no help from the hapless dean, Kirkpatrick curled her lip, turned on her heels, and surrendered to the mob.

The scene shook me deeply: Was the harassment of an unpopular speaker the legacy of the Berkeley-campus Free Speech Movement, when students demanded the right to canvass for any and all political causes on the campus's Sproul Plaza? Wasn't free speech a liberal value? How, I wondered, could this thought police call itself liberal? As I raced back to the threadbare offices of the *Daily Cal*, where we tapped out stories on half-sheets of paper hunched over manual typewriters, my adrenaline was pumping. I knew I had the day's lead story. For the rest of the academic year, a controversy raged in the faculty senate and within the board of regents, where several of former Governor Reagan's appointees still sat, over whether the campus administration should have done more to secure Kirkpatrick's ability to speak freely. The few outspoken conservatives on the faculty, and the Reagan regents, raised their voices in support of Kirkpatrick's free speech rights. The liberals seemed to me to be defending censorship.

Later that year, I declared a major in history with an emphasis on European and American diplomacy. Repelled by the Berkeley left, especially in the months following the Kirkpatrick incident, I gravitated toward the few conservatives on the faculty who had taken up the cudgels against the anti-Kirkpatrick protesters. Through my studies, including seminars with Walter McDougall, a young, mustachioed foreign policy hawk and occasional contributor to conservative intellectual William F. Buckley's *National Review*, I formed some early ideas about the need for vigilant American defense policies, and under his tutelage I developed a strong anti-Communist viewpoint.

Outside the classroom, my political education consisted of devouring copies of Norman Podhoretz's *Commentary*, the leading monthly magazine of the ex-liberals known as neoconservatives. I stumbled upon an issue of *Commentary* on a library reading rack and charged off into the stacks of Moffitt Library, where I read back issues for days. Like Podhoretz's famous piece "The Present Danger," *Commentary* specialized in alarming essays on the Soviet threat, some of them by Kirkpatrick herself. The intellectual vigor and fiery polemics appealed to me more than the foppish, Anglophilic bent of *National Review* or the *American Spectator*, the other leading conservative magazines of the day. *Commentary* seemed to speak to everything I was learning in class at that young age—the need for a strong military was so plain, if you studied history—and also to everything that troubled me about Berkeley's political extremism. I couldn't get enough.

I loved writing for the *Daily Cal*, and I thrived there as a reporter, fitting in easily with the brainy newspaper crowd. In my junior year, I was elected by the staff to a top-level news-editing post. I won election because I had worked hard breaking stories, including a series of investigative articles proving that a university vice president had misappropriated university resources to benefit a private company he ran on the side. The articles forced his resignation. I was a respected reporter on the staff, and as an aspiring young journalist exposing corruption, I was gratified to win my first scalp.

With my new post came a seat on the paper's editorial board and the opportunity to write signed op-ed columns. For some weeks, the editorial page editor had been after me to contribute a column for the paper's international opinion page. The October 1983 U.S. invasion of Grenada, where American forces overthrew a Marxist-leaning regime, seemed like an obvious chance to hone my polemical skills. Inspired by a McDougall seminar on "just war" theory, and a bracing op-ed in the *New York Times* by right-wing columnist William Safire, I sat in Café Roma and scribbled out in longhand a ringing endorsement of the "liberation" of Grenada from the Soviet sphere of influence that steamrolled over legitimate arguments against the invasion. To me, the column was an academic exercise; I hadn't realized that it would be received in Berkeley as a political thunderclap. While I wasn't knowingly playing the part of provocateur, when the column was published on a Monday morning, all hell broke loose.

By the early 1980s, most of the thirty-thousand-plus Berkeley student body had no interest in carrying on the scruffy activist traditions of the 1960s. They were tall and blond and from places like Orange County and had keg parties at their frats. Or they were the studious children of immigrants, devoted to their engineering books. While most students seemed unconcerned with events in Grenada, the military operation was deeply unpopular with Berkeley's small but very vocal population of activists, who saw it as an example of rapacious American imperialism and had taken to the streets with flag-burning protests. My column stoked the flames of the local fires, and I rather unintentionally became the focus for the protesters' rage.

The main opposition to my column came from some lefty faculty members, like Charlie Schultze, the award-winning chemist who was always protesting at the Livermore weapons lab, and the city of Berkeley's political establishment—Mayor Gus Newport, an avowed socialist, and liberal Democratic Congressman Ron Dellums, whose staff had close relations with Maurice Bishop's ousted Grenadan regime. There was opposition, too, within the *Daily Cal*, an off-campus cooperative run independently of the university, led by the general manager, Marty Rabkin, one of those '60s types who had come to Berkeley and never left. "How *could* you?" an indignant Marty said to me in his office as we watched the desecration of the American flag in the streets below.

How could *I?* I wasn't the one burning the flag. Though critics, including Rabkin, were outraged by what they saw as the grave injustices of U.S. foreign policy in Grenada, I didn't see their point of view, just as I had been unable to credit the position of the anti-Kirkpatrick demonstrators, who believed that her policies condoned murder. All I understood was that I was being targeted in a campaign by the left to recall me from my post as editor for speaking my mind. I remember rushing by, feeling vulnerable and turning my face away in embarrassment, as huge rolls of brown paper petitions against me were unfurled on Sproul Plaza.

To me, liberals were flatly and unapologetically advocating censorship of opinions they considered illegitimate and immoral, a rerun of the Kirkpatrick incident. The argument went: An editor at a newspaper with a 150-year progressive tradition should not be allowed to publish such obscene views. I was branded a warmonger, a fascist, and worse. I was determined to stand my ground and fight, all the more so because, as I saw it, the fight was not about Grenada, but about the First Amendment. Viewing it this way, as a moral rather than an ideological struggle, I became as self-righteous and rigid as my critics, who in my eyes were not just wrong but un-American.

I survived the threatened recall only on a technicality. The bylaws governing the cooperative had no provision for removing editors, and they could be amended only at the end of the academic year when new editors were elected. Continuing on as editor, I accepted and even embraced the controversy I incited, willfully doing everything I could to enhance my outsider status. I baited my liberal adversaries, publishing a diatribe against a board of regents proposal to strengthen affirmative action programs. Meanwhile, every editorial decision I made was seen by many on the staff as motivated by an evil right-wing plot. Being an outspoken conservative in Berkeley got me noticed, which I relished. I imagined myself as David against the liberal Goliath.

By the end of my junior year, I had become both a hated—and, I'm sorry to say, something of a hateful—figure in the newsroom. I demonized my enemies on the staff, led by a bubbly blond from Pasadena and a brooding Hispanic fellow, both of whom I openly and wrongly scorned as witless affirmative action hires. I was also caught in an embarrassing lie. A small cadre of loyalists had stuck by me through the Grenada controversy. As a way of building up my power base, when a problem arose in a story one of them had written after it was published, I sought to tarnish the reputation of one of my foes, who had edited the piece. I told the editor in chief that the vice chancellor had called to complain about the story. She immediately called the university official and found out the truth: He hadn't called. When the editor confronted me about the lie, I froze, speechless, and walked away. Soon enough, everyone in the newsroom knew I had lied. Though my poor cadre knew about my lie and voted for me anyway, I lost overwhelmingly in my campaign to be elected editor in chief. For good measure, the bylaws were amended to provide for the removal of editors on a majority vote of the staff: the Brock Amendment.

Though my discomfort with the extremist elements in Berkeley was understandable and in some ways valid, it was distorted by an emotional overreaction to the Grenada controversy. Like most political arguments in college, the episode had a distinctly personal edge. Rather than settling in some reasonable middle ground between left and right, my feelings of persecution caused me to swing to the right. To hold myself together during the campaign to recall me, I dug in my heels, assumed a warlike posture, and closed my mind and my heart to all things left and liberal for good. Moreover, I now viewed politics as a knife fight, my critics as blood enemies. My still-nascent ideological commitments acquired a vengeful overlay: *I'll get them.*

At the same time, I was able to find comfort—a sense of belonging and a measure of stature—in the sectarian right-wing Berkeley campus underground that rose up to defend and embrace me. In addition to historian Walter McDougall, there was the witty political scientist Paul Seabury, whose lectures were sometimes protested because he was a member of Reagan's Foreign Intelligence Advisory Board. The bald, bespectacled Seabury was a smoker, and after class I would sit with him as he indulged himself and told me of his political journey from left to right, in reaction to the radical anti-Americanism and what he called "the fascistic style" of the 1960s left. I also became a research assistant to Aaron Wildavsky, a renowned neoconservative social theorist, on his book *The Beleaguered Presidency*, in which he argued that the Democrats were becoming "a party that delegitimized the nation's second-largest constituency—white, working, Christian males." I romanticized these faculty conservatives as stalwart defenders of constitutional protections, civility, and tolerance, never once wondering if they might have jumped into the fray to defend Jeane Kirkpatrick and me for ideological reasons. With McDougall, Seabury, and Wildavsky taking me under their wings, happy to have a bright new recruit with a sharp pen in the cause, I settled comfortably into conservatism.

I fell easily under the spell of my surrogate father figures, as though anyone who gave me attention could dictate my beliefs. From them I found the moral and ideological clarity, the critical affirmation and acceptance, and the firm sense of who I was that my fragile psyche yearned for. I slapped the label of the entire conservative movement on my lapel, gave it authority over my being, without even understanding what it meant. Stumbling into a fight over Grenada at the age of twenty, I came out of it playing the role of right-wing ideologue—right-wing robot, really—to the hilt. I jumped on a conservative trajectory that would cause me to live my life along a certain but wrong course for the next fifteen years.

My earliest political memory is of the 1976 presidential campaign. My father, Raymond, a conservative Irish Catholic in the mold of Patrick Buchanan who hadn't voted for a Democrat since JFK, had been an early supporter of Ronald Reagan; he switched to President Gerald Ford when Ford captured the GOP nomination. My mother, Dorothea, a stay-at-home mom caring for my younger sister, Regina, and me, had been born in Connecticut to a family of staunch New Deal Democrats. She was a swing voter and, about Ford, was on the fence.

Me, at age fourteen, I was enamored of Democratic nominee Jimmy Carter, touched by the moral convictions and humanity that seemed to anchor his politics. I taped Carter's campaign commercials off a huge console television set in our living room on my white plastic cassette recorder and played them over and over again in my room:

He-talks-about-the-government,
and-how-good-it-could-be,
for-you-and-me.

What cinched my support for Jimmy Carter was his post-Watergate promise to never tell a lie to the American people. Even then, I loved the game of politics. My playful scheme was to lobby for the vote of my mother, bringing her back into the Democratic fold after her 1972 vote for Nixon and canceling out my father's ballot. My father woke me gently early in the morning after election night, before I had to catch the bus to school, to tell me the news: My guy won. I remember the warmth of the moment well. Talking politics helped me relate to my otherwise remote dad; it was the only way I felt I could attract his attention and evoke his affection.

My father looked like the 1970s talk show host Mike Douglas, and he had the same genial, unassuming manner when dealing with the outside world. He was a good man in every sense, a devoted husband and zealous churchgoer who worked hard to provide ample material support for our family. Sadly, more often than not, that was all he seemed able to provide. At home, he was one of those not altogether atypical dads of his generation who seemed emotionally dead. After a long day at the office, he spent the evening closed off in a small den in front of a TV. We spent so little time together, just the two of us, that I still remember my father treating me to a Flintstones movie one Saturday afternoon, and the time he took me into his office, where I traced maps with colored marking pens, as if they were yesterday.

Born and raised in a lower-middle-class neighborhood in Jersey City, New Jersey, the first member of his family to attend college, now a pipe-smoking marketing executive settled in the comfortable New Jersey suburbs, Ray Brock had been part of an early migration of northeastern Democratic ethnics into the Republican Party of Richard Nixon. His politics, his cultural outlook, even his religious beliefs, were fervently right-wing: anti-Communist, pro-life, anti-busing, pro–death penalty. Dad had even gone a big step further to the right than Patrick Buchanan, seceding from the Catholic Church in protest of the liberal reforms of the 1960s. He joined a rump sect forty miles from home that continued to celebrate Sunday Mass in Latin under the auspices of an excommunicated French archbishop, Marcel Lefebvre. Dad was a winger through and through.

Far less politically minded than Dad, Mom had worked in the chambers of a respected judge before marriage. She put her career on hold until Regina and I were well into our teens, serving instead as a dedicated and attentive homemaker. From an age before I could speak English, my mom, an Italian American opera buff who looked like she could have been the somewhat more imposing sister of the actress Olympia Dukakis, sat me in a baby's chair on a beautifully polished maple wood dining table and taught me Italian. Eschewing baby-sitters, even close relatives, every Saturday night she dressed us up and took us along on her weekly dinner date with my father at a fancy neighborhood restaurant, where Dad had a few Manhattans, Mom had one whiskey sour, and my sister and I ordered ginger ale cocktails decorated with maraschino cherries.

An articulate, well-read woman, possessed of a mordant wit, my mother coached me to excel academically, encouraged me to write, and instilled in me a yen for worldly success, in what may have been at least partly an expression of her own unfulfilled ambitions. Like Dad, Mom was undemonstrative and emotionally closed off, though she showed her caring in other ways. As if she were the curator of a valuable archive, she preserved and filed every piece of writing I produced from the very earliest age, including a kindergarten essay called "Archie the Ant" and an elementary school autobiography titled "All About David." The autobiography was preoccupied with elaborate descriptions of seemingly every one of the innumerable Christmas and birthday gifts I had ever received, and it was illustrated with photos of my smiling parents—my father's smile was natural, my mother's was a bit forced—and of my sweet little sister playing in the yard with our snow-white toy poodle, Pierre. I concluded by predicting that I would grow up to become a "lawyer as a way of going into politics." The story seemed to be that of a relatively content, earnest, if somewhat self-possessed, kid.

Of course, there was more to the story than that. Because of her upbringing in a hypercritical household, my mother was tightly wound, sometimes unsure, and a little too concerned with outward appearances, traits that I soon took on myself. For instance, I remember walking to my Catholic elementary school, Our Lady of the Assumption, in Wood-Ridge, New Jersey, a suburb just outside New York City, each morning with a neighbor, Lynn, who lived up the street a few houses away. In what became an anxious ritual, on cloudy days when it looked like a chance of rain, my mother instructed me to stand in the vestibule of our home and wait and see if Lynn had her umbrella. If Lynn had it, I was conditioned to grab mine; if she didn't, I knew to leave it at home. My mother was unable to make the simple decision herself or to allow me to make up my own mind. I was taught to defer to what others did and to tailor my behavior accordingly.

My mother was also stressed about the fact that my sister and I were adopted. After my parents had tried and failed for a few years to conceive naturally, they chose to adopt me as a baby, and Regina followed two years later. Thirty years ago, adopting children carried a stigma; adoptive parents often were seen as inadequate, and adoptive children were considered "second best." Though we were told that we were adopted as soon as we were old enough to comprehend it, Mom insisted that Regina and I hide this fact from anyone outside the family. With my strong jaw and jet black hair and eyes, I was constantly told by my mother how much I looked like her.

Regina, a petite, hazel-eyed girl with fine features and dirty-blond hair, was coached to say she looked like Dad. As part of the deception that we were our parents' natural children, my sister and I told all of our friends that we were half Italian and half Irish. One day, Regina came home from a ballet lesson and told my mother that she had made an innocent slip and revealed to her ballet instructor that she was adopted. Panicked that the whole ballet class would find out, Mom redoubled her efforts to hush us up. Living with the secrecy and lies, I acquired an unusual ability to block out and avoid the truth and to live my life with no inner questioning. So ingrained was the lesson that I never told even my closest friends about my adoption until my father passed away when I was thirty-seven years old.

Adding to the sense of secrecy and shame surrounding my adoptive status was the typical confusion of the adopted child about his or her identity. In my case, the mystery was deepened by comments I overheard at a very young age made by my mother's sometimes bellicose Italian American relatives to the effect that I was Jewish. I took the comments literally and believed well into my adulthood that I was likely of Jewish ancestry. Many years later, when I finally got up the nerve to ask her about it after my father died, my mom told me that teasing me about being Jewish was her family's shorthand way of explaining the fact that I was a well-mannered, precocious child, especially in contrast to my boisterous, fun-loving Italian American cousins. I was such a "stick-in-the-mud," another description frequently applied to me by these same relatives, that I refused to eat my own birthday cake, preferring instead to munch on a bag of pretzels.

Not that I minded thinking I was Jewish, for this allowed me to indulge the fantasy I had of being an aberration in my own family. I'm not sure which came first, the sense of not belonging, or of not wanting to belong, but in any event, I spent a lot more time fantasizing about the grand life I might have had than being present in the ordinary one I did have. Even into my early twenties, I made up stories to myself, and occasionally to others, about where I might have come from.

Besides my adoption, I had another fact to hide, another reason to fear and avoid self-evaluation. At the age of eleven, I became powerfully aroused during a game of touch football with the neighborhood boys at a nearby park. When I got home, thinking about one of the players, I had my first orgasm. I didn't know the terms "homosexual" or "gay," but from that moment on, I knew I was sexually interested in men. I was a wispy adolescent, overly concerned with my costume—my father and I had a bitter exchange when I insisted he buy me a very expensive three-piece, glen check Pierre Cardin suit for my eighth-grade graduation—and when I arrived at my all-male high school, Paramus Catholic High School in Paramus, New Jersey, I was singled out and ridiculed for being different. My best friend's name was Brett, and soon enough we were hazed as "Brett and Brock." As I came to understand what homosexuality was, I feared that both of my parents, especially my religiously devout father, would reject me all the more if they knew this truth. I concealed what was at that age the most important thing I knew for sure about myself.

It's little wonder that no matter how quiescent I may have seemed to others, I was an overstressed child. Beginning when I was five or six and continuing through my teenage years, I suffered from periodic bouts of eczema, an inflammatory skin condition that often results from anxiety. When it flared up severely, the eczema covered my fingers and toes with red, wildly itchy, oozing lesions. When the lesions became hard and scaly, my digits became so encrusted I could barely move them.

In 1977, in the middle of my sophomore year in high school, our family moved from the East Coast to a newly developed suburb, filled with huge, cookie-cutter tract homes, near Dallas, Texas, where Dad's company had relocated. I was enrolled in one of those newfangled public high schools, Newman Smith High School in Carrollton, where the oddly angled walls are carpeted in bright colors and the air is rank because the windows are sealed shut. Having studied in small, traditional northeastern Catholic schools all my life—where I achieved a certain status by flourishing academically and, though I was somewhat withdrawn and uncertain, always had a few close pals and a strong rapport with my instructors—I went into culture shock in a land of pickup trucks and burritos. Unaccustomed to the Texas twang, I could barely make out my teachers' lessons, much less relate to my fellow

classmates. Suddenly, I was flunking out of algebra, and I didn't have a friend
in the world. With my small, thin frame and dark coloring, even my appearance set me apart from my peers, who looked to me like gangly albinos. I
wasn't about to trade my three-piece suit for cowboy boots. I wanted out.

Around this time, my relations with my father took a hostile turn. As I
grew older, my father's unavailability, emotional and otherwise, had begun
to feel punitive, all the more so as I pinned the blame for the painful move
to Texas on him. Dad won a promotion in the move to Texas, but I failed to
see why he couldn't have landed a job that was equally good or better in
New York. The older I got, the more his limitations caused me to disrespect
him, while at the same time the more irritated he became with a son who
at age fifteen could already outargue him. Keeping her head down in the
verbal cross fire, and unhappy in Texas herself, my mom was suddenly
unavailable for the first time ever, retreating behind closed doors with terrible migraine headaches. Rather than try to conform or to please others to
meld with my surroundings, I oscillated to the other extreme, adopting a
combative frame of mind and rebelling against both my dad and my strange
new home state any way I could.

In an outburst of contrarianism, I poured my energies into editing the
moribund student newspaper, the *Odyssey*, which I fashioned into a crusading liberal weekly in the heart of the Reaganite Sunbelt. The paper took
top awards in statewide competition, but it made me—or rather, I made
myself—a pariah at school as I campaigned against a "bloated" school ath-
letics budget in a state where Friday night football was sacrosanct, and
attacked the "do-nothing" student government. The style of argument was
one that I had learned in debating politics with my father—rigidly uncompromising, and dogmatically black and white. The frustration and rage I felt
toward my father and toward Texas came pouring out on the page.

Sex was another emotional outlet. Shortly after moving to Texas, I had
begun to date girls—to experiment sexually, follow social convention, and
perhaps to ease the psychic discomfort of being gay in a school that seemed
much more alien to me—in other words, much more straight—than did my
all-male New Jersey high school. I couldn't find another Brett to bond with.
I was quite sexually active with one Texas classmate, who was mature for

her age and a transplant to Texas. A year or so later, I found my second sexual partner. At a state journalism conference in Austin, where we had gone to pick up our newspaper award, I began a torrid affair with my sophisticated raven-haired journalism teacher, a woman in her late twenties who was a bit of a fish out of water in the school herself. The affair began late one night in her parked blue Buick, during a talk in which I tearfully expressed feelings of emotional abandonment and loneliness. She loved me, she said, words I don't remember having ever heard before. I was rather easily seduced. The relationship lasted for several months until school let out, and I boarded a plane for my Washington internship.

Before departing, I delivered a vigorous, thumb-in-your-eye valedictory speech as editor of the high school paper. I outlined "stories to be covered and causes to fight for," including two then-popular liberal causes, the Equal Rights Amendment for women and opposition to a local nuclear power plant. I concluded by exhorting my colleagues on the paper, "It is the duty of the student journalist to look beyond the status quo and to actively pursue progressive ideas . . . as journalists we must be advocates." On graduation night, my family's house was egged by fellow students, whom I had upset with my journalistic crusading. The attack scared the hell out of my two visiting grandmothers, asleep in the front bedrooms of the house, and it reinforced my hostility to Texas and everything it represented.

I chose Berkeley partly because it was a bitter pill for my father to swallow and was as far away from Dallas as I could imagine. My experiences there in the early 1980s were not as solitary as they seemed. Budding young conservatives throughout the country, particularly on elite liberal campuses, were an embattled, despised minority—often deservedly so. Though as a broader political force the left was teetering on the brink of irrelevance, on college campuses the left was the establishment. We were the radicals, the counter-counterculture, the ones battling university administrations, questioning authority, rejecting orthodoxies, writing crusading editorials, staging protests. We even had an upstart group, Accuracy in Academia, targeting for intimidation left-wing professors in classrooms across the country. Ben Hart, whom I would soon meet in Washington, wrote a book called *Poison Ivy* about this conservative student revolt at Dartmouth. He might as well have been writing about Harvard, Yale, or Berkeley. Something about the sanctimony of the PC campus of the mid-1980s gave conservatives in my generation a focus as we passed through the typical youthful phases of rebelliousness, anger, and confusion about identity.

We were the ones voting for Ronald Reagan in droves. In 1984, I pulled the lever for Reagan. His strongest voting group that year was among people like me, eighteen to twenty-four years old. In the early '80s, the national Young Republicans organization ballooned to more than half a million members. Being for Reagan, a reviled figure in university circles, and perhaps no place more reviled than at Berkeley, was a way of standing out. But there was more behind this realignment among the young than that; there was self-interest and fear. We were the generation caught between the baby boomers of the '60s and the generation-Xers of the '90s. Unlike the boomers, who grew up in a time of U.S. leadership abroad and prosperity at home, we faced the limits of American power in the 1970s. America had lost the war in Vietnam and was being challenged to a nuclear arms race by an emboldened Soviet Union. There were gas lines, stagflation, and Americans held hostage in Iran. We were the first generation of young white males to feel that the significant advances being made by women and racial and ethnic minorities threatened our own futures.

We knew what we were against more than what we were for. We were against the discredited Democratic Party, the party of appeasement and redistributing the money of hardworking taxpayers. We were against all the isms: Communism, feminism, multiculturalism. Reagan's optimistic rhetoric—peace through strength, morning in America—was music to our ears. So were his jokes, like the open-mike one about bombing the Russians in five minutes.

Most all of us were involved in alternative campus publications—in the '80s, "alternative" meant conservative—funded by a right-wing outfit in Washington called the Institute for Educational Affairs. The foundation was chartered in 1978 by former Nixon and Ford treasury secretary William Simon and Irving Kristol, the ex-Trotskyite intellectual known as the godfather of neoconservatism, in a bid to recruit and program cadres of young people and send them forth into ideological battle. While it appeared to us as if the left was an all-powerful force, the truth is that in terms of movement building, the left didn't have the money, the discipline, or the single-mindedness of the right. The right-wing reviews constituted a powerful network of like-minded youth. At the University of Chicago, two young conservatives with whom I would later work closely in Washington, John Podhoretz (son of Norman) and Tod Lindberg, John's roommate, founded *Counterpoint*, a conservative literary journal. At Dartmouth, future friends Ben Hart, Dinesh D'Souza, and Laura Ingraham took a more confrontational course, consciously aping the outrageous rhetoric and radical tactics of the '60s, in publishing the infamous *Dartmouth Review*. *Review* staffers took sledgehammers to a symbolic shantytown constructed to protest South African apartheid. They published a column written by a fictitious African American Dartmouth student under the headline "Dis Sho' Ain't No Jive, Bro." And they infiltrated a meeting of the campus gay and lesbian association and outed its members.

At Berkeley, I had no cause to associate conservatism with prejudice against gays. In the early '80s, gay issues weren't polarizing our campus. The avid sexual escapades of my high school days in Texas notwithstanding, since arriving in Berkeley I no longer put aside my deeper desires. With some hesitation, during my freshman year, I went on uneasy dates and had hurried sexual encounters with other guys in neighboring dorms. By the end of the year, I considered myself gay and had surprisingly little trouble accepting that reality, perhaps because I had gotten used to the idea of being different in Texas; yet I had no idea of how to live as an openly gay young man.

During my freshman summer, before I fell in with the Berkeley campus conservatives, I naturally gravitated to work for the Ralph Nader group on campus, the California Public Interest Research Group, doing fund-raising for a statewide recycling initiative. On the job, I met Andrew,* a blond, blue-eyed dreamboat of the Brad Pitt variety, a Boston native who had transferred to Berkeley from the University of Massachusetts at Amherst. One of the

---

*Andrew is a pseudonym for privacy's sake.

first times I laid eyes on Andrew, he came tumbling out of the back of a beat-up van, driven by lesbian friends of his from nearby Monterey, toking on a joint, barefoot, and wearing nothing but farmer's jeans. Andrew was openly gay and more sexually experienced than I was. He had already had one live-in boyfriend for a year in Boston. We became close friends instantly, and through Andrew I learned all about the gay world—and how to be honest about who I was. After we had known each other for about ten months, Andrew moved into my off-campus studio apartment, and we began to live as boyfriends. I was in love. In our junior year, we moved to a flat in San Francisco's Haight-Ashbury district, happily commuting to school each morning in our VW Bug. By the time I was elected editor, I was openly gay at the *Daily Cal*, and it didn't seem to faze anyone.

I got a stiffer reaction when I came out to my parents during my freshman summer when they visited Berkeley from Texas. After a few days in California, my mother sensed something, as mothers do, and asked at dinner one night if I was gay. When I said I was, Mom excused herself from the table for a few minutes. Dad's reaction could have been far worse than it was: He just stared off into the distance, glowering, and never said a word to me about it, then or ever. Eventually, my mother was much more supportive and came to accept the situation so long as I didn't tell the rest of the family about it; so far as I knew, my father never did accept it and the revelation drove us even further apart. In our continuing political debates, even as I moved to the right, it seemed now that he was trying to incite and punish me more than the other way around. Still, at the time, so long as I was out from under their roof and comfortable being gay, I told myself their opprobrium didn't matter.

As an openly gay student at Berkeley, I *was* warned about the right-wing company I was keeping. One of the University of California's regents was an openly gay man named Sheldon Andelson, a prominent Los Angeles banker and Democratic activist who had been appointed to the board by Governor Jerry Brown. After one regents meeting that I covered for the *Daily Cal*, Andelson invited me back to his fancy suite at San Francisco's Clift Hotel for a chat. He had noticed that I seemed to have a special rapport with the conservative regents. Stripping down to his boxer shorts and climbing into an enormous bed for a power nap, Andelson lightly cross-examined me. "What are you doing with these Reagan people?" Shelly asked me in his teasing way. "Don't you know they hate people like us?" In my experience, his admonition just didn't register. Shelly was from another generation; he didn't understand.

After my tumultuous year as an editor at the *Daily Cal*, in the summer of 1984 I was approached about editing the *Berkeley Review*, an even cruder version of its sister publication at Dartmouth. Though I was a strong anti-Communist and was convinced that conservatives, in contrast to the politically correct left, stood for my core values of individual liberty and intellectual freedom, I was by no means a racist, homophobic *Berkeley*—or *Dartmouth*—*Review* conservative. On social issues like abortion, in fact, I remained as liberal as I had been when I first arrived in Berkeley. And as a young, openly gay man living in San Francisco, I was no cultural conservative. Though the overture was tempting, the *Review* just didn't seem a good fit for me. I was strong enough to make these critical distinctions, and comfortable enough in my own skin to reject the post and make a fresh start. Feeling responsible for some *Daily Cal* colleagues who were blackballed at the paper because of their affiliation with me, I helped found another outlet, a dignified, neoconservative weekly magazine we called the *Berkeley Journal*. We raised money from conservative alumni by convincing them that the campus needed a voice more in tune with the mainstream politics of '80s students.

I also wrote my first piece for a national publication, which I submitted to *Policy Review*, the theoretical organ of the right-wing Heritage Foundation in Washington. I had a relationship with the magazine through an interview I had done with the editor of *Policy Review*, Adam Meyerson, for a summer internship there. A painfully awkward man in his early thirties, the kind of fellow who may have been too damn brilliant to connect comfortably with others, Meyerson, a former editor at the conservative *Wall Street Journal* editorial page and at the *American Spectator*, was known as an influential shadow mentor to young conservatives such as Dinesh D'Souza. My article, "The Big Chill: A Report Card on Campus Censorship," was a survey of incidents on other campuses where conservative speakers like Henry Kissinger and Caspar Weinberger had been shouted down by left-wing protesters. The *Policy*

Review article led to a lead op-ed column, "Combating Those Campus Marxists," on the editorial page of the *Wall Street Journal,* then and still now the most prized venue for a young conservative writer on the make.

As graduation approached, I knew I wanted to write and to advocate, and I loved politics. Though I graduated with a solid record, I skipped out of much of my academic career to file stories at the *Daily Cal,* and I figured journalism was one way to be involved in public affairs with no more schooling. Like most journalists, I was turned on by seeing my byline in print. Yet given the bitterness surrounding my time at the *Daily Cal,* I had no desire to work anywhere but in the conservative press. With my politics, what would be the point of struggling in a job in the mainstream media? I had turned down the *Policy Review* internship in favor of one in the news department of the *Journal* in New York. Because the *Journal's* editorial page was staunchly conservative, I felt the newspaper as a whole would be hospitable to conservative views. The stint in New York had gone well, and the paper normally hired its successful interns. But as I was leaving college, I ran up against a *Journal* hiring freeze. That was the only gig in mainstream journalism I would have considered.

At twenty-two, I was eager to join the conservative outriders, to further a cause that was, along with my nascent relationship with Andrew, the defining aspect of my life. Conservatism provided me with everything—a way of making sense of the world, of fitting in to it, even a self-image that I would not question for years to come. With the *Journal* option foreclosed, I considered working on a conservative editorial page, maybe in San Diego or Detroit or even in Dallas. But the *Journal* piece caught the eye of John Podhoretz, who had recently been hired by the conservative *Washington Times* to create a national newsmagazine for the publishing conglomerate owned by the Reverend Sun Myung Moon. Working as a writer in Washington for Norman Podhoretz's son seemed like the ideal job. John called me in California, flew me in for an interview, and, after talking things over with Andrew, who had no particular career plans and agreed to come with me, I was soon happily packing my bags for D.C.

CHAPTER TWO

THE THIRD GENERATION

As I arrived in Washington in 1986, the conservative era ushered in by Ronald Reagan's election was fading fast. On the issue that overshadowed everything else—American aid to the guerrillas in Nicaragua who were trying to overthrow the Marxist-Leninist Sandinista regime there—the Reaganites were in a defensive crouch. Not since Vietnam had the left been so galvanized over an issue of foreign policy. Each year, it had gotten harder for the White House to round up the votes needed to pass a military aid package through the Democrat-controlled House. Washington was a town divided. The old principle that politics stopped at the water's edge was dead and buried; so was the tradition of respecting one's political opponents. The battle lines were clear: Reagan's illegal war! Communist sympathizers!

This is the cauldron I stepped into when, at age twenty-three, I entered the grand marble and brass lobby of the *Washington Times* building, a renovated warehouse on the outskirts of town, to report for work. When the Time Inc.–owned *Washington Star* went out of business in 1981, shortly after Reagan's election, Reverend Moon and his disciples saw an opportunity to gain influence in the capital by founding a newspaper. The first issue of the *Times* rolled off the presses in 1982, and though its circulation of one hundred thousand was dwarfed by the *Washington Post*'s eight hundred thousand, the fiercely anti-Communist paper soon emerged as a key ally of the Reagan administration—Reagan said it was his favorite paper—and a powerful voice in the conservative movement.

Yes, that's what we called it. The conservative movement. Or usually just "the movement." When I moved to D.C., I hadn't known I was signing up for a movement, a well-financed, tightly run political machine intensely devoted to enacting a rigid ideological orthodoxy in the political realm. I knew nothing of the movement's history: its roots in GOP Senator Joseph McCarthy's anti-Communist witch-hunts of the 1950s; its takeover of the Republican Party in Senator Barry Goldwater's losing bid for the presidency in 1964; its exploitation of racial fears and cultural divisions in Richard Nixon's victories; and the installation of one of its own into the presidency, Ronald Reagan, by fusing its secular anti-Communist, antiliberal wing with a burgeoning fundamentalist religious wing. Had I been drawn to liberalism, rather than conservatism, I would have found no self-identified, hardwired "liberal movement" in the 1980s; indeed, the right would prove to be far more rigidly doctrinaire than the PC crowd that had so offended me in Berkeley. Yet having been embraced by the conservative campus under-ground at Berkeley, I settled in among these clannish political renegades without reservation.

The dominant figure at the *Times* was the editor in chief, Arnaud de Borchgrave, *Newsweek*'s former chief foreign correspondent. Arnaud had had an illustrious career as a globe-trotting reporter, but at least in his telling, by the late '70s his hard-line anti-Soviet views put him at odds with the powers that be at *Newsweek*. He left the magazine, which is owned by the Washington Post Company, in 1980, a refugee from what he called the "DMC," the dominant media culture. With Robert Moss, Arnaud wrote a novel, *The Spike*, about a journalist who exposes KGB infiltration of the American media. Now running the *Times*, Arnaud had a chance to even the score with the Posties.

The son of a Belgian count, and the husband of a much younger, porcelain-skinned wife, Alexandra, an accomplished photographer and the great-granddaughter of the esteemed book publisher Henry Villard, Arnaud was culturally about as far as one could get from Bible Belt fundamental-ism. A short, trim, impeccably tailored man in gold-rimmed aviator glasses, he exuded the sophistication and personal vanity of a European aristocrat. He name-dropped incessantly, chain-smoked Winstons, drank wine at lunch, and could occasionally be glimpsed doing early morning push-ups in his underwear in his office, or sunning himself with a foil reflector in the arbore-tum adjacent to the *Times* building, maintaining a perennial orange glow.

The first thing I remember Arnaud saying to me, in his staccato voice, was a compliment about a pale-blue spread-collar shirt I had bought with my mother's credit card at Neiman Marcus before moving to D.C.: "Young man, who is your shirtmaker?"

Arnaud was the least of the eccentrics at the *Times*. There was the paper's president, Bo Hi Pak, a member of Moon's Unification Church and a former Korean army colonel who also headed a secretive Moon-funded anti-Communist lobby called Causa International that financed right-wing paramilitary groups around the globe. Pak described his challenge this way: "It is a total war, basically war of ideas, war of minds. The battlefield is the human mind. That's where the battle is fought. So in this war, the entire thing will be mobilized—political means, social means, economic means and propagandistic means—trying to take over the other person's mind. That is what the Third World War is all about." There was the shadowy *Times* publisher, Dr. Ronald Godwin, Dr. God-ball to us, formerly the Reverend Jerry Falwell's right-hand man at the Moral Majority, the Christian Right organization. And there was Arnaud's No. 2, Wesley Pruden, a taciturn Arkansan whose father was a chaplain to the White Citizens Council of Arkansas, an adjunct to the Ku Klux Klan.

Then there was Moon himself—the Rev, we called him—the head of the South Korea–based Unification Church, who claimed to be the second coming of Christ, the true Messiah, dedicated to uniting the world—both Eastern and Western civilizations—under a single theocratic leader, himself. Moon was seen as an ally of American conservatives in that he saw the defeat of godless Communism, especially in North Korea, as a necessary step in achieving his dream of marrying politics to religion. Moon, who sought to control several worldwide media outlets as a vehicle for advancing his cause, surfaced occasionally, usually on weekends when the newsroom was quiet. He delivered violent, table-pounding anti-Communist exhortations to top management and the several dozen church members placed in strategic positions at the *Times*.

The alliance between the conservative Christians and the neoconservative Jews who helped run his publishing empire in Washington was hard to fathom except in coldly utilitarian terms on all sides. Moon founded his church in 1954 in Korea—which he believes is God's chosen nation. He teaches that Christian churches further Satan's power and has said that God punished Israel and the Jews in the Holocaust for rejecting Jesus.

Moon was the head of a religious cult whose one-world theology, mass weddings of complete strangers chosen by him, and unsavory tactics were repellent. Whispered tales of brainwashings administered to wayward church members regularly coursed through the building. But if this troubled me, I never talked about it with anyone—and vice versa. Thriving at the *Times* entailed walling ourselves off from uncomfortable truths about our bosses. Then, too, respected conservatives like Arnaud, many years my senior, and GOP Senator Orrin Hatch of Utah, a Mormon, who had gone so far as to call Moon's theology "a religious alternative to Communism," had made the judgment that in the war against Communism, one couldn't pick and choose one's allies. Pumping hundreds of millions from his business operations in Korea and Japan into the paper, as well as generous subsidies from a rich Japanese patron who had founded a fascist political party in the 1930s, Moon was a ready source of cash. There were no other moneybags on the scene clamoring to lose $50 million a year to underwrite an unprofitable conservative newspaper.

In theory, the *Times* was supposed to be no more conservative than other newspapers were liberal: Its political point of view would be confined to the editorial pages, while the news columns would be fair, balanced, and objective. In practice, the *Times* was closer to a European-style newspaper, where one political stance or another openly infuses the entire publication, than it was to the conventions of American journalism. Though the conservative movement operated outside the Republican Party while seeking influence within it, in the Reagan era, the movement's agenda—and therefore that of the *Times*—was pretty much Reagan's: militant anti-Communism, tax cuts to benefit corporations and the rich, dismantlement of affirmative action and social welfare programs, deregulation, and union-busting. In high school, at the RFK Foundation, and at Berkeley, the crusading style of journalism was one that I had emulated; I had taken no journalism courses in college that would have shown me another way.

Moon unabashedly mixed politics and journalism. While publishing the

Times, he also directed the American Freedom Coalition, a pro-Reagan, grassroots political lobby. When Congress cut off aid to the Nicaraguan counterrevolutionaries, or contras, Arnaud wrote an editorial announcing a *Times* fund-raising drive for a Nicaraguan Freedom Fund, endowed with a $100,000 check from Bo Hi Pak. To the horror of many in the newsroom, Arnaud insisted on splashing the editorial across the front page. Arnaud's action came two months after Reagan aide Oliver North had drafted a secret memo calling for the establishment of such a fund. Four editors quit the paper, accusing Arnaud of ordering changes in an editorial on South Korea after he discussed the subject with one of the owners, violating guarantees of editorial independence for the news department. Wire service copy was doctored in stories dealing with the Rev's felony conviction for tax evasion. And there were endless controversies and resignations over what became known as "Prudenizing" news copy—slanting it in a conservative direction. In this culture, I cut my reporter's teeth.

The political bias was more blatant on the weekly *Times* newsmagazine, *Insight*, where I was assigned as a news reporter. In contrast to the paper, the magazine's top editorial staff, including editor John Podhoretz—or Pod, as we called him—had both youthful zeal and no journalistic experience: Pod's college roommate at Chicago, Tod Lindberg, edited the news pages, and frizzy-haired Liz Kristol—the daughter of neoconservative éminence grise Irving Kristol—edited the cultural pages of the book. Mini-cons, the trio was dubbed.

I had taken the job in no small part because John was the son of Norman Podhoretz, whose magazine had so impressed me at Berkeley and whose own writing, both in style and substance, I had found so lucid and compelling. In contrast, John, a year or two older than me, was a big disappointment, an overbearing know-it-all with the looks, manners, and all the subtlety of John Belushi. He seemed cursed by the desire to overcome a deep well of insecurity often seen in the offspring of highly accomplished parents—John's mother, Midge Decter, was as formidable a thinker and writer as Norman. Though John had flashes of skill as an assigning editor, he

routinely injected politics into our copy; and his own writing, in which he
interpreted pop culture through a crudely propagandistic lens, was embarrassing. A typical example was a six-page Pod essay on the return of the "real
man" in American film, a celebration of Sylvester Stallone's "pectorals" and
Don Johnson's "displaying his manliness by wearing a perpetual three days'
growth of beard."

Despite what I thought of him, I opportunistically stayed in Pod's good
graces, and through him, I received all the right introductions into the young
conservative social scene in D.C. I became a regular at the weekend house
parties of Grover Norquist, the burly, bearded, bespectacled activist and
consigliere to the fiery right-wing backbencher from Georgia, GOP
Congressman Newt Gingrich. The parties often were thrown to launch a
book or raise money for Republican candidates for office. Grover had
attended Harvard in the 1970s, where he was known for advancing unpopular right-wing positions at the *Crimson* newspaper. He drew to his Capitol
Hill row house a movement crowd from the Hill, the conservative lobby
groups, and the think tanks—people like *Dartmouth Review* alumni Ben
Hart and his wife, Betsy, Reagan speechwriter (and future congressman)
Dana Rohrabacher, and, always, Grover's best friend, *Wall Street Journal* editorial writer John Fund, in one of his brown double-knit suits. Though he
was a few years older than most of us, Grover had never married, his home
looked like a frat house, and he seemed incapable of talking about anything
but movement politics—to the point that his own guests spent most of the
evening trying to avoid being trapped in conversation with their single-
minded host. That is, when they weren't trying to avoid the flat beer being
pumped from kegs in the kitchen. Incongruously, Peter, Paul, and Mary tunes
played on the stereo. Listening to the iconic 1960s group was permissible,
Grover would say, in all seriousness, "now that the left is being destroyed."

Ill at ease at these "revenge of the nerds" gatherings, basically introverted,
and unsure of how to handle the issue of my sexuality, I drifted in late and
out early, usually accompanied by a woman colleague from the *Times*, never
Andrew, who had moved to Washington with me from San Francisco. No
matter how much I drank, I couldn't loosen up in this setting. Though I
wanted nothing more than to make my home among these conservatives,

even after a dozen nights at Grover's, I couldn't trust or truly connect with any of them as friends. I traversed the room like a zombie.

John also brought me to the airy Connecticut Avenue apartment of Nick and Mary Eberstadt, who ran a salon for the young neoconservatives. Nick was a scholar at the American Enterprise Institute, a conservative think tank that housed the leading intellectual lights of the Reagan era, and Mary was the editor of Irving Kristol's new foreign policy magazine, the *National Interest*. Here, the food and drink were markedly better, and a more writerly crowd gathered, including Christopher Buckley, the son of William F. Buckley, and the humorist P. J. O'Rourke, who entertained us with riffs on the latest liberal outrage. I was a bit more at home in this company, but I still felt self-conscious and sullen in what was, ostensibly, my crowd of con-servative scribes.

Insight was modeled on *Time* and *Newsweek*. I quickly learned what it took to be one of Pod's golden boys: a mix of reported fact laced with a heavy dose of conservative—preferably neoconservative—spin. We made no bones about the magazine's ideological biases around the office, which we justified as balancing out the liberal biases that so infuriated us in the pages of the major newsweeklies. Yet in the doublespeak that I was coached in at the *Times*, the magazine was marketed as objective journalism, and this is how we presented ourselves to the reading public.

I could see that those who hewed to the party line got plum assignments and rose through the ranks. One young comer was Danny Wattenberg, the son of neocon columnist Ben Wattenberg and a former speechwriter for the architect of Reagan's contra policy, Elliott Abrams. Abrams also happened to be Pod's brother-in-law. On the other hand, those who didn't inject pol-itics into their work—and there were plenty of regular, old-school journal-ists on both the paper and the magazine—had their copy mangled by Pod and were shunted to the sidelines by the mini-cons.

Though I was acutely aware that I didn't have Wattenberg's pedigree, the formula came easily to me. For one of my first pieces, an enthusiastic analy-sis of the Reagan Doctrine—the idea of turning back Soviet gains in the Third World by financing proxy wars of insurgency—I interviewed John's father, Norman, whose magazine had done much to advance the doctrine in

conservative policy circles, and whose wife, Midge Decter, headed an organization of hawkish intellectuals, the Committee for the Free World, that
agitated on behalf of these "freedom fighter" armies. Norman reported back
to his son, who then reported to me, that my questions had been unusually
astute. The piece also elicited my first Arnaud-gram, a handwritten con-
gratulatory missive on yellow cardboard.

My stock was rising. Soon, I was a senior writer, promoted on political
grounds ahead of people who had thirty years in the business on me, covering the congressional debate on aid for the Nicaraguan contras, and traveling to Managua for firsthand reports on Sandinista atrocities. I also
endeavored to look like an old fogy in training, donning a bow tie and horn-
rimmed glasses and, ludicrously, puffing on a pipe and occasionally even carrying a walking stick.

In Nicaragua, I could see that since taking power in a military coup in
1979, the Sandinistas had trampled on human rights, denied democratic
freedoms, and impoverished their people. The failed revolution was all
around me in the barrios of Managua. The contras, many of whom had ties
to the right-wing dictatorship that had been ousted by the Sandinistas, had
their own authoritarian bent, I learned, but the true democrats I met on my
trips, people like Violeta Chamorro, editor of the newspaper *La Prensa*,
were offering them guarded support as a means of bringing free elections to
their country. With the Cold Warriors in the United States fervently behind
the contra war, the Nicaraguan democrats had little choice in the matter.
They had no power to pursue an alternative strategy that might well have
meant less carnage to the region.

My generation had never been called to serve in the military; we were too
young to be drafted. To me, the Cold War was a global chess game, remote
and intangible. In totalitarian Nicaragua, not far from the Mexican border,
the Cold War was brought home, and I imagined that I was doing my own
small part to win it. My anti-Communism became suffused with bitter emotion as I grew to feel nothing but contempt for the Democrats in Congress
who, I was convinced, were propping up an evil regime by failing to fund
the resistance.

So wild-eyed was my anti-Communism that I cultivated a relationship with Chile's ambassador in Washington, and parlayed that into a "world exclusive" interview with Chilean military dictator Augusto Pinochet, whom liberals regarded as the devil incarnate. In the late 1970s, Jeane Kirkpatrick, in a series of influential essays in *Commentary*, had laid down the line that authoritarian dictatorships were capable of evolving into democracies, while totalitarian ones were not. The theory justified U.S. support for repressive right-wing regimes in the Third World like Pinochet's. With a plebiscite on Pinochet's regime approaching in 1987, I donned a bulletproof vest and boarded the Chilean equivalent of Air Force One, joining Pinochet and his generals on a campaign swing to Easter Island, far off the Chilean coast in the Pacific. I filed a long cover story on the strategic importance to the United States of maintaining an anti-Communist regime in Chile, and a companion piece lauding Chile's free-market economy.

In seeking out and executing this assignment, I was flippantly engaging in the extremist one-upmanship that characterized not only me, but many young conservatives of the era. Supporting the contras was one thing, but defending Pinochet? You couldn't get any more hard core than that. Though I had been shaken by published reports of Pinochet's record of torturing and even murdering political opponents, as a result of my own discomposure and impaired judgment, I did not investigate or confront the subject in my ten-thousand-word takeout. An early lesson, but one that wouldn't sink in for years: As a young zealot, I disciplined myself to ignore the soft tug of my own conscience, and see only what I was supposed to see. In fighting for what I saw as a larger good, in this case anti-Communism and the moral superiority of democratic capitalism, I turned a blind eye to facts that did not suit my political aims. With little awareness of what I was doing, I proved myself capable of papering over monstrous moral wrongs in the service of the perceived morality of my cause.

My unquestioned devotion to the movement line earned the trust of the *Times* hierarchy, and I was next given the sensitive assignment of covering the transition to democracy in South Korea, the first free election of a president there since Chun Doo Hwan had taken power in a military coup. On this trip, I was disheartened to see that Moon's interest in owning a newspaper in the capital of the most powerful country in the free world was not really advancing conservative ideology, but rather fostering the perception of influence and prestige and credibility for Unificationism in places like Korea and Japan, where, unlike in the United States, his church had both a sizable following and, perhaps more to the point, a sizable conglomerate of media, real estate, high technology, and industrial holdings. In a sign of Moon's political clout abroad, Yonhap, the South Korean government news agency, regularly quoted the *Washington Times* as if it were on a par with the *Washington Post*. Here's what Moon's millions were buying: When I gave a local Seoul tailor my business card, without missing a beat he nodded enthusiastically and cried out, "Oh, Reverend Moon!"

Pod promoted me to senior editor in charge of the national and international sections of the magazine. Under the demands of the job, I became a committed smoker, buying a pack of cigarettes on my way into the office and knowing that it was time to go home when the pack was empty. Soon, seeing what my bosses wanted, I was doing my own version of "Prudenizing" copy, and conspiring to run recalcitrant liberals off the staff. When I harassed and humiliated one woman, targeted as a liberal, to the point that she stormed into my office in tears, dumped two feet of research files into my lap, and quit, John and Tod high-fived me.

Pod soon moved to a higher level post on the newspaper, which entailed a reshuffling of the major assignments and favored beats at *Insight*. The fear among the staff was that those writers who had won Pod's favor might be in for demotions. Under Pod's reign, the lead foreign, national, and business reporters were either strikingly handsome or pedigreed straight men or closeted homosexuals like me. Yet when Pod left and Tod took the job, I moved up another notch.

As he announced at one editorial planning session, Tod considered himself a "twenty-nine-year-old urban hipster," and his interests did range beyond right-wing politics to include music and fashion. Tod was a pleasure to work for, but Pod's departure triggered a fierce turf war between the top dog at *Insight*, a man named Kirk Oberfeld, and de Borchgrave, who retained nominal control of *Insight*'s operations and was everything Kirk wasn't— savvy, accomplished, connected, and involved in a marriage that, at least from the outside, appeared ideal.

The upper management tier at *Insight* was a nightmarish cult of personality within the Moonie cult, which I now experienced personally because I was one of them. Kirk was married to a woman named Linda Moore, *Insight*'s managing editor, who was so degrading and foul-mouthed that no one wanted to speak to her, much less work for her. It could not have helped Linda's disposition that Kirk abused his power by openly courting another woman editor right under Linda's nose. Kirk introduced me to a prototype of a certain kind of right-wing man, married or not, that I would encounter at the very highest levels of the movement in the years to come. To Kirk, women, including his wife, Linda, were "cunts," or "fucking cunts." Arnaud either had "no balls," or Kirk threatened to "cut his balls off." Men who didn't follow Kirk's orders were "prissy," "sissies," "faggots," "cocksuckers," or "fudge-packers." Kirk had a problem with alcohol abuse, rarely showing up at work until 4 or 5 P.M., when we all jumped to attention and plotted to circumvent or upstage Arnaud.

Now part of the editorial hierarchy, I was invited to lunches in the executive dining room with the likes of CIA director William Casey, though I could never quite decipher what he was saying through his infamous mumbling. I also attended weekly editorial meetings in Arnaud's impressive, glass-enclosed executive suite, where we munched on Pepperidge Farm Goldfish served in silver bowls and listened to Arnaud denounce the DMC. If we were having trouble getting big-name interviews, Arnaud would bark to his secretary, "Get me Jack Kemp on the phone," and we'd have our quote.

Jack Kemp, a veteran guru of supply-side tax cuts for the rich, was one of our heroes. Like him, we were serious about ideas, or, more tellingly, what we called "the battle of ideas." We read Charles Murray's *Losing Ground*, which claimed that increases in social spending for the poor actually had made their plight worse. We read *Illiberal Education*, Dinesh D'Souza's exposé on the follies of political correctness. And we read Allan Bloom's defense of the Western canon, *The Closing of the American Mind*. (John actually sent me to Chicago to interview his mentor for a cover story.) There, I found a sensitive, engaging, chain-smoking intellectual the likes of which I had never met. For three hours in his book-lined apartment, Bloom remained in a manic state as he downed espressos, cigarette ash falling all over a black double-breasted suit coat. I followed him to a lecture, which he delivered as a seductively brilliant panic attack. Years later, after Bloom died, his friend Saul Bellow outed him as a homosexual.

There was electricity on the right, the same sense of bravely flouting convention—of subverting the dominant culture—that I had first felt in Texas and then at Berkeley. We loved Star Wars—not the movie, but the fantastic space shield against Soviet nukes. Our taste in movies ran to *Top Gun*, starring Tom Cruise as a derring-do Navy jet fighter pilot shooting down Soviet MiGs. We went to weekly Wednesday night gatherings of like-minded, under-thirty conservatives at the Heritage Foundation, Washington's leading right-wing think tank, called the Third Generation. Barry Goldwater made the GOP a conservative party; Ronald Reagan made it a winning electoral majority; now it was our turn. The crowd was often standing room only, filled with fresh-faced activists in blue blazers and rep ties ready to go the gentlemanly first and second generations one better by taking up arms in behalf of our ideology. Well, that was the spirit, anyway. Led by Ben Hart of the Dartmouth mafia, we actually jawboned about arcane subjects like the presidential line-item veto and drank a lot of Coors beer, donated by Heritage benefactor Holly Coors. We revered writers like William F. Buckley and George Will, and when we went on C-SPAN, we tried to imitate them. Tod Lindberg even coached me on how to sit like Buckley, in a magnificent half-recline.

There was something ersatz about this Third Generation of conservatives, symbolized by the yawning gap between the talents and achievements of Norman Podhoretz and his son John. As the ex-conservative writer Michael Lind noted in his book *Up from Conservatism*, our group produced no great thinkers or writers, no classic books or landmark articles, no successors to the elder Buckley or Kristol or Podhoretz. The most successful among us would one day end up as top functionaries in right-wing Australian tycoon Rupert Murdoch's media empire, or as hosts of cable TV chat shows. Others would give up intellectual pretensions altogether and go straight into politics, like Ralph Reed, the young mastermind behind the Christian Coalition.

In the age of Reagan, conservatism had cachet, thus many of us drifted into it easily, without really having to think our way there. The leaders of our generation had been drawn to Washington, rather than New York, where politics, not ideas, are central. Yet we were different as well from past generations who had come to the capital to make their mark. High-minded ideals of public service and journalism were little in evidence, nor was there much concern or compassion for those less fortunate than us. For all our ferocious intensity, our hatred of big government and big media, our ideology was in a way empty, more an attitude, a kind of playground politics, than a philosophy of government.

I typified the group in these respects. I was content to think what everybody else was thinking. I knew whom to idealize, and whom, conversely, to trash. Though I was genuinely moved by the goal of helping other countries adopt democratic values, in the main I had come to Washington not to save the world, but to continue fighting the war against the left that I had gotten caught up in at Berkeley. Unlike the Berkeley profs who recruited me into conservatism, I had no deep understanding of conservative ideology. If I had been asked why I was part of a movement that consistently sided with the interests of the very wealthiest Americans, or that wanted to strip away environmental protections at the behest of big business, I would have spouted the party-line sound bites, but there would have been no real conviction behind them. I also had no extraordinary talents. I was smart, but not terribly well educated. I had an activist, rather than a reflective, temperament; and my ability to understand and judge was clouded by the ideological biases of an elder generation. Nor was I any great shakes as a writer, though in a class of second- and third-raters, I would find easy success. Fervor, and a lot of elbow grease, were enough.

Traveling in Pod's posse, I considered myself a young neocon. It was often said that the neoconservatives—the ex-liberals, or, as Irving Kristol had famously remarked, "liberals who were mugged by reality"—spent most of their time defining what they were not. We were not the Old Right, the cultural conservatives who were fearful of the economic and social effects of unfettered capitalism and immigration, and skeptical of American engagement abroad. That was Pat Buchanan. We were not what was then known as the New Right, now called the religious or Christian Right, with their ironclad antiabortion stance and support of prayer in the public schools. That was Jesse Helms. Nor were we libertarians, people who simply wanted the government out of everything, including world affairs.

Though we were all part of the broad Reagan coalition, glued together in our anti-Communism, these doctrinal distinctions, finely parsed in the little conservative journals, mattered. They mattered because they made it possible for us to see ourselves as not part of them. One of my first pieces in 1987 as a freelance book critic for *Commentary* was a scorching review of Pat Buchanan's autobiography, *Right from the Beginning.* "Buchanan's language of 'religious war,' leaving as it does no room for compromise or diversity, threatens the new conservative coalition and could yet trigger a corrosive and ultimately self-defeating battle within the Republican Party," I concluded. No, that was not us.

By breaking with their former colleagaues on the left, the neoconservatives were able to position themselves into a place of cultural and political power based on a fundamental deception. Originally, they broke with the left over Vietnam and what they saw as anti-American and cultural radicalism that was a by-product of the antiwar movement. Many left academia when university administrations accommodated the demands of student activists. As Reagan came to power and began a major arms buildup, however, the neoconservatives, skilled polemicists with access to prestige media like the *New York Times,* were able to label everyone in the liberal camp who disagreed with them as dangerous leftists and even as un-American. Through rhetorical sleight of hand, the neocons made it appear as though principled anti-Communism had ceased to exist in liberal, Democratic ranks. Though Kristol's *Public Interest* had been founded in the 1960s to discuss how best to reform government programs for the poor, by the 1980s the magazine was celebrating writers like Charles Murray, who wanted to gut such programs. What began as support among the neocons for the liberal civil rights tradition of Lyndon B. Johnson and Hubert Humphrey became hostility to affirmative action in all forms. Claiming to be the true and only heirs to the vaunted tradition of the "New York intellectuals," the neocons' defense of traditional standards of scholarship in the university became a device to shut out and discredit legitimate diverse curricula as "politically correct." The one issue on which the neocons remained true to liberalism was abortion rights. Most were pro-choice, as I was; even among those who said they were pro-life, their hearts didn't seem to be in criminalizing abortion.

The Third Generation included working women, divorced singles, and even a few gays. We weren't what the right called "traditionalists" in our personal lives. Indeed, I never thought any one of my conservative women friends, even those who espoused pro-life views publicly, would fail to avail themselves of the right to choose abortion if need be. Almost everyone in my set seemed to favor smaller government, free markets, and individual freedom. Put another way, they—we—were Lockean liberals. We did not wish to enforce a strict moral code through government action. As much as possible, we wanted the government to leave us alone.

In part because I was gay, I always was more socially liberal than the 1960s-bashing neoconservatives. Libertarianism was perhaps a better fit for me then, but during the Cold War, isolationism struck me as irresponsible. Then, too, I gravitated toward power, and by the middle '80s, although Reagan himself seemed to me to represent the Goldwater tradition of anti-Communism abroad and live-and-let-live libertarianism at home, this tradition had little standing among the party's intellectuals. The libertarians, housed in Washington's obscure Cato Institute, had essentially withdrawn from the conservative movement. The neocons, by contrast, were Reagan's court intellectuals. They ran the important magazines, and they controlled the important right-wing foundations.

My affinity for the neocons was also a matter of tone and style. For many years, Norman Podhoretz had called himself a centrist or even a neoliberal. The neocons were sophisticated, urban intellectuals, secular rather than religious. They wrote with an analytical precision that awed me; what I didn't see then were the unspoken passions underneath. Though his son John told me that his father's politics were deeply entwined with his conceptions of "manliness," in *Breaking Ranks*, the most famous neocon manifesto, the short, flabby elder Podhoretz did not acknowledge that his defection bore any relation to his inner life. While revealing nothing about himself, Podhoretz claimed that he was forced to defect from liberalism by the intellectual weaknesses, cowardice, and sexual experimentation of his former friends. Yet the neocons didn't strike me as scary, like the two New Right types at the *Times;* I knew myself enough to avoid them like the plague. Sam Francis, an immensely obese, chain-smoking editorial writer, advocated a "white pride" philosophy and warned against a liberal "war against the white race." And born-again Christian columnist John Lofton, who skulked through the building in dark glasses, charged that "homosexuals, adulterers, and fornicators" staffed the paper. They left under pressure, too Neanderthal even for the *Times.*

In the mid-1980s, one had to wade into the deepest fever swamps of the right wing to hear this sort of bigotry. I didn't regard Francis and Lofton as part of any movement I was in. The magic of Reagan's political appeal was that Sam Francis and John Lofton could think Reagan was their president, I could think he was my president, and lots of Democrats could think he was their president, too. My experience of Reagan was as a second-term president, not the extremist candidate of the 1970s who mocked "welfare queens," questioned evolution, and ran with the early backing of the Reverend Jerry Falwell's Moral Majority. I saw Reagan as a strong leader who stood for the first principles of anti-Communism, limited government, and individual liberty.

Significantly for me, Reagan was also an ex-Democrat, a divorced, non-religious, ex–Hollywood actor who seemed to do little more than give lip service to legislating the social agenda of the right. Though he came to power with the support of the social right, Reagan always conveyed to me a sense that he was far less censorious a man than the likes of Jesse Helms, whose politics were punctuated by antiabortion, anti–civil rights, and anti-gay sentiment. Reagan's failure to do anything for the antiabortion cause but speak to an annual pro-life rally on the Mall (via a public address system from the Oval Office) was an open joke in our circles. Even Reagan's moralism seemed positive: He didn't demonize. Republican strategist Lee Atwater, who ridiculed hard-core conservatives as "the extra chromosome crowd," called this philosophy of inclusiveness the "Big Tent." As to private sexual matters, I remembered reading that Reagan once had said it didn't matter what you did, so long as you didn't do it in the street and scare the horses.

On arriving in Washington from San Francisco, Andrew and I moved into a small loft apartment in the funky Adams Morgan section of the city. I wasn't in town long before I was introduced to closeted gays and lesbians working in Republican politics. The many closeted gays who served in the senior-most ranks of the Reagan administration called themselves the "laissez fairies." Gay Republicans were everywhere, even in the city's bars, long considered a kind of free zone where gay Republicans could let down their guard without much fear of being outed. When I walked into J.R.'s, a popular bar in the heart of D.C.'s gay Dupont Circle strip, it seemed that every other person I met was a Republican. There was Terry Dolan, founder of the hard-right National Conservative Political Action Committee, which was responsible for the GOP wresting control of the Senate in 1980, and whose brother, Tony, was Reagan's chief speechwriter. There was Marvin Liebman, one of Bill Buckley's closest friends and a founder of the Young Americans for Freedom, a network of conservative organizations on college campuses that served as training grounds for virtually the entire movement leadership. One night, I saw a well-known Reagan imagemaker playing pool in his cowboy boots at the Lost & Found, a gay dance club in southeast D.C. In a city that is more like a small southern town, where everyone may not know everyone, but everyone knows *about* everyone, the word was that this fellow kept a boyfriend in a town house on Capitol Hill, and a wife and kids in another location, and no one leaked a word of it.

What I didn't know until years later, while reviewing material to write this book, was how influential the closeted gay conservatives had been years before I arrived on the conservative scene in the same condition. More than any other conservative, it had been the closeted homosexual Liebman, working closely with Buckley, who extinguished the libertarian strain in modern conservatism and turned the party into a vehicle for radical activism. In a book called *The Other Side of the Sixties: Young Americans for Freedom and the Rise of Conservative Politics*, reviewed in the libertarian magazine *Reason* in February 1998, historian John A. Andrew III wrote that students on both the left and the right were radicalized in the 1960s. The radical right-wing students connected themselves to the Liebman group, Young Americans for Freedom. YAF "emerged to offer an ideological and structural critique of the reigning liberalism. They sought to reject, not reform, the consensus liberalism," Andrew wrote. The *Reason* reviewer, Nick Gillespie, continued, "The brainchild of William F. Buckley Jr. and a few other prominent conservatives (including then–*National Review* publisher William Rusher, conservative journalist M. Stanton Evans, and Republican fund-raiser Marvin Liebman), YAF was designed to combat the bland centrist modern Republicanism that Dwight Eisenhower, Nelson Rockefeller, and even Richard Nixon had brought into the GOP." To meet the Communist threat, YAF "supported the peacetime draft and defended before Congress the loyalty-oath provisions of the National Defense Act, arguing that state intervention was justified in the name of national security," Gillespie wrote. YAF provided a training ground for scores of conservative leaders, including Rep. Robert Bauman (who, like Liebman, came out as gay years later), fund-raiser Richard Viguerie, Pat Buchanan, and Howard Phillips, cofounder of the Conservative Caucus. Ultimately, YAF itself split apart by the late 1960s, with Buckley in-law and former Goldwater speechwriter L. Brent Bozell leading the most extreme faction, publicly condemning libertarians for failing to endorse government measures to protect "traditional" society and for opposing the Vietnam War.

Being a gay conservative provided me with access to a second social life, very separate from the one Podhoretz had introduced me to, that revolved around fancy dinner parties in the Kalorama homes of prosperous gay lobbyists and lawyers and political operatives, officials of the Republican National Committee, top aides to Republicans on Capitol Hill, and even a member of Congress or two. I was a frequent guest at dinners hosted in a chic Kalorama condo by a high-powered Republican lobbyist for arms manufacturers named Peter Malatesta, whose mother had married Bob Hope. Then in his early fifties, Peter was a larger-than-life character and a marvelous cook who knew how to throw a party. I learned a lot from Peter about what happened in Washington, and in Hollywood, behind closed doors.

In Italian, Malatesta means "bad temperament," and Peter didn't disappoint on that score either. He bore all the marks of some gay men of a certain age who have forced themselves to live a double life: He had a surfeit of unhappiness and self-loathing that came rushing to the fore whenever he had downed the requisite amount of Scotch. Andrew and I traveled with Peter to Palm Springs, where we stayed at Bob Hope's guesthouse, a few miles from the main property, but soon enough we realized that socializing with Peter had its limits. He worried all weekend that he would be "found out" if someone saw us cavorting by the pool in our Speedo swim trunks. While Peter could be avuncular and amusingly flamboyant one minute, his anxiety about being in the closet could turn him bitter and ugly, in violent, profanity-laced temper tantrums, the next. With the exception of *Insight*'s Kirk Oberfeld, I had never heard such abusive language. We tired of trying to figure out when the tide might turn.

Peter was only one of many closeted gay right-wing Republicans I would come to know in my years in Washington. Perhaps because they were trying too hard to fit into GOP ranks, they often embodied the worst attributes of the extreme right—racism, sexism, and anti-Semitism. While I was well acquainted with the hidden subculture within a subculture of conservative gay life, as a journalist I was never brought fully into the closely guarded fold. And I was never sure I wanted to be, either. The secretiveness, not to mention the binge drinking and the common use of male prostitutes, lent a disturbing quality to it all. These relationships, like the ones with Pod and company, remained an extension of my political life. My only connection to other gay people was among these closeted gay Republicans, and with Andrew, an apolitical loner who had taken a job as an appraiser of rare books and prints. After a strong dose of Malatesta, Andrew had little interest in either my gay or straight conservative political worlds.

My social isolation from the rest of the gay community, which I chose to avoid on grounds that it was overwhelmingly Democratic and liberal, meant that there was no one in my life to challenge my position as a gay man working in the conservative movement. If there was any conflict between advancing the conservative agenda and being gay, the closeted gay men and women in my orbit either didn't recognize it, or more likely just didn't talk about it. Any troubling contradictions were walled off or rationalized in the same way we never talked about the Moonies at the *Times*.

The only person at the *Times* with whom I socialized outside the office during these early years, my only real friend other than Andrew, was a tall, blond, brassy southern woman who thought conservatism was "horseshit" and could never understand how I had gotten mixed up with the movement as a gay man. Katie Tyndall, a talented writer in her mid-thirties, was one of those liberals at *Insight* who labored at the bottom of the totem pole. I tried to take in stride Katie's good-natured ribbing, often over long dinners with Andrew, whom she nicknamed Dennis the Menace. Our relationship was full of fun, a ray of sunshine in an otherwise desolate right-wing social scene, but I ended up pushing Katie away because I couldn't abide her prodding about the contradiction between the David she knew and what I was doing with my career.

In time, I did develop an internal dialogue about being a gay conservative, and it went something like this: Being conservatives, we valued modesty, we'd just as soon keep private matters private, we rejected the identity politics and victimology of the left. We did not see ourselves as part of a group with the same set of politics and interests, but rather as individuals who happened to be gay. Just as some of us, as the cliché went, happened to be left-handed. Why should what you do in bed have anything to do with your position on marginal tax rates? Of course, it was easier to maintain this position in the mid-1980s, before the extent of Reagan's neglect of the AIDS crisis became an undeniable fact. Also, though the Reverend Jerry Falwell's Moral Majority was hostile toward gays, the Christian Coalition, which would have much greater success in placing an indelible antigay stamp on the GOP, had not yet been founded. Had I come out of college as an openly gay man ten years later, I doubt I would have fallen in with the by-then transparently antigay GOP.

While I didn't feel unwelcome in the Republican Party, and I learned to rationalize my place in it, I lived with an implicit deal—I was welcome as long as I wasn't honest about my sexual identity. I knew no Republicans who were publicly out. Most conservative gays I knew, especially the older set, were in a constant state of panic about being discovered. One *Times* colleague waited three years to gingerly broach the subject with me at lunch, for fear either that I might not be gay, or that I might tell the wrong person that he was. We were out only to each other. Being much older than I was, the closeted gays at the paper were more easily singled out as gay. They held lower positions than I did, and I came to believe that their sexuality had been held against them by management. These fears were all the more reason to take some steps to protect myself from exposure.

I could see what it took to survive, and without thinking through the implications, I instinctively regressed from the open way I had handled my sexuality at Berkeley and retreated into the closet, adopting my own policy of "don't ask, don't tell." Hardly anyone who wasn't gay ever asked, and I rarely brought the subject up unless I was sure it was safe. A stressed, bifurcated existence though it certainly was, I attributed the need to stay closeted to social norms, not conservative politics. Gays in all walks of life made such compromises, I told myself, especially in a city of ambition and pretense like Washington, where everyone, gay and straight, seemed to look over their shoulders and hedge their bets as they rose through the power ranks.

Of course, although our straight counterparts didn't know for sure that we were gay, for the most part they did know. The confirmed bachelor in his fifties, the eligible guy in his thirties who never had a girlfriend—they weren't hard to identify as gay. Most conservatives in my world didn't seem terribly interested in the subject, at least no more than the average person might be—or so I tried to think. One exception was John Podhoretz, who seemed obsessed with homosexuality. When they heard I worked for John, older gay conservatives often referred me to a piece published in *Commentary* in 1980 by John's mother, Midge Decter, a biting homophobic diatribe about gay life on New York's Fire Island called "The Boys on the Beach." Had I read it then, the article would have shown me that antigay bigotry was not confined to the fever swamps after all. The sophisticated-seeming neocon intellectuals were right-wing cultural reactionaries. Somehow, I had missed the Decter essay in the library stacks at Berkeley, and because I suspected it might reveal an unpleasant reality about the people I had associated myself with, who were promoting my career, I never found the time to look it up.

One day, before I left the office on my way to interview a *Commentary* writer for a story I was working on, John warned me, with a sneer, to be "careful" because this "queer" was certain to make a pass at me. (He didn't.) I was embarrassed into silence. Was this John's way of telling me that he knew I was "queer" too? I was stung again, and felt betrayed, when I learned from a mutual conservative acquaintance of ours that John was, in fact, one of those who "knew" that I was gay, and, golden boy or no, he and a few other conservatives had many laughs ridiculing me behind my back at the Eberstadts' salon. Nick was in on the gay bashing, and presumably also Mary, who soon retired from editing and writing, surfacing only very rarely with long essays on an odd preoccupation: homosexual pedophilia. (I should admit that we conservative gays had a few chuckles psychoanalyzing John— Podenfreude, as the practice was known around the newsroom—when he began writing a column for the *Washington Times* under the drag name "Tiffany Midgeson.")

I remember where I was at the moment the Reagan regime teetered on the brink of falling: sitting in my office at the *Times*, watching pensively as Attorney General Edwin Meese announced that American arms sales to Iran had been secretly funneled to the Nicaraguan contras in defiance of a congressional ban on U.S. military aid to the contras. Meese announced the appointment of a fact-finding panel headed by Texas Senator John Tower. Soon, independent counsel Lawrence Walsh launched a massive criminal investigation, and an acrimonious congressional probe got under way. The charges were the most serious since Watergate. Violations of law. Lying to Congress. Evidence shredded. The Constitution subverted.

Despite evidence of serious wrongdoing in the Iran-contra affair, we saw it as just another knife fight. We said that the congressional Democrats, frustrated by Reagan's popularity and checkmated in policy battles, had perfected the art of scandal politics. We considered the large number of Reagan associates who were under investigation for ethical indiscretions to be falsely accused by the liberal opposition. After all, we maintained, they had passed the independent counsel statute that institutionalized the criminalization of politics, and they padded the congressional committee staffs with investigators to harass the executive branch. As if amnesia had set in, left unmentioned was the fact that all of these safeguards had been established after the abuses of the Nixon administration were exposed.

With the Democrats winning control of the Senate in 1986, they had the president himself in their sights, and the conservative movement was in a state of siege. Impeachment was in the air. "What liberalism and the left have in mind is the second ruination of a Republican Presidency within a generation," thundered Reagan communications chief and former Nixon speechwriter Patrick Buchanan in a *Washington Post* op-ed, voicing the view of conservatives that the Democrats were deploying the scandal artillery to win what they had lost in the 1984 elections. Raising the specter of a coup d'état, Representative Newt Gingrich said: "The left has started a no-holds-barred struggle to see if they can retain power in the country. . . . If Reagan is the Reagan of mythology, it's time to strap on the guns and reenact 'Death Valley Days.' "

In fighting back, we weren't just defending our president. In the broadest sense, we saw Iran-contra through the prism of the Cold War, the dividing line between freedom and totalitarianism. We were certain we were on the right side of history. No matter how many incriminating facts the investigations turned up, we simply weren't about to let a decade of anti-Communist policies be discredited by the liberal Democrats and their allies in the media. But to save Reagan and his policies, we had to defend the illegal contra resupply effort and spin the lies told to Congress by top Reagan officials as unimportant technicalities. The tables were turned on Reagan's opponents—and the strategy put into place—by Oliver North, the young lieutenant colonel who ran the rogue contra resupply operation from the White House basement. North lit up the television cameras with his in-your-face congressional testimony, casting himself as an average patriotic American against a craven political elite. North seemed to imply: So what if some laws were broken? What mattered was the historic struggle in Central America. Ollie mania swept the country, and we young conservatives had our first real hero. (Unlike our elders, we had never loved Reagan unconditionally. By now, in fact, it was common for us to compare Reagan's romancing of Soviet leader Mikhail Gorbachev unfavorably with North's unflinching anti-Communism.)

To be sure, not all conservatives embraced North: *New York Times* columnist William Safire, another Nixon aide, said North should be jailed for violating the Constitution. But most conservatives followed the lead of House Judiciary Committee member Henry Hyde of Illinois, who defended North's illicit activities in the name of a higher moral good. "All of us at some time confront conflicts between rights and duties, between choices that are evil and less evil, and one hardly exhausts moral imagination by labeling every untruth and every deception an outrage," Hyde wrote in the minority report of the Iran-contra committee.

I fell in lockstep behind North and Hyde. Like all of the institutions of the conservative movement, the *Washington Times* put on a full-court press to defend North and the pro-contra policy, even if it meant essentially endorsing lying under oath and obstructing justice on a critical matter of national security. I covered the congressional hearings for *Insight*, and at the ripe old age of twenty-six I made my first appearances on television as a bow-tied talking head, abetting the cover-up by bashing the Democrats and the media as Communist sympathizers. When I attempted the Buckley half-recline, though, I nearly fell off my chair.

Though the public rallied to the administration's side, and the Democrats backed down from the idea of impeaching Reagan against the popular will, the investigations paralyzed the Reagan White House politically for almost two years and bloodied brethren like Elliott Abrams, who pled guilty to two counts of misleading Congress and was later pardoned by President George H. W. Bush. In a memorable interview, Abrams's wife, Rachel, expressed the desire we all felt—to mow down her husband's liberal detractors with a machine gun. For my conservative friends and me, the lessons of Iran-contra were twofold. Scandal politics—turning opponents into criminals—was strikingly effective. And conservative respect for the rule of law and constitutional principles and civility in politics could be sacrificed to the right ends.

The 1987 nomination of Judge Robert Bork to the Supreme Court was another indelible political moment. If we loved Ollie, we loved Bork even more. Unlike North, Bork and his wife, Mary Ellen, were members of the conservative intellectual set; his children, Ellen and Bob Jr., were part of the Third Generation. In later years, after Bork's defeat, I would be informed by one of the Bork children to stock my bar with their father's favorite Scotch—Glenfiddich, if I'm not mistaken—in the event that he showed up at my house in Georgetown for a post-dinner libation, as many prominent conservatives developed a habit of doing.

More than any single figure, for the right, Bork's nomination represented the culmination of a strategy put in place at the beginning of the Reagan administration to force a right-wing economic and social agenda on the country by judicial fiat. Judicial conservatism—the respectable idea of a limited role for the judiciary in a democracy—was abandoned by these right-wing judicial extremists, who belonged to a secretive legal network called the Federalist Society, which was devoted to restricting privacy rights and reproductive freedoms, rolling back civil rights gains, and thwarting the authority of government to regulate industry in the public interest. In the Reagan administration, Federalist lawyers, including Attorney General Edwin Meese, William Bradford Reynolds, Theodore Olson, and Kenneth Starr in the Justice Department, Kenneth Cribb in the White House, and Clarence Thomas at the Equal Employment Opportunity Commission, among many others, worked to strip away civil rights, voting rights, and environmental and consumer protections, and to defend discriminatory practices by cities, local schools, and religious institutions. Reagan-appointed Federalist judges like Bork, Antonin Scalia, and Laurence Silberman did the same from the federal bench. After years of pitched battles over the selection of judges in the Reagan era, the elevation of Bork was seen as a way to turn back decades of liberal jurisprudence by tipping the balance on the high court toward the right for years to come.

The left considered Bork, who first came to national attention when he agreed to carry out Nixon's order to fire Watergate prosecutor Archibald

Cox in what became known as the Saturday Night Massacre, public enemy number one. Leading liberal politicians and interest groups pulled out all the stops to defeat him: media buys, direct mail, opinion polls, and phone banks, all designed to expose Bork's judicial philosophy as a smoke screen for what it was: a dangerous political agenda. While the liberal opponents of Bork were correct that he had a record of hostility to civil rights and was a threat to women's rights on reproductive matters, at the time I took the line of the Republican right, which held that the left was unfairly trashing Bork— "borking" him, in the term coined by Bork supporters. I wrote and edited major stories for *Insight* on the Bork confirmation, and, swept up in the partisan battle, I did not question what side of the line in the sand I stood on. I defended Bork as part of the conservative movement's broader power struggle with the left. I exercised no independent judgment of my own, and did no investigation of Bork's record for myself as I tapped out my prescripted lines.

Looking back, I know that my support of Bork was more a flaring up of the aimless partisanship of my generation, and my own tendency to drift along a set path, than it was a matter of genuine support for his ideas. What is more, even then, on all of the issues at stake in the culture war that the Bork nomination set off—from prayer in the schools, to the regulation of pornography, to the decriminalization of certain drugs, to civil rights, privacy rights, and abortion rights—my own latent values were "intellectual class values . . . egalitarian and socially permissive," as Bork derisively described the views of his opponents in his book on the nomination struggle, *The Tempting of America*. I did not share the cultural values of Bork or his supporters. Though I may have been at least vaguely aware of this cleavage at the time, I can't be sure it even registered. My intense desire to succeed in my chosen career as a conservative writer, and to belong to my tribe, obscured any other feelings or values that would have complicated the picture, and I buried many of my beliefs to fit into the movement.

Like many younger conservatives who had been scarred and damaged in skirmishes with the left on our college campuses, I *did* identify with Bork as the victim of what we saw as a left-wing smear campaign. For us in the Third Generation, the Bork battle reawakened memories of personal injury and reignited spiteful impulses, marking an end to Reagan's sunny style of GOP politics. In our view, Bork's opponents conducted a campaign of personal demonization and moral delegitimation to defeat him, and they won, leaving him for dead by the side of the road. For the conservative movement, the hardball tactics of the anti-Bork effort would give license to mount a decade-long campaign of revenge and retribution against liberals and their media collaborators, all of it justified and legitimized as payback. In a 1988 speech decrying the left's campaign against Bork, Newt Gingrich captured well how we saw things in the movement: "The left at its core understands in a way Grant understood after Shiloh that this is a civil war, that only one side will prevail, and that the other side will be relegated to history. This war has to be fought with the scale and duration and savagery that is only true of civil wars. While we are lucky in this country that our civil wars are fought at the ballot box, not on the battlefields, nonetheless it is a civil war."

CHAPTER THREE

LENINISTS OF THE RIGHT

We conservatives could never be happy. After a decade of conservative control of the White House, we still saw ourselves as losers. Ronald Reagan had failed to deliver, the evil empire was still a threat, and so was big government. Some said Reagan had softened in his dotage, or perhaps the Democrats, who were more firmly entrenched on Capitol Hill at the end of his term than they were in 1981, were just more cutthroat than we were.

Yet for all of the Gipper's shortcomings, there was no one to fill his shoes. Even before he left office, a sense of nostalgia for Reagan's presidency, and a dread realization that we would never see his like again, set in. The most popular figures in the movement were Ollie North and Judge Bork, symbols of battles past. In the '88 primaries, the young conservatives I knew either supported Jack Kemp, the New York congressman, or flirted with Governor Pete Dupont of Delaware, both of whom seemed to represent the faith in individual freedom and soaring confidence of Reaganism. The religious right was barely a blip on our radar screen: I remember a Young Republicans convention in Chicago where televangelist Pat Robertson, making a bid for the presidency, was booed. The race came down to Vice President George Bush and Senate Minority Leader Bob Dole, two establishment figures we regarded as ideological pretenders.

Bare-knuckled Bush campaign strategists Lee Atwater and Roger Ailes won the election for Bush with blunt attacks on Democratic nominee Michael Dukakis's patriotism and a racially tinged ad that exploited Dukakis's support for a prison furlough program in which a convicted black rapist, Willie Horton, was set free. Though my partisan juices were flowing at the time, looking back on it, the campaign against Dukakis, who was portrayed not only as unfit to be commander in chief but essentially as un-American, was the first time the so-called wedge cultural issues that divide Americans, backed by big money and slick advertising, had defined a presidential race.

Once in office, Bush implicitly repudiated his hard-edged campaign, reverting to what he called "kinder and gentler" form. We called Bush a "squish," an old Cold War adjective, and we seethed as we watched him throw in the towel on the only thing he stood for—no new taxes—and endorse a range of liberal legislation from an affirmative action bill to new environmental restrictions in concert with a Democratic majority in Congress. "The issue," *National Review* editorialized, "is whether the decade of Reaganism meant anything, or whether Mr. Bush merely thought his promises were a vehicle to the Oval Office, to be discarded at his convenience." The career compromisers and deal makers who led the Republicans in Congress, Bob Dole in the Senate, and Bob Michel in the House, we saw as softer than Bush.

Bush's actions on the domestic front undercut Reaganite appeals against government spending, high taxes, and federal regulation. When the Berlin Wall fell, ushering in an era of post–Cold War politics, the reliable Republican issue of anti-Communism, the only plank in the Republican platform that I had anything approaching real belief in, was also lost. Everywhere Communism was collapsing—in Poland, in Nicaragua, even in the Soviet Union itself. The old battle cries—such as Jeane Kirkpatrick's blasting of the Democrats as the "blame America first" crowd—suddenly meant nothing. Anti-Communism, as the conservatives conceived it, was never supposed to be a winning crusade. Now, the passion behind our politics was gone. The loss of anti-Communism as a rallying point "left [conservatives] in a sinking boat without a motor," said Thomas Fleming, editor of the conservative magazine *Chronicles*. "It's a joke among some of my friends that our purpose in life is now fulfilled and abolished. Those who went into politics or went into journalism particularly to fight this fight [against Communism] may want to move on and become carpenters," observed conservative columnist Charles Krauthammer, a former psychiatrist.

Among the Cold Warriors, there was little triumphalism, only anomie. We—Reagan and his supporters—thought we had won the great struggle of the century with our militant anti-Communism, and yet there was an uneasy feeling that our vanquished enemy would be sorely missed. Neocon writer Francis Fukuyama, in an article for Kristol's *National Interest*, described Communism's collapse and the ascendance of democratic capitalism around the globe as "the end of history." Many conservatives resisted this idea—perhaps because the end of history meant the end of us?—and went into denial about the changes afoot in the Kremlin and in Eastern Europe. Soon, though, reality set in. At a conference of Midge Decter's Committee for the Free World—where, starstruck as I was, I took a seat at the back of the room—I remember scratching my head along with the rest of the audience as Norman Podhoretz, Irving Kristol, Jeane Kirkpatrick, and Hilton Kramer heatedly argued with one another over the question "Does 'the West' Still Exist?" To ask the question was to answer it. The Cold War really was over.

Shorty after the conference concluded, Midge Decter announced in a letter to its international network of anti-Communist intellectuals that the Committee for the Free World, which bemoaned in its 1981 charter "the climate of confusion and complacency, apathy and self-denigration, that has done so much to weaken the Western democracies," was suddenly going out of business. Among the names affiliated with the committee were Norman Podhoretz; Irving Kristol; and Hilton Kramer, the editor of the *New Criterion*. "Except in certain enclaves of absurdity and irrelevance, such as the universities and the Public Broadcasting System," Decter wrote, "virtually no one in the world believes anymore that there is a system preferable to ours: more benign, more equitable, more productive. Another way people liked to refer to what we were doing is waging a 'battle of ideas.' That battle, at least among serious people, is now over. We have won it." Decter went on to identify a new enemy: the American education system, which she said contained attacks on Western civilization and poisoned children's minds with theories on "self-esteem."

Political movements arise from the spadework of intellectuals, not politicians. The older generation of conservative intellectuals who had framed the political culture that brought Reagan to power and sustained his administration—

the Norman Podhoretzes, the Charles Murrays, the theorists of supply-side economics at the *Wall Street Journal* editorial page—were spent. Whatever one thought of their ideas, they were serious thinkers, and there was no one of their caliber to replace them in the Bush era. The one bright spot on the horizon was quickly extinguished. Aside from William Bennett, the Bush drug czar who had made a name for himself as Reagan's pugnacious education secretary, the only movement conservative named to Bush's pinstriped cabinet of Republican businessmen was Jack Kemp. As secretary of housing and urban development, Kemp declared war on domestic poverty, trying to tackle social problems through the free market by establishing incentives for businesses to invest in the inner cities. These promising proposals, representing a so-called New Paradigm, had been dreamed up by a longhaired, exceedingly tall policy expert named Jim Pinkerton, who worked on domestic policy in the Bush White House. Kemp was hailed by the *New Republic* as a "bleeding heart conservative," but Edwin Feulner, one of the founders of the Heritage Foundation, the leading right-wing think tank, made clear that the guardians of conservative dogma were cutting Kemp off at the knees: "We [conservatives] just don't believe in being compassionate with other people's money."

Our generation had sharp-tongued publicists and sharp-elbowed operatives, but we had few original thinkers like Pinkerton, who truly seemed devoted to crafting a conservative program to help the poor. One illustration of the phenomenon was the case of Bill Kristol, the son of Irving Kristol, founder of the *Public Interest*, an important social policy journal dedicated to critical examination of the Great Society's legacy, and Gertrude Himmelfarb, the esteemed historian who argued that the rejection of Victorian values led to Britain's demise as a world power. Bill Kristol became a conservative at Harvard in the early 1970s during the anti–Vietnam War protests. As he described it, his initial attraction to conservatism was more a matter of temperament than intellect. "It was always just more fun to be in the minority than the majority in those years," he told the *New York Times Magazine*. "I was able to rebel against my generation instead of against my parents." At Harvard, Kristol, a self-identified "radical conservative," was one of the early contributing editors to the *Alternative*, an irreverent, liberal-bashing publication that was later renamed the *American Spectator*.

As a young Harvard professor, Bill had the ability and the connections to inherit the family business, writing scholarly articles on political philosophy, but he got the Washington bug in the mid-1980s and traded the potential for the kind of enduring influence his parents had for more immediate political power and, eventually, a lot more visibility as a TV talking head. Retaining the air of an arrogant academic intellectual, Bill went to work for William Bennett, a protégé of his father's, in the Reagan Education Department, and he now served as chief of staff to Vice President Dan Quayle. Quayle was widely perceived as dim-witted, and Kristol earned the unenviable sobriquet "Dan Quayle's brain." Rather than devoting his considerable intellectual firepower to crafting a constructive conservative platform, Kristol approved a speech in which Quayle attacked a popular television sitcom character, Murphy Brown, a successful career woman who decided to have a child as a single mother after having an affair with an old boyfriend. Kristol was a follower of the philosopher Leo Strauss, who argued that the goal of political life ought to be an objective sense of virtue and social order, rather than freedom and tolerance. Alone in the Bush White House, Kristol presciently identified perceived moral collapse and a reassertion of sexual traditionalism as issues through which Republican politics might be revived after the Cold War.

Other churning forces in the conservative movement also sought to find a political issue in using the state to police private lives. One was the American Conservative Union, a group representing interests from pro-life to gun rights that had been formed after the Goldwater defeat to fuse anti-Communist, economic, and moral traditionalist conservative factions under one banner. At an ACU board meeting, theorist Jeffrey Bell, a former aide to both Reagan and Kemp, argued that since conservatives had defeated Communism and won the debate on free-market economics, the "big unfinished agenda is the social issues, especially abortion. The liberals are saying to us, 'You've won on growth economics and anti-Communism. The only thing you have left is abortion on which you're unpopular with the public, so why don't you shrivel up and go away?'" At another fractious conservative summit where the movement's line was set, chaired by William F. Buckley, New Right leader Paul Weyrich called on conservatives to take on "the role of defending and fostering basic American values." Meanwhile, at the *Washington Times,* our owner, the Reverend Moon, declared in a speech, "A man's sexual organ belongs to his wife, this truth will never change! Anyone who doesn't agree is crazy!" (Moon, who was married in 1944 and divorced in 1950, was reported to be a ritual womanizer. Young girls reportedly underwent sexual initiation into his cult to cleanse them of "Satanic spirits.") Around this time, the *Times* began gay bashing in its pages, which became the subject of concerned interoffice messaging among the closeted gays at the paper; I was too busy climbing the editorial ladder to participate in the exchanges.

Paul Weyrich, a tall, rotund, pink-skinned man who for some reason always wore a black undertaker's suit, avoided the press and worked largely behind the scenes, but he was a familiar figure to me from around town, where he was revered as one of the architects of the modern conservative movement. Beginning in the early 1970s, when he left the staff of a conservative U.S. senator from Colorado, Gordon Allot, Weyrich set out to create an infrastructure on the right—political and legal interest groups, coalitions, think tanks, magazines, and political action committees—to rival that of the left. With $250,000 from Colorado brewer Joe Coors, and help from direct-mail fund-raising wizard Richard Viguerie, Weyrich founded the Heritage Foundation and made it into the premier research institution on the right. He then started the Free Congress Foundation and its PACs, dedicated to reversing entrenched Democratic rule on Capitol Hill. Within a decade, Weyrich's operation dwarfed anything like it on the left, making it possible for people like me to flock to Washington in droves and find jobs.

While Weyrich's organizational abilities were impressive, I was put off by his conservative populism—anti–New Deal, anti–civil rights, antiabortion, antigay. One of the first conservatives to see that southern evangelical Christians and northeastern ethnic Catholics alienated from the Democratic Party over civil rights and cultural issues could provide grassroots troops for the GOP, in 1979 Weyrich supplied the name for the Reverend Jerry Falwell's New Right group—the Moral Majority. In the 1980s, when I joined the movement, the Christian Right's political activities focused heavily on building support for anti-Communist guerrilla insurgencies around the globe. With godless Communism now vanquished, Weyrich's attention turned to mobilizing resentments for the domestic fight against the liberal culture, as defined by such things as abortion rights, gay rights, feminism, liberal judges, pornography, multiculturalism, affirmative action, and sex education in schools. Weyrich's Free Congress Foundation, for example, published a tract called *The Homosexual Network*, which warned direly of "a widening homosexual power grab in our society."*

By his own words, Weyrich revealed that he wasn't really a conservative at all in the older sense of the term. "We are no longer working to preserve the status quo. We are radicals, working to overturn the present power structure of the country," he declared. Weyrich described his views as "Maoist. I believe you have to control the countryside, and the capital will eventually fall." He advocated no-holds-barred tactics. "I am struck by the fact that we have lots of people who want to be nicer than God. If you read Scripture, Jesus was not some sort of milquetoast person with supreme charity," Weyrich said. "He cut people in two." One booklet on political tactics published by the Weyrich organization included a section saying that for the right reasons lying was to be regarded as a permissible "mental reservation." (Moon, too, taught that lying is necessary, even under oath, when one is doing "God's work.")

What no one expected was that the first casualty of Weyrich's campaign to restore "basic values" would be a Republican. In a move that stunned conservative Washington, Weyrich testified before the Senate that Bush's nominee for defense secretary, Senator John Tower of Texas, was a drunk and a womanizer. "I have encountered the nominee in a condition—a lack of sobriety— as well as with women to whom he was not married," Weyrich told the Senate. Word in movement circles was that Weyrich was flexing his muscles with a new, more moderate administration that might be tempted otherwise to

---

*In 2001, Weyrich, who had a history of associating with anti-Semites and racists that dated to his involvement with George Wallace's American Independent Party, was embroiled in a controversy over whether he himself was anti-Semitic. In an Easter essay, Weyrich, who called himself a "Melkite Greek Catholic deacon," wrote that "Christ was killed by the Jews." Weyrich was accused by conservative writer Evan Gahr of being a "demented anti-Semite."

ignore him. Tower also may have provoked Weyrich's ire because he was pro-choice. Though unproven, the charges were widely believed and sunk the nominee, who was unmarried at the time.

Though the Tower scandal is largely forgotten today, coming not long after Gary Hart dropped out of the 1988 Democratic presidential primaries when allegations of marital infidelity surfaced in the press, it fundamentally changed the way political battles were fought in Washington, seriously erod-ing the barrier between public and private. Though most Beltway conser-vatives were aghast at what Weyrich had done, he identified a dormant culturally conservative constituency in the Christian Right that believed the private lives of public people mattered just as much, perhaps even more, than their policy views. Weyrich's vicious attack on Tower demonstrated the new power of sexual politics, of making accusations with no proof, and of using ill-defined issues of "judgment" and "character" to discredit opponents based solely on alleged personal behavior. Sexual McCarthyism had been introduced into modern right-wing politics.

Another sign of the changing face of conservatism in the post-Reagan era, this one from outside the Washington Beltway, was the rise of Rush Limbaugh. A native of Missouri, hailing from a family of influential Republicans, Limbaugh was something of a ne'er-do-well, bouncing from job to job, until he found his niche during the Reagan years, delivering bombastic right-wing commentary on the news of the day at a local radio station in Sacramento, California. Taking the show national in 1988, Limbaugh's listenership more than dou-bled as he soared from 58 radio stations to 450, evidence that conservatives were hankering for a harder edge, and evidence, as well, that there was big money in bashing the left.

Limbaugh was a talented showman and originally considered himself more a comedian and entertainer than a political commentator. Rather than sticking to comedy, though, Limbaugh began calling himself a "journalist in relentless pursuit of the truth." Limbaugh's genius was in recognizing a vast market among conservatives who detested the liberal media and eagerly would gobble up an alternative source of information from a like-minded broadcaster. As Limbaugh once explained it: "The American people were fed up with the single version of events they were getting from the mainstream elite media. Someone on the air—me—has finally started saying what millions of people believed all their lives." He called his network Excellence in Broadcasting, but this was a misnomer, for under the guise of facts and evidence and logic he was really putting out disinformation to his hungry fans. A litany of his serious factual errors—from his claim that no one had been indicted in the Iran-contra affair, when in fact there had been fourteen indictments, to his suggestion that Congress had opposed the American use of force in the Persian Gulf, though both houses had authorized it—appeared in the *New Republic* under the headline "Rush Limbaugh's Lies." Limbaugh was undaunted.

In a period of social change unloosed in the 1960s and 1970s, and economic uncertainty brought on by globalization and the declining industrial sector in the 1980s, Limbaugh's simplicity was comforting to many. The self-described "most dangerous man in America" was an old-fashioned demagogue, staking a claim of moral superiority for those on "the right side," as he interpreted even the smallest developments in the news in a rigid evil/liberal versus good/conservative context. He instructed his millions of listeners, who called themselves "ditto heads" and tuned in to the show at noon in Rush Rooms around the country, not to bother reading the newspapers. "I will do all your reading, and I will tell you what to think about it," he declared.

Limbaugh cast the world as a war between "our" values and "theirs," a paradigm of the Cold War now applied to America itself, and he used vituperative language to draw the lines. He didn't spend much time on the Reagan agenda of smaller government, free markets, and a strong defense, playing instead to cultural animosities against women, minorities, and gays, and to right-wing fears of the sexual revolution—a bellwether of the demonizing themes the party was turning to. Limbaugh introduced himself to audiences as "your epitome of morality and virtue. A man you could totally trust with your wife, your daughter, and even your son in a Motel Six overnight." He told his listeners, "The American people are more and more turning to what is called traditional family values, rejecting what is abnormal or perverted" including "commie libs," "feminazis," "environmental wackos," the homeless, for whom he advocated spaying, and especially gays. He ran "gay community updates," introduced by a recording of Dionne Warwick belting out "I'll Never Love This Way Again," in which he lectured that gays had only themselves to blame for AIDS. And he opened segments on openly gay congressman Barney Frank, a frequent target, with the song "My Boy Lollipop."

Limbaugh essentially was taking a page from the *Dartmouth Review*—including regular skits where he would speak in "black English"—and broadcasting it nationally on the radio. He was often accused of racism. "Have you ever noticed how all newspaper composite pictures of wanted criminals resemble Jesse Jackson?" he once asked on the air. "Take that bone out of your nose and call me back," he told another caller. In response to a caller who said that black voices needed to be heard, Limbaugh snapped, "They are twelve percent of the population. Who the hell cares?" Many callers—women needed to send photos of themselves to make it through the screening process—vented similar prejudices. "Abortion is the baptism of feminism and lesbianism is their community," said one. Limbaugh himself staged "caller abortions," in which he switched on the sound of a vacuum cleaner as he hung up on those with whom he disagreed. Sexual dirt was a staple of Limbaugh's repertoire. His "Ted Kennedy Update," sung to the tune of "The Wanderer," included the lines "'Cause I'm a Kennedy / Yes, I'm Ted Kennedy / I sleep around, around, around, around."

With the notable exception of William Bennett, who called Limbaugh "possibly our greatest living American . . . extremely sophisticated, extremely smart . . . very serious intellectually," the Republican establishment was slow to embrace Limbaugh's routine. Though no one I knew in D.C. took the time to listen to the broadcast, he was striking a chord with listeners outside the political class. I first heard of Limbaugh from my dad in Texas, who thought Rush was just about the most compelling figure on the national scene since Father Charles Coughlin, the reactionary radio priest of the 1930s. On the other hand, Andrew, who was otherwise politically disengaged, couldn't resist occasionally tuning in to Rush on the car radio, in disbelief that such antigay bigotry was being broadcast on the airwaves.

Talk radio would soon emerge as a transformative political organizing tool for the right, with Rush Limbaugh the most famous and influential among dozens of hugely popular imitators from coast to coast. William F. Buckley, the *National Review* founder and prolific author, had a successor after all. Buckley's erudite, gentlemanly brand of principled conservatism, which had instructed the movement since the 1950s, had gone out of fashion. And the sort of ugly extremism Buckley had tried to rid the movement of—by such actions as condemning the red-baiting, racist John Birch Society—had won over a new generation of conservatives.

By 1992, Limbaugh was attracting attention among party strategists and pundits who were worried that Bush would take the party down to defeat in the November elections. The right-wing monthly the *American Spectator* featured Limbaugh on its cover, announcing the arrival of "Rush Limbaugh's Revolution." The article concluded by saying that "what Limbaugh has done is fill a political-cultural void created by the departure of Ronald Reagan, the last figure to speak unapologetically for American conservatism." Soon, the well-connected conservative columnists Rowland Evans and Robert Novak were reporting that a Bush aide had made a "tape of Limbaughisms that the boss might study." Evans and Novak agreed that "President Bush would do well to imitate the style of Rush Limbaugh." Two years hence, after becoming the first Republican Speaker of the House in forty years, Newt Gingrich would devote an entire chapter to Limbaugh in his book *To Renew America*, titled "Why Rush Limbaugh and His Friends Matter."

By the late 1980s and early 1990s, the politics of an urbane, Jewish, neoconservative insider like Bill Kristol, a Christian Right grassroots organizer like Paul Weyrich, and a right-wing midwestern demagogue with an angry following in the Republican rank and file like Rush Limbaugh had begun to converge around the partisan strategy of demonizing and condemning those Americans who were "different." The culture war of the Bork hearings was breaking out again, this time with much greater force. The politician on the scene who would tether the culture war to the political war was a "systematic revolutionary," as he called himself—Newt Gingrich. With conservatism adrift, the round-faced, gray-thatched Georgian supplied an anchor on Capitol Hill.

We were drawn to Newt in part because he wasn't a country club Republican like the Californian multimillionaire industrialists who comprised Reagan's kitchen cabinet. We had nothing but disdain for the airhead Republican set, the Biffs and the Buffys, who, with the exception of strategically placed Federalist Society lawyers, for the most part staffed the Bush White House. By contrast, the young conservative activists I knew—the D'Souzas, the Kristols, the Ingrahams—were not, for the most part, well-off WASPs. We had not inherited our Republicanism, or much else—we were mostly the offspring of middle-class, ethnic ex-Democrats. With a tinge of class resentment, perhaps, we almost always used the word "conservative" rather than "Republican" when describing ourselves. We were movement loyalists first, party loyalists second. In this respect, Newt's background seemed more like ex-Democrat and Eureka College graduate Ronald Reagan's (and ours) than Bush's, a Republican blue blood about whom we used to joke that no Yale grad with four names could ever be trusted. The son of an Army man, Newt broke with family tradition and joined the Republican Party in Georgia in 1960.

Newt cut an atypical Republican profile, earning a Ph.D. at Tulane, becoming a college history professor, and seeking office as a congressman who could toss off erudite references to Winston Churchill, Teddy Roosevelt, and the Kondratieff wave. When he talked about how the Third Wave information age would free the individual, stoke entrepreneurialism, and lead to the decentralization of state power, he could be inspirational. Newt not only read books, from Toynbee to Asimov, he wrote them. Newt thought big. He held great promise. We saw him as the natural successor to Reagan—a younger Reagan with a handle on the future, a leader both smarter and tougher. Describing a passage from a speech he heard Gingrich give, writer John Taylor observed in a profile for *Esquire*: "Breathtaking, dazzling, slightly dizzying, 124 words long yet syntactically coherent, this quintessentially Gingrichian sentence linked management theorists, a board chairman, a military hero, academic studies, historical documents, and a movie in a single sweeping concept. There was, to at least a few in the audience, something actually awe-inspiring about the speaker's performance. And it was not simply the air of erudition. He can convey, more than any other politician in America today, the sense that he grasps the historical moment he occupies."

Yet, looking back on it, Newt's fascinating and unpredictable intellectual interests, his futuristic cyberspeak, and his musings on the cycles of history never were joined to a new agenda for conservatism. Though he was known as a man of ideas, no one really knew what Newt stood for. Some feared that in his heart of hearts he was an opportunist, a nihilist even, using conservatism as a vehicle to win power. After the Republicans lost twenty-six seats in the 1982 elections, working with then Representatives Trent Lott of Mississippi and Dick Cheney of Wyoming, Gingrich had founded a new House caucus, the Conservative Opportunity Society, to do the unthinkable—shape the Republicans into a congressional majority. Yet since the issues were the same warmed-over GOP fare—balanced budget, crime, welfare reform, Star Wars missile defense—COS was more a new slogan than a new governing program. Newt, as it turned out, wasn't really interested in governing at all. He was interested in leading an insurrection against government itself and all of its functions except defense, a cause even more radically draconian than that contemplated by the neoconservative policy experts or enacted by the tax- and budget-cutters of the Reagan years. The only idea embedded in the rhetoric was a very old one: unregulated capitalism combined with an attack on altruism. ". . . Gingrich does have ideas," John Taylor wrote in *Esquire*. "Gingrich is essentially a proponent of social Darwinism, which initially took hold in the late nineteenth century—a time, much as today is, of massive immigration, racial tension, and the absence of compelling ideological differences in politics. Like Gingrich, the Victorian social Darwinists worshiped entrepreneurship; they actually celebrated the unfairness of life."

Newt also introduced a new style of Republicanism, based on confronting and demonizing the liberal culture that supported the big government idea. Newt understood that conservatism thrives only when it has an enemy, and in the Cold War's wake, Newt declared war again, this time on the *domestic* enemy, the Democratic Party and the "corrupt liberal welfare state" it sustained. Newt's analogy of American liberalism to world Communism made it possible for us to continue to divide the world into white hats and black hats, to channel our fears in a new direction. No longer would the Democrats simply be opposed; they would be destroyed. In this pathology, Gingrich was some years ahead of the party's chief ideologists. Not until 1993, after Bill Clinton's election as president, did Irving Kristol write in the *National Interest:* "There is no 'after the Cold War' for me. So far from having ended, my Cold War has increased in intensity, as sector after sector has been ruthlessly corrupted by the liberal ethos. Now that the other 'Cold War' is over, the real Cold War has begun. We are far less prepared for this Cold War, far more vulnerable to our enemy, than was the case with our victorious war against a global Communist threat."

Newt's overarching strategy was to portray the differences between the two parties as at root moral, not political, laying the rhetorical groundwork for an offensive that would play out in Washington over the next several years. As early as 1978, in his first race for Congress, Gingrich, who had trained in one of Paul Weyrich's seminars, called for a "return to moral values." He used certain outrageously stigmatizing language, long a hallmark of right-wing political organizing, to caricature the opposition as immoral, even evil. "People like me are what stand between us and Auschwitz," Gingrich declared. "I see evil around me every day." Newt called the Democrats "sick," "grotesque," "loony," "stupid," "corrupt," "anti-family," and "traitors." Describing the "value structure" of the left, Gingrich charged, "We were promised all the multi-partner sex you wanted and penicillin would take care of it. We were promised all the recreational drugs you wanted and it wouldn't be dangerous, wouldn't be addictive . . . The left-wing Democrats represent the party of total hedonism, total exhibitionism, total bizarreness, total weirdness, and the total right to cripple innocent people in the name of letting hooligans loose." In *Esquire*, Taylor concluded, ". . . Gingrich offers up a history of American values in a scheme so hysterically partisan, so transparently dishonest, so willfully stupid, that it's impossible to believe even Newt himself would expect anyone to take it seriously."

But Newt *did* take himself seriously, as did legions of other right-wingers across the country, including me. I can't speak for others, but to me, Newt's appeal was based less on political philosophy or ideology than on raw emotion. I instinctively identified with his fanatical hatred of the left. I thought name-calling was cool. This had seemed to be the lesson of the '88 campaign: We won when we talked about stuff like the Pledge of Allegiance and portrayed the other guy as having alien values. I liked Newt because, unlike the Burkean caution of Ronald Reagan that seemed to have failed us, he had the style of the angry campus revolutionary. I also have to wonder if adopting Newt's aggressive, warlike stance wasn't a way of releasing other pent-up frustrations: After all, I was in the closet, alienated from myself, and I was also a social misfit, unable to feel as though I was in the right place, no matter how many times I said and wrote all the right things and sported those silly bow ties. The apocalyptic "us versus them" paradigm was gratifying, for it held out the promise of assuaging my insecurities and giving me a sense of finally belonging.

Gingrich himself was plagued by many of the same demons. As Taylor wrote in *Esquire*, ". . . Gingrich has learned not just to endure rejection but to thrive on it. Separated from his biological father, he was also, when he was only a few days old, almost lost forever to his mother because of a mix-up in the maternity ward. His adoptive father, Bob Gingrich, who joined the Army after money problems forced him to drop out of medical school, was a harsh, unyielding man. Frustrated in his own ambitions (he had retired from the Army at age forty-nine to become a security guard and toll collector), he seemed to harbor a particular resentment toward his precocious adopted son. Moving from base to base, forced to make new friends every few years, Gingrich grew up the perennial outsider. Like the new kid on the playground, he has the garrulous desire to impress as well as the resentment of the persistently excluded. His cult of personal strength evolved as a survival strategy . . . ."

What I didn't see then was that a politics built on hatred of those who were not straight, white, God-fearing men in nuclear families would, as a matter of logic, turn against me and mine; I didn't see it because the disjuncture between what I was hearing from the conservative movement, and what I was seeing in it, allowed me to fool myself. I didn't take the culture war seriously because those who were espousing it all around me didn't seem to take it seriously, either. Rush Limbaugh, for instance, was not who he seemed to be on air. In the otherwise celebratory *Spectator* profile, the writer introduced one discordant note, describing Limbaugh as "an unlikely conservative warrior." While Limbaugh regularly denounces "lifestyle liber-alism," he is "twice divorced with no children . . . [and] does not go to church."

And Limbaugh seemed to be the rule rather than the exception. Of all of the editors I worked with during this period, my editor at *Commentary* (not Podhoretz) taught me more than anyone about how to write a sen-tence. He also schooled me in the uncompromising moral traditionalism of neocon orthodoxy. So I was surprised and troubled when I learned from an editor at another conservative magazine that he was engulfed in a scandal in New York literary circles over an extramarital affair with one of his young writers. I learned from this, at still an impressionable young age, that it was okay to lead public and private lives that bore little resemblance to each other.

As for Gingrich, I was never an intimate of his, but I was enough of an insider to see that Newt didn't seem like the kind of guy who would impose a fundamentalist view of morality on the rest of us. He struck me as another member of the decadent and hypocritical conservative elite, using whatever rhetorical flourishes he thought necessary to inflame cultural animosities in the right-wing base of the party. Through my connections in the world of closeted gay conservatives, I knew that Newt had top gay and lesbian advis-ers. He and his wife, Marianne, were especially close to Steve Gunderson, who then was one of a handful of closeted gay Republicans in Congress. And, despite his moral chest thumping, Newt seemed a product of the per-missive culture he was attacking. He had admitted smoking marijuana, avoided service in Vietnam, and divorced his first wife, Jackie, while she was sick with cancer.* If widespread reports from Gingrich's inner circle could be believed, he was an unfaithful husband to his second wife, Marianne. The story, persistent among Gingrich intimates, was that Newt was having an affair with a female aide to Steve Gunderson, which turned out to be true.

---

*In court papers, Jackie Gingrich charged in 1980 that Gingrich failed to provide enough money to pay for support of their children, and she said the electric company was about to shut off power. She eventually won a judgment requiring Gingrich to increase his payments.

Socially permissive as I was, to me Newt's private life made him seem less judgmental and more human, and I hoped to receive the same kind of understanding from him and other conservatives with regard to my own personal life. What I underestimated was Newt's capacity for hypocrisy: his ability to live his personal life as he wished, his embrace of his own closeted gay posse, while leading a scorched-earth crusade to have the government enforce right-wing political and social values—the very opposite of the ideals of liberty and limited government he claimed to espouse.

Among younger conservatives like me, Newt Gingrich attracted a cadre of loyal acolytes. Foremost among these was the automaton Grover Norquist— or Grosser Nosetwist to his detractors inside the movement. To meet him, you might think Grover was a typical nose-to-the-grindstone D.C. policy wonk, but Grover wasn't at all a typical wonk in his fierce dedication to his causes, whether it was anti-Communism or hostility to government in all forms. As a youngster, Grover had been deeply impressed by the 1950s conservative classic *Witness*, written by Whittaker Chambers. When Grover first came to Washington from Harvard in 1978, the sight of imposing federal buildings made him "physically ill," he explained to the *Washington Post*. "They took people's money to build those things, people who were just getting by, [they] stole their money and built those things out of marble. . . . Neo-American fascism, stuff that looks like Albert Speer designed it."

As a leader of a movement marked by pessimism and paranoia, Grover was remarkably confident and, even in the face of setbacks, relentlessly optimistic about our ultimate triumph. After Harvard, Grover took a job at the College Republicans, an adjunct of the Republican National Committee, where, among other things, he mentored a young Ralph Reed. By the time I met him, Grover had started his own corporate-funded group, which he called Americans for Tax Reform, to drum up grassroots conservative support for Reagan's 1986 tax plan. Grover told the *New Republic*, which called him "the Che Guevara of the Republican Revolution," that he inherited his fiscal conservatism from his parents, who raised him in a wealthy Massachusetts suburb. Each time they went out for ice cream, his father would bite into Grover's cone, punctuating the bites with "sales tax," "income tax," and "estate tax." In Washington, Grover found a soul mate in Newt Gingrich, often taking long early morning walks with the congressman to plot strategy.

Like his fellow radical conservatives, Norquist believed politics was an extension of war by other means. If Newt had identified the post-Soviet enemy as the "corrupt," "treasonous" Democratic Party, Grover's job was to map out the battle plan. His organizational meetings were held in an office building on Dupont Circle every Wednesday morning and were attended by a who's who of conservative activists in town, representing about seventy interest groups, each with effective grassroots operations, including the National Taxpayers Union, the National Right to Life Committee, the National Rifle Association, and the Christian Coalition. Also in attendance at these so-called Wednesday Group functions were writers from conservative publications like the *Washington Times* and *National Review*, which essentially functioned as appendages of the movement.

Grover would have been a comic figure if he hadn't been so deadly serious. At the Wednesday Group sessions, Grover announced that in dismantling the "liberal welfare state," we would target "the weakest parts of the empire"—legal services for the poor and government support for the arts— just as the Cold War had been fought in remote villages in Mozambique. As if to underscore the point, Norquist showed off photos of himself in combat fatigues and brandishing assault rifles, regaling the group with tales of his travels with anti-Communist guerrillas in Afghanistan and Angola, trying to kill what he invariably called "the other team."

Grover's simple anti-Communist, antistatist platform was the essence of Reaganism as I understood it then. What those outside the movement failed to understand about Grover was that his antitax fervor was based not on principle—a desire to ease the tax burden on the American family—but on cynical partisanship. Cutting taxes, he often said, was a way to "defund the left." When government grew, Grover theorized, so did the voting rolls of government bureaucrats, who cast their ballots for the Democrats. Single-mindedly focused on attaining power, Norquist sought to demolish not only the Democratic power structure, but also the established Republican one.

The moderate-conservative House minority leader Bob Michel had to be deposed, Norquist liked to say, because Michel didn't wake up every morning "wanting to hurt the other team."

There was nothing traditionally conservative in Grover's approach. As I conformed myself to the movement, I was being inculcated into a radical cult that bore none of the positive attributes of classical conservatism—a sense of limits, fair play, Tory civility, and respect for individual freedom. On the contrary, Grover admired the iron dedication of Lenin, whose dictum "Probe with bayonets, looking for weakness" he often quoted, and whose majestic portrait hung in Grover's Washington living room. Grover kept a pet boa constrictor, named after turn-of-the-century anarchist Lysander Spooner. He fed the snake mice, all of them named David Bonior, the outspoken liberal House whip. And he studied the writings of Antonio Gramsci, a leading Italian Communist, who had argued that to change society, a political movement must first "capture the culture."

Of all of the intellectual mentors Grover cited, the life of Antonio Gramsci is perhaps the most instructive in understanding the character of the young radical conservative. Like Gramsci, Grover was possessed of a superior intellect and a militant persona. Gramsci was alienated from his father and originally embraced socialism because his older brother had. Gramsci had a hunched back and stood not even five feet high. While in school, Gramsci's father cut him off financially, leading to further deterioration in their relations and plaguing the young intellectual with untreated nervous disorders. Despite his promise as an academic, Gramsci became active in the Socialist Party and launched a career as a fierce pamphleteer, making himself a voice to be reckoned with throughout Italian political circles. Inspired by the Bolshevik Revolution in October 1917, Gramsci sided with the Communist minority within the Socialist Party and built up the Italian Communist Party at the dawn of the Italian fascist movement. After serving as Italy's delegate in Moscow to the Communist International, he was elected general secretary of the Communist Party in Italy. Soon thereafter, Gramsci was arrested by the government in Rome and spent ten years in prison producing his most influential revolutionary writings, in the form of notebooks and letters, before dying of a cerebral hemorrhage in 1937. Two decades later, his writings were studied carefully by the radical left throughout the world, particularly by leaders of revolutionary movements in the Third World—and by the anti-Communist Grover Norquist.

In their ferocious attacks on the liberal Democratic opposition, the Gingrichians adopted the exaggerated "by any means necessary" philosophy of the '60s radicals that they said they abhorred. In his book *Rock the House*, about the 1994 GOP takeover of Congress he helped Gingrich engineer, Norquist wrote: "How do you ever expect to gain allies saying 'I'm standing in the train tracks, and the train is going to run me over, but the right and virtuous thing for you to do is to stand with me while we lose.' I think you should run up 100 yards and blow up the train tracks and then see what the train thinks about that."

A few years back, Gingrich had been deeply impressed by the results of private GOP polling showing that Democratic criticism of Reagan attorney general Ed Meese's ethics badly damaged him. Paul Weyrich advised Gingrich that he would never rise to power within the GOP unless he also targeted a powerful figure for defeat. By the late 1980s, Gingrich and Norquist had developed a strategy to portray the Democratic leadership of the House as a corrupt feudal hierarchy, and they used the good government ethics reforms of the 1970s, passed by the Democrats after Watergate, to take it down. Calling House Speaker Jim Wright "the most unethical Speaker in the history of the House," Gingrich—with virtually no backing from his House colleagues—buried him in an avalanche of ethics charges, focusing mainly on private financial dealings. Miraculously, a couple stuck: Gingrich called it "a fishing expedition that caught a whale." Though by pre-Watergate standards, Wright hadn't really done anything wrong, Newt understood how to exploit the new rules to impugn Wright's personal integrity. Soon after the ethics committee found that Wright had violated House rules in his business arrangements with a Texas friend, and had gotten around limits on speaking fees by selling copies of a book he wrote to lobbyists, Wright resigned, but not before denouncing Gingrich for introducing "mindless cannibalism" into the chamber.

Conservatives long had defended a critical distinction between public and private realms, while the idea that the "personal is political" had been a slogan of the 1960s New Left. Along with leaders like Paul Weyrich, Gingrich took conservatism on a sharply different course, embracing and twisting this notion of the 1960s radicals to their own ends, using sexual innuendo to smear people who stood in his path. With Wright beheaded, Newt's operation struck at his successor, Tom Foley of Washington. Mark Goodin, the communications director of the RNC, put out a memo called "Tom Foley: Out of the Liberal Closet," comparing Foley's voting record with openly gay Congressman Barney Frank's. Gingrich was forced to apologize to Foley and Goodin was forced to resign, but another low, dishonest precedent was set.

Even within conservatism, Newt was a renegade. He had a cadre of young storm troopers in his camp, but most traditional conservatives were appalled by Gingrich's tactics and suspicious of his motives. Columnist George Will compared Gingrich to Senator Joseph McCarthy. "Some ideologically intoxicated Republicans think the Democrats are not merely mistaken but sinful. Such Republicans believe the Earth must be scorched and sown with salt before the Heavenly City can be built," Will wrote. Representative Dan Coats, an original member of Gingrich's Conservative Opportunity Society, quit the group, saying that "Newt's belief" that "you almost had to destroy the system so that you could rebuild it" was "kind of scary stuff." Reflecting the discomfort of the Republican Old Guard with Gingrich and his guerrillas, Senate minority leader Dole said, "They aren't the Republican Party, and they aren't going to be." "The young hypocrites," he called them—no, us.

Over time, such warnings would be muted as Newt advanced through Republican ranks. By toppling Wright, Gingrich demonstrated that scandal politics was our path to power, and he became, if not yet the leader of the GOP, the unofficial leader of the House Republicans. The Young Turks in the House, people like Trent Lott, and Tom DeLay and Dick Armey of Texas, who had come into office with Reagan, saw Newt as one of them; he also won some support from younger Republicans like Bill Paxon, Vin Weber, and Steve Gunderson, who were hankering for power. In a race for House whip in 1989 on the heels of Jim Wright's resignation, a slot that opened up when Dick Cheney was named defense secretary after the defeat of John

Tower, Gingrich ran against Congressman Ed Madigan. Madigan, who had the backing of the Old Bulls, Bob Michel and the pre-Reagan GOP establishment, fell short by only two votes. "Ed Madigan is a nice guy, and nice guys aren't what we're looking for," explained Representative Charles Douglas of New Hampshire.

After Reagan's election as president, Newt's ascension into the House leadership was the most pivotal event in modern movement history. He quickly moved to extend his power base, using his corporate-financed political action committee, GOPAC, and its offshoots—"Newt's world," as it was known—to help fund and train like-minded GOP House candidates around the country, and to consciously remake the Republican caucus in his own image, something Reagan—whose sharper corners had been smoothed over by the Doles and the Michels—never managed to do. Newt himself taught a class called "Renewing American Civilization" at two colleges in Georgia that was broadcast nationally via satellite; tapes were sold to GOP recruits by GOPAC. One GOPAC training tape suggested using "contrast words" to describe opponents, including "decay, failure, shallow, traitors, pathetic, corrupt, incompetent, sick." The college course, and another organization called the American Campaign Academy, whose goal was to activate 200,000 citizen-activists throughout the country, were housed under the auspices of two tax-exempt foundations. The law required that the activities not be political in nature. Yet the American Campaign Academy operated with $1 million in financing from the Republican Congressional Trust, and Gingrich operative Joe Gaylord was paid $1 million through GOPAC to develop it as a vehicle to professionalize the training of GOP activists.

Newt's chief counselor in these efforts was Gaylord, who had served as executive director of the National Republican Congressional Committee in 1983, about the time Newt founded the Conservative Opportunity Society. Originally from Iowa, Gaylord was given his major training in politics by a man named Eddie Mahe, Gaylord's predecessor as political director of the NRCC. If Grover Norquist represented the movement side of Gingrich's operation, Gaylord, a handsome man with wavy white hair and sharp features, was the nuts-and-bolts political mechanic. Gaylord knew

every House race in the country, district by district, and he had helped
Newt win his first race in 1978. In a pamphlet called *Flying Upside Down*,
written for the NRCC on how to beat the Democrats, Gaylord advised
candidates to go negative, often and early.

But under Gaylord's leadership in 1984, 1986, and 1988, the
Republicans performed poorly in House races. Gaylord soon left his post,
setting up shop at Gingrich's GOPAC, becoming a consultant to the group
for candidate recruitment and training—and much more. In one memo to
GOPAC's chairman, Newt wrote: "Joe Gaylord is empowered to supervise
my activities, set my schedule, advise me on all aspects of my life and
career. He is my chief counselor and one of my closest friends." From his
perch at GOPAC, Gaylord was able to engineer Newt's defeat of Madigan
by calling in chits from members from his days at the NRCC. Gaylord then
installed Gingrich people into the leadership slots and the campaign committees of the Republicans in the House, eventually forcing Bob Michel's
retirement as minority leader. Newt was positioned to succeed Michel and
assume the levers of power in the GOP, becoming, in Newt's words, "an
old-time political boss."

CHAPTER FOUR

"A COUNTER-INTELLIGENTSIA"

Midway through the Bush administration, I left my job at the *Times* to serve at the Heritage Foundation in a yearlong fellowship underwritten by the John M. Olin Foundation, a philanthropy supported by the Olin family petrochemical fortune. From this sinecure, working for the first time not among writers and editors but among hard-core movement activists, I saw how right-wing ideology was manufactured and controlled by a small group of powerful foundations like Olin, the Adolph Coors Foundation, the Smith-Richardson Foundation, the Scaife Family Trusts, and others that lavishly underwrote the effort. William Simon, a rock-ribbed conservative and high-profile leveraged buyout king who had been treasury secretary under Presidents Nixon and Ford, became president of Olin in 1976 with the explicit intention of redirecting its grant making to achieving partisan political results for the right. He also founded the Institute for Educational Affairs, which bankrolled the right-wing campus reviews. "The only thing that can save the Republican Party . . . is a counter-intelligentsia," Simon said.

Following the Watergate scandal and the economic recession of the mid-1970s, major American corporations, especially in the West, teamed up with the Wall Street venture capital class to coordinate their political activities. They gave targeted donations in the tens of millions to conservative political action committees like Terry Dolan's National Conservative Political Action Committee and Paul Weyrich's Free Congress PACs; and they promoted right-wing ideology through a network of think tanks and issue lobbies and publications advocating free-market capitalism, deregulation, and lower corporate taxes. In his 1978 book *A Time for Truth*, Simon called on business leaders and corporate foundation executives to fund "intellectual refuges for the non-egalitarian scholars and writers in our society who today work largely alone in the face of overwhelming indifference or hostility. They must be given grants, grants, and more grants in exchange for books, books, and more books."

With Simon on its board, the American Enterprise Institute in Washington, a conservative think tank that housed Irving Kristol, Robert Bork, Jeane Kirkpatrick, and Charles Murray, among others, doubled its operating budget by the late 1970s. In the 1980s, Heritage's annual income soared from $1 million to $18 million. While the corporations were primarily interested in funding antiregulatory, antitax, and anti–labor union research and advocacy, many of them also saw the need to protect and expand overseas investment opportunities by underwriting the anti-Communist cause. Though the alliance was at times uneasy, the socially conservative New Rightists, coming into a position of dominance within the broader conservative movement, were well placed to take advantage of the corporate largesse.

No institution better exemplified the convergence of various strains of conservatism than Heritage, founded by Paul Weyrich and Edwin Feulner, with start-up money from Coors and additional backing from a range of corporate sponsors, including oil and gas, electronics, and pharmaceutical interests. Companies like RJ Reynolds tobacco and the consumer goods giant Amway were major donors. The foundation recruited for its board Richard Mellon Scaife, an heir to the Mellon banking fortune; Lewis Lehrman, a drugstore magnate; Dr. Robert Krieble, founder of the worldwide chemical corporation Loctite; and writer Midge Decter. Lavishing six-figure fellowships on such figures as Edwin Meese and William Bennett, Heritage promoted aggressive anti-Communism, laissez-faire economics, and the moral traditionalism of the New Right. Heritage made its first mark in 1981 with a volume called *Mandate for Leadership* that became the ideological blueprint for the new Reagan administration. Heritage is a tax-exempt foundation, requiring that it not engage in activities or lobbying benefiting a political party. However, the organization functioned as a de facto arm of the GOP, churning out slick position papers, called Heritage Backgrounders, that were then marketed on Capitol Hill by a specially designated congressional relations shop. The authors of the papers were nominally independent researchers, but in the argot of Grover Norquist, they were expected to behave as loyal members of the conservative movement "team." Essentially, the papers backed up an already fixed ideological viewpoint, dictated directly by a tier of Heritage executives who decided the organization's position on a given issue, and indirectly by the outside foundations that held Heritage's purse strings.

Olin seemed eager to credit and finance the research of promising young conservatives, who then fanned out across the nation's op-ed pages and television airwaves (direct from an in-house studio), promoting the movement agenda with a scholarly veneer. Though I had no advanced degrees, I assumed the grandiose title of John M. Olin Fellow in Congressional Studies, which, if nothing else, certainly impressed my parents when I sent them a copy of the Heritage press release announcing my appointment. At this straitlaced, corporate-style think tank, I had a much harder time finding my footing than I had among journalists at the *Times*. I showed up for work each day grimly retreating to my office behind a closed door, and I forged virtually no personal relationships, with one exception. To get through some social obligations without arousing suspicions about my sexuality, I feigned interest in an attractive young woman, Meg Hunt, who worked across the hall and deployed her as my escort. The relationship went no further than that; either she thought I was the perfect gentleman, or maybe she knew better and simply welcomed the company. Still, I was aware of the deception involved, and I felt chagrined and increasingly panicked as I actively adopted a false pose for the first time since coming to Washington.

I was assigned to the legislative affairs section, but, feeling alienated by my surroundings, purposely missed their early Friday morning strategy sessions. It appeared to me that no one really knew what went on in the upper tier of Heritage's management. Feulner—Dr. Feulner, as he was called—spent most of his time on the road raising money, in the United States and abroad. Heritage raised a significant amount of money from conservative business interests in South Korea, Taiwan, and Japan. Over time, even within the movement, many concluded that foreign money corrupted the scholarly work Heritage put out on foreign policy. One of the strangest things I learned for sure at Heritage was that the organization was the least efficient bureaucracy—surely worse than any government agency—I would ever encounter. Literally three requisition forms were required of me before I could get a replacement bulb for my desk lamp.

My assignment was to write a monograph, which I hoped to publish as a book, challenging the conservative orthodoxy on the proper relationship between the executive and legislative branches of government. Given the exigencies of the Cold War, and especially during the controversy over funding for the anti-Communist guerrilla movements in the Third World, a conservative consensus had gelled that congressional involvement in foreign policy was an unconstitutional usurpation of executive authority. My idea was that with the Cold War over and a squish like Bush in the White House, this principled conservative preference for a strong executive and a weak Congress should give way to the political reality that the conservative agenda could be best advanced by renegade conservatives on Capitol Hill. At Heritage, where Bush was regarded with suspicion, if not contempt, the argument would be well received. In one celebrated incident, a Heritage executive, Ben Hart's wife, Betsy, had presided over a meeting where a replica of Bush's head was presented on a silver platter.

I spent much of my research time in 1990 and 1991 scrawling down notes and drinking beer at the Monocle, a popular Capitol Hill watering hole, with senior Senate and House staffers assigned to the House Republican Study Committee and the Senate Steering Committee. The two groups were founded by Paul Weyrich, working with then-congressman Trent Lott, to push the congressional Republican caucus in a more conservative direction and punish wayward Republicans when they "sold out" the movement. These radical activists believed that conservatives should grab power anywhere they could get it in the political system, even if it meant flouting the constitutional separation of powers and other established processes of government.

It said something about my agitated frame of mind that I chose as my mentors on the Heritage project two notorious right-wing activists. David Sullivan was a chubby, spectacled fellow in his mid-forties who had spent the 1980s trying to undermine the Reagan administration's arms control deals with the Soviets from his post on the Senate Foreign Relations Committee under Senator Jesse Helms. Nicknamed "Mad Dog," Sullivan, a Harvard graduate with a master's degree from Columbia who was also a lieutenant colonel in the U.S. Marine Corps Reserves, was perhaps the most skilled obstructionist on the Hill, a master of bureaucratic intrigue and strategic leaking to the press—"rat fucking" the enemy, in Sullivan's words. My other mentor, Michael Pillsbury, an adviser to right-wingers in the House, including Gingrich, looked like the Hannibal Lecter character in the film *The Silence of the Lambs*. Dr. Pillsbury was fluent in Mandarin Chinese and had an encyclopedic knowledge of every minor wrinkle in American foreign policy during the Cold War. In 1986, in a bit of derring-do, he had been forced out of the Reagan Pentagon for doing an end run around his own superiors in a bid to provide Stinger missiles for the anti-Communist guerrillas fighting the Soviet-backed regime in Afghanistan. I revered them both.

At the end of my year at Heritage, I was approached by Adam Meyerson, who had published my "Big Chill" article while I was still at Berkeley back in 1985, and asked to write up my findings for Heritage's influential journal, *Policy Review*. I ended the *Policy Review* article by standing on its head the case for a strong executive I had made in defending the Reagan administration's Iran-contra policies: "The biggest fear for conservatives should not be of congressional overreaching in foreign policy. It should be that their own political leaders and opinion-setters will continue to sit on their hands, blithely reciting passages from *The Federalist* in deference to executive power, while ceding the foreign-policy field to the congressional left. It would be far more effective for conservatives to get in the trenches and throw more grenades."

My time at Heritage marked a significant turning point in my career. Dating back to my days in Berkeley, I saw myself as a participant in the political wars, and coming of age when I did, in a period of conservative decline and ideological confusion, the partisan blood lust and underhanded tactics of everyone from Ollie North to Newt Gingrich to Paul Weyrich to Mad Dog Sullivan held real appeal. I was soon taking my own advice; my writing began to reflect a propensity for grenade throwing.

I had been grateful a few years back to be invited into the pages of *Commentary* and the *Wall Street Journal*, a feat for someone my age, and my writings in those sober venues, while hewing to the party line, reflected a certain intellectual integrity and high-mindedness. I defended Dan Quayle in *Commentary* ("Quayle So Far"), defended free trade in the *National Interest* ("The Theory and Practice of Japan-Bashing"), and defended SDI in the *Journal*. In these early years in Washington, I was also a model of discipline and restraint. Though I was ambitious, my ego was in check, and so was my avarice. I kept my head down, and did my work, just like all the other young conservative scribes. Why this wasn't enough for me, I'm still not exactly sure, but I do know that my move in an opposite direction wasn't a decision; it was an emotional impulse. Perhaps I sensed I didn't have the ability, or temperament, or patience, to make a name for myself writing for highbrow publications like *Commentary*. I felt confined and bored by the staid form of the essay and the op-ed; I wanted to get my hands dirty, to do some real reporting. The vibe from the movement was radicalizing me, too.

Then, as well, just at this time my personal life turned tumultuous. My relationship with Andrew had always been rocky, partly because I had lied to him about my family background when we first met, trying to hide my adoptive status. But as we lived together through the years, he came to realize that the story I told him didn't hold together. In 1987, my sister Regina, then in her mid-twenties, came to Washington for a visit. Something about her instant bond with Andrew ate away at me. One night, worried and depressed, I went to bed while they went out for drinks after dinner. My mother had told me that she and my father had decided to hide from my sister the fact that I was gay after they first learned of it from me in 1982. Over drinks, my sister asked Andrew if we were gay and he said yes. Perhaps liberated by that truth, Regina told Andrew that she and I were adopted.

I can only imagine the impact this conversation had on Andrew, who had been living with a liar. Since he had grown to love me, Andrew must have wrestled with the issue and weighed it together with other problems we were having. He never said a word to me about it until years later. Within a few months, he told me that the only way we could continue to live together was as friends, in a larger space, in separate bedrooms. An emotional mess over the breakup, I agreed to move to hold on to any piece of Andrew I could. I was in intense pain because he had left me—inexplicably.

Andrew and I moved to larger quarters, a rickety rental house that he chose in the quiet, leafy Woodley Park section of the city, and we lived relatively amicably for four more years as the closest of friends. In every way but romantically we were just like the couple we had always been. Soon, we both began to date other men. Of course, Andrew had a much easier time of making the transition than I did. I managed to date a few men sporadically in the late 1980s and early 1990s while living with Andrew, but being a closeted right-winger this was perilous business, all the more so during my time at Heritage, where I had a divided persona—taking Meg Hunt to a Christmas party at Ben and Betsy Hart's home in the Virginia suburbs one night, and going on dates with men on other nights. I was lucky to find a young architect named Kevin, whom I saw for about a year until early 1991, which included the period of my Heritage fellowship, when my politics became more right wing, and my way of expressing it became so vehement it bordered on the vicious. When Kevin and I parted as friends in January 1991, he made a multicolored carving, dated 26 January 1991, that carried a hidden inscription on the back, which I never saw until ten years later, when I lifted it out of its frame. Kevin had written:

As it happens, I am giving this Christmas present to you on the same weekend that we met one year ago. As you are reading this, it is probably some time, maybe years later. I hope that your books have become best-sellers, especially the one about your lightning-bolt conversion to neoliberalism . . . In any case, I truly hope that we have grown as friends and have shared many more good times together. Your friend always, Love, Kevin.

I suppose Kevin could see a soul worth knowing beneath it all. He moved to Texas to do graduate work, and I immediately missed his presence in my life. He had been one of the few self-aware gay men who had been willing to put up with my right-wing ranting. However, I was far more devastated by Andrew's abrupt announcement at this very time that he was moving back to California.

I was furious and depressed about being left alone in D.C. I had no real friends or meaningful relationships of my own, and my relations with my family, especially my father, were cool at best. Andrew was all I had in the world. With him out of the picture, I tried to suppress all traces of gayness and poured all my energies into my career. With the benefit of hindsight it's clear that I had set myself up, once again, to displace my emotional life and channel my personal misery into my writing. Rather than relaxing over dinner with Andrew in the evening and maybe going to a gay bar for a beer, every night I sat alone in that rickety house, at a small, mission-style wooden desk in a cramped bedroom, brooding about a life I knew was out there but couldn't have as I feverishly pecked away on the computer. A mad dog, an emotional monster, was about to be unleashed.

For all these reasons, in some combination, I was rather suddenly drawn to the psychic thrill of relentless partisan attack, and to an altogether new genre of malicious right-wing muckraking.

In approaching the *American Spectator* to do some freelance writing, I had in mind furthering the conservative cause by consciously imitating the advocacy journalism of the New Left, pioneered in such publications as the *Village Voice* and *Ramparts* magazine. These leftists, like Upton Sinclair and Lincoln Steffens before them, suspended the rules of conventional journalism, taking a crusading role in the events they wrote about. Though I didn't have the skills or judgment of Sinclair or Steffens, I nonetheless set about writing for a magazine that would allow me to be more overtly political than I had been at *Insight*, which kept up the form and style of a newsmagazine. Advocacy journalism can be done well, by a balanced person. But by an unbalanced one—well, the results were disastrous.

While muckraking may have been too outré for the rest of the buttoned-up conservative press, it was the right fit for the feisty, irreverent monthly that had been founded as an alternative student publication—originally called the *Alternative*—at the University of Indiana by R. Emmett Tyrrell Jr. The year was 1967, and Tyrrell was protesting the election of a student body president who was a member of the New Left movement Students for a Democratic Society. Two decades before my generation would rise up against the same forces, the *Spectator* had been founded in the spirit of youthful rebellion against campus leftism. An Irish Catholic native of Chicago, Tyrrell had been able to keep the student magazine going after college by cultivating older conservatives like William F. Buckley and Irving Kristol. Like the other conservative opinion journals, the *Spectator* was a money-losing proposition dependent on monied interests to keep it afloat. Buckley and Kristol helped persuade rich benefactors like textile magnate Roger Milliken and Wall Street venture capitalist Theodore Forstmann, corporations like Philip Morris tobacco, and several foundations to underwrite the *Spectator*—among others, the list included the Olin Foundation, the Lynde and Harry Bradley Foundation, the Smith-Richardson Foundation, and the Scaife foundations. (The same Four Sisters, as they were known, also bankrolled Heritage.)

By far the most important benefactor in the *Spectator*'s firmament was Richard Mellon Scaife, the eccentric, Pittsburgh-based Mellon banking and oil heir. Scaife's mother, Sarah, was the granddaughter of Thomas Mellon, founder of the family fortune. Beginning in the mid-1960s when Sarah Scaife died, her son Richard gained control of four family trusts, and he began to direct hundreds of millions of dollars from them into building an infrastructure for the then-nascent conservative movement. The left didn't have anything close to as dedicated a sugar daddy as Scaife. His idea was to mirror liberal organizations by setting up think tanks such as Heritage; legal foundations and litigation groups to fight civil libertarians and environmentalists like the Landmark Legal Foundation; a network of Cold War national security and intelligence centers; watchdog groups like Accuracy in Media; and publications like the *American Spectator*.

Scaife's crusade, which he described as a "war over American values," was born of Barry Goldwater's defeat in the 1964 presidential campaign, which left Scaife bitterly determined to fight liberalism and discredit its idea of achieving social advances through government. He gave $1 million to Richard Nixon in 1972 (in 334 separate checks to avoid gift taxes), but after Watergate, a dejected Scaife began to funnel his money into institutions rather than individuals. In the early 1970s, Scaife dabbled in publishing of a sort. According to published reports, at the behest of the CIA, Scaife subsidized a London-based news service called Forum World Features that disseminated CIA propaganda, promoting agency causes and attacking its enemies, in newspapers around the globe. During this period, the news service was charged by British intelligence officers with ginning up phony personal scandals against Labour Party members to boost the electoral fortunes of the Conservatives.

According to calculations made by the *Washington Post*, Scaife gave more than $200 million to conservative institutions between 1974 and 1992 in an attempt to influence government policy and train personnel. Though he operated in the shadows, Scaife was the most important single figure in building the modern conservative movement and spreading its ideas into the political realm. In a speech to the Heritage Foundation's Presidents' Club, Newt Gingrich saluted two people "who have really created modern conservatism—Dick Scaife and [Heritage President] Ed Feulner." Gingrich went on: "Scaife is a remarkable citizen who has spent many years as a key force in sustaining conservative ideas and who has played a major, major role on Heritage's board, and he's been a good friend and good ally for a very long time, and I remember working with him starting in the late 1970s." A remote figure, Scaife operated his four foundations—the Allegheny, Carthage, Scaife Family, and Sarah M. Scaife foundations—through two deputies and rarely spoke to the press. Approached by a reporter for the *Columbia Journalism Review* who tried to question him, Scaife railed, "You fucking Communist cunt, get out of here."

Scaife was an unlikely general in a war to restore traditional values. According to the *Washington Post*, Scaife openly kept a companion on the side for years during his first marriage. Scaife eventually divorced and married the longtime companion, who continued to live apart from him in the nearby house where Scaife had kept her. Scaife's problems with alcoholism became so severe that he almost drank himself to death more than once, the newspaper said. The *Post* quoted Scaife's sister, Cordelia, as saying that Sarah Mellon Scaife was "just a gutter drunk . . . So was Dick . . . So was I." The *Post* also reported that Scaife's family relations were terrible; he was on speaking terms with neither his daughter nor his sister. Scaife's sister had stopped speaking to him twenty-five years earlier, when her husband was found dead. Richard Scaife had bitterly opposed the marriage. The death was ruled an accident or a suicide, but the *Post* reported Scaife's sister suspected at the time that her brother Richard was somehow involved.

Many years later, in 1999, Scaife was linked to another death. By this time, Scaife had been identified as a central figure in a special project run by the *Spectator*, which he funded, to drive President Clinton from office. According to the *Washington Post*, Scaife had feared that he was a target of a Las Vegas man who regularly denounced him on the Internet, and Scaife had hired a private detective to investigate rather than call the police. The Scaife critic eventually showed up in the building in Pittsburgh where Scaife keeps his office, toting a gun. Soon thereafter, he was found dead in a men's room in the building. The death was ruled a suicide. When a competing Pittsburgh newspaper reported on the suspicious death, the reporter was denounced in the Scaife-owned Pittsburgh *Tribune-Review* as a "Scaife hater" who should have realized that the dead man was "an unstable man who became fully unhinged [and] was pushed over the top by liberals . . . who joined the Clinton White House and their friends to demonize Dick Scaife."

To older conservatives like Scaife, the *Spectator*, a kind of right-wing *National Lampoon*, was an encouraging sign that the right was making inroads with the young. Bob Tyrrell took as his mentor the American satirist H. L. Mencken, known for his wicked pen, and originally infused the pages of the magazine, which he modeled after Mencken's 1920s-era *American Mercury*, with a high-spirited skepticism of all ideologies and agendas. In the early years, the magazine attracted writers ranging from democratic socialist Sidney Hook, to liberal Harvard professor Roger Rosenblatt, to a young writer named George Will, who called himself a Whig. The humorist P. J. O'Rourke also got his start at the magazine. In the late '70s, *Time* had named Tyrrell—we called him Bob—"one of the future 50 leaders of America." Bob imagined himself as the Buckley of his generation.

Since moving the magazine from a run-down farmhouse called the Establishment outside the midwestern college town of Bloomington, Indiana, in 1986, to offices inside the Washington Beltway in suburban Virginia, the *Spectator*, renamed after a 1930s literary magazine published by George J. Nathan and evoking the stuffy London *Spectator*, had shed its freewheeling, individualist roots, when the magazine seemed to insist on little beyond drinking spirits. The magazine's offices, which could have been those of a small insurance office, were dominated by a giant lithograph of Barry Goldwater and lined along the halls with black-and-white photos of Bob posing with conservative moneybags like Lewis Lehrman—Bob's version of the Washington vanity wall. As Bob sought to become an influential figure in the movement, the magazine became more predictable, joining the conformist chorus of first Cold War, and then culture war, conservatives. The ubiquitous trio of Jeane Kirkpatrick, Midge Decter, and Irving Kristol joined the editorial board.

By 1988, Ronald Reagan was being celebrated at a dinner at Bob's home among the faux Georgian mansions of suburban Virginia, a world away from the eccentric days of the Establishment, where Bob lived like a kind of right-wing bohemian. When he moved to Washington, however, Bob put on airs and gave the impression that he was from big family money. The *Spectator* was published by a tax-exempt, nonprofit (and theoretically nonpartisan) foundation that Bob headed and began to milk like a private trust fund. Tax laws governing such organizations limit the use of tax-exempt funds for any insider's "private inurement" to "reasonable compensation." Though Bob did little editorial work, in addition to his salary of about $200,000 a year, the foundation paid one-third of the purchase price of his home in the D.C. suburbs and provided him with a 500 Series Mercedes-Benz; leased an apartment for him on New York's Upper East Side; and covered his lavish personal expenses, including regular trips to London, limousines, gardeners, utility bills at his home, and staggering liquor bills.

A short, athletic man with an impish face, twinkling blue eyes, and a noto-riously high-pitched voice, underneath his studied nonchalance and zany antics, such as carrying trick walnuts in his suit pocket with condoms inside them, Bob was intensely competitive and thin-skinned. He was having little success gaining the respect of the capital's political class, even among con-servatives. Rather than engaging with his opponents' arguments, as a young writer Bob had made a name for himself by poking fun at them, on the the-ory that reasoned debate with left-wingers was a waste of time. To the inside-the-Beltway folks, though, his zingers seemed puerile: Liberals were "gas-bags," feminists were "bed-wetters," neoliberals were "a commune of transsexuals who, halfway through their surgical refurbishment, had a change of heart."

Like Rush Limbaugh, Newt Gingrich, and Richard Mellon Scaife, Bob was another leading conservative who said one thing in public and did the oppo-site in private. In 1989, the *Washington Post* canceled Bob's weekly column, sending him into a tailspin of depression and afflicting him with a bad case of writer's block. His lawyer-wife, Judy, divorced him as he took up the life of a bon vivant, drinking away the hours in his Savile Row suits and Turnbull & Asser shirts and ties in London and New York nightclubs. In his words, Bob was pursuing "physiologically well-appointed women." Commenting on the acrimonious divorce, Bob would say, "Lose a family, gain a nightclub." One of Bob's frequent companions in his romps through international hot spots was right-wing Greek gossip columnist Taki Theodoracopulos, who had been convicted on cocaine smuggling charges in England and did time in jail.

Because I had no social life whatsoever, I chose to ignore Bob the public moralist and embrace the fun-loving libertine. *Vanity Fair* critic James Wolcott described the *Spectator* circle as "young farts . . . a loose clique of wet blankets and party poopers." While this may have been fair from the point of view of a New Yorker, Bob and the *Spectator* crowd passed for cool and sophisticated in the conservative subculture of Washington wonks like Grover Norquist and forbidding moralists like Paul Weyrich. We knew how to party. Though there wasn't much to my relationship with Bob other than our mutual disdain for the left, and a taste for insolence, everything about

Bob that Washington considered unserious—his iconoclasm, his infectious joie de vivre, his sense of style, even his boozy catting around—made him great fun to hang out with, often over a champagne-soaked dinner at the exclusive Jockey Club. Bob was the first movement figure with whom I could relax somewhat and halfway enjoy myself. Soon I found myself wanting the material comforts he had. I even began imitating Bob, buying Turnbull & Asser shirts and switching from cigarettes to cigars.

I did this despite Tyrrell's penchant for picking on gays, which made the *Spectator* one of the odder places in the conservative movement for me to have ended up. "Cephalic indices and empirical observations of homosexuals at public demonstrations and on Halloween night in San Francisco have established that many homosexuals develop heads shaped very much like squash . . . ," Tyrrell wrote. "Let us henceforth speak of our homosexuals as squashes. Let the universities hold their Squash Rights Week. And let us accord proper respect to the Squash Community." I wasn't aware of the *Spectator*'s antigay bent when I began writing for it, though given my all-consuming desire to make it in the movement, and my capacity to accommodate or deny anything that stood in the way, it would not have made a difference. In time, I convinced myself that the antigay slurs were not on gays as individuals, but on the gay rights movement, which I had been taught to regard as no different from any other left-wing special interest group—the feminists, the civil rights lobby, the enviros, they were all on the other team.

Besides, many contributors to the *Spectator* were part of the conservative gay underground, which legitimized the affiliation in my eyes. When I first came to Washington, I occasionally had seen one *Spectator* board member at gay bars around Washington. And one of the top deputies to Richard Mellon Scaife was also a member of the club, though a very uneasy one. Back in the late 1980s, when I first started freelancing for the magazine, I ran into Scaife's deputy in a gay bar in Rehoboth Beach, Delaware, a vacation spot for many gay Washingtonians. When he learned of my connection to the magazine, he darted away like a cockroach. As I got more involved with the *Spectator*, I began to wonder if he knew something I didn't. Because the

Spectator was more aggressively homophobic than the *Times*, I slowly but surely ended my dating life altogether, taking a step further back into the closet from the position I had occupied at the *Times*. By the early 1990s, with Andrew gone, I, too, was living like a cockroach.

As his writing career languished, Bob turned the running of the magazine over to his deputy, Wlady Plesczynski. The son of Polish immigrants who had fled the Nazis, Wlady, then in his late thirties, had worked under Bob for the better part of two decades since the magazine's founding in Indiana. If Bob was a show horse, Wlady was a workhorse, a self-effacing type content to toil behind the scenes while the boss and his writers soaked up the limelight. In person, he was Bob's opposite number, shy, socially bumbling, peering out from behind owlish black-framed glasses, and shabbily dressed in big brown corduroy jackets and clodhoppers. While Bob, a former competitive swimmer, seemed to spend half his time pumping iron and playing handball, Wlady shuffled through the *Spectator*'s offices as if he had no joints, an endearing human Gumby. Wlady had several wonderful qualities—he was always a gentleman, almost deferential in manner, and loyal to a fault. If Bob's side of the *Spectator* was all satire and sarcasm, Wlady was responsible for the other side, commissioning and editing the many serious pieces in the magazine, essays and book reviews by such writers as Maurice Cranston, Kenneth Lynn, George Gilder, and James Q. Wilson. He nurtured several younger writers who went on to prominence as conservative commentators. His writers loved him, and in time I did, too.

But I was younger than even the young contributors, and I needed someone with sounder judgment than Wlady to guide me. When dealing with his stable of scholars and aspiring pundits, Wlady was a talented and decent editor. What set me apart from virtually all of my colleagues was that I was trying to break news stories, something Wlady knew nothing about. My agenda was bolder, and more fraught with peril, than the essay and review writing being done at *Commentary, National Review,* and even the *Spectator.* These missives were merely opinion pieces, and were regarded as such. I considered myself a right-wing reporter dealing in fact, the likes of which had not been seen since Victor Lasky wrote in the 1960s, and I was proposing a

direct attack on the monopoly that I believed left-liberals held—and vigi-
lantly guarded—over the news business. Like Wlady, I wasn't ready for
prime time.*

Wlady seemed to manage and edit me through osmosis. I never knew him
to give a clear directive. We did much of our business on the telephone, and
Wlady was so nervous that I often imagined that he had taken the call while
hiding under his desk. He was a harried editor, most months putting out the
entire magazine himself, and also a credulous one, rarely questioning the
reporting in a piece, so long as it bludgeoned the predictable liberal targets.
He did nothing to check my growing instinct for the jugular. Like Grover
Norquist, Wlady had a deep suspicion of weak-kneed Republicans and a
blunt "us versus them" mentality, but unlike Grover, Wlady was more typical of the conservatives in his fatalism. As he saw it, the liberal culture—Bob
called it the Kultursmog—coddled the Dems and tore down the
Republicans at every turn. Certain that we were losers no matter what we
did, destined to remain on the outer fringes of respectable debate, Wlady
encouraged taking potshots at the enemy. For Wlady, accepting what I wrote
about his political foes, no matter how unflattering or unbelievable, was simply a matter of faith.

The magazine employed no fact checkers of the kind I later learned was
the norm for reputable magazines. As for legal review, Bob often boasted
that he retained a libel lawyer merely so that he could overrule him and
publish whatever he wanted. Bob had magazines to sell to bloodthirsty conservatives, and rich ideological patrons to please. He had no time for legal
niceties or niggling facts. In terms of working with professional journalists,
in going from the *Washington Times* to the *American Spectator,* I'd gone from
a culture of "Prudenizing" to one of willful malpractice. My first big story
for the magazine, "The Real Anita Hill," was a case in point.

---

*Neither, of course, was Lasky, who wrote a series of "The Man and the Myth" books in
which he attempted to discredit leading liberals such as John F. Kennedy, Robert F.
Kennedy, and Jimmy Carter. Lasky also wrote a book in 1950 defending Joe McCarthy
and the anti-Communist witch-hunts, *The Seeds of Treason*, and an apologia for Nixon's
crimes in Watergate, which hit the best-seller list in 1977. His work was not taken seriously by journalists or historians outside the right wing.

CHAPTER FIVE

THE REAL ANITA HILL

A decade has passed, and given the sensational sex scandals that rocked Washington in the years following, it's hard to capture how riveted the country was when law professor Anita Hill came forward in a Senate confirmation hearing and accused her former boss, Supreme Court nominee Clarence Thomas, of sexual harassment. For us in Washington, the Thomas-Hill hearing was more than a shocking media spectacle; it was part of a broader struggle for political power between conservatism and liberalism that split our world in two. Thomas and Hill instantly came to represent issues much larger than themselves. Liberals viewed Thomas as an enemy of civil rights, an Uncle Tom who acted as Reagan's hatchet man, a sexual predator who bore the collective guilt of all harassers. For them, Hill was every woman, the Rosa Parks of sexual harassment, who had endured Thomas's bullying only to be bullied again when she came forward before a male-dominated Senate chamber that refused to take her charges seriously. For us, Hill's charges were nothing more than an eleventh-hour political hit orchestrated by desperate liberal groups opposed to Thomas; the feminist movement, we believed, then seized on her story to forward its agenda, expanding the sexual harassment laws and redefining the legal and social relationship between men and women. For both sides, everything from the subordination of women to civil rights policies, abortion, pornography, racial attitudes, and gender politics seemed suddenly at stake in the Thomas-Hill controversy.

If a previous generation had been defined by the cataclysmic struggle between Whittaker Chambers and Alger Hiss over whether Hiss was a Soviet spy, my generation had Clarence Thomas versus Anita Hill. Shortly

after the hearings ended in October 1991, with Thomas narrowly confirmed, the telephone rang at my office at the *Washington Times*, where I
had returned following my stint at Heritage. Wlady, on the line from the
Spectator, mentioned that the magazine had received a contribution from
Elizabeth Brady Lurie, an eccentric, chain-smoking heiress who lived in a
remote area of North Carolina and who served on the board of one of Paul
Weyrich's organizations. Lurie wanted to finance a "special investigation"
into the affair. Was I game? Wlady wanted to know. I saw the offer, my introduction to right-wing checkbook journalism, as a big break. I wasn't one of
the magazine's marquee names. After several years on the conservative sidelines, I now had a chance to prove myself as a combatant in the culture wars.

With the exception of the Gulf War, nominating Clarence Thomas to the
Supreme Court was the only worthwhile thing George Bush did in office,
so far as most conservatives were concerned. After Bush's first high court
appointee, Justice David Souter, joined the majority in upholding abortion
rights, when the next court slot came open, Bush was under tremendous
pressure from the right to pick a reflexive conservative like Thomas. Well
known for his strident opposition to all forms of affirmative action to redress
racial or gender discrimination (even though he had benefited from it himself), Thomas also could be counted as a vote to overturn the *Roe v. Wade*
decision legalizing abortion. Thomas was beloved by the right, a prized symbol whose presence in the GOP legitimized conservative attacks on civil
rights policies. When he served as the chairman of the Equal Employment
Opportunity Commission under President Reagan, critics charged Thomas
with lax enforcement of antidiscrimination laws.

My own support of Thomas was as unrooted in ideological belief as my
support of Judge Bork had been. On the judicial issues that Thomas would
face on the bench, my views—civil libertarian, pro-choice, strong support of
separation of church and state—were closer to those of the anti-Thomas
coalition than they were to Thomas's. Yet as in the Bork case, I fell in line
with people whose social values were anathema to mine. My acceptance of
the *Spectator* assignment was motivated by a mix of partisanship and opportunistic careerism. For one thing was certain: The Republican right had a
heavy investment in Clarence Thomas; in my five years in Washington, no

issue had inflamed the right into paroxysms of rage the way his nomination struggle did. Defending his reputation was sure to bring its rewards.

In choosing Thomas, two lawyers advised Bush in the White House— Bush counsel C. Boyden Gray, a patrician tobacco heir who looked like Ichabod Crane and kept a pet pig in his Georgetown mansion, and Lee Liberman, a diminutive woman in Coke-bottle glasses who was known as "Rasputin" for her immense, behind-the-scenes influence over Bush's judicial picks. Working closely with Thomas himself, the duo made a cynical calculation. The only way to slide a hard-right conservative through the Senate was to choose a "black Bork," driving a wedge through the civil rights community, and picking up support from a bloc of Democratic southerners with large African American constituencies. Despite Bush's famous claim that Thomas, whom he had nominated as an appellate judge on the important D.C. Circuit Court just a year before, was "the most qualified" jurist in America to sit on the high court, Thomas was really the only one who fit the ingenious confirmation strategy devised by Gray and Liberman.

Though we conservatives derided him as a moderate, by ceding legal policy and judicial picks to a network of right-wing lawyers, George Bush did much to preserve the dominion of the conservative movement in the 1990s. The right would soon lose control of the executive branch, but the movement would hold sway through control of the nation's top courts. This counterrevolution in the law, which aimed to roll back decades of liberal jurisprudence in areas such as civil rights, property rights, due process rights, and reproductive freedom, was led by members of the Federalist Society for Law and Public Policy Studies, a group of conservative lawyers and academics that took its name from President James Madison's writings in the Federalist papers, which had emphasized the powers of individuals and states under the federal system. Two law students had founded the Federalist Society in the early 1980s: Bush judge-picker Lee Liberman at Yale, and Spencer Abraham, the future Michigan senator and energy secretary, at Harvard, both of whom had been frustrated that ideas like separation of powers, "strict constructionism," and states' rights were getting short shrift from their more liberal-minded professors. Society affiliates quickly sprang up on campuses around the country.

As the newly minted right-wing lawyers moved to Washington, the society's monthly lunches at a restaurant in D.C.'s Chinatown became a hotbed of political organizing, networking, and ritualistic denunciations of the "imperial" liberal judiciary and its rulings. In its literature, the society called for "reordering priorities in the legal system to place a premium on individual liberty, traditional values, and the rule of law." Describing the relationship between the Federalist Society and the GOP, Republican lawyer and special prosecutor Lawrence Walsh, whose Iran-contra convictions of Reagan officials for lying and obstructing justice were overturned by Federalist Society judges, likened the group to "the Communist front groups of the 1940s and 1950s, whose members were committed to the Communist cause, and subject to Communist direction, but were not members of the Communist party."

I could easily pick out society members and sympathizers around town; they were the ones wearing fat silk ties with small silhouettes of James Madison on them. In addition to Boyden Gray and Lee Liberman, those affiliated with the society included two Supreme Court justices, William Rehnquist and Antonin Scalia, and their clerks; at least four judges and many of their clerks from the D.C. Circuit Court of Appeals—Robert Bork, Laurence Silberman, David Sentelle, and Kenneth Starr, the latter named by Bush to be his solicitor general; Edwin Meese; Senator Orrin Hatch; and the president of the Washington Federalist chapter, Republican appellate lawyer Theodore Olson, who had served in Reagan's Justice Department. Richard Mellon Scaife and high-dollar individual donors—including Gray, Starr, and Olson, who formed the James Madison Club—backed the organization financially. Having failed to elevate Bork, with the Thomas nomination the society again maneuvered to place another of its own onto the high court, where he would provide a decisive fifth vote for the conservative bloc.

Once Thomas got the nod, conservatives were determined to do anything necessary to get him confirmed. Ad hoc advocacy groups like Women for Judge Thomas sprang up to check the opposition of women's rights organizations. Bill Kristol cooked up the idea of a Citizens Committee to Confirm Clarence Thomas, modeled explicitly on the grassroots activities of the anti-Bork coalition and headed by his friend and former Reagan aide Gary Bauer of the Family Research Council, a leading Christian Right organization. Pat Robertson and Ralph Reed announced a $1 million Christian Coalition pro-Thomas ad campaign. Conservative activist Floyd Brown, who had produced the Willie Horton ads in the '88 Bush presidential race, targeted Thomas opponent Ted Kennedy in an ad that featured a headline from the *New York Post*, "Teddy's Sexy Romp"—a reference to the alleged goings-on in Palm Beach, Florida, during the weekend when his nephew was accused (and later acquitted) of rape. Most important was Paul Weyrich's network of antiabortion, antipornography, pro–school prayer activists stretching across the country. Weyrich set up a war room in his Washington offices, where every allegation raised against Thomas was rebutted the moment it surfaced.

Liberal interest groups like People for the American Way, the National Abortion Rights Action League, and the National Organization for Women were galvanized also, working overtime to defeat the nominee, but Thomas was able to bob and weave his way through the barrage of charges and appeared headed for confirmation. Unlike Bork, who was unapologetic in stating his true views to the committee, Thomas had been coached by the Federalist Society confirmation team to give the Judiciary Committee answers to questions that may have been technically true but seemed purposely misleading. Asked about his views on *Roe v. Wade*, for example, Thomas claimed, "I cannot remember personally engaging" in any discussion of *Roe*. Thomas's own sister contradicted his denial under oath that he had referred to her as a "welfare queen." On the eve of the Senate vote, Anita Hill, a professor of law at the University of Oklahoma, came forward with allegations that she had been sexually harassed by Thomas, her boss at Reagan's Equal Employment Opportunity Commission, ten years before. When Hill's sensational claims were leaked to the press, Thomas hemorrhaged massively.

What no one except the two protagonists knew for sure was whether Hill's highly detailed, sexually graphic charges were true. Hill claimed that Thomas had pressed her for dates and taunted her with lewd references to pornographic movies. I watched Hill testify on a Friday morning with a dozen conservative colleagues at the *Washington Times*. Hill testified for hours in vivid detail about what Thomas had said and done to her. Looking a bit like a deer caught in the headlights, she testfied with great specificity about times, and dates, and circumstances, and she provided direct quotes from Thomas. She also supplied the committee with detailed accounts of contemporaneous conversations she had had about Thomas's behavior with others. When she finished, I shocked my colleagues by saying that I intuitively believed her. That Hill's charges were a political dirty trick seemed far-fetched to me; in fact, I had already concluded, before Hill testified, that Thomas had likely perjured himself before the committee on *Roe* and other issues. I was the only one in the room who thought Hill was telling the truth—or who would admit to thinking so.

By early evening, Thomas's handlers in the White House decided to stop the senators' questioning of Hill's account—which had only gotten more detailed and persuasive as the day wore on—and Thomas took the witness chair. Thomas had long believed that those who disagreed with him on an issue hated him, and he hated them in return. On Friday evening, an enraged Thomas denounced the entire confirmation proceeding as a "high-tech lynching for uppity blacks who in any way deign to think for themselves." He told the committee that he had not bothered to watch Hill's nationally televised testimony, implying that it had all been a bald-faced lie or a sick fantasy. Yet when confronted by Senator Patrick Leahy, a Democrat from Vermont, with specific questions—Did he watch pornography and discuss it with any women?—Thomas gave the same sort of cagey answers he had given to the *Roe* query. "I will categorically say that I have not had any such discussions with Professor Hill," Thomas answered.

When Hill returned for further cross-examination on Saturday morning, the Republicans were loaded for bear. The Federalist team had worked through the night to attack and discredit specific aspects of Hill's testimony. One of the most striking anecdotes that Hill had related was a story in which Thomas had turned to her in his office and said, "Who put this pubic hair on my Coke?" *The Exorcist* contained a scene involving pubic hair and a glass of gin, and sure enough, Senator Hatch held up a copy of the book, whose theme involved the exorcism of Satanic spirits, and accused Hill of lifting that detail in her testimony from the novel. Hill cited a particular character from a pornographic movie she said Thomas had mentioned to her, "Long Dong Silver." Federalist lawyers dug up an obscure sexual harassment case filed in 1988 in Kansas in a district court that mentioned the character—again suggesting that Hill and her "slick lawyers," as Orrin Hatch put it, had created a bizarre story about Thomas by culling bits and pieces from publicly available documents. Senator Arlen Specter, who had angered the right by opposing Bork, accused Hill of "flat-out perjury." And Senator Alan Simpson hinted darkly about derogatory personal material on Hill he had received "over the transom."

And so it went as Hill and her panel of fact witnesses were nitpicked about their recollections from a decade ago by Republican senators, fed by an attack machine set up in Boyden Gray's White House office. Where exactly were you sitting, Professor Hill, when Judge Thomas mentioned Long Dong Silver? What was the precise date, Professor Hill, that you called your friend Susan Hoerchner to report Judge Thomas's conduct? In a courtroom, the specificity of Hill's charges and her contemporaneous evidence would have helped prove her case. But the Federalists understood something that the lawyers who helped prepare Hill and her witnesses did not—like the Bork battle, the Thomas battle would be fought in a court of public opinion. By catching Hill on the faded memories and small inconsistencies that are always present in a claim of sexual harassment, the Republicans could make Hill look like a liar on national television. By the end of the weekend, as Hill's testimony was disputed by the right, and as the contest became so heavily freighted with ideological symbolism for each side, my first impressions receded, and my partisan loyalties caused me to side with Thomas. So did more than half the country. He was confirmed by four votes.

This time, we won. But there was still a battle to be waged. The Republicans were running scared in the 1992 election season, dubbed the "Year of the Woman." They were facing a voter backlash against the way Hill had been treated by the Republicans on the Senate committee that would culminate in the election of four Democratic women to the Senate and help Bill Clinton win the White House. At the 1992 Republican convention, delegates would hold up signs saying "Anita Hill: Feminist Fraud," and hounded

Nina Totenberg, the National Public Radio correspondent who broke the Hill story, with the epithet "whore." Sexual harassment claims were skyrocketing, and sexual harassment laws were being tightened. Republican Senator Bob Packwood was ridden out of office on sexual harassment charges. Conservatism itself seemed threatened by this second wave of feminism.

In accepting Wlady's invitation to write about the Thomas-Hill saga, I hoped to turn back this feminist tide, exposing the treachery of what we saw as a liberal cabal that leaked Hill's uncorroborated charges into the public domain and forced her public testimony. I planned to write an anatomy of a partisan knifing and to argue that because Hill's charges were unproven, they did not constitute grounds for rejecting Thomas as unfit for office. In framing the article, I would also play to the deeply ingrained conservative suspicion that the liberal media, as part of the pro-Hill faction, hid the political motivations behind Hill's case. Arnaud de Borchgrave had called it the "DMC," Bob Tyrrell called it "the one-party media." Rather than lampoon the press, or try to somehow infiltrate it from within, my idea was to bypass it altogether. We needed our own media, our own reporters, and our own means of getting out our side of the story. Elizabeth Lurie's trope of a "special investigation" suited my purposes perfectly.

In their treatment of Anita Hill, the Senate Republicans set a new low in the threshold for public discourse in the capital, and I would go lower still, checking whatever independence I had at the door and making myself part of the right's extensive political machinery. Researching the subject took me, for the first time, inside the Republican halls of power, and, now in my late twenties, the heady experience made me all the more eager to do their bidding. Putting aside my discomfort with their right-wing social agenda to get my story, I worked hand in glove with Weyrich's people at Free Congress. Aides to Republican senators forked over previously unreleased Senate depositions, FBI interviews, and all the filthy rumors that had slipped in under the Judiciary Committee's heavy wooden doors. My eyes widened.

Sexual harassment cases turn on the credibility of the accused and the accuser. On national television, the Republicans trashed Anita Hill's reputation—but they knew their constituents would let them go only so far. I had no such constraints. I did a demolition job on the character of Hill and her witnesses. I suddenly had access to everything that Senator Simpson described as coming in "over the transom." One young White House lawyer working for Gray, Mark Paoletta, had obtained an affidavit from a psychiatrist who watched Hill's testimony on television and concluded that she suffered from "erotomania." Then there was the famous "pube" affidavit. After the hearings concluded, the Republicans passed along to me assorted wild sexual rumors about Hill that they said they had heard about during the hearings, but never mentioned publicly, with the exception of an insinuating reference by Senator Simpson to Hill's "proclivities." The Republicans, including Simpson's staff and Paoletta from the White House, told me precisely how to hunt the rumors down—they came from two former students of Hill's, whose names were given to me—and I did it. One of the students claimed in a sworn affidavit that Hill had returned his and a fellow student's exam paper with pubic hairs sprinkled throughout it. GOP staffers turned the affidavit over to me. When I contacted him, the second student refused to back the first student's story up. I published the "pube affidavit" anyway.

If Republican aides were eager to abet my savaging Hill, so were Thomas's closest friends. Among others, they included fellow D.C. Circuit Court Judge Laurence Silberman; his wife, Ricky, who served as vice chair of the Equal Employment Opportunity Commission under Thomas and headed Women for Judge Thomas; Armstrong Williams, a former Thomas aide at the employment commission who would soon host a right-wing radio talk show; and Paoletta. Though the confirmation battle had been won, they told me that a full-scale defense of Thomas was still necessary to confer legitimacy upon his Supreme Court tenure. These people who knew Thomas best in the world, now my sources and soon-to-be friends of mine, told me nothing had happened between Thomas and Hill. No asking for dates. No dirty talk. No porn. Nothing. They conveyed a very convincing impression that they knew in their bones that Hill's story was a monstrous lie. And they were still in wild-eyed fury about it. Judge Silberman speculated that Hill was a lesbian, "acting out."

Besides, Silberman confided, Thomas would have never asked Hill for a date: Did I know she had bad breath?

These friends of Thomas seemed much more warmly welcoming and personally engaging than any group of conservatives I had met in five years in Washington. I became particularly close with the Silbermans, thinking of them as surrogate parents—or perhaps, in the back of my mind, as the emotive, erudite, highly accomplished Jewish parents I never knew.

Larry had been a liberal Republican in the Nixon Labor Department, where he devised the so-called Philadelphia Plan, imposing racial hiring goals on federal contractors. In the late '70s, he swung to the right with the zeal of the converted, publicly repudiated the affirmative action policies he had created, and served on Governor Reagan's foreign-policy team. When Reagan appointed Larry to the second-highest federal court in the land, just below the Supreme Court, the nomination was briefly held up over whether Silberman was forthcoming with the committee about his tenure at a San Francisco bank that was heavily fined for failing to report billions in cash transactions. Silberman was confirmed to the court, where he established himself, along with Robert Bork and Antonin Scalia, as a leader of the judicial right wing. He overturned felony convictions rendered against Oliver North in the Iran-contra affair, a controversial decision that was thought to have damaged his chances of being nominated to the Supreme Court. In the small circle of right-wing legal beagles in the capital, the bald, bespectacled judge, a ringer for my Berkeley professor Paul Seabury, was considered as smart as Bork or Scalia—and more uncompromising. I hadn't had as brilliant and interested a teacher as Judge Silberman since Seabury, and he was to have a far more profound influence on me than my college professors.

A consummate Washington insider for more than two decades, Larry would often preface his advice to me with the wry demurrer that judges shouldn't get involved in politics—"That would be improper," he'd say— and then forge ahead anyway.* He was a behind-the-scenes adviser to the

---

*Silberman appeared to be referring to the codes of ethical conduct governing judges that contain direct prohibitions on political activities.

conservative editors of the *Wall Street Journal* editorial page, and he delighted conservative audiences with his acid critiques of the liberal press. In a speech to the lawyers of the Federalist Society, he had coined the phrase "the Greenhouse effect" for the pressure he believed *New York Times* Supreme Court correspondent Linda Greenhouse exerted in her reporting on Supreme Court justices to tailor their opinions in a liberal direction. Larry told me the same malevolent media forces were at work in the smearing of Thomas.

In her designer knit suits and Hermès pumps, Ricky Silberman was a buoyant, silver-haired, social lioness cum den mother of the right. By day, she slipped on half-glasses and was credited as Thomas's intellectual tutor at the EEOC, steeping him in right-wing ideology as they worked to limit the scope of federal discrimination protections for women and minorities. The easily incited Ricky was out for revenge against the mob of feminists—"extreminists," she called them—who had lynched her friend Clarence. She proved as dedicated a coach as Larry. "This is about an eye for an eye!" she exclaimed, fist raised to the sky, as she fed me tea and sugar cookies—and dished the dirt on Anita Hill—in the French country–style kitchen of her impeccable Georgetown town house.

I didn't disappoint. My *Spectator* article was published in March 1992 under the headline "The Real Anita Hill." It ran with a full-page cover caricature of Hill, her African American features exaggerated, that was so over the top even Ricky said it was racist. She overcame her reservations as soon as she flipped open the cover.

In the style of right-wing conspiracist tracts, complete with extensive citations, quotations, and footnotes, "The Real Anita Hill" recast the accepted narrative of the hearing as a liberal conspiracy to frame Thomas on false charges. The first section of the twenty-two-thousand-word takeout was a lawyerly dissection of the testimony of Hill's main corroborating witness, Susan Hoerchner, exploiting inconsistencies in her previously unreleased Senate deposition leaked to me by GOP staff to advance a theory that Hill had complained to Hoerchner of sexual harassment months *before* Hill had gone to work for Thomas. I had been told of this theory by Nelson Lund, a

Federalist Society academic on the Bush White House staff, who had devised it with Quayle aide William Kristol during the hearings, and I studied the hearing record intensely to make it work. In the second section, I sought to expose what I claimed was Hill's political agenda in opposing Thomas. Though it had no bearing on the veracity of her testimony, I voraciously pored over every word written about Hill in the weeks before and since the hearing. When I found one article in which she expressed vaguely feminist leanings—no surprise, especially after the hearing—I presented the quote as treasonous. Finally, I hit pay dirt in one obscure interview where Hill indicated she disagreed with Thomas's views on abortion and affirmative action. I turned this truth against her, assailing her as a vicious leftist who perjured herself to advance her own political agenda.

While these two sections were skewed, they were plausible interpretations of the written record. As is always the case with sexual harassment, there were weak spots in the story told by Hill and her witnesses, and I portrayed them as intentional lies. But I still had a problem that caused me to overreach. If Thomas was completely innocent, Anita Hill would have had to be insane to go on national television and tell a lie under oath. Grasping for an explanation of the inexplicable, doing everything I could to ruin Hill's credibility, I took a scattershot approach, dumping virtually every derogatory—and often contradictory—allegation I had collected on Hill from the Thomas camp into the mix. Hill was an ambitious incompetent passed over by Thomas for a promotion. She was "kooky." She was a man-hater. She had a "perverse desire for male attention." She had a "love-hate" complex with Thomas. She made "bizarre" sexual comments to students and coworkers. She sprinkled pubic hairs in her law students' term papers. She was, in my words, "a little bit nutty and a little bit slutty."

For what was then a lighthearted magazine, the full-throated tenor of the attack, and especially its tabloid bent, was a major departure. Surely, this was an impossible story to tell without explicit references to sex; but no respectable publication, not even the *Spectator*, had ever seen the likes of the sexist imagery and sexual innuendo I confected to discredit Anita Hill. These were but two ingredients in a witches' brew of fact, allegation, hearsay, speculation, opinion, and invective labeled by my editors as "investigative journalism." And, well, it did *look* like journalism. By taking portions of the record and quoting previously unreleased Senate material, I was able to create the illusion that the article was based on established fact, solid evidence, and extensive documentation. The editors weren't careful with the magazine's reputation, much less mine. Wlady, the managing editor, hardly questioned a word I filed. All women were "emotional" and thus prone to fabrication, Wlady said.

Yet there is a critical distinction between what I thought I was doing—my intentions—and the sloppy, skewed, slanderous material that spilled off my keyboard. I was able to go at the other side like a bloodhound because I believed every word of my reporting was solid and true. For many readers, my inability to take in other points of view was, perversely, the source of my strength as a political writer. I was possessed of "the moral certainty of a young warrior," as Howard Kurtz would write in a *Washington Post* profile. I sincerely believed my own propaganda.

The truth is that with my woefully inadequate training at the *Washington Times* and the *American Spectator,* I didn't know what good reporting was. Like a kid playing with a loaded gun, I didn't appreciate the difference between a substantiated charge and an unsubstantiated one. The cardinal rule of the journalism profession, that every allegation must have at least two sources before it may be printed, was not enforced at the *Times,* and it was unheard of at the *Spectator.* My sources *did* tell me all the things I quoted them as telling me. I didn't have the judgment to know that people will say anything, particularly in an incendiary conflict such as this one. Every source I relied on either thought Thomas walked on water or had a virulent animus toward Hill. Already conditioned to think the best of Thomas and the worst of Hill, I did nothing to test these sources or question their motives. That almost all of the "kooky" quotes were voiced from behind a shield of anonymity gave me no pause. My incompetence was compounded by an uninformed bias, by the grip of a partisan tunnel vision that was by now such a part of my nature that it distorted my work, disabling me from finding the truth, without my even knowing it.

Of course, to most readers outside the conservative world my reportage was self-discrediting. But my piece had a certain power in its presentation.

Despite my roiling emotions, the cognitive part of my brain was built like a steel trap. Though I was really nothing more than a promising Republican operative in training, what made me unique was that I was in a position to put their legalistic, highly analytical theories, defensive hair-splitting, derogatory gossip, and political spin into print, where I presented it all as fact. Alone among them, I considered myself a reporter. I was a clear writer, so many people read the piece and believed it.

Soon after the article appeared, Rush Limbaugh began reading entire sections of it for several days running on his nationally syndicated broadcast, complete with a squeaky-voiced impression of Susan Hoerchner. With his audience of over 2 million listeners, the largest audience of any radio show then on the air, Limbaugh put the *Spectator*—and me—on the map. Overnight, every right-winger in America knew my name, or so it seemed. Limbaugh, whom Justice Thomas would later befriend to the point of officiating at Limbaugh's wedding, was the perfect audience for my attack on Anita Hill. Above his workstation, he had posted the following admonition: "Sexual Harassment at This Work-Station Will Not Be Reported, However, It Will Be Graded." Limbaugh was making me famous for calling Anita Hill a slut.

Some conservative friends outside the *Spectator* did warn me quietly that the "little bit nutty and a little bit slutty" line, a reference to the classic nuts-and-sluts defense in sexual harassment cases, was in poor taste, or at least politically foolish, in that it handed my critics a club with which to beat me. The phrase certainly stuck, and it would be unearthed and brandished in my face in all future controversies over my work. Clearly, the ugliness that the *Dartmouth Review* had introduced to conservatism, and that I had once rejected back in Berkeley as irresponsible, now came easily to me. I *did* give it a second thought, but when I suggested to Wlady that maybe the line was too much, we agreed to keep it in. I had fallen in with radicals of the Gingrich-Limbaugh stripe. After all, how far was the "nutty/slutty" line from Newt's rants about the "grotesque" and "sick" Democrats, or Limbaugh's slurs on blacks and women? Then, too, the "nutty/slutty" line was not completely out of character with the *Spectator*'s gonzo house style. Conceivably,

Bob Tyrrell could have written the line in a satirical column. But in a piece that was otherwise presented as serious reporting, the line was not amusing; it was degraded sarcasm—inexcusable, disgusting.

Back at the *Spectator,* the editors had never seen anything like the raw emotional reaction in the conservative grass roots to Limbaugh's promotion of the article, which he introduced with the song "She's Come Undone," by the Guess Who. For perhaps the first time in its history, the magazine went back to press to meet the demand at the newsstands. While old-line conservative magazines like *National Review* refused to lower their standards and pander to Limbaugh's audience, the *Spectator* began advertising on the Limbaugh broadcast, and subscriptions poured in. Before the year was out, circulation had soared 300 percent to 114,000. I had stumbled onto something big, a symbiotic relationship that would help create a highly profitable, right-wing Big Lie machine that flourished in book publishing, on talk radio, and on the Internet through the '90s.

To keep a good thing going after the overwhelming reader response to "The Real Anita Hill," the magazine became a forerunner in the intellectual corruption of the right as it moved away from the thoughtful essays and scholarly reviews and humor pieces that had been its stock-in-trade and toward Anita Hill–style hit jobs, replete with anything-goes allegations and a more squalid brand of "humor." One attention grabber, a foreshadowing of things to come, was a profile by my old *Insight* colleague, "investigative writer" Danny Wattenberg, of Hillary Rodham Clinton, whom the magazine called "the Lady Macbeth of Little Rock" and "the Winnie Mandela of American Politics." The article included the testimony of unidentified "wicked gossips in Little Rock."

Shortly after the Hillary Clinton piece ran, I had a chat in the office hallway with Ron Burr, the magazine's longtime publisher, who had been a classmate of Tyrrell's at the University of Indiana. An easygoing, middle-aged preppy who, like Bob, looked much younger than his years, Ron was in charge of marketing the magazine and raising money from supporters to subsidize it. Ron was a stand-up guy who didn't have a mean bone in his body, but he had a job to do. Gazing up at a row of framed magazine covers, Ron told me that we had discovered a formula for selling magazines to the conservative grass roots. "Can't you find any more women to attack?" he asked with a chuckle.

In response to the sotto voce criticism about the "slutty" line from conservative colleagues, I said nothing, but this is what I thought: To the extent that incendiary rhetoric and literary gimmickry attracted attention, even negative attention, well, wasn't that the point of breaking through the liberal media filter? I was doing good, getting out the truth by any means necessary. My article was the one creating a buzz in conservative circles, the one being furiously faxed around town like samizdat, not those gray essays in the *Journal* and *Commentary*. Fuck them, I thought, I'm blazing a trail.

It may seem surprising that, literally in a matter of weeks, I had gone from believing Anita Hill, to agnosticism on the charges, to portraying Hill as a deranged liar. But in retrospect, perhaps it's not so surprising. After all, my career path rewarded party-line polemics, not independent thinking. In defending Pinochet, and in supporting Bork, I had already shown an ability to sequester my conscience and sublimate my own values so that I could belong to the movement, just as I now disregarded my own intuition that Hill was a credible witness. Seeking a channel for my ambition, I was a perfect—and perfectly willing—instrument for the wishes of others and for agendas I didn't share.

In some ways, I was still acting out my personal drama from Berkeley—conservative David against the liberal Goliath. Ginni Thomas's view of the hearings as a battle of "good versus evil," as she put it to *People* magazine, must have reminded me of my own struggle against the "evil" left wing in Berkeley. I was eager to find meaning and purpose in my life as an ideological warrior, to make Newt's words, and Grover's, about the "enemy" Democratic Party real. I imagined that a political movement—one that I knew absolutely nothing about, and had never had the slightest contact with—had done Thomas a grave injustice. In helping to clear Thomas's name for the history books and turn back the feminist tide, I now had a grand mission to fill the empty space that had been left by the end of the Cold War. Thomas's tormentors stood in for the evil empire—my own version of the paranoid style of politics swirling all around me in the movement.

There was also emptiness inside me. Even though I spent all of my time in and around it, I had no close personal bond with anyone in the conservative movement. While I was able to pretend this wasn't so, I felt self-conscious and vulnerable, and I was deeply uncomfortable in the movement; yet I also had no relationships outside of it, except for Andrew, who was on the other coast. As I look at the matrix now, it's apparent that the peculiar mix of my politics, my profession, and my homosexuality perpetuated my isolation. Because I was a journalist, I was never a full-fledged member of the closeted Republican gay underground; I felt too gay for my straight right-wing peers, around whom I was afraid to be my honest self; and I was too closeted and too right-wing to allow myself to connect with almost anybody else, gay or straight, which meant no real friends, no dating, and only furtive sex.

Even then, I knew there was something odd about how badly I wanted Thomas's allies as my comrades in arms, though I didn't know how to account for it. The sad reality is that I was trying to fill my unmet, private emotional needs through my professional life. I saw the kinship that the Thomas camp seemed willing to provide me as a way of filling my tortured need for friendship and affection and acceptance, as a salve for my loneliness. Through them, I was trying to find not only kindred spirits in a cause, a comforting sense of being cosseted by true believers, but also a happy place. I was looking to others, rather than within, for affirmation.

Yet at the same time, I quite consciously feared that my homosexuality stood in the way of my ever being fully accepted in the conservative movement. The steady undercurrent of bigotry—from the writings of Midge Decter, to my dealings with her son, John, to Newt Gingrich's smearing of Tom Foley, to Bob Tyrrell's flippant gay bashing—was a clear signal of this. I began to resent the fact that I was gay, though I never connected this to the need to impress, to overcompensate, to prove myself good enough and tough enough to the conservatives that I also was feeling. While at the time it seemed like nothing more than finding my groove as a writer, a palpable anger imbued my prose in a way that it never had before. The doctrinaire absolutism, the thunderous extremism, the wildness of expression—these qualities were not uncommon among other closeted right-wing homosexuals I had known, nor, for that matter, among some extreme right-wing minorities, of whom Clarence Thomas was the foremost example. And it may well have been on this basis that I found myself instinctively empathizing with Thomas. At the bottom of my rage there must have been a loathing, not of liberals, but of myself. By giving voice to their hatred of Anita Hill, I was trying to force the conservatives to love a faggot whether they liked it or not.

The March 1992 Anita Hill article became the basis for my first book. When the piece came out, I had been working on a scholarly book on Congress at the Heritage Foundation that my agents had been able to sell to HarperCollins Publishers for a small advance. Given the buzz around the *Spectator* piece in conservative circles, I decided to switch book topics. An Anita Hill book, I figured, could take the message of Thomas's innocence to a wider audience. On the advice of John Podhoretz, I had hired as my agents Glen Hartley and Lynn Chu, a husband-and-wife team who had created a market niche in representing conservative writers like John's father, Norman. It's wonderful to have agents who believe in you, and Lynn and Glen were dyed-in-the-wool ideologues. Only a few years older than I was, they had come to their conservatism in much the same way I had, in reaction to collegiate PC liberalism in the late '70s and early '80s. Deceivingly petite, Lynn, a University of Chicago–trained lawyer, was so fierce in her diatribes against feminism and affirmative action that she sometimes frightened even me. Glen, for his part, wanted to change the title of the project from the ambiguous *The Real Anita Hill* to the blunter *Why She Lied*.

When they took the project to my editor at HarperCollins, a tweedy, courtly executive named Ed Burlingame, he told them if I wrote a book trashing Anita Hill, I would ruin my career. That was all I needed to hear. I prided myself on doing nothing to tailor my views to the journalistic mainstream. I believed this was my strength, giving me great freedom of action, and making me a lethal adversary. Unfortunately, what I then romanticized as fearlessness turned out to be recklessness. Ed Burlingame would be proven right.

Lynn and Glen knew just where to go next. They had a close relationship with Erwin Glikes, an editor at Free Press, then an imprint at Macmillan Publishers, who published the books of many of their clients. Erwin was another neoconservative. A native of Antwerp, Belgium, the son of Jewish refugees from Hitler, Glikes had been educated at Harvard and settled into a comfortable life in academia as a professor of English and assistant dean of Columbia College. The student protests in the late 1960s, however, caused him, like many liberals, to reconsider his political beliefs and affiliations. Glikes began his publishing career working for Irving Kristol, then an editor at Basic Books, and went on to become head of trade book publishing at Simon & Schuster. In the early 1980s, he left Simon & Schuster, furious that he wasn't getting support from his colleagues to publish successfully the conservative books on his list. To illustrate the problem, Erwin liked to tell the story of having once been accidentally informed by an S&S sales representative (who didn't know who Glikes was) that "no one was going to a lift a finger" to sell Norman Podhoretz's 1981 book *The Present Danger.* For Glikes, the comment was the last straw. At Free Press, Macmillan would give him his own marketing and publicity shop.

Angry and volatile, Erwin began waging a one-man war against the politics of the book industry in New York. A brilliant man and a savvy publisher, he invented a certain kind of ideological publishing that became very hot in the late '80s and early '90s. He seemed to have a magician's power in developing a theretofore-unknown market for conservative books, making bestsellers of books by George Will, Bob Bork, Allan Bloom, Francis Fukuyama, and Dinesh D'Souza. *The Real Anita Hill* would be another in that line, and I would see from the inside how the trick was done. For Glikes, making money was just icing on the cake: Each book was a cause. As it happened, when Lynn and Glen approached Erwin, he had been carrying my Anita Hill article in his briefcase for weeks, pushing it on anyone who would listen. Gender politics, in particular, enraged Erwin. I can still hear him railing, between bites of chocolate layer cake in the executive dining room at Macmillan, that the feminists, "in their iron hoop skirts," had seized control of New York publishing. What better way to smite them than by signing up my book for $120,000, more than ten times the advance I had been paid by HarperCollins? So much for ruining my career, I thought.

At Free Press, Erwin Glikes assigned the editing of the book to a bright young editor, Adam Bellow, the son of Nobel laureate Saul Bellow. Adam's claim to fame was having edited Dinesh D'Souza's first book, *Illiberal Education*, a broadside against political correctness on the nation's campuses. D'Souza had been an editor of the *Dartmouth Review* when it published its racist "jive" column, and for his work he had earned the nickname "Distort D'Newsa." *Illiberal Education*, however, was well reviewed and became a surprise best-seller. In the next go-around, D'Souza's history caught up with him. The first print run of his second book for Adam, *The End of Racism*, which explored supposed connections between the social problems facing African Americans and low IQ, had to be trashed when the circulation of galleys prompted a threat of libel action from one of its subjects.

Erwin never criticized my *Spectator* piece, but I understood that he had little regard for the magazine; Adam's job was to "dry-clean" me for a more discerning audience, as Adam explained it to me. Even more than Erwin, Adam had an instinctive knack for how to cover a conservative argument with a patina to make it appealing to the liberal eye. Adam's most successful authors were wolves in sheep's clothing, for he had learned from Erwin to approach the marketing of his books, as he did D'Souza's, like a political campaign. At the time, the power of right-wing talk radio to sell books had yet to be demonstrated, and New York publishers were skeptical that a philistine like Rush Limbaugh had a literate audience. So the key to success, Adam explained to me, as if he had a secret formula, was to "capture" the center with rhetorical sleight of hand, just as a right-wing pol might lure swing voters. Persuading the liberal or moderate reader that a conservative book's point of view was "reasonable" would give it a crack at a favorable review in the *New York Times* and elsewhere. Respectful reviews, in turn, would establish the book with the mostly liberal, urban audience who bought serious nonfiction books. The climb up the best-seller lists would be aided by having an author with the talent for presenting extreme views in a "reasonable" fashion on the book promotion tour, as D'Souza did.

Before my book tour in the spring of 1993, I practiced my shtick with a media trainer hired for me by Erwin. Because the liberal media was out to discredit conservatives, Erwin coached me, the price of media credibility, of being taken seriously as a journalist, was to call black "white," to deny that I had a political agenda. I wound myself up, marched into the TV studios, and spouted the line so often, I almost managed to convince myself of my own spin. "Katie," I told *Today* show host Katie Couric, leaning in for effect, "character assassination is wrong," whether it happens to a liberal or a conservative. When I returned to my hotel room, the telephone was ringing. "You hit the ball out of the park," Ricky Silberman cried.

To me, contemptuous of anything that smacked of being mainstream or respectable, proud to be toiling in the conservative ghetto against the liberal establishment, Erwin's tactics were entirely new, and at first discomfiting. As a first-time, no-name author, at best I had hoped my book would be a minor success with conservatives; I expected to be completely ignored by the liberal media, and I couldn't have cared less. Now, I was on the *Today* show! Erwin and Adam taught me to set my sights higher, and they also introduced me to the concept that piles of money could be made while advancing the cause. They had a much slicker notion of Gramsci's "capturing the culture" than did poor Grover Norquist.

I was never certain about Adam's commitment to conservatism. His political stance struck me as a pose, perhaps adopted to fit the views of Erwin, his much more strong-willed and self-assured mentor in book publishing. Adam owed everything to Erwin, who had enabled him to establish a professional identity as someone other than Saul Bellow's son. Whether I detected in Adam a lack of sincerity, or whether he was more subtle in expressing his views than my friends in Washington, didn't really matter to me because I had enough fire in the belly for us both. What did matter was Adam's undeniable gift with an editing pencil. When it was finished, *The Real Anita Hill* bore only a passing resemblance to the *Spectator* article. The main change was that I bent over backward to adopt a more respectful tone toward Hill, a tactic urged on me by Adam, who knew that for the first time I had a potentially wide audience, and could expect scrutiny from critics. "Think of the reader as you would a juror," Adam coached me. "The tone should be more in sorrow than in anger." In this sanitized retelling, Hill was no longer a nut or a slut. The book was framed more as a defense of Thomas than an attack on Hill, who was portrayed more as a victim than a victim-izer, a confused pawn pressured to turn an old white lie into false Senate testimony by ruthless liberal Senate staffers and feminist supporters. Of course, I had never met one of these staffers or feminists, nor, such was my isolation in these years in Washington, had I ever even met a Democrat working in politics. Yet my hatred was refocused on these imaginary villains who had broadcast Hill's lies on national television.

I approached the book in the same way I had approached the article; my goal was to write a truthful account. Tainted by bias, and already committed to a flawed interpretation of events in print, I got no closer to the truth in the book. In fact, nine years after I wrote it, when I finally reread the book in 1999 while struggling to write this one, I could see that all the scrubbing, smooth-ing, and polishing done by the editors only ended up producing a more per-suasive—and therefore more insidious—form of propaganda between hard covers. As in the *Spectator* article, I failed to weigh my findings against the fact that all of my sources were pro-Thomas partisans. By the same token, the screeching *Spectator* article ensured that I had no access to Hill's supporters, and therefore no understanding of their motivations, no responses to any of my charges, and no knowledge of whatever incriminating evidence they might have gathered against Thomas that was not introduced in the hearing. They all did the right things in refusing to talk to a biased writer like me. As for the traits ascribed to Hill that might have motivated her to lie—ambitious, will-ful, and even vengeful—they were culled by me from the Thomas camp. Everyone I spoke to *hated* the woman. As media critic Howard Kurtz adroitly summarized it in the *Washington Post:* "Brock quotes detractors (many of them anonymous) who describe Hill as 'untrustworthy,' 'selfish,' 'bitter,' 'mil-itantly anti-male,' 'holier-than-thou,' 'obsessively concerned with race and gender issues,' 'subject to wild mood swings,' 'a full-fledged campus radical,' 'obsessed with oral sex,' and 'the world's kinkiest law professor.'"

The book had four principal coauthors. In the Bush White House were Lee Liberman and Mark Paoletta. Lee, a former clerk to Antonin Scalia, had

called me at the *Times* after my *Spectator* piece was published, offering further assistance for the book. I called her regularly to match wits as I pored
over the voluminous hearing record, working day and night from my home
in Woodley Park. Lee was always a gentle, lovely person in my dealings with
her, but she was also a fierce pro-life advocate with close ties to the antiabortion movement. I often called Lee in the morning, after a long night of
obsessing over the record, to check the legal reasoning for our theory of the
case. The conversations were clipped; I told her of this or that tidbit and
asked if this or that supposition from the record made sense to her. She
rarely gave me an instant answer, often calling back a few hours later. If Lee
said the theory worked, as it usually did, I developed it further; if it didn't
work, it was back to the drawing board for me. Lee was always available, but
she was cautious by nature and cool emotionally.

Over time, I became much closer personally to Mark. Mark was a few
years younger than I was, and not quite as formidable intellectually as Lee,
which permitted me to think that Mark was working for me. Unlike Lee,
who had grown up in Manhattan, was set financially, and had gone to Yale,
Mark was in debt with college loans and had no Ivy League pedigree. He
came from a working-class family in the Northeast. His father, whom I met
on occasion, lived in Connecticut and was a conservative Catholic just like
mine was. Mark told me his mother had abandoned the family and left his
father to raise Mark as an only child. During the six years I knew him well,
Mark was barely on speaking terms with his mother. Of course, since I never
told Mark of my adoption, it seemed as though we had even more in common than we did: My mom was Italian American, and she had cousins with
the name Paoletti, and Mark and I joked that we might be distant cousins.
To use an apt cliché, Mark was the epitome of tall, dark, and handsome, and
I soon met his pretty wife, Tricia, another Republican lawyer. The Paolettas
eventually had several children, all of whom came to my house in Washington, and later to my beach house in Delaware, to play. Mark and Tricia, in
turn, invited me to dinner at their small cottage in the Virginia suburbs; they
met and accepted Andrew into the fold when he visited from California,
as had Ricky and Larry. Mark and I talked constantly, day and night, by

telephone—so much so that Tricia joked that her husband was neglecting her
for me.

If Lee acted as my lawyer, Mark performed a different function. Seeking
to prove that Hill had a poor employment history with a private law firm
before she went to work for Thomas, Mark helped me to get a crucial bit of
information out of a reluctant source. The source was Judith Hope, a prominent Republican lawyer who was nominated by Reagan for a federal judgeship on the D.C. Circuit but never confirmed by the Democratic-controlled
Senate. The post was filled by Clarence Thomas when Bush won the election in 1988. During the Thomas-Hill hearing, Hope had expressed some
private doubts to Boyden Gray and others about whether Hill had been
truthful when Hill testified she had not been asked to leave the law firm
before she went to work for Thomas. Hope came under enormous pressure
to testify to her recollections, but she had no firsthand knowledge of Hill's
employment reviews, and she was too unsure herself of what exactly had
caused Hill to leave the firm to go on record under oath. Essentially, Hope
had done nothing more than pass along ten-year-old gossip from the firm
about Hill's performance to her GOP lawyer friends.

Mark filled me in on the details of what Hope had conveyed to the White
House. Seeking to nail Hill as a fabricator, Mark and I agreed that I should
sweat Hope down and get her secondhand information on the record for my
book. I had several tense confrontations on the telephone with Hope, who
clearly didn't want to talk, before I finally was able to badger her into meeting with me by implying that I had the full force of the Federalist Society
behind me. When I again hit a brick wall in our meeting, Hope looked as
though she might burst into tears when I bluffed her into talking by saying
that I already had her conversations with White House lawyers on the
record and was determined to publish them one way or the other. I then
took Hope's shaky memories and built them up into a charge that the top
partners in Hill's old firm—most of whom were politically active liberal
Democrats who had let Hill use their law office for meetings with her
lawyers before she testified publicly—had abetted Hill's perjury by backing
up Hill's account of how she left the firm.

The more I worked with Mark and Lee, the farther into Thomas's tight inner circle I was drawn. It was not a trusting group. The Thomas loyalists, I learned, had their own back channels and secret strategy sessions through-out the nomination struggle. Attorney General Richard Thornburgh was out of the loop, because, I was told, he had expressed misgivings about Thomas's nomination. Former Reagan chief of staff Kenneth Duberstein, who was brought in by the White House to coordinate nomination strategy, was a moderate Republican not to be trusted. Bill Kristol was edged out because he talked too much to the press. Even Senator John Danforth, Thomas's Senate sponsor, was also viewed with suspicion. The Silbermans, too, were one step removed, once Hill's charges became public and they gave Thomas what Mark called "crazy advice." I never learned what the advice was, but whatever happened caused Mark to grimace whenever I mentioned my sur-rogate parents, and it may have caused the Silbermans to "boycott," as Larry put it, Lee Liberman's wedding to Republican lawyer Bill Otis.

In addition to Boyden Gray and Mark and Lee at the White House, the inner circle included three Justice Department officials: J. Michael Luttig, the top Justice official handling the nomination; his deputy Tim Flanigan; and John Mackey, a deputy attorney general. During the Thomas hearings, Luttig was nominated and confirmed for an appellate judgeship but remained actively involved as a Thomas adviser. He was replaced in the administration by Flanigan. It was a very hard circle to penetrate, but I managed to do it when I took up the issue of another witness and ex–Thomas employee, Angela Wright, who never testified in the public hearing, but had accused Thomas of pressing her for dates and making crude remarks to her on the job in a Senate deposition. The discrediting of Wright was seen by the Thomas loyalists as per-haps the most important part of my book, for it had been widely believed by both sides in the struggle that if Wright had testified, the nomination would have been doomed. Why she didn't testify remained a mystery. The campaign of intimidating women from saying what they knew about Thomas during hearings and smearing their reputations would continue through my book.

I was told by Mark Paoletta and Lee Liberman that when Wright's name surfaced, the FBI had done a background check on her as a potential witness, and that the FBI file contained information that could be used to undermine Wright's credibility. Though disclosure of the file was potentially criminal, Mark sent me to John Mackey at the Justice Department, who was a liaison with the FBI, to find out about getting it. Lee had me call and visit Tim Flanigan to discuss how the file might be leaked to me. Both Mackey and Flanigan were encouraging. Following this round of inquiries, Mark had me call an aide to Senator Strom Thurmond, Duke Short, who apparently had access to Wright's file during the hearing, and Terry Wooten, Thurmond's chief counsel, who had cross-examined Wright in her Senate deposition. Wooten agreed to see me in an office on Capitol Hill. When I arrived, Short greeted me, took me to a small, nondescript office where Wooten was waiting, and disappeared. Closing the door, Wooten took a seat and we discussed Angela Wright for less than an hour. On the desk in front of him, Wooten had copies of several pages from Wright's raw FBI file. I was thrilled to lay my hands on the documents. With his agreement, I took the pages home and got to work. The interviews Wooten gave me were of Wright's former employers and colleagues who had criticized her to the FBI. I reprinted sections of the file in my book, including one interview in which Wright was described as "vengeful, angry, and immature," and another that labeled her a "seductive-type person" who "would invite the sexual advances of a man and then brag about having guys hit on her." The FBI file, which contained unfiltered and unverified information, enabled me to do to Wright what I had already done to Hill. (Wooten has publicly denied giving me the file.)

The disclosure of the confidential file by high Republican officials was highly unusual, and it was also an instance where the Republicans actually carried out the misdeeds that they had accused the Democrats of perpetrating. During the hearing there was a hue and cry from the right that someone hostile to Thomas had tipped the press off to Hill's confidential charges, which led to Hill's public testimony. In one section of the book, I was publicizing leaked charges, and in another I sought to identify the Democratic leaker who could be blamed for the entire mess and would forever be tarred by the right as a devil figure. I worked very hard to come up with a villain: Democratic Senator Paul Simon of Illinois. I accused Simon of illegally leaking Hill's confidential Judiciary Committee affidavit to the press, a conclusion for which I had no sources. I merely made a deduction from the record, not nearly the kind of evidence one needed to lodge a charge against a senator that, if true, warranted an Ethics Committee investigation. In his autobiography, published in 1999, Simon took issue with much of what I wrote about him. He told the story of meeting Judge Patricia Wald of the D.C. Circuit, a liberal whom I claimed was "close" to Simon and portrayed as a conspirator in the campaign against Thomas. After my book was published, Wald was scheduled to testify before one of Simon's subcommittees. Before she began speaking, Wald walked up to Simon and said, "Since we are close, I thought I should introduce myself." The two had never met. Simon was kind enough to conclude in his book that I was "a young man with more ability than judgment."

Of course it had been none other than Judge Silberman who gave me the false information on his colleague Pat Wald, whom he hated with a passion. Shortly after I dropped off the chapter called "Trial by Leak" late one evening at the Silbermans' Georgetown home, stuffing it through the mail slot in their door like a surprise gift, my telephone rang in Woodley Park. Ricky and Larry were literally squealing with joy about the case I had constructed implicating Simon, a vocal critic of Silberman's during the judge's own confirmation hearing. They were passing the phone to each other, marveling at my "genius" at the top of their lungs. "You got him. You nailed him. You fucked him. You killed him," they sang. The state of manic euphoria that gripped the Silbermans that evening is impossible to describe to a normal person, but I would see more and more of it—in others, and eventually in myself—as I rose through the ranks. (In a similar vein, Ricky Silberman passed to me an unverified quote from her nemesis in the feminist legal community, Judith Lichtman of the Women's Legal Defense Fund; the quote was a fabrication.)

In time, I came to understand precisely what I had done in *The Real Anita Hill*. Clichés are based in truth, and one of the oldest of them is that writers can write well only if they are writing about what they know, what they see, and what they experience firsthand. The conspiracy theory I invented about the Thomas-Hill case could not possibly have been true, because I had absolutely no access to any of the supposed liberal conspirators. As in the case of Silberman and Wald, all of my impressions of the characters I was writing about were filtered through their conservative antagonists, all of whom I believed without question. Therefore, the case made in the book was not only wrong and false, it was almost precisely the opposite of the truth. I described James Brudney, an aide to Senator Howard Metzenbaum, as "evidently driven by a mix of ideology and power" and charged that "like most instrumentalists, in politics as elsewhere, Brudney was known for cutting ethical corners and compromising personal relationships to achieve desired results." That could have been any number of Republican operatives I knew well, but it could not have been Brudney, about whom I knew nothing. With her "guerrilla tactics," I wrote, Nina Totenberg "would stretch the ethical standards of her profession to get a story." That was me, certainly not Totenberg, a respected professional whom I never met. And who was the slimy senator nicknamed "Metz" by his GOP foes? That could have been any GOP official connected to Boyden Gray's attack machine. But it wasn't a recognizable portrait of Howard Metzenbaum to anyone who knew him. Instead of doing real reporting and undertaking a legitimate investigation, I unconsciously projected onto the liberals what I knew and saw and learned of the right wing's operations.

Erwin Glikes would have made a great general. Nervous about the reviews a week before the publication date, Erwin launched a preemptive strike, personally flying to Washington to take the book to George Will. Erwin hoped that Will, a right-wing commentator with a prominent place in the established media culture, would launch the book from his platform in *Newsweek*, a magazine no one could dismiss as a right-wing rag. Will took the bait, writing, "Brock assembles an avalanche of evidence that Hill lied— about her career and her relations with Thomas." Next came a long excerpt taking up almost the entire editorial page of the *Wall Street Journal*. Erwin's imprimatur counted for a lot more than the *Spectator*'s; this time, the conservatives openly embraced my work.

And not only the conservatives. When I learned that the book was under review at the *New York Times* by Christopher Lehmann-Haupt, the paper's senior reviewer, I remembered that Lehmann-Haupt, though he was no conservative, had launched Allan Bloom's *Closing of the American Mind* with an enthusiastic notice. I had a friend who had a friend on the night desk of the *Times* who agreed to fax the review to me at home when it became available in the computer system the night before it was scheduled to run. As it came through the fax, I was chatting on the phone with two of Thomas's close friends, Washington lawyer Richard Leon and his wife, Christine. I could scarcely believe my eyes. Was this some kind of cruel practical joke? The review called my book "well-written, carefully reasoned, and powerful in its logic . . . must reading for anyone remotely touched by the case . . ." Tears clouded my vision as I hung up with the Leons and dialed Adam at home. "We win!" I yelled.

The moment shook me. The *Times* review was a huge and unfathomable victory. "Winning" may seem like an odd choice of words to describe a book review, but it was a revealing one, for that is how my fellow conservatives and I really saw it. *The Real Anita Hill* was much more than a book to us; it was another shot across the bow in the ongoing war with the left. Taking our fight into the heart of the liberal establishment and getting a rave review for our side—well, it didn't get any better than that. Adam's strategy had worked like a charm. I was on a roll. Reviewers from other respected publications also praised the book. The reviews spurred thousands of orders, and the book shot up the best-seller lists, where it stayed for a dozen weeks.*

Why did the majority of mainstream reviewers fall into line? For one thing, the intricate fact war—in which the mountain of assertions on each side could be disputed, rebutted, or explained away by the other side—had proven especially suited to my analytical mental bias. I knew the ins and outs of the case better than anyone; I'd obsessed over them night and day for months in that cramped Woodley Park bedroom, figuring out just how to twist and turn the facts to advantage my side. As the Republicans had done

---

*The book was also a finalist for the *Los Angeles Times* book prize, the result, according to Adam Bellow, of a campaign by a fellow of the right-wing Claremont Institute in California, who was involved in nominations.

on television, in print I created an even more convincing appearance that I had caught Hill lying under oath. The argument I made was logically sound, and it seemed to fit the available evidence to those who had not studied it or reported on the case themselves. On this last criterion, though, reviewers had to place a great degree of trust in my reliability as a reporter, and unfortunately, I let them down.

If some of my reviewers suspended their skepticism, one plausible explanation for the lapse may have been their moral sense, not confined to conservatives, that the sudden airing of unproven sexual charges was unjust and poisonous to the political system. Then there was the unusual *Rashomon*-like quality of the Thomas-Hill psychodrama. In a fundamental sense, there was no such thing as an impartial reviewer in this case; everyone's judgment was subjectively influenced by where they stood in the cultural conflict, or by their own life experiences—in other words, by whether they were predisposed, for whatever reason, consciously or not, to believe what I wrote. To the extent that the case incited a war of the sexes, it might also be worth noting that my favorable reviewers were mostly men.

With the book a critical and commercial success—a crucial beachhead for the right in the culture wars—I knew it was only a matter of time before a counterattack was mounted. *Wall Street Journal* reporters Jill Abramson and Jane Mayer, who were working on their own book on the hearings, soon came after me in the *New Yorker*, publishing a piece called "The Surreal Anita Hill." The pair wrote that they were weighing in on the subject because other reviewers' "essentially uncritical acceptance of the facts . . . threatens to do a disservice to history." Noting my background in conservative publications, they wrote, "[He] pretends to be neutral when he's not." They then launched into a scathing critique of the book, conceding me no ground whatsoever, and unearthing several factual errors—forcing the Free Press, in one instance, to issue a correction on a fact that I was unable to argue my way out of. I claimed that feminist scholar Catharine MacKinnon had advised Hill's legal team; she had not.

Armed with the *New Yorker* review by two crack investigative reporters, Molly Ivins published a column, "Save Yourself $24.95," that some independent booksellers in Manhattan posted near displays of my book. "If this book is unbiased, Richard Nixon never told a lie," she wrote. *Times* columnist Anna Quindlen faulted my "overwhelmingly one-sided reporting" and pointed out that I had received $11,000 in money from conservative foundations—Olin and Bradley—to support my research. "The book is not only steeped in ideology, it was financed by it." Writing in the *Nation*, Deirdre English concluded that the book was "a sham and a scandal, marking a journalistic standard so low that no reputable publisher should have touched it." Ellen Goodman wrote that the book was not, "as the subtitle declares, 'The Untold Story.' It's 'the Untrue Story.'" A Manhattan bookseller compared *The Real Anita Hill* to *Mein Kampf.*

One morning I opened the *Times* to find an Anthony Lewis column with a headline blazing "Sleaze with Footnotes." "A farrago of the preposterous and the vicious," a "model of the politics of character assassination," Lewis thundered. The sleaze in question was a sly and baseless hint in the text that Hill might have had a sexual relationship with Metzenbaum aide James Brudney. The footnote cited an obscure pro-Thomas newspaper published in Washington's African American community that claimed, with no sourcing, that Hill and the aide had been roommates at Yale. Lewis quoted my footnote: "Though there is no evidence to support such a conclusion [that the two had had an affair], conspiracy theorists might be tempted to conclude that these close links preclude coincidence."

I got a knot in my stomach as I read. I had no idea why, but I was upset and embarrassed. I curled up on the couch and closed my eyes. For a brief few minutes, I began to question what I had done: "Sleaze with Footnotes." When I felt well enough to place a telephone call, I reached Erwin at home in Manhattan, telling him I was ill and wanted to cancel book promotion plans for that morning. He sounded as if he were dancing on tabletops. "You'll go from number six on the list to number two," he crowed prophetically. (Rush Limbaugh's *The Way Things Ought to Be* occupied the top perch.) "Getting attacked—that's what this business is all about. They'd like to ignore you, but they can't. The response is proportionate to the damage you've done. Fuck his 'facts.' You've taken casualties."

Erwin's pep talk helped me go into denial about the merits of the criticism coming my way. Regard the slings and arrows from the left as badges of honor, Erwin implored me—David versus Goliath all over again. Seeing that the bad reviews were commercially useful, Erwin reprinted the attacks in full-page ads in the *Times* over the headline "Read it. Then, you decide." Erwin, my agents Lynn and Glen clucked proudly, had "brass balls." Meanwhile, he launched the kind of blitzkrieg that could succeed only with the backing of a tightly knit political operation, circulating an "Anita Hill Update" to dozens of conservative opinion makers to keep them abreast of news from the front lines and supplying them with copies of my deviously clever ten-thousand-word refutation of the *New Yorker* review, which I published in the *Spectator.* This inspired still more conservatives to come to my defense—William F. Buckley, Thomas Sowell, Cal Thomas, Mona Charen, and the editorial pages of the *New York Post* and the *Washington Times.*

The only time during the entire controversy that Erwin came unglued was when *National Review* unexpectedly panned the book. Calling from his cell phone on a Friday afternoon as he drove to his country house, he fumed, "We need this shit from our friends?" Though *National Review* rightly may have been resisting the unreliable and distasteful journalistic method I had introduced into conservatism, Erwin and I decided professional jealousy was at work. After all, I thought, in a bout of punch-drunk egoism, with a major best-seller under my belt my first time out, I not only dusted my thirty-something peers in conservative publishing, I also accomplished a feat that most of my elders—the Kristols, the Podhoretzes, the Tyrrells—couldn't even dream of.

Though the book had no dedication, and no mention of my family in the acknowledgments, in my world of conservative Washington, I was a hero overnight. The right's celebration of the book cushioned the blows from the left, but I took the praise personally. My newfound celebrity allowed me, or so it seemed, to let go of some of my self-doubt and self-loathing; I thought I was accepted among my political comrades because I was suddenly a star and a stud. My friend Ann Coulter, a conservative lawyer and future TV pundit and author, told me that when I walked into a room full of conservatives, it was like Mick Jagger had arrived. Ann was joking, but I believed her.

My social circle expanded well beyond the other young writers, editors, and Capitol Hill wonks of the Third Generation. Not yet thirty, I was now a junior member of the capital's conservative elite, a sought-after guest at exclusive dinners where GOP lawmakers and top judges and famous columnists came together to hash out strategy and trade off-the-record confidences. One of these dinners was an elite monthly confab hosted by Bob Tyrrell called the Saturday Evening Club, named for a regular dinner H. L. Mencken had hosted. Bob—who had never invited me to the dinner in my four years of freelancing much tamer pieces for the *Spectator* that garnered little attention—finally took me into the fold.

At the Saturday Evening Club, held around a long, rectangular table in a private dining room of the fancy French restaurant La Brasserie on Capitol Hill, I rubbed elbows with Robert Novak, Fred Barnes, Bill Kristol, Lally Weymouth, Brit Hume, Arianna Huffington, and their dinner guests, ranging on any given night from members of the Bush cabinet to members of the GOP congressional leadership, to Supreme Court justices. As dinner commenced, we took turns announcing to the assembled group our names and affiliations. One evening, when former secretary of state Henry Kissinger was the guest, I said my name, Kissinger paused dramatically, gazed down the long table through his horn-rimmed glasses, and grumbled in his gravelly signature accent, "Oh, you're David Brock. I've read your work." I was impressed, and so was Bob Novak. "Kissinger knew who you were," Novak whispered to me in amazement.

Outside the Beltway, on a speaking tour of college campuses, I drew standing-room-only crowds, joining an illustrious group of conservatives like Antonin Scalia, Ken Starr, and Ed Meese, whose speeches had been underwritten by the Federalist Society. Over homemade lentil soup in her Georgetown kitchen, I honed my speech on the Thomas nomination with Ricky Silberman, who, ironically, had once been a speechwriter for Bob Packwood. Ricky wanted to be sure the speech was high-toned, no *Spectator*-like low blows. At Dartmouth, *National Review* editor and professor Jeffrey Hart undid Ricky's handiwork in his effusive introduction of me with a horribly crude reference to Chappaquiddick. At Yale, special security measures were taken to shield me from hundreds of jeering left-wing protesters. It felt good to be back in Berkeley.

My book party at the Embassy Row Ritz-Carlton Hotel was one of the conservative social events of the year, but more important, at least I felt at the time, it was an outpouring of affection and camaraderie. Everyone came—Senator Danforth, Judges David Sentelle and Larry Silberman, Judge Bork and his wife, the entire Kristol clan, Arnaud de Borchgrave, Boyden Gray, Charles Krauthammer, Brit Hume, Mad Dog Sullivan—and, in a moment that meant more to me than any other, Ginni Thomas made a surprise appearance and tearfully embraced me. Andrew, who had flown in from California for the event, took me aside and said, "Gee, David, they really love you."

I was well on my way to achieving everything I wanted: a warm, secure place in the conservative movement; fame and success as a writer, on my own terms; a starring role, an identity, as a radical right-wing outlaw; as well as something I had never wanted but that would prove quite useful in the years to come—sanction for my mission from some mainstream media. The pangs of conscience I had felt when reading Anthony Lewis were safely buried. Mick Jagger was all warmed up for the next act.

CHAPTER SIX

HOLY WAR

In a review of Pat Buchanan's memoirs for the neoconservative magazine *Commentary* back in 1987, I had warned of the corrosive dangers to the Republican Party of a divisive right-wing holy war that aimed to fan the flames of nativism, bigotry, and social intolerance. By 1992, after four years of conservative disunity, frustration, and disappointment during the Bush presidency, in the midst of an economic downturn, a backlash against the gains of women and minorities, and a resurgent religious revival in what became known as the year of the "angry white male," the holy war broke out. Through organization and sheer force of numbers, the religious right had won control of the conservative movement, and the movement, in turn, now was dictating Republican Party policy. In a search for post-Communist bogeymen, Republicans officially embraced right-wing fundamentalism as their own. The party branded its opponents as immoral and un-American, schemed to probe their private lives, and virtually launched an antigay pogrom. I drifted along.

The roots of the GOP holy war could be found in the racial appeals of Richard Nixon's "southern strategy"; the movements against abortion rights and the Equal Rights Amendment in the 1970s; the political organizing of Paul Weyrich and of the Reverend Jerry Falwell, who in 1979 had declared America a "Christian nation"; and the election of Ronald Reagan in 1980. But more than anything else, the sea change in Republican politics was affected by the Reverend Pat Robertson, who lost the presidential nomination race in 1988, but took his contributor lists and founded the Christian Coalition to advance what he called "restoring the greatness of America through moral strength." Unlike the now-defunct Falwell organization, which could not muster the clout to pass its legislative priorities on abortion or school prayer in the Reagan years, Robertson's fledgling group grew like topsy, fulfilling the potential that Paul Weyrich had seen more than a decade before and making the word "Christian" synonymous with right-wing politics.

Fueled by opposition to abortion and gay rights as the centerpiece of its "traditional values" agenda, by 1992 fundamentalist Christians had taken control of the state GOP parties in as many as a dozen states and had working majorities on perhaps hundreds of local school boards around the country, where decisions on everything from curricula to condoms were made. They were armed with often misleading voter guides, passed through evangelical churches, designed to identify which candidates did or did not support the "Christian" position. The coalition financed antigay initiatives in Maine, Colorado, and Oregon (Oregon's ballot branded homosexuality "abnormal and perverse"), and it fought an Equal Rights Amendment for women in Iowa, which, Robertson wrote, would advance "a feminist agenda . . . that would encourage women to leave their husbands, kill their children, practice witchcraft, destroy capitalism, and become lesbians."

Robertson hired a talented young conservative and committed Christian named Ralph Reed to head up his national office. Reed had been executive director of the national College Republicans during Reagan's reelection in 1984, worked for Gingrich protégé Grover Norquist, and then earned a doctorate in American history from Emory University. Though he later found it necessary to soften the Christian Coalition's image (and did so successfully), Reed, a slight, baby-faced man in a coat and tie who might have had trouble punching his way out of a paper bag, seemed to relish the war metaphors frequently employed by tough-talking political consultants. In his autobiography, *Active Faith*, published by the Free Press and edited by Adam Bellow, Reed wrote: "We are not revolutionaries, but counterrevolutionaries, seeking to resist the left's agenda and to keep them from imposing their values on our homes, churches, and families." Like the Gingrich revolutionaries, Reed admired the tactics of the 1960s radicals he claimed to disdain. "Just as Tom Hayden and the SDS had transformed American politics in the '60s and early '70s by turning the youth vote into a potent political force," Reed wrote, "we hoped to create a generation of committed conservatives that would be a mirror image of the New Left." Bragging that the group's activists carried out its political activities by "flying under radar," Reed remarked, infamously, "I paint my face and travel at night. You don't know it's over until you're in a body bag. You don't know until election night."

As befit their grassroots strength, fundamentalist Christians were a major force at the 1992 GOP convention in Houston, making up as much as 42 percent of the delegates. Announcing a $13 million drive to elect "pro-family Christians" to office that year, Robertson declared that his goal was to achieve "working control" of the GOP by 1996. He was given an honored place among the lineup of GOP convention speakers in Houston, warning "unless America returns to her Christian roots . . . she will continue to legalize sodomy, slaughter innocent babies, destroy the minds of the children, squander her resources, and sink into oblivion."

Robertson's speech was eclipsed by the prime-time performance of Pat Buchanan, who had challenged George Bush in the Republican primaries, winning nearly a third of the vote. While the conservative Catholic Buchanan and the Christian Coalition leadership differed on several issues, particularly in foreign policy, his call for a "religious war for the soul of America . . . as critical to the kind of nation we will one day be as the Cold War itself" was well received by the rank-and-file delegates. Invoking the specter of a race war in a reference to rioting by African Americans in Los Angeles, Buchanan said: "As [the troops] took back the streets of L.A., block by block, so we must take back our cities, and take back our culture, and take back our country."

After his 1990 retreat on his "no new taxes" pledge, and facing a third-party candidacy from Dallas billionaire H. Ross Perot, President Bush, feeling compelled to mollify the religious right, invited Pat Robertson to sit in the presidential box in Houston. Two weeks after the convention, Bush attended a Christian Coalition rally in Virginia Beach, where he castigated the Democrats for failing to mention "the word God" in their platform. Vice President Quayle was the featured speaker at a Christian Coalition "God and Country" rally at the GOP convention. Republican National Committee chairman Rich Bond, bringing the civil war rhetoric of Newt Gingrich and

Irving Kristol to prime time, stood on the convention floor and said: "We are America. Those other people are not." When Massachusetts Governor William Weld strode to the Houston podium and extolled the view of almost everyone I knew in Washington—"keep[ing] government out of people's pocketbooks and out of their bedrooms"—convention delegates roundly booed him.

Though conservatives like H. L. Mencken had once written critically of Christian fundamentalists, the party's intellectuals now signed on to Pat Buchanan's religious war. William McGurn of *National Review*, which had endorsed Buchanan's insurgent candidacy (as had Rush Limbaugh), lauded Buchanan's convention speech and suggested that only Republicans had real families. Buchanan "was right to point out that this year's election is more than a choice between two presidential candidates: It is a choice between two distinct cultures fighting for the soul of America. . . . Democrats may insert a clause about family values in their platform, but Republicans come with actual families." Robert Bartley, the editor of the editorial page of the *Wall Street Journal*, also defended Buchanan: "The way that the Houston convention was characterized set a stereotype. . . . But to say that his [Buchanan's] speech was intemperate and inflammatory . . . that just doesn't ring true." Both neoconservative Irving Kristol and Grover Norquist wrote pieces cheering the influence of the fundamentalist Christians in the GOP. Kristol may have been genuinely sympathetic to the movement's cultural conservatism, though for Grover, who had always struck me as libertarian, it seemed more a cynical sellout to the Christian conservatives, who had the troops.

The year 1992 marked the first time gay rights was elevated as a national campaign issue. The Democratic platform called for an end to discrimination against gays in the military, and Bill Clinton became the first presidential candidate ever to mention gay rights in his convention acceptance speech. Conservative leaders also abruptly changed their tone toward gays. In their embrace of Robertson and Buchanan, Republican leaders revealed that bashing gays was now an explicit party strategy, and Newt Gingrich, whom I had mistakenly viewed as tolerant on the gay issue, was reportedly behind it. "Some Republicans, such as Rep. Newt Gingrich of Georgia, are urging in the private councils of the Bush campaign for a 'decapitation' of the Democrats by an attack on Mr. Clinton's character and a new gay-bashing offensive," the *Wall Street Journal* reported. Speaking to the convention, Pat Buchanan denounced the "amoral idea that gay and lesbian couples should have the same standing in law as married men and women." To justify the party's anti-gay stance, respected conservative voices argued that homosexuality is a "learned behavior," as Dan Quayle put it. *Commentary* published an article by a Harvard psychologist who advocated discrimination against gays on the dubious theory that most young homosexuals are actually "waverers"—they could go either way—and thus could be coerced by social disapproval into leading heterosexual lives. And in a syndicated column about the outing of right-wing activist Phyllis Schlafly's son John in a gay magazine, Cal Thomas suggested that "behavioral therapies used to treat mental disorders" could cure Schlafly of his malady.

I watched Buchanan's convention speech from a vacation home in Provincetown, Massachusetts, a popular gay resort, that Andrew had rented for the summer while his home in California was being renovated. Afterward Andrew and I made our nightly tour of Provincetown's gay bars. I didn't dare tell anyone what I really thought of the convention proceedings, but I could see that the party was making a tectonic shift: preaching hatred of government on the one hand, and calling for government enforcement of religiously ordained standards of personal conduct on the other. It no longer seemed like the party I had joined in the mid-1980s. The people Lee Atwater once had derided as the "extra chromosome crowd" were taking over. Though most of the gay Republicans I knew had come into the party at a very young age through family and home state political connections and were in no position to leave their careers in the party in middle age, many of them privately voted for Clinton—as would many other Republicans and Independents appalled by the Houston spectacle, and the party leadership's tacit endorsement of it. A group of gay Republicans was banned from testifying at the party's platform hearings, as they had in 1988. As a result, the gay group, the Log Cabin Republicans, which worked for gay rights within the GOP, refused to endorse the Bush-Quayle ticket. Reacting to the Houston convention, longtime William F. Buckley protégé Marvin

Liebman came out of the closet—"I started feeling like a Jew in Hitler's Army," he explained—and expressed his hope that the Republican ticket would be defeated in November.

Rationalization and denial were no longer possible. The proverbial scales were starting to fall from my eyes. I was now on notice that my relationship to the conservative movement was not an alliance, but a misalliance. Yet I had gone to Provincetown to work on a draft of *The Real Anita Hill*. With the impending publication of my first book, a book that would exploit the rhetoric of the culture war, and whose constituency was in large measure the social conservatives who had supported Clarence Thomas, I was not about to jump ship on principle. What principle would that have been, after all? I was not a Log Cabin Republican, the openly gay men and women trying to liberalize GOP ranks. I was a closeted opportunist. I had no interior life to speak of—my sole focus was outside myself, on my career, my book, my place in the conservative movement, my now tight relations with a circle of conservative friends. I had so little sense of self, particularly as a gay man, that I had no principle to defend. The die was cast. I chose to turn a blind eye to rhetoric and intentions that I knew were wrong. My book cemented my place on the wrong side in a culture war that was officially declaring gays as targets, objects of scorn, even persecution. I again put my conscience in abeyance, this time knowingly.

Had I been looking at the election as a voter, I could have been a Clinton Republican. A son of the South who had come out of the Democratic Leadership Council faction that was trying to move the party away from the left-liberalism of the 1970s and 1980s, Bill Clinton was a pro-growth free trader and was pro-immigration. He promised to enact a middle-class tax cut, to restore fiscal discipline, and to reform the welfare system. He was tough on crime—he had gone back to Arkansas in the middle of the Democratic primaries to execute a convicted murderer—and, though the Communist threat was now gone, Clinton had supported the Gulf War and criticized George Bush as soft on the Chinese. Like me, he also was a social liberal—pro–civil rights, pro-choice, pro-gay, and antigun.

The Republican right would fight Clinton, the most talented and popular Democratic politician to come along in twenty-five years, with unprecedented fervor. By moderating on key fiscal, defense, and crime issues, while at the same time proposing to lead through government activism in health care, the environment, and education, Clinton, with his awesome powers of intellect and charisma, represented a unique challenge. He threatened both to split the right *and* to win a mandate to change things in a direction that many conservatives and their corporate backers, from the tobacco lobby to the gun lobby, strongly opposed. If Clinton and Clintonism succeeded, the right would be marginalized for a generation.

The right's opposition to the Clintons was characterized by a level of malice that transcended normal partisan opposition. In effect, Clinton and his wife, Hillary, the first two-career, baby-boomer couple who had come of age in the 1960s to vie seriously for the White House, became accidental culture warriors. After the Cold War, and Bush's forfeiture of the tax-and-spend issue, conservative leaders opted for a new political tack, defining themselves against the "moral decay" of the 1960s.

The plan was hatched by the GOP political leadership during the 1992 presidential campaign and spread through the right-wing media. The Clintons were made into metaphors for all of the social changes of the past thirty years that the right-wing base in the country hated. Clinton was charged with having an affair with lounge singer Gennifer Flowers; with smoking marijuana; and with dodging the Vietnam draft. As Pat Buchanan, who had gotten out of service in Vietnam because of a bad knee, put it in his convention speech, Clinton was "a draft-dodging, pro-gay greenhorn, married to a radical feminist." Marilyn Quayle, whose husband, Dan, went into the National Guard rather than serve in Vietnam, charged, "Not everyone demonstrated, dropped out, took drugs, joined the sexual revolution or dodged the draft." At the GOP convention, the Arkansas delegation distributed lapel stickers that said: "Smile if you have had an affair with Bill Clinton." Some conservatives went further, charging Clinton with sedition. Congressman Randy Cunningham compared a visit Clinton made to Moscow in 1969 while he was studying at Oxford to the treasonous Tokyo Rose during World War II. (For good measure, Cunningham said the entire

Democratic Congressional leadership "should be lined up and shot.") The Republican National Committee charged that Clinton had been recruited as "an agent of [Communist] influence." Future congressman Sonny Bono called Clinton a "Communist." The country was being conditioned to see an invention made up entirely by the Republican right: "Bill" and "Hillary" Clinton. Thus, from virtually the first moment that they stepped out of Arkansas and onto the national stage, the country never again saw the Clintons.

Hate, of course, is an emotional aversion, not an intellectual one. In my personal experience, when I spent enough time talking with a Clinton-hater, I found the problem in the emotional life of the hater. The hatred of the Clintons was very real; it was not a political gimmick deployed for dramatic effect. It could be heard in the angry voice of even a silly goose like *Spectator* editor Bob Tyrrell, who would play a leading role in the right-wing *Kulturkampf* against the Clintons. Without a trace of self-consciousness, but perhaps more than a trace of boomer self-loathing, Tyrrell, who, unlike the Clintons, had been unable to keep his own family intact, would tell the *Philadelphia Inquirer:* "This is a cultural thing. Clinton is of my generation and when I was at Indiana University, he and Hillary and their people were tearing down the great American institutions. They had within them the seeds of social destruction. And now, 30 years later, they have borne out what I feared then."

These right-wing attacks did not resonate with my social liberalism. I may have worn the clothes of a social conservative, but they didn't fit. Like the majority of the country, I didn't much care whether Clinton had smoked pot, served in the military, or had strayed from his marital vows. Moreover, at this juncture, there was far less ideological affinity between the GOP and me than when I had first come to Washington. The party had left me and many other libertarian-leaning conservatives back in Houston.

Yet in pursuit of my budding career as a right-wing muckraker, I let myself get mixed up in a bizarre and at times ludicrous attempt by well-financed right-wing operatives to tar Clinton with sleazy personal allegations. Operating in conjunction with, but outside of, official GOP or movement organizations, and well below the radar of the American public and the press corps as the election campaign unfolded, the effort went far beyond the opposition research typically conducted in political campaigns— not only in its secretiveness and its single-mindedness, but also in its lack of fidelity to any standard of proof, principle, or propriety. These activities, for which there was no precedent in modern American politics, were a very early hint of how far the political right would go in the coming decade to try to destroy the Clintons.

At the center of the ad hoc operations was a man named Peter Smith, whom I had first spoken to in 1991, when he called out of the blue to compliment me on a freelance piece I had done for the *American Spectator* attacking President Bush's secretary of state, James Baker. Baker was a pragmatic establishment Republican and a bête noir of conservative activists who thought he had undercut them when he served as President Reagan's White House chief of staff. In an otherwise sober analysis of the failures of Baker's tenure at State, I added an unverified aside that implied Baker was having an affair with a longtime aide. Smith savored that morsel above any other.

Soon after the Baker piece appeared, I met Smith for breakfast at the posh Hay-Adams Hotel across the street from the White House. At breakfast, Smith took my measure as we engaged in political small talk. He let me know only that he was a very successful investor of some sort based on Chicago's Gold Coast. A small man with wiry white hair and perfectly manicured hands, he exuded the air of a staunch Republican millionaire with his bespoke navy blue suit and Hermès tie. He chatted quietly about his frustration with the squishiness of Baker-type Republicans and talked hopefully of the day that Gingrich would be national leader for the party. As for me, all I remember telling Peter at breakfast was my dream of one day becoming a prominent right-wing reporter like Bob Novak, the political columnist and "Prince of Darkness" talking head. (Novak's many critics referred to the reporting team of Evans and Novak as "Errors and No Facts.")

I also told Peter that I had long found Gingrich to be an inspiration in my work. One of the first freelance pieces I had done for the *American Spectator* was based on a letter Gingrich sent to Nicaraguan leader Daniel Ortega in which Gingrich challenged the patriotism of opponents of the guerrilla war that was being waged against the Nicaraguan government. One of Gingrich's keen observations was that "fights make news," and, sure enough, Speaker Tip O'Neill denounced the Gingrich letter as "the lowest thing I've ever seen in my thirty-two years in Congress."

Smith then suggested we go to his room for coffee. Sitting in a wing-back chair in the elegant suite, he quickly got to the point of his visit. Peter was soft-spoken but his voice carried with it a certain steeliness. He was one of the top contributors in the country to Newt Gingrich's GOPAC and said he had taken it upon himself to fight the liberal bias in the media by funding conservative journalism of the sort I was doing at the *Spectator*. He mentioned several of my earlier *Spectator* pieces in which I red-baited liberal Democrats for failing to support Reagan's foreign policy initiatives. He was ready to write a check to the *Spectator* within a few days if I thought it would help launch his journalism project. He mentioned figures—$30,000? $50,000?—what would it take?

I told Peter I knew little about the *Spectator's* financing and was in no position to take him up on the offer, though I did say I could put him in touch with *Spectator* publisher, Ron Burr. A few days later, I gave Smith Burr's number. When I called Smith's office with the information on who Burr was and how to reach him, I used a business card Smith had given me when we parted that said simply "Peter Smith & Co." Peter had told me always to ask for his assistant, Gail—no one else—when attempting to reach him. He almost always came on the line, or called back within a few minutes. Clearly, Peter's project was important to him. What I didn't realize then was what the project was: Peter was recruiting me into what Hillary Clinton later called "the vast right-wing conspiracy."

I didn't hear again from Peter for another year, when he called me, in September 1992, as I was working at home on the Anita Hill book. He said he had a story tip he wished to pass on to me concerning Clinton's Arkansas past that was being covered up by the pro-Clinton press. With the election only eight weeks away, there was a sense of urgency in Smith's request, as if he thought he could stop Clinton's election. But Peter was no Deep Throat, and I was certainly no Bob Woodward.

Though I wasn't covering the race, and I'd committed to a crash book deadline, I agreed to hear Peter out. Whenever the liberal press was bashed, a sentiment that had given rise to Rush Limbaugh and the investigative exposés in the *Spectator,* I was programmed to spring to action like a trained seal. I met with Peter because I was trying to make a name for myself as a conservative writer by following up on the Anita Hill article. Also, Peter offered me $5,000 for my trouble, not through the *Spectator* but paid directly to me by check; getting by on my Anita Hill book advance, I was a whore for the cash. Although accepting a payment like this was most unusual and unethical for a journalist, in my mind it was no different from taking money from politically interested parties like the Olin and Bradley foundations.

Peter was unfailingly polite, confident, and direct. He seemed like a serious guy, and given his role at GOPAC, as well as his financial support of the Republican National Committee and the Heritage Foundation, he was obviously well connected and had lots of money to throw around. I later learned that Peter had spent $80,000 for a GOP dirty-tricks operation in 1992 to finance a small army of consultants and researchers—and who knew whom else—to troll through Arkansas's byways looking for damaging material on the Clintons.

Peter asked me to meet him at the Capitol Hill offices of Republican political consultant Eddie Mahe, who I knew was a close Gingrich protégé ever since Mahe had volunteered in Newt's first race for Congress in 1974. A bald, hardened southerner with bottle-thick glasses, Mahe had been the political director of the National Republican Campaign Committee in the late 1970s, where he trained and mentored the man who would succeed him in the NRCC post and become Gingrich's closest political adviser, Joe Gaylord. In 1984, Mahe had established a tax-exempt think tank, the American Opportunity Foundation, that housed "Newt's world," his research and education projects. Now, Mahe was on Peter Smith's secret payroll. Also attending the meeting would be Hugh Newton, a former official of the antilabor National Right to Work Committee. Newton was now a publicist whom I had known since my days at the Heritage Foundation, a Newton client.

Though Peter seemed to relish the skulduggery, there was a hint of nervousness in his voice when he told me the meeting was to be kept in the strictest confidence. When I arrived at Mahe's Capitol Hill office, I could hardly believe the bad joke I had walked into. Splashed across the conference table were copies of the *Globe* supermarket tabloid, featuring a story about a woman purporting to be a Little Rock prostitute by the name of Bobbie Ann Williams. The article made the wild claim that Clinton was the father of a boy whom the African American prostitute had given birth to some years ago, after being impregnated at a sex orgy at the Hot Springs home of Clinton's mother, Virginia Kelley. The *Globe* reproduced a fuzzy likeness of a young mulatto boy who was said to be a dead ringer for Clinton. Peter told me that he was trying to find a lawyer in Arkansas to represent the woman and arrange a press conference in which she would challenge Clinton to submit to a paternity test. Mahe promised to put me in touch with another operative, whom he identified only as "Mr. Pepper"—I never learned his identity—who could help me ambush the boy for a photo shoot. For his part, Newton was supposed to help me place and publicize the article. I tried not to laugh as I jotted down a few notes and promised—tongue planted firmly in cheek—to get right on the story.

Peter, though, meant business. Why he had taken the lead in managing this dirty war against Clinton he never really said. Nor did he reveal the extent to which Gingrich may have known what he was up to, for Peter was a man of few words. Eddie Mahe's role in the operation, of course, suggested a close Gingrich connection. Clearly, Peter was a fervent Republican partisan who was willing to go to extraordinary lengths to see to it that Clinton did not win the White House. Beyond that, he seemed animated by a furious denunciation of the liberal press that he said was refusing to report negative personal stories about Clinton to protect the Democratic nominee. Grumbling about press bias was nothing new to me; it was a staple of right-wing paranoia. What I had never seen before was the kind of red-faced rage Peter displayed when he talked about how Clinton was getting away with so much. Slick Willie, as his Arkansas detractors had dubbed Clinton, was driving Peter nuts.

A few telephone calls to Arkansas allowed me to determine the origins of the Bobbie Ann Williams story. In a bit of Arkansas political theater that

I would become all too familiar with in the future, the Bobbie Ann Williams rumors were circulated by a fellow named Robert Say McIntosh, who had leafleted Little Rock with photos of a young boy that were labeled "Clinton's love child." McIntosh apparently bore a grudge against the Clinton administration, which had refused him a state development grant to support his sweet potato pie business. The McIntosh leaflets prompted an enterprising impostor to identify herself as Bobbie Ann Williams and sell the "Clinton love child" story to the *Globe*. The article was accompanied by a photo not of Bobbie Ann Williams, but of her sister. When the story was recycled years later in the *Washington Times*, the real Bobbie Ann Williams came forward to say that she was not a prostitute and had never met Bill Clinton. In 1999, the *Star* tabloid announced that it had performed a paternity test on the boy identified in the McIntosh leaflets, and he was not Clinton's son. The *Globe* story was fake. "Mr. Pepper" also proved to be less impressive than advertised. Though he called me several times dangling the meeting with the boy, he never pulled it off.

Peter Smith's tabloid sleuthing had a self-parodic quality that made it easy to dismiss at the time and I was happy to pocket Peter's $5,000 and go back to work on *The Real Anita Hill*. Though nothing came of the "love child" story, what seemed like a chance connection to Smith would soon result in a series of improbable events and mishaps that would help change the face of political conflict in the Clinton era. The holy war rhetoric emanating from Houston dovetailed nicely with the anti-Clinton jihad that Peter Smith and I were about to launch.

CHAPTER SEVEN

TROOPERGATE

Following the publication of *The Real Anita Hill*, I leapt at an offer from the *American Spectator* to become a full-time "investigative writer" with the mission of doing more Anita Hill–style hits on the left—my dream job. With the proceeds from the best-selling book, I moved out of my Woodley Park rental and bought in the posh Georgetown section of the city, around the corner from my surrogate parents, the Silbermans. I glided across Washington's Key Bridge each morning to the *Spectator*'s offices in Arlington, peering over the dashboard of a large new black Mercedes, a slightly smaller model than the one Bob Tyrrell drove.

With Bill Clinton in the White House, the climate in the conservative movement reached fever pitch. When Ricky Silberman toasted my book in April 1993, she gave voice to something I had sensed about the book's reception during the promotion tour. Conservatives seemed to be buying the book as a protest, not only against Anita Hill and her feminist supporters, but also against the victory of liberalism in Clinton's election four months before. In a declaration of war against the new administration, Ricky boomed, "When the chronicles of the counterrevolution are written, the first page will be *The Real Anita Hill*."

Ricky wasn't the only one in a fighting mood. Republicans had controlled the White House for twenty of the last twenty-four years: That was the order of things. The election of Clinton bonded the Republican leadership and the conservative movement for the first time since the Reagan years. On the night of Clinton's election, Senate minority leader Bob Dole laid down the gauntlet, declaring that the president-elect had no mandate to govern: "Put our votes together with Ross Perot, and we have a majority of the

American people." Dole branded Clinton's presidency, won with 43 percent of the vote, as illegitimate. The new president was a usurper. The Christian Coalition went further, calling Clinton's inauguration "a repudiation of our forefathers' covenant with God." Paul Weyrich declared, "The nation deserves the hatred of God under Clinton."

In the weeks before the inauguration, Republican strategists privately decided not to allow Clinton the honeymoon normally afforded to incoming presidents by both parties in Congress. "Clinton will be debilitated," predicted former Bush White House counsel C. Boyden Gray. The sharp ideological divisions in the Republican Party, the recriminations over why Bush lost the election, and the questions about a future agenda for the GOP were all covered over by a new common cause: The Republican right would deny Clinton the chance to be president.

Always happier as an oppositional, out-of-power protest movement, conservatives were relieved to be rid of President Bush. The mood in the movement was reflected at an annual gathering of the Conservative Political Action Committee, when grassroots political organizers from around the country convene in Washington to get their marching orders from the movement's leading politicians and intellectuals. The hall at the Omni Shoreham Hotel was covered with signs saying "No More Bushit." In a rousing address, William Bennett, who would become one of the leading voices of moralizing conservatism in post-Bush GOP politics, made the now commonplace analogy of the Democrats to Communists: "Conservatives seemed to be flying in all directions after the demise of Communism. I've just discovered what will hold the Republican Party together. I've seen the party coalesce in the last twenty-four or forty-eight hours in opposition to the Clinton proposals."

The early Clinton proposals all touched on elements of culture—he intended to lift the ban on gays in the military and on the use of fetal tissue in medical research, and appointed Hillary Rodham Clinton to head the administration's sweeping efforts to reform the health care system. Thus, the extreme right, with its portrayal of the Clintons as the apotheosis of the 1960s, was able to set the terms of engagement against the new administration. In a symposium in Heritage's *Policy Review,* former Reagan aide Gary Bauer instructed conservatives to use gays in the military and health care to "regalvanize pro-family sentiment in the electorate." Henry Hyde, the white-maned Republican congressman from Illinois, warned apocalyptically in *Policy Review:* "We should be prepared to resist the coercive Balkanization of society likely to follow the new administration's aggressive pursuit of the militant gay agenda and lifestyle radicalism. Fundamentally, the question is whether the U.S. will, in its third century, exist in any recognizable moral and cultural continuity with its founding." Not to put too fine a point on it, Republican House whip Dick Armey called Hillary Clinton a Marxist.

The tight network of right-wing foundations also declared war. The nor-mally circumspect Michael Joyce, who headed the Lynde and Harry Bradley Foundation in Milwaukee, called Clinton's election a "cultural coup d'état," and vowed, "We're fighting the dominant liberal culture, the towering insti-tution of an elitist liberalism which despises ordinary Americans' daily life." The Bradley Foundation was an influential neoconservative organization named for Harry Bradley, an electronics components manufacturer who had been an active member of the John Birch Society. In a speech to a conser-vative summit meeting in Washington sponsored by *National Review,* Joyce, who had supported my research on the Anita Hill book with a small grant, embraced a style of politics that was overtly radical. He spoke of cultivating a "new generation of muckrakers," concluding: "It may sound as if I'm sug-gesting that conservatives should now engage in the sort of countercultural activities that previously dismayed us. I am. Given the structure of power in America today, it is time we realized we are indeed the counterculture. We are revolutionaries."

The early skirmishes between the Clinton administration and the right wing involved several administration nominees who were targeted for defeat by conservative interest groups. I knew the key architects of these attacks through my work on the Anita Hill case, and they told me that their anti-Clintonism was powered by a desire to avenge the Bork and Thomas hear-ings. One conservative leader was Clint Bolick, a bald, cherub-faced former special assistant to Clarence Thomas at the Equal Employment Opportunity Commission (Thomas was the godfather of one of his children) who went on to become a protégé of William Bradford Reynolds, who had fought to roll back civil rights protections in the Reagan Justice Department. Bolick was an affable sort who now ran the Institute for Justice, a public-interest law firm backed by the Koch oil and gas family of Kansas that opposed affirmative action programs for women and ethnic minorities. Almost single-handedly, Bolick defeated Lani Guinier, Clinton's nominee to be assistant attorney general for civil rights, by branding her, in an op-ed piece in the *Wall Street Journal*, a "quota queen," a play on the racist "welfare queen" epithet. In an effort to show that Guinier's views were "breathtakingly radical," Bolick's group combed through hundreds of scholarly articles Guinier had written in search of quotes that could be pulled from their context and made to look damaging. Bolick openly admitted that he was playing the same game of distortion and innuendo that he claimed was at work in the Bork and Thomas cases.

Other nominees came in for rougher treatment. The Southern Baptist Convention labeled Surgeon General Jocelyn Elders, an advocate of abortion rights and sex education, a "eugenicist." Senator Jesse Helms called Roberta Achtenberg, the openly gay nominee to head the Department of Housing and Urban Development, a "damn lesbian." And when attorney general nominee Janet Reno's record as a Dade County, Florida, prosecutor yielded no fertile ground for attack, Tom Jipping, who handled legal issues at Paul Weyrich's powerful Free Congress Foundation, tried to interest me in rumors started by a crackpot Reno foe in Florida that Reno had a history of drunk driving. Jipping, a friend from the Thomas hearings, told me he carefully studied a how-to book on the Bork nomination written by two left-wing activists. To stop the confirmation of Reno, whose appointment would affect everything from civil rights policy to judicial selection, Jipping and his allies were prepared to do just about anything. Tips funneled to the *Washington Times* resulted in calls to several Reno associates inquiring about her sexual orientation. When a lobbyist for the National Rifle Association brought the drunk driving rumors to a staff meeting of top GOP Senate aides, the FBI was asked to investigate and found the stories to be "unfounded and scurrilous."

In these early days of the Clinton administration, Republican leaders condemned such tactics; Senator Hatch denounced the attacks on Reno as "despicable to my mind," and the NRA fired its lobbyist. But the episodes showed that in my circle of radical activists, no tactic—even malicious sexual gossip—was out of bounds. The scandal popularly referred to as Troopergate was born in this savage climate. With a moral obtuseness that, when I think back on it, still astounds me, I would use the very means I had so recently and passionately deplored in the Clarence Thomas case— unproven sexual charges, promoted by partisan enemies—to mount an assault on Bill and Hillary Clinton's moral and political authority that would dog them until their final days in the White House.

In mid-August of 1993, once again I received a call at my *Spectator* office from Peter Smith. Peter told me that he had a contact in Arkansas, a lawyer named Cliff Jackson, who could put me in touch with several Arkansas state troopers who had served on then-Governor Clinton's security staff and wanted to go public with stories of Clinton's womanizing. They were look- ing for an author to collaborate with them on a book, and Peter had rec- ommended me to Jackson. Would I get on the next plane to Little Rock? Peter wanted to know.

After the wild goose chase Peter had sent me on for Clinton's "love child," I was skeptical of his trooper tip, but checking out dirt on the Democrats was my job. So I shrugged my shoulders and arranged with Peter for Cliff to meet me at the Little Rock airport, where I was told to come off the plane holding a copy of the *Washington Post* under my left arm so that Cliff would recog- nize me. As we drove in his old Mercedes to a nearby Holiday Inn, Jackson, a plain-talking country lawyer in his late forties, breathlessly outlined what he described as an "explosive" story. The bodyguards, as he called them, had observed Clinton in a variety of compromising positions with women over the years, and they were ready to turn on their ex-boss. I listened closely, but I wasn't expecting much to come of the story until Cliff told me that a reporter for the *Los Angeles Times,* Bill Rempel, who had worked with Cliff on stories dealing with Clinton's draft record in 1992, had left Little Rock the day before, after spending several hours debriefing the troopers. Maybe this wasn't a phantom story after all.

I checked into the hotel, and things immediately got weird: Cliff disappeared to collect the troopers and told me they would sneak into my room via an outside staircase rather than use the lobby entrance. Cliff was convinced the troopers were being followed, though by whom he never said— my first brush with the paranoid political fantasy that the Clintons ran death squads against their political enemies. A knock at the door, and four hulking state troopers filed in, trailed by Cliff and Lynn Davis, a former chief of the Arkansas State Police and failed GOP politician who also was advising the men. After brief introductions, the troopers sat down and began to swap what they called, quite appropriately, "sleaze" stories about the Clintons— and I began my descent down a path of twists and turns and consequences.

Two of the troopers—Larry Patterson, a tall, loquacious man with an icy stare, and Roger Perry, a fat, pockmarked tough guy with a mop of black hair—did much of the talking. A third trooper, pale, mustachioed Danny Ferguson, and a fourth, roly-poly Ronnie Anderson, chimed in with some piquant anecdotes of their own, but they seemed uncomfortable ratting out their former boss. According to the troopers, as I would subsequently report in the *Spectator*, Clinton had affairs with at least seven women during his marriage (including Gennifer Flowers, who had made the allegation herself during the 1992 presidential campaign in an interview she sold to the *Star* tabloid), as well as a series of onetime sexual trysts the troopers said they arranged for him. They also made the incredible claim that they witnessed a couple of the sexual encounters: once, through a surveillance camera on the grounds of the governor's mansion where Clinton allegedly received oral sex in a pickup truck; another time, standing guard outside a parked car in Chelsea Clinton's deserted schoolyard as Clinton again received oral sex. On the night before President-elect Clinton departed Little Rock for his inauguration in Washington, the troopers claimed, they escorted one of Clinton's girlfriends, disguised in a trench coat and baseball cap, into the basement of the governor's residence for a good-bye assignation.

The troopers' wicked portrait of Hillary Clinton was a jumble of contradictions. In one scene, she was a man-hating feminist whose marriage to Clinton was a cynical pact for political power; in another, she was an anguished spouse, distraught over her husband's unfaithfulness. The couple often fought violently about Clinton's misbehavior within their earshot, the troopers said. They spoke vividly of one night when Clinton supposedly had slipped out of the residence after Hillary had gone to sleep, borrowed one of the troopers' vehicles, and driven off to visit one of his girlfriends. An hour or so later, Hillary suddenly awoke and called down to the guard shack to ask where her husband was. "The sorry damn son of a bitch," she yelled, slamming down the phone. When Roger Perry called Clinton at the woman's home, he said Clinton stammered, "Oh, God, God, God. What did you tell [Hillary]?" When Clinton returned to the mansion, he and Hillary had a profane dustup, in which Hillary supposedly shrieked at Bill, "I need to be fucked more than twice a year!" The interview grew increasingly farcical as the troopers described Clinton's method of eating apples whole, core and all, and Hillary's habit of calling from her law firm and ordering the troopers to fetch her feminine napkins.

As the troopers talked, I was speechless. Why say anything when I was having a great time scribbling down what I thought were the Clintons' intimate family secrets. Women in trench coats! Sex caught on camera! Feminine napkins! For me, working for the *Spectator*, not the *New York Times*, this was a journalistic gold mine: the wilder and more outrageous and even knee-slappingly absurd the stories were, the better. Nothing of the sort ever had been printed about an American president—and for good reason, as it would turn out.

Initially, it was Cliff Jackson, not me, who was mindful of the pitfalls involved in handling such dicey material. A sly negotiator who had plied the mainstream press in 1992 with anti-Clinton stories, Cliff proceeded to tell me how the trooper story could be "packaged" so that it would not be strictly about consensual sex, generally a taboo subject for the media. As Cliff conceived the story, Clinton had abused his power as governor and misused state resources by ordering the troopers to arrange and cover up his extramarital affairs. Although it sounded like a stretch to me—a way of justifying printing a sex story with a phony news hook about misappropriation of funds—the *Los Angeles Times* guy liked the angle, Cliff said. This was important, because according to Cliff's plan, the *Times* was to be used to break the initial story, which would serve to pump up the value of the book proposal that I was to write with the troopers' cooperation.

Though I had relied on partisan sources in the past, I was still concerned enough about the character of the people I was dealing with to take a deep breath. I just didn't trust these slippery Arkansans the way I had the conservative Washington insiders who dirtied Anita Hill. Ringleader Cliff Jackson was a well-known Clinton critic and Republican activist in Arkansas. He had befriended Clinton at Oxford, where Clinton was a Rhodes scholar and Jackson was studying on a Fulbright scholarship. The two were friendly competitors, but the relationship soured when they returned to Arkansas, as Clinton embarked on a path that made him the youngest governor in the state's history in 1978, and Jackson ran unsuccessfully for a county prosecutor's job and settled into a personal injury law practice in Little Rock.

In the '92 campaign, Jackson released to the media personal correspondence with Clinton from the late 1960s, which was interpreted by the press as casting doubt on the candidate's version of events surrounding his military draft status. (Jackson himself had gotten a medical deferment.) During the New Hampshire primary, a group formed by Jackson and funded in part by Peter Smith called the Alliance for the Rebirth of an Independent America, or ARIAS, took out ads labeling Clinton a draft dodger. I knew that Jackson's efforts to derail Clinton went deeper than the draft issue. According to Peter Smith, Jackson had been his Little Rock connection on the "love child" story, working behind the scenes to find a lawyer to issue the paternity challenge to Clinton.

Seeing Jackson up close, it was apparent to me that he was dedicated to destroying Clinton at all costs; it was in his bones. Though he was a Republican, he represented his opposition to Clinton as a matter of character rather than ideology. A Christian fundamentalist, Cliff's broad-brushed attack on Clinton's moral turpitude seemed disproportionate to the facts, even as alleged by the troopers. Though there was no evidence in any of the troopers' accounts, or in anything Cliff had told me, to suggest that Clinton's relations with women were anything but fully consensual, Cliff insisted that the alleged affairs were "an abuse of women." This is the way it had always been, he sputtered, even back at Oxford when Clinton two-timed his girlfriend. Clinton had no integrity; he was immoral and dangerous, Cliff seethed, shaking with indignation.

For Cliff, revealing this hidden truth about Clinton was a noble cause. He was aiming for nothing less than overturning the 1992 election. If only the American people could learn the truth! Clinton would be impeached! I was unimpressed by Cliff's talk of overturning elections and unmoved by his tirade against Clinton. In fact, the more I listened to him, the more I came to believe that Cliff's hatred of Bill Clinton sprang from envy: Cliff was envious of Clinton's success as a pol, and even of his way with the opposite sex.

The troopers, too, had suspect motives. Having supposedly done Clinton's dirty work for years—"We helped him cheat on his wife and he treated us like dogs," as Larry Patterson put it—they were embittered that Clinton had gone to Washington and failed to buy their loyalty with cushy jobs. And they all despised Hillary Clinton and everything she symbolized as a professional woman and committed feminist—they would revel in her humiliation. At bottom, Cliff made clear, the troopers saw dollar signs in exposing the Clintons. Soon after Clinton left them behind in Arkansas, the troopers began plotting among themselves to sell their story. A few reporters had approached them in '92 sniffing around for Clinton sex stories, and they'd refused to talk, but things were different now. In the spring of 1993, they had gone for advice to Lynn Davis, their former boss, who took them to Jackson, who they hoped had the media savvy to strike a lucrative book deal. Though Cliff hid it from me, he had signed a contract guaranteeing him a portion of royalties from any book or TV deals coming out of the trooper story. According to Ronnie Anderson's later statements, Lynn Davis told the four troopers that they "could earn $2.5 million in royalties." The promise of such lucrative deals, as much as ideological opposition, fueled the story. Lots of folks in Arkansas, I soon learned, had a piece of Bill Clinton they were willing to sell for the right price.

I returned to Washington, transcribed my notes, and called my agents to discuss a possible book. The options were unappealing. If I wrote a book about the Clintons under my own name, drawing on the troopers' material, there was no way to cut them in on a deal; that would be paying sources to talk, which I knew would discredit the book. If the troopers themselves sold the book, I would be relegated to the role of ghostwriter.

I flew back to Little Rock in mid-September, met with Cliff and the troopers, and explained the difficulties with the book project. I didn't want to walk away from the story; my appetite was whetted. My goal was to blunt the question of the troopers' unsavory motives by talking the group into allowing me to write up their story as a magazine piece for the *Spectator* with no money changing hands. If they were paid up front to talk, I argued, the story would be dismissed as trash for cash. Go public, gauge the reaction, and if there's a book deal down the road, hire a ghostwriter then, I argued. I lucked out, for by now, Cliff hinted, there were problems getting the *L.A. Times* story to print. Several layers of editors had to clear the piece, and even if the troopers were deemed credible, the *Times* was understandably skittish about exposing the sex life of the president without a legitimate news hook. Thus the *Spectator,* which had a political reason to put the story out, and where there was very little editorial control, became a convenient second track for Cliff.

With Cliff and the troopers on board, I now had to ask myself: Should I really publish this salacious bombshell? Cliff Jackson was right: Even though the line between public and private behavior had been blurred in the Hart, Tower, and Thomas episodes, a public figure's dirty personal linen was not considered newsworthy unless there was demonstrable hypocrisy involved. So I began to sketch out some rationales for why Clinton's extramarital affairs might be relevant to the public domain. I did this in good faith, though I really was subconsciously justifying what I wanted to do. I jumped through the same hoops, developed the same rationales, that other reporters would repeat in future Clinton sex stories. If the troopers were right about Gennifer Flowers, Clinton had misled the public in the '92 campaign in denying the affair. Lying was a legitimate story. The sheer number of affairs and Clinton's indiscretion with his bodyguards suggested poor judgment, even recklessness—also newsworthy. Though I passed no moral judgment on Clinton's personal life, public opinion polls showed 15 percent of the electorate would not vote for an adulterer, and how could I as a reporter withhold the information from them?

I was still queasy about the whole thing. Something was missing in Troopergate—a sense of higher ideological purpose that made it feel wrong even at the time. My laundry list of justifications for publishing the trooper piece notwithstanding, the only conceivable idea behind this story—that Clinton's private moral failings disqualified him from leading the country— was something that I did not believe. Even if the stories were true, Clinton hadn't broken any laws; he hadn't invited reporters to examine his private life, as Gary Hart had; and he could not be charged credibly with hypocrisy, a widely accepted news hook.

I didn't tell my bosses at the *Spectator* what was up, only that I was work- ing on a secret project involving Clinton, because I didn't trust Bob or Wlady to give me sound advice on how to proceed. Instead, I turned to a small group of people who were several cuts above the *Spectator* crew intellectu- ally and whom I respected enormously—but all of whom were fervent anti- Clinton partisans with no journalistic background. I canvassed the group that helped me trash Anita Hill.

One of my informal advisers was the leading Republican operative Bill Kristol, the former chief of staff to Dan Quayle who was heading up a new group called the Project for the Republican Future with seed money from Michael Joyce at the Bradley Foundation. Kristol's stated goal was to help Republicans identify issues—from crime to welfare reform to Haiti policy— that could be turned to the Republicans' advantage. Kristol's work, which amounted to little more than shooting down Democratic initiatives, showed how vexing it was for Republicans to come up with any issues or ideas in the age of Clinton. "In politics, as in life generally, a lot of what one does is oppose bad ideas," he told the *New York Times.* "Opposition is worthwhile for its own sake, good for the country." With the GOP out of power, Kristol had his major success with what he called "cheerful obstructionism" of the Clinton health care plan. At a time when even Senator Dole was in agree- ment with the Clinton administration that the country faced a "health care crisis," the glib Kristol coined a counterslogan: "There is no health care cri- sis." Eventually, this became the official GOP mantra.

Kristol's concern had less to do with the health care system than with derailing the Clinton plan as a means of defeating and humiliating the pres- ident. Kristol feared that a new middle-class entitlement would seal Clinton's hold over crucial swing voters. The Clinton plan's "rejection by

Congress and the public would be a monumental setback for the president," Kristol wrote in one of his blast faxes circulated among Republicans on the Hill, "and an incontestable piece of evidence that Democratic welfare-state liberalism remains firmly in retreat." In an interview, Kristol conceded his cynicism: "Frankly, there's a political opportunity here. If we can really defeat Clinton on health care, which is at the center of both his political and policy agendas, that can lay the groundwork for defeating Clintonism across the board. And that, in turn, can lay the agenda for advancing a conserva- tive reform agenda in '95 and '96."

Though we were not close personally, I decided to call Kristol and ask his advice because, though he had radical sympathies, he seemed to have the most savvy political judgment of anyone I knew on the hard right. He was cool and unflappable and seemed also to have a healthy sense of humor about the political world, a rarity in my circle. But more than anything else, I prized Kristol's opinion because he had an instinctive feel for the rhythms of the elite media and a reputation as an accomplished spinmeister in the Bush White House (though often on behalf of himself and at the expense of the administration). Kristol immediately grasped the potential political significance of the trooper story—it would throw sand in the gears of Clinton's legislative program—but he seemed dubious about using private sexual information to stymie the president. The neocons took a backseat to no one in fighting the culture wars, but there was still an old-fashioned con- servative sensibility, reflected in Bill's reticence, that led them to steer clear of the gutter. Bill told me that conservatives should focus on substantive dis- agreements with the Clinton administration, and he warned that the piece could stigmatize me as a tabloid journalist.

I next telephoned Lee Liberman, who would soon go to work as a lawyer on the staff of her Federalist Society cofounder Spencer Abraham, who won a Senate seat from Michigan. During the Anita Hill hearings, Lee had sold me on the line that the opponents of Thomas were engaged in "personal destruction." So she told me to publish Troopergate in an artful way. After I supplied the rough outlines of the piece, without missing a beat, Lee told me flatly that while she was opposed to personal attacks on principle, she had come to the conclusion that the only way the "cycle of personal attacks" in Washington would ever be broken was to make the other side "cry uncle."

I then turned to the Silbermans. Ricky thought the terrain was too perilous and advised me to drop the story. I knew she was concerned with protecting the reputation of the Anita Hill book above all else, and if I went with the story, I would never have the future she imagined for me, getting a slot on the highly respected MacNeil-Lehrer NewsHour on PBS like another conservative protégé of her husband's, *Wall Street Journal* columnist Paul Gigot. For virtually every ambitious conservative I knew, mainstreaming yourself, getting out of the conservative ghetto, was the ultimate goal, yet I couldn't imagine a worse fate. To me, *Spectator*-style extremism was pure; Gigot was a sellout. I dismissed Ricky's advice.

Though he was a sitting federal judge who would rule on matters to which the Clinton administration was a party, Larry strongly urged me to go forward. By now, after his almost daily dealings with me as I wrote *The Real Anita Hill*, Larry must have known I always deferred to his judgment. He also had keen psychological insight. He wrapped his advice in an appeal to my ego. The trooper story would be much bigger than the Anita Hill book, he predicted. Clinton would be "devastated," and therefore the story could only greatly enhance my reputation. Sitting in his favorite tan leather club chair, Scotch in hand, the judge told me he felt sure that if the same story had been written about Ronald Reagan, it would have toppled him from office. Clinton, he surmised, might be toppled as well. Of course, the liberal media might ignore the story to protect Clinton, but in conservative circles, I would be king. When I heard that, I was over the fence. I left the Silbermans' house with a racing pulse.

Fortified by Larry's advice, I was now determined to get the story, but back in Arkansas I learned that two of the four troopers were backing out. Cliff said Ronnie Anderson told him that he had received a telephone call from a man named Buddy Young, warning him against talking. Young had supervised the troopers on Clinton's security detail and now held a presidential appointment in Dallas. Simultaneously, Roger Perry told me that Danny

Ferguson had told him that Clinton had called Ferguson personally and dangled job offers to both Perry and Ferguson in an effort to shut down the story. According to Perry, Ferguson suddenly wasn't going public, either.

The news of the presidential phone call, while secondhand, was tantalizing. If Perry's account of Clinton's offer to Ferguson were true, it could constitute a bribe, and therefore possibly an impeachable offense. I was beginning to feel as if I had more than a sex story: I might be sitting on a story right out of *All the President's Men*. In my overexcitement, I convinced myself that Ferguson and Anderson, though I had never spoken with either of them about it directly, must have been intimidated by Clinton and Young to stop a true story. I never considered the equally plausible explanation that the troopers got cold feet because they had no solid information to offer. By the same token, Clinton may have called the troopers because he was concerned about lies being spread. (Notes of the Ferguson call taken by Clinton that surfaced in the sexual harassment lawsuit brought against the president by Paula Jones said: "Troopers being talked to by lawyer—offered big $. He says GOP in on—now talking about 100G/7 years—job and whatever get from book . . . [H]e and R. Anderson know it's wrong, they don't know anything, all rumors not good for their families or mine.")

Meanwhile, the two troopers who were committed to telling their stories, Larry Patterson and Roger Perry, hadn't given up on the idea of getting paid to talk. As we drove back to the Holiday Inn after dinner one night at a Little Rock restaurant (called, appropriately, Sir Loins), Cliff stopped at a convenience store so the troopers could buy beer. When they stepped out of the car, Cliff told me that he was knee deep in negotiations with Peter Smith to get them money. As Clinton's notes reflected, various iterations of deals were flying back and forth via fax between Little Rock and Chicago. In one, Peter agreed to set up a defense fund should the troopers incur legal expenses as a result of going public, while another guaranteed that Peter would relocate them out of the state, and find them jobs at commensurate wages, if they were fired from their trooper posts. There were also murmurs of direct cash payoffs to the troopers from Peter.

I hit the roof. The credibility of the whole enterprise was on the line. Fuming, I told Cliff I wasn't going to let the troopers ruin my reputation along with their own. I returned to Washington and phoned Peter in Chicago, explaining to him that if money was involved, the story would be tainted. If he didn't call off the negotiations, I coolly threatened, I'd pull the plug on the piece I intended to write and would write a different one— exposing the whole scheme in print and burning Smith in the process.

Peter insisted that no deal had been inked, and pledged to work with me toward the common goal of getting the article to bed. Since I had first talked with him in the summer, Peter had somehow convinced himself, perhaps in too many talks with Cliff, that Clinton's illicit affairs made him a security risk and that the country was imperiled every day he sat in the Oval Office. Like Judge Silberman, Peter, too, thought the piece might bring Clinton down.

To calm me further, Peter suggested that I relay my concerns to two lawyers who were advising him on the trooper matter. I now realized that I had walked into what was starting to look like a plot by high-level Republicans to oust Clinton from office; Peter wasn't freelancing, after all. Peter asked me to call Richard Porter, a protégé of Bush White House counsel Boyden Gray's who had worked on opposition research for the Bush-Quayle campaign and was now at a Chicago-based law firm, Kirkland & Ellis. I had friends at the Washington office of Porter's firm: a group of young conservative lawyers working for partner Kenneth Starr. I called Porter and expressed my reservations about the payoffs; he took it all in and said little. Peter also arranged for me to meet personally with a Washington attorney named Dan Swillinger, who had drafted the agreements with the troopers on Peter's behalf. I was surprised to learn from Swillinger, a slight man with a trim black mustache, that he was a lawyer for GOPAC and for Newt Gingrich personally. Another lawyer retained by Smith, Mark Braden, had been a counsel to the Republican National Committee. Were these guys insane? Hadn't they ever heard of the concept of "deniability"?

It was at this juncture that Mark Paoletta reentered the picture. Back in August, when I first heard from Peter Smith, I called Mark immediately with the news, and I told him of my progress on the story in intricate detail every step of the way. When Bush lost the White House to Clinton—an event that enraged Mark—he had gone into private practice at a Washington law and lobbying firm called O'Connor & Hannon. Mark had hoped to land a higher-level post in a second Bush administration and was unhappy to be out of the political fray in the law firm. When I first mentioned to Mark that I was having trouble getting the troopers to go forward, he told me that our conversation, and all future ones, would be protected by the attorney-client privilege. We began plotting strategy to get the story into print no matter what.

I kept one eye on Cliff and Peter as I drafted the eleven-thousand-word article. I knew the stakes in taking on a president, or at least as much as you can know before doing it, and I tried to get the story right. Having been burned on some factual errors in the Anita Hill controversy, I took more care this time, flying back and forth to Little Rock twice more to cross-examine the troopers. They sat for hours, completing each other's sentences as they told the same vulgar stories again and again. The performance was impressive, though I hadn't known that many cops are talented raconteurs, often embellishing their exploits for the sake of a good story. I cross-referenced all names and places the troopers mentioned, looking for holes in their stories, and I called everyone named in the piece for comment. But at the end of the day, the allegations couldn't be verified, the troopers hadn't been able to affix specific dates or times to any of the events described, and I had to make a leap of faith in accepting their word.

I bought it all because I wanted to. War for war's sake was really the only way I knew since coming to Washington seven years before. I also had career considerations. The Anita Hill experience was still fresh in my mind; it had left me on a high, I had slain a liberal Goliath, and I was casting around for the next big prey. That Clinton was the first Democratic president in my adult lifetime—personally reviled by the movement, my audience, even if not by me—made him an especially inviting target.

Yet I didn't hate the Clintons, as did Cliff Jackson and legions of Republicans. I certainly did not share the sense of Michael Joyce and others that the Clintons were a threat to "ordinary Americans." In fact, I was so busy fighting my own battles in 1993 over *The Real Anita Hill* that I had hardly given them a second thought, or written a word about them, since the election.

On an emotional level, however, I saw the Clintons as proxies for my liberal critics. In the controversy over Anita Hill, I had been scarred by attacks from the left, I was in a vindictive mood, and there could hardly have been a sweeter way to avenge these enemies and vent my hatred of them than by exposing their president in a tawdry sex scandal that made the Thomas hearings look tame by comparison. My partisanship was no longer theoretical. I was a full-scale combatant, I had war wounds to show for it, and I needed the thrill of another round of battle. Indeed, Troopergate can perhaps best be understood as having nothing to do with the Clintons, but rather as an extension of a form of warfare I had learned to perfect in writing *The Real Anita Hill*—a cruel smear disguised as a thorough "investigation." As I had heedlessly appropriated the Republican attacks on women witnesses in the Thomas hearing, so did I appropriate the troopers' misogynistic rendering of Hillary Clinton. Having invented a "kinky" sex life for Anita Hill, I had little trouble making what may have been a few extramarital dalliances by Clinton appear deviant and strange. "Bill Clinton is a bizarre guy," I said with a smirk, appearing on CNN's *Crossfire* to debate the trooper piece. But it was me, a sexually repressed closeted gay man, detailing Clinton's alleged infidelities to forward the right-wing political agenda, who was the bizarre guy.

Unlike in the Anita Hill case, I did deliberate over whether to publish Troopergate. But my faculties were seriously impaired—by my lack of training, by the corrupting influence of partisanship, by the ego trip of bestsellerdom at thirty-one, and perhaps most of all by a sick sense of my own identity. This time, I was not acting to defend Clarence Thomas against perceived injustice; or to protect the conservative movement from the onslaught of feminism; or to advance any set of ideas; or even to satisfy my yearning to belong to the conservative movement, which I thought I had already achieved by publishing *The Real Anita Hill*. I pushed ahead because my role at the *Spectator*—as a right-wing hit man, a hired gun in every sense of the term now—was more than a job; it was who I was. I had a hit to pull off.

By now, the *L.A. Times* had dispatched a second reporter, Doug Frantz, to Little Rock to work with Bill Rempel on the story, and I felt sure that even if the *Times* brass was dragging its feet, a daily paper with far more resources than the *Spectator* would beat me to press. Cliff had shown me affidavits the troopers had sworn out to the *Times*, so I had a good idea of the angle Rempel and Frantz were pursuing. They had hewed closely to Cliff's "it's not about sex" sales pitch, emphasizing allegations like Clinton's use of the troopers to procure women on state time, and Clinton's use of an official cell phone to call an alleged girlfriend. The graphic descriptions of sex, and many other gratuitous goodies, appeared headed for the cutting room floor at the *Times.*

On the assumption that my piece would be a second read at best, I threw in every last titillating morsel and dirty quote the troopers served up. I even published what the troopers conceded was their idle conjecture, such as the claim that Hillary had been having an affair with her former law partner Vince Foster, who had come to Washington as a deputy White House lawyer and committed suicide in July 1993. The troopers' evidence for the allegation was a scene in a public restaurant in Little Rock, where Foster had supposedly fondled Hillary. With my gonzo spirit on overdrive, I tossed it all into the piece, details that had no conceivable news value—devoured apple cores, feminine napkins, Socks the cat's battle against hairballs, everything but the story of Clinton once farting in an elevator and blaming it on Roger Perry. I had my standards, after all.

The right-wing construct of "Bill" and "Hillary" now had "facts" to back it up. My article depicted "Bill" as a sexually voracious sociopathic cipher, while "Hillary" appeared as a foulmouthed, castrating, power-mad harpy, joined together in a sham power marriage. The piece left such an indelible image in the minds of the media and the public as it led network newscasts and became a staple of Jay Leno monologues and *Saturday Night Live* skits that it would be possible in the future to say and write and broadcast any crazy thing about the first couple and get away with it. The Clintons were moral monsters.

In the first year of the Clinton administration, the *Spectator* had contented itself with serious critiques of Clinton policy. There had been no effort to destroy the Clintons personally, and the *Spectator* had never run an exposé on a politician's private life, much less that of a sitting president. Yet when I filed the piece in December 1993, Wlady seemed no more flustered than he always did on deadline. He asked a few perfunctory questions and set it in type. The galleys were kept from Bob for as long as possible because we didn't want the piece to leak. We felt sure Bob would be on the phone blabbing the news all over town. A pro forma libel review followed, resulting in few if any changes to the manuscript.

The *Spectator* worried little about libel, employed no fact checkers, and was not closely edited—and the Troopergate piece was no exception. One section of the article that escaped everyone's notice was an anecdote told to me by Danny Ferguson before Ferguson decided not to put it on the record. The story was meant to describe Clinton's modus operandi of sometimes securing hotel rooms around Little Rock for his sexual liaisons. According to Ferguson, one day in May 1991, Clinton had taken a room at the Excelsior Hotel in downtown Little Rock after giving a speech there. Clinton had asked Ferguson to invite a woman, a state employee manning a booth at a job fair in the hotel lobby, to come up to his room. The woman "made his knees knock," Clinton allegedly told Ferguson. Ferguson identified the woman to me only as Paula. He said he escorted Paula to Clinton's room, and waited outside for less than an hour. When Paula emerged from the room, Ferguson claimed, she commented that she was willing to be Clinton's "regular girlfriend."

This anecdote, which would prompt the woman, Paula Jones, to come forward and sue President Clinton for sexual harassment, got into print through a fateful comedy of errors that probably could have played out only at the *Spectator.* After Ferguson bowed out of the story, I should have cut out the Paula anecdote, because he was the only firsthand source for it. But Ferguson also had mentioned the story of Paula to Roger Perry at the time it occurred. So I left it in, unchallenged by editors or lawyers, with second-hand source Perry as the only one vouching for its accuracy.

Separately, I made a decision not to name any of the women whom the troopers linked to Clinton. When I contacted the women, some of them denied the charge, and others refused comment. So far as I could see, naming them, violating their privacy, and disrupting their lives served no purpose. I hit the delete key everywhere in the piece where a woman had been named. The Paula story slipped by me because Paula didn't have a last name, and it didn't occur to me that, if there was even a grain of truth to the anecdote, in a small town like Little Rock just a first name might be enough to identify someone. I never even bothered to ask Ferguson if Paula had a last name. A throwaway line, that's all Paula was.

I took the edited draft back to Little Rock so that Larry and Roger could review it for factual accuracy. I had agreed to show it to them for my own protection, for if my sources weren't prepared to stand by everything they had told me, I would be in deep trouble. When they showed up at my hotel room to read the draft, Roger took his gun out of his holster and placed it on a nearby side table. A state trooper could get away with murder, Roger, a former narcotics officer, explained matter-of-factly. "You can pull someone off the road, shoot them, then throw a gun, and some drugs, in the car." This seemed to be Roger's idea of a joke, and the absurdity of an armed trooper standing over my manuscript wasn't lost on me, but it put me on edge nonetheless. They quietly read the galleys, suggested a few small corrections, and left.

Later that night, Cliff learned from Peter that I was trying to undermine the financial deals he had in the works. Livid, Cliff called me in my room to tell me the entire story was off; the troopers weren't going forward without "protection." At this tense juncture, having spent three months working on a story that seemed about to slip away, I decided to fill in my boss at the *Spectator.* I reached Bob over Thanksgiving week at a vacation home in Kitty Hawk, North Carolina, and told him that my investigation of Clinton had hit a brick wall because the sources wanted to be paid to talk. "How much do they want?" Bob screeched into the phone. "I'll write them a check!" Not much help there.

Early the next morning, Lynn Davis showed up unannounced at my room, demanding that I surrender the tapes of my interviews with Larry and Roger. I told him it was too late to drop the story, I hadn't spent three months working on it for nothing, and I'd publish it with or without their permission. As for the tapes, he could have them, but there were copies back in Washington. When Davis stalked off, I called a cab for the airport, leaving my rental car behind. Maybe I had spent too much time in conspiratorial Arkansas, but I actually thought Roger Perry might pull me off the road and kill me.

Of course, before I made each of the prior decisions, I checked in with Mark in Washington, who urged me to betray everyone involved in the trooper mess to get the story to press. For the next few weeks, in overheated conversations with Cliff, Lynn, and Peter, whom I hounded on a Florida vacation, I continued to threaten to publish the piece without the troopers' okay. By convincing them I was a madman, I hoped to intimidate the troopers into going forward, while scaring the hell out of Peter so he wouldn't cut any checks. Cliff faxed an incendiary letter to Bob, complaining that I was harassing and bullying his clients and threatening to seek a criminal complaint against me under an Arkansas law prohibiting threats and coercion. When Bob laughed off the letter, Cliff cracked. He'd do it my way. The troopers would go public with no money changing hands.

Once the concession was won, Mark helped draft a written agreement for the troopers to sign in which they guaranteed me that they had not been paid to talk to me. There was a rather large loophole in this agreement, which Mark and I were fully aware of, but that we really had no way of guarding against, short of pulling the article: Future payments to the troopers could well be made. To cover myself, I disclosed the agreement in a footnote to the article. Not until four years later did I learn that within a few months after the piece appeared, Peter Smith had written checks of $6,700 to each of the two troopers (more than 10 percent of their yearly salaries) and of $6,600 each to Lynn Davis and Cliff Jackson, violating the spirit, if not the letter, of our deal.

In return for green-lighting the article, Cliff asked that the January 1994 issue of the *Spectator*, which would feature the story, not be prereleased to the media before it appeared on newsstands in late December. That would give the *L.A. Times*, which was still hot on the story, a few more weeks to break it first, in accord with our original agreement. I wasn't happy about giving the *Times* a break, but it seemed like a fair trade-off to get the piece out. About ten days passed with no news from the *Times* as Cliff told me of a titanic struggle within the paper over whether or not to go with it. I guessed that the *Times* would spike the story, so, unbeknownst to anyone but Mark, I took matters into my own hands, breaking my word to Cliff.

I had learned at the knee of Erwin Glikes, the publisher of *The Real Anita Hill*, that right-wing journalism had to be injected into the bloodstream of the liberal media for maximum effect, so I set out to coax an established media venue into repeating the troopers' charges, leaking the galleys to a friend at CNN from my days at the *Washington Times*, with the proviso that CNN couldn't go on air without my say-so. My friend grabbed the first plane to Atlanta and took the galleys to top CNN executives, and I was astonished to see how easy it was to suck in CNN. My effort to penetrate the major media was in some ways as important as the story itself, for it demonstrated an appetite in the press for Clinton scandal stories, even when they came from clearly biased venues, and broke down a barrier that would make the job of future anti-Clinton provocateurs much easier. When the *Spectator* staff learned that the magazine's embargo had broken, there was an effort to find the perpetrator. Through a fax transmission discovered by an editor, I was found out. When confronted, I came up with a clearly implausible lie, but once I denied it, the matter was instantly dropped and everyone went back to work and continued to treat me as they always had— as if they had learned nothing about my character.

Events moved beyond my control because the story was too radioactive to be kept under wraps. Copies began floating through CNN headquarters and soon leaked out to the Clinton camp. Clinton operative Betsey Wright, who had described her role in the '92 Clinton campaign as knocking down false stories of Clinton's womanizing—"bimbo patrol," she called it—got a copy and slid it under the hotel room door of *L.A. Times* reporter Bill Rempel, who was in Washington lobbying his editors for his piece to run. Wright apparently hoped that Rempel would think twice about the story now that he would be playing second fiddle to a vile right-wing rag. Meanwhile, CNN had landed in Little Rock and contacted Cliff, who called me, hysterical about the leak, about which I feigned ignorance. "You might as well just get it out," he yelled, slamming down the phone. It was Sunday morning, December 18—Christmas week. I called Wlady at home, and ordered him to start faxing out galleys of "His Cheatin' Heart," a cover article showing a red-faced Bill Clinton tiptoeing from the governor's mansion under cover of nightfall.

That evening, on its 6 P.M. broadcast, CNN led with the trooper story. Correspondent Bob Franken set the scene, a send-off ceremony for the Clintons at the Little Rock airport as they departed for Washington in January 1993. Franken quoted Larry Patterson's claim that Clinton had asked him to escort one of his girlfriends to the event. Patterson appeared on tape, saying that Hillary had turned to him at the event and said, "I know who that whore is, get her out of here." I couldn't believe my eyes or ears. I called Ricky and Larry Silberman at a holiday party and held the phone to the television. I was literally jumping for joy.

For a few days, the story was everywhere. Larry Silberman was right—this was a much bigger deal than *The Real Anita Hill*. White House counselor David Gergen called CNN to get the story yanked, but he was too late. The Associated Press had picked it up, and it made the *Washington Post* Monday morning. On Tuesday morning, the *L.A. Times* unleashed its story, which I had mentioned in my piece, hoping to force it out. By the time the *L.A. Times* reporters appeared on *Nightline* later that evening, they looked sullen, and Frantz would soon quit the paper in what some saw as a protest of his story having been held. I had beaten them to the punch, and because their piece was more restrained, a more professional job appearing in a more respectable outlet, Clinton's defenders gave me all the credit—or blame—for breaking the story. Journalist Sidney Blumenthal appeared opposite Rempel and Frantz, deftly turning the subject back to me. "This all started with David Brock, a right-wing . . . well, I hesitate to call him a journalist," Blumenthal said. At a White House Christmas party, Hillary Clinton branded the piece "outrageous, terrible," and charged that it was the handiwork of her husband's political enemies, though she hadn't known the half of it. In a halting voice in a radio interview, Clinton, now in the untenable position of having to prove his innocence, said the troopers' stories were "outrageous, and they're not so."

Under press scrutiny, the only serious allegation raised in both my story and the *Times*'s—Clinton's job offer to the troopers—was shaken. After Betsey Wright flew to Little Rock and confronted Ferguson about the allegation of the job offer from Clinton, which Wright had reportedly said "could get the man impeached," Ferguson's lawyer issued an affidavit backing off the claim. The *Boston Globe* and *Newsday* noted that Trooper Ferguson had never put the allegation on the record himself. Rempel, Frantz, and I used it based on what Roger Perry said Ferguson had told him. None of the trooper allegations that could be independently checked turned out to be true. About the woman in the trench coat, for example, the Secret Service disputed the troopers' contention that its security checkpoint had been breached. Though the troopers claimed that Hillary had ordered gate logs at the governor's mansion destroyed to cover up Clinton's contacts with Gennifer Flowers, the *Arkansas Democrat-Gazette* discovered that no such logs had been kept. The paper also reported that the event at which Foster had allegedly fondled Hillary had never occurred. The Associated Press sent a reporter to the troopers' guard shack to check out their claim that they had seen Clinton receiving oral sex in a truck on the mansion grounds through a video surveillance camera, and the reporter concluded that the camera could not have captured a clear image from inside a vehicle. Finally, Perry and Patterson were forced to acknowledge lying to investigators for an insurance company about the circumstances of their having wrecked a state police car after a night of drunken carousing—both to protect themselves and to defraud the insurance company of $100,000.

Media commentators were unanimous in condemning the decision to publish the troopers' unverified assertions. R.W. Apple, the Washington bureau chief of the *New York Times*, stated dryly: "I'm not interested in Bill Clinton's sex life as governor of Arkansas." David Shaw, the respected media critic of the *Los Angeles Times*, said of his own paper: "It's a tough call, but if I'd been the editor I wouldn't have run it." In *Newsweek*, Joe Klein wrote: "Not to put too fine a point on it, but the story is trash." He called the troopers' portrait of Hillary "a Neanderthal fantasy of what feminists are really like." Anthony Lewis in the *New York Times* referred to me as "the man . . . who has made himself chief manure spreader for the extreme right." Paul Duke, the moderator of PBS's *Washington Week in Review,* called me the "loser" of the year, for writing "that slimy magazine article that revived all those old charges about Bill Clinton's private behavior." Historian Garry Wills labeled me "not only a sleazebag, but the occasion in others for sleazebaggery." *Newsweek's* "Conventional Wisdom" box contained a down arrow next to my name: "D. Brock—Am Spectator 'journalist' swallows any pond scum that fits his right-wing agenda." The *New Republic* did a parody of the piece under the byline David Crock.

Though Norman Podhoretz privately lauded me as "our Bob Woodward," there was ample criticism of Troopergate, too, from the conservative establishment. John O'Sullivan, editor in chief of William F. Buckley's *National Review,* said he would not have published the article. Even culture warrior Pat Buchanan, apparently still honoring traditional conservative respect for privacy, chided me for releasing "poison gas canisters" into the political debate. "I've never seen this kind of detail in a respectable magazine. This is the kind of stuff that used to be confined to the supermarket tabloids. It's very lurid and lewd, and I think it's degrading to the national debate on issues like NAFTA and health care, which is where we ought to be putting our energies," Buchanan told the *New York Times.* Bill Kristol's Project for the Republican Future put out a statement warning that conservatives' pursuit of scandal would be a distraction from important policy battles. I was told that Jack Kemp had run into my colleague Danny Wattenberg's father Ben at a New Year's celebration and told him he thought the piece set a destructive precedent.

Back at the *Spectator,* Wlady, a stalwart supporter during the Anita Hill contretemps, didn't flinch during the shelling. He told me my fellow conservatives were gutless wonders who were knocking the piece because of their own personal peccadilloes, which he proceeded to list. I didn't notice it then, but that was just the point: If sexual monogamy were now a prerequisite for public service, Republicans as well as Democrats would be vulnerable. Bob went public with his own odd defense of me, telling the *New York Times* that while there were errors in both my Anita Hill and Troopergate pieces—"I'm surprised there were so few," he said in his airy manner—what mattered is that "the main point is true." His comments infuriated me. I believed I had made no significant errors (I attributed the mistakes in the piece to quibbling by pro-Clinton journalists), and I wrote a letter to the *Times* for Bob's signature, retracting what he had said, and told him to sign it. Yet Bob had let the truth slip out about my work. Troopergate contained at least a kernel of truth—sex would turn out to be an Achilles' heel for Clinton—but it was not fit to print. The article was a mix of circumstantial observation and rumor—and no one would ever be able to tell which parts of it may have been accurate and which parts were not. That didn't bother Bob, who honestly had stated his philosophy of journalism: for the *Spectator*, getting the gist of the story was good enough. The real aim was not journalistic but political.

Despite the attacks from the liberal pundits and brickbats from my own camp, I was having the time of my life. With the *Spectator*'s circulation tripling once again, I got a big, fat raise—half a million dollars, to be paid out over the next four years. And I loved nothing more than running against the liberal press pack and defying the cultural powers that be. I had learned during the Thomas-Hill controversy to shrug off and brazen out valid criticism, and I was able to do so again. I fantasized about carpet-bombing the White House on Christmas Eve. That's how deranged I had become.

Perhaps because Bill Clinton already had a widely rumored reputation in the Washington press corps as an oversexed country bumpkin that matched the stereotype of Hillary as a conniving bitch, no one in the major press ever culled the many errors in my piece into a comprehensive factual refutation. The problems surfaced in dribs and drabs in widely scattered news outlets over the course of several weeks. Troopergate was described as tasteless and irrelevant, but it was allowed to enter the media ether as if it were true. As Michael Kinsley put it in his *New Republic* column, "The responsible press has been whipsawed into publicizing Brock's allegations." I pulled off the hit successfully. As for the conservatives, I accepted Wlady's view that my critics were cowards. And they would all come around soon enough, casting aside their reservations about Troopergate as the anti-Clinton crusade heated up.

CHAPTER EIGHT

OUT OF THE CLOSET

Congressman Bob Dornan, a ferociously anti-Clinton right-winger from Orange County, California, was sitting in for Rush Limbaugh on the day my trooper piece was published. Dornan devoted the entire three-hour broadcast to my story, and in a departure from the show's format, I appeared as a special guest, lighting up the switchboards as I gleefully described Clinton's sexual shenanigans. When I arrived at the studio, Dornan's wife, Sally—who had once yelled "Shut up, faggot!" to a gay protester—greeted me with a big hug.

During one of the breaks, the congressman told me that while I was reporting the trooper story, Cliff Jackson had contacted him in an attempt to line up political support for the troopers once they went public. In approaching Dornan, I suppose Cliff had sensed that the natural constituency for the trooper story was the extreme right, particularly the Christian Right, which would use the piece to try to shred Clinton's moral authority to govern. While the more secular wings of the conservative movement weren't sure what to make of Troopergate, for the Christian Right, the political war against Clinton had theological underpinnings. As Ralph Reed noted in his book *Active Faith*, the "Christian nation" or "Reconstructionist" movements of the Christian Right believed in "legislating the ancient Jewish law laid out in the Old Testament: stoning adulterers, executing homosexuals, even mandating dietary laws." These evangelical extremists were trying to bring down Clinton in the name of God.

By now, the *Spectator* was wired into an extensive, nationwide network of right-wing talk radio shows that could be activated irrespective of whether the established media publicized its articles. I blanketed Christian talk radio across the country, shows with millions of listeners hosted by Marlin

Maddoux in Dallas and the Reverend James Dobson of Focus on the Family, a Christian Right organization with an annual budget of over $100 million and its own zip code in Colorado. I flew to Virginia Beach for a live appearance on the Reverend Pat Robertson's *700 Club*. I also received a number of speaking invitations and personal honors from far-right organizations. I denounced Clinton as an immoralist at the annual Conservative Political Action Committee meeting—where, according to a write-up of the conference, I received a more rousing ovation than Ollie North—and I did the same at the Christian Coalition's annual Road to Victory conference in Washington, walking past antigay booths as I made my way to the podium. Glancing furtively at my image on a huge screen in the Washington Hilton ballroom, I roused thousands of stomping Christian activists from their seats.

I flew to St. Louis to receive the Winston Churchill Award, presented for "Courageous and Committed Service to the Conservative Cause," from the Council for National Policy, a kind of right-wing Trilateral Commission, founded in 1981 to coordinate the efforts of various religious right organizations. The identities of the four hundred or so people who comprise the organization's board of governors—conservative activists, elected officials, and retired military men—were kept a tight secret. Founders of the council included direct-mail fund-raiser Richard Viguerie; Howard Phillips of the Conservative Caucus; Paul Weyrich; brewer Joe Coors; the Reverend Jerry Falwell; and the Reverend Tim LaHaye, at the time the president of the Moral Majority in California, who, with his pro-life activist wife, Beverly, of the group Concerned Women for America, advocated "Biblical principles for family living." The council still meets clandestinely four or five times a year; among its members have been several prominent Republican politicians, including Senators Trent Lott, Jesse Helms, and John Ashcroft, and Representatives Dick Armey, Tom DeLay, and Bob Dornan.

At the St. Louis session, I dined with, among others, Ed Meese; Edwin Feulner; Ollie North; Ralph Reed; anti-ERA activist and former John Birch Society member Phyllis Schlafly; and Larry Pratt, who quit as cochairman of Pat Buchanan's presidential campaign because of his ties to white supremacist and antigovernment hate groups. Morton Blackwell, a longtime associate in Virginia politics of Reverend Falwell, presented my award.

I knew nothing of the CNP's origins when I accepted their invitation, and in typical fashion, I did nothing to educate myself about it. When I arrived at my hotel in St. Louis, though, I was reminded of the early days at the *Washington Times* when I had steered clear of right-wing extremists like John Lofton and Sam Francis and publicly criticized Pat Buchanan. Now, I was toasting them and accepting their awards. I knew I didn't belong behind that podium at CNP, gazing out at Phyllis Schlafly's bee-hive hairdo. Rushing through a short acceptance speech, I tried to smile, but I couldn't. I was miserable. Yet this was how I made my living and it was who I had become. The conservatives had bought my brain.

What no one in the room that night at CNP knew was that had I spent my Saturday night in Washington, I would have been prowling through the dark corridors of gay dance clubs. When he hosted me on the Limbaugh broadcast, Bob Dornan—who had outed GOP Congressman Steve Gunderson on the floor of the House, declaring of gays, "They're destroying the country, to say nothing about the party, and we have a moral obligation to expose and destroy them"—didn't know I was a closeted homosexual. Virulent homophobes Pat Robertson, Marlin Maddoux, and James Dobson didn't know. Nor did a for-mer Arkansas state supreme court justice and the state's leading segregation-ist, a man by the name of Jim Johnson, who had shared a platform with me at the Conservative Political Action Committee meeting. Johnson had called Clinton a "President of the United States who is a queer-mongering, whore-hopping adulterer; a baby-killing, dope-tolerating, lying two-faced treasonist activist." As Johnson's speech demonstrated, Troopergate was inflaming fun-damentalist passions against homosexuality, and I was now, as Marvin Liebman had referred to himself earlier, a Jew in Hitler's army. Knee deep in this profound moral conflict, I wouldn't recognize it, for recognizing it would have forced me to question my own beliefs and discover my own self-loathing. I was only interested in self-promotion. Bob Dornan wasn't a bigot, he was my fan.

Almost as soon as Troopergate broke, the *Spectator* switchboard received several calls from gay newspapers around the country claiming to have

information on my sex life—my very own "bimbo eruptions," in the parlance
of Betsey Wright. An anonymous letter disclosing the fact that I was known
to frequent a popular Washington gay bar called Badlands near Dupont
Circle was circulated to gossip columnists working for the major daily newspapers. Though closeted, for years I had gone out to bars looking for one-
night hookups with some frequency, always by myself, very late at night,
with few knowing, and no one caring, who I was. That was catching up with
me now that Troopergate was exploding nationally, and I wasn't sure how
to handle it. I was scared stiff.

In early January 1994, I was house sitting in California for Andrew, where
I had gone to wait for Troopergate to blow over. One morning at 5 A.M., the
phone rang. I groped for the receiver, and heard a bone-chilling scream from
a closeted conservative friend in D.C.: "You've been outed!" I needed to see
a column published that morning in the *New York Times*, my breathless
friend informed me. I told him to calm down and fax me the piece, which
I read, bleary-eyed, before throwing myself back into bed.

When I got up a few hours later, I reread the piece by Frank Rich headlined "David Brock's Women." Of my exposés on Anita Hill and the Clintons,
Rich wrote: "It's women, not liberals, who really get him going. The slightest
sighting of female sexuality whips him into a frenzy of misogynist zeal. All
women are the same to Mr. Brock: terrifying, gutter-tongued sexual omni-
vores." I wasn't quite sure what to make of the column. I didn't want to
believe that I had been outed. Rich didn't say I was gay, he said I was a misogynist, and, although some considered misogynist to be a clichéd code word
that a generation ago implied homosexual, one didn't necessarily translate
into the other. In subsequent interviews Rich, a strong supporter of gay rights
who often tackled gay issues with the utmost sensitivity and humanity, maintained that he had known nothing about my personal life when he wrote the
column, and I had no reason to think he did. "There are straight and gay
misogynists and I don't know or care what kind David Brock is," Rich would
tell the *Washington Post*.

Yet that morning in California, after making several phone calls back east
to see how bad the damage was, it was clear to me that it didn't matter what
was in Frank Rich's mind when he wrote his column. Even if he had not

intended to, because I *was* gay, and some people obviously knew it, Rich had ignited a controversy over the question of my sexuality in the gossip mills of New York and Washington, especially among conservatives, who were quick to tell me that Rich had outed me in the *New York Times*, even though I had never told any of them that I was gay. "You know what he's getting at, don't you?" Ricky Silberman roared into the phone. I stammered, saying little. I was angry and embarrassed that these personal questions had been raised. What did my sex life have to do with my journalism? Why was my privacy being violated? Of course, I had no one to blame but myself for this turn of events. Privacy? Propriety? Discretion? Troopergate had destroyed all that. I had invited every bit of what I was being put through.

In considering whether to publish Troopergate, in the back of my mind I realized that I was playing with fire, for surely someone would conclude that if I was investigating Bill Clinton's consensual sex life and proclaiming it newsworthy, the incongruity of my private life and my professional one—as a closeted gay man at the *American Spectator* "outing" Clinton— also was newsworthy. I suspected that my political enemies might plot to out me, presumably dooming my future with the Republican right; I had already survived one outing scare during the Anita Hill controversy, when I heard that feminist author Susan Faludi was planning to out me in *Vanity Fair*, though nothing came of that rumor. I believed that the image of a closeted right-wing homosexual in the tradition of J. Edgar Hoover and Joe McCarthy aide Roy Cohn was one that the left, not entirely without reason, would have loved to stick me with. Yet abandoning the trooper article to protect myself went against my self-conception as a fearless foe of the left, and it was not in my nature then to back down from a challenge, even at my own peril. Unconsciously, perhaps the risk involved in being "found out" even added to the psychic thrill of publishing Troopergate.

A few days after the Rich piece ran, Howard Kurtz, the media critic of the *Washington Post*, telephoned me in California. For me, a conservative journalistic outlaw, a call from Howie was always trouble. Kurtz was doing a wrap-up of the fallout from Troopergate, and he wanted my response to the litany of criticisms made by Kinsley, Klein et al. When he asked about the Rich column, I responded carefully to the literal text—of course there was no animus toward women in my work, some of my best friends were women, I told Kurtz—but I pointedly ignored the insinuations about my private life that my conservative friends had detected in the Rich column. Later in the interview, as we were reviewing my educational history and the like, Kurtz suddenly asked me if I was "publicly gay"; I recognized the loophole in Kurtz's formulation, I wasn't publicly gay, and so I said no. Kurtz sounded unsatisfied—it turned out he had been told that I was openly gay at Berkeley by former classmates of mine—but he didn't press the point. We hung up, agreeing to talk again later in the day.

I went for a swim and started to freak out about the Kurtz interview. Clearly, Kurtz had heard that I was gay. He was probably going to ask me about it again in our follow-up talk, but I didn't think he would out me against my will. This was the *Washington Post*, after all. By asking if I was "publicly gay," Kurtz seemed to be giving me the option of outing myself by saying yes, or dodging the question of my sexuality by saying no. I concluded that evading the question probably put me in the clear, at least for the time being.

But what about all those outing threats coming in to the *Spectator* switchboard? Sooner or later I knew I would have to confront the question head-on, and I wondered if I should just tell Kurtz for the record that I was gay.

The public discourse on the right about gays had gotten worse since I first came to Washington in 1986. As I swam, I was terrified about telling Kurtz the truth. In college I was comfortable and happy being openly gay, but I soon repressed and denied this fundamental part of myself to get ahead in the movement. My mind began to race with thoughts about what my political mentors and associates thought about homosexuality. With the collapse of Communism, and the rise of Christian fundamentalists as a force in the Republican Party, conservative leaders and politicians were seeking to use gays to advance politically. The evidence of a resurgent antigay bigotry was mounting all around me, not only in the wider world of Republican politics, but also in my own small world of Washington conservatives. Newt Gingrich, who had inspired my first *Spectator* piece, had compared gays to alcoholics. Commenting on the decision of his longtime friend Marvin Liebman to come out, William F. Buckley had written that homosexuality was not "normal or healthy." In an essay in *Commentary* on a Queens, New York, elementary school curriculum that taught tolerance of gays, Midge Decter, whose son gave me my first job, implied that it would encourage recruitment of schoolchildren into homosexuality. Questioning the value of a vaccine for AIDS, Norman Podhoretz, who published me in *Commentary*, wrote that it would permit homosexuals "to resume buggering each other by the hundreds with complete medical impunity." And in an interview with the *New York Times Magazine*, Bill Kristol, whose advice I had sought on Troopergate, said, "I do not think society can or should treat homosexuality the same as heterosexuality."

At the *Spectator*, my workplace, the situation was even grimmer. In his monthly column, "Continuing Crisis," Bob continued to make jokes at the expense of gays—referring to AIDS as "Rock Hudson's disease." British writer Christopher Monckton suggested quarantining people who tested positive for the AIDS-related virus, HIV. *Spectator* columnist Tom Bethell wrote, "I wonder if gays may not have been gayer when they were still in the closet." In a piece called "Manhattan Swish" about a New York law guaranteeing homosexuals freedom from housing discrimination, P. J. O'Rourke defended discrimination against gays by people who believe that "homosexuality is a horrid transgression against God's plan. Do these people have to live and work with a man whose activities they detest?" Michael Fumento, another Third Generation journalist and frequent *Spectator* contributor, advanced the theory that there was no AIDS crisis in the heterosexual community at a time when AIDS rates were in fact rising at an alarming rate among the poor and blacks. Fumento, a favorite client of my literary agents, Lynn Chu and Glen Hartley, had written in *National Review*: "If AIDS is the plague of the 1980s, then homosexuals are the rats who are the carriers."

I also knew that the *Spectator* had a history of controversy involving one gay conservative writer. In his 1993 book *A Place at the Table*, the *Spectator*'s movie reviewer, Bruce Bawer, wrote that he left the magazine when he refused to delete a passing reference to homosexuality in a review of the play *Prelude to a Kiss*. Bawer said that upon submitting the review, Wlady had informed him that the magazine had a policy against running anything about AIDS or homosexuality, but since the *Spectator* did run several articles on these subjects, Bawer concluded that Wlady meant that the magazine would print only antigay or homophobic material. When Bawer refused to delete the reference and Wlady insisted, Bawer quit. After reading Bawer's book, I somehow managed to bring the subject up with Wlady, who awkwardly denied Bawer's account. I shrugged it off and probed no further, since I didn't really want to know the truth. Having already established myself in the *Spectator's* firmament and developed a loyalty to Wlady during the Anita Hill and Troopergate flaps, which I felt he had returned, I wasn't going to let possible prejudice against another writer, whom I did not know, upset my world. Some gays can be awfully hypersensitive, I told myself. So long as I stayed in the closet, being gay had never hampered my career on the right, and that was my only concern.

Now, I was emotionally unraveling at the prospect of my career going up in smoke. In seven years in Washington, I had been more or less in the closet, but I had never flat out lied to anyone about my sexuality, and I didn't want to start now. I even had breached my own "don't ask, don't tell" policy on a very few occasions with straight colleagues in the conservative movement when I felt we had become close enough that they should know. Since I never asked anyone to keep the confidence, I was sure that word had spread around town. Thus, anyone in my circle who cared to know that I was gay probably already did. Though we had never discussed it, I was certain that both Bob and Wlady had heard rumors on the conservative grapevine that I was gay, and despite all of the antigay material in the magazine, I didn't think the rumors diminished me in their eyes. I had been wounded by some antigay bigotry, notably in my experiences with John Podhoretz, but I thought that he was an anomaly. What I did fear, so much so that I could hardly bear the thought of it, was the reaction to the truth outside my circle. A few dozen conservative insiders presuming among themselves that I was gay was one thing; but it was quite another for my grassroots audience, several hundred thousand *Spectator* subscribers and contributors and millions of Rush's dittoheads, to be confronted with a public proclamation that I was gay.

I was also powerfully upset thinking about the reaction I expected from my family back in Texas. Though I later learned that my mom was privately distressed about the brutal tone I had taken in my work toward both Anita Hill and the Clintons, my father and I had become much closer since I had become a well-known conservative, establishing a tenuous bond that I did not want to break. Indeed, in hindsight, I've often wondered whether my original attraction to conservatism back in Berkeley wasn't in some way motivated by a subconscious need to repair the breach in our obdurate relationship, which had reached a feverish antagonistic pitch first with my decision to attend Berkeley and then with the revelation that I was gay. Rather than leaving Berkeley as a leftist, as Dad feared, I had oscillated from embracing RFK to Ronald Reagan as my political hero, giving me some hope that we might share common ground.

Dad, who had listened to Rush Limbaugh long before Rush became a household name, was thrilled when the talk show host began promoting my career. When *The Real Anita Hill* was published, he visited local bookstores in Dallas, asking clerks to display the book prominently. His congressman in Texas, Dick Armey, wrote him a letter praising my work. When I went back to Texas for the holidays, my father and I still spoke of little beyond politics, but we were joined now on the same side, chatting amiably about that liar Anita Hill, or those god-awful Clintons. I finally had my father's attention, acceptance, and respect, and I had made him proud. Though we never discussed my sexuality after that conversation a decade ago in Berkeley, I knew from my mother that my father disapproved of my homosexuality and told himself that it had been a passing youthful phase due to my proximity to San Francisco. I didn't want to rub his face in it now and lose him again.

After my conversation with Howard Kurtz, I had to call my mother and told her I was considering coming out. I didn't expect much support, knowing how concerned she was with privacy and appearances, and how relieved she had been that the tensions between my father and me had finally abated as a result of our political entente. When I described my predicament, without missing a beat, Mom, keeper of the family secrets, said, "Why can't you be like Clinton and lie about it?" Then she cracked that she didn't mind what I told the *Post*, since she didn't know anyone in Washington anyway. Not exactly a vote of confidence, the conversation depressed me, and momentarily sent me off in the wrong direction. Maybe I *could* lie my way out of it. If I dodged Kurtz's question and was then outed by the gay press, I calculated, the mainstream press probably wouldn't touch the story, and even if it did, I could flatly deny that I was gay. The right would have enough cover to stick by me, and my relationship with my father could continue.

My mother's reaction sent me into a frenzied tailspin as I tried to reach my political friends. In seeking their advice, I presented the dilemma not as a struggle for self-respect and personal honor by telling the truth about who I was, but as I then saw it: a matter of political damage control. I first called Ricky Silberman, who had already broached the subject with me in her comments about the Rich column. "Call Larry!" she exclaimed, and hung up. I called Judge Silberman's chambers and was put right through. "Don't do it," he said. But when I mentioned the outing threats from the gay press, he said it might be better to "get it out first."

I then called Erwin Glikes and Adam Bellow in New York. After letting loose a furious denunciation of the liberal press, Erwin told me that I was young, the issue would dog me throughout my career, and I should "get it over with now." He then told me to call Adam for advice on how to handle Rich. When Adam came on the line, he told me that he and Erwin had decided I should go on the offensive, charging publicly that Rich had outed me, and thereby turning the tables on the *New York Times* to make myself look like a victim of Rich's bigotry and hypocrisy. Adam said he would work up a quote for me to give. Adam soon called back with the following statement, an attempt to redeem myself with conservatives: "My sexual orientation has never been a factor in my journalism and it never will be. Having said that, any sophisticated reader would interpret the Rich column as a thinly veiled outing. I think one has to look at the journalistic ethics of playing to antigay stereotypes and engaging in third-grade psychologizing. It's particularly dismaying that the *New York Times* would publish such a vulgar attack, and it will be interesting to see if the mainstream media regard it as acceptable because it was aimed at a conservative."

As I studied Adam's words, I could see the tactical advantages to outing myself at this moment. By dishonestly moving the focus onto Rich, I could take the sting out of his charges of misogyny and get the monkey of my sexuality off my back while turning the story line into a controversy about whether a conservative writer had been outed by a prominent, pro-gay liberal columnist. Though I didn't harbor any personal animus toward women, there is little question but that after several years of schooling inside the conservative movement, misogynistic imagery and rhetoric did mark both my writings on Anita Hill and Hillary Clinton. I was, at least subconsciously, following the directive I had received from the *Spectator*'s publisher, Ron Burr—"Can't you find any more women to attack?"—and playing to the misogynistic biases of my right-wing audience. And despite Adam's clever wordplay, there was a psychological issue embedded in my work, not in my homosexuality per se, but in the distortions of the closet.

I reached Mark Paoletta at his law office, telling him I had a plan to defuse the issue of my sexuality by acknowledging that I was gay while slamming Rich. Though I was sure my sexual orientation wasn't news to Mark, he was nervous and noncommittal about my going public. He walked me through who might know the truth, as we assessed the chances of getting caught if I lied to the press. When I told Mark I didn't want to lie, he told me quietly that he was going to "call Thomas and see if it's okay." Kurtz was on deadline, so I had no time to wait for Thomas's opinion. When Mark called me later that night and told me Thomas had said it was "okay," I was relieved. If Thomas thought it was okay, maybe it would be.

With the help of a few shots of vodka, I called Kurtz back and read him the Adam Bellow statement. I hung up, thinking the deed was done, took a deep breath, and plopped onto the nearest sofa, drink in hand. But I wasn't done. The *Post* saw right through Adam's carefully ambiguous language. A few minutes later, Kurtz called me back to say an editor felt the quote sidestepped the issue and wanted me to state flatly that I was gay. Fine, I said, I was already out on a limb, I may as well jump. Kurtz assured me the matter would be handled delicately, and he was true to his word.

Having made the decision, I called Wlady to inform him. He tried to talk me out of it. When I wouldn't budge, he hung up. He called back soon to say that he had spoken to *Spectator* editorial board member Fred Barnes, who advised "stonewalling." My heart sank.

The next morning, my mother was mortified. Brian Lamb discussed the *Post* piece on C-SPAN and the *New York Post* ran a banner headline. Now, the whole world knew. I didn't dare ask what my father thought.

Back in D.C., the response on the right was overwhelmingly supportive. Tom Jipping of the virulently antigay Paul Weyrich organization, who had fought in the trenches with me for Clarence Thomas, called and invited me to discuss the issue on Weyrich's new conservative television network, National Empowerment Television. Calls flooded in from people like Bill Kristol, a savvy media player, who told me I had handled the issue deftly. I had been invited to speak, but I hadn't yet appeared, at the Christian Coalition conference. I called the conference organizer, offering to quietly withdraw so as not to embarrass the group, but she told me she wouldn't hear of it because I was the membership's most requested speaker. When I showed up at the *Spectator*'s offices, not knowing what to expect, David Henderson, a longtime board member, apologized to me for having told an antigay joke in my presence—a joke that I didn't even remember hearing, so deeply was I in denial about my surroundings. Even the notoriously antigay California congressman William Dannemeyer approached me at a conservative gathering in Los Angeles where I was being honored, shook my hand, and said I'd given him something to think about.

My unconscious strategy for gaining acceptance in the movement as a gay man seemed to have worked. Had I been a less valued conservative writer, my career might have been over, but by making myself indispensable as the man who took on Anita Hill and Bill Clinton, I had forced the conservatives to embrace me. By playing victim to Frank Rich, I had given conservatives all the more reason to rally to my side. Writing in *National Review*, editor John O'Sullivan chided Rich for outing me: "Mr. Rich, the *Times* theater critic until his rebirth as an op-ed columnist, makes an unlikely skinhead. But some things are more important than combating homophobia; in Mr. Rich's case, protecting feminist icons such as Hillary Clinton and Anita Hill from the iconoclasm of David Brock and the *American Spectator.*"

I also won the support of the ex–New Leftist turned vehement neoconservative David Horowitz. Horowitz had edited the radical magazine *Ramparts* in the 1960s, but fifteen years later, together with his writing partner Peter Collier, he endorsed Ronald Reagan's election in a piece called

"Lefties for Reagan." I had come to know Horowitz, a squat man with fly-away hair and a Lenin-like beard, in the late 1980s, when he ran something called the Second Thoughts Conference, an annual neocon gathering in D.C. From there, Horowitz used his formidable marketing and polemical skills to emerge as a well-paid conservative pamphleteer underwritten by an array of right-wing foundations, including those controlled by Richard Mellon Scaife. Settling in Los Angeles, he founded the Center for Popular Culture, which devoted itself to fostering conservative values and politics in the entertainment industry.

In his books *Radical Son* and *Destructive Generation*, Horowitz renounced the extremist doctrines and violent tactics of the 1960s radicals he once practiced. The tragedy of Horowitz was that thirty years later, he was the same violent person, working in behalf of another extreme ideology. In a later book, a Machiavellian political manual for the right called *The Art of War and Other Radical Pursuits*, he sought to school the right in the same tactics he had once described as illegitimate and immoral. He favorably cited the dictum of Al Capone, "When they come at you with a knife, you go at them with a gun."

Horowitz also publishes the conservative journal *Heterodoxy*, which rushed to my defense in the wake of the Frank Rich controversy. "What do conservatives, generally thought to be 'homophobic' or anti-gay, think about one of their most celebrated and respected members coming out? For many on the right, Rich's column of sexual innuendo about Brock and the consequences that followed it were simply attempts by the liberal press to bring down America's hottest conservative voice this side of Rush Limbaugh and the only investigative journalist of note on the right. . . . The revelation that Brock is a homosexual has indeed sent shock waves through just about every segment of the political journalism community. . . . For the most part, however, conservatives have said 'So what?' "

The *Spectator*, it was clear, was going to stand by me, too. The *New Republic* used the occasion of my coming out to tweak the *Spectator* for its history of running antigay articles by P. J. O'Rourke and Tom Bethell. The *Spectator* had emerged as "a path-breaking publication whose two most recent blockbusters were written by an openly gay man," the editorial noted, and Bob supplied this tongue-in-cheek response, trying to defuse the controversy with humor:

"It goes without saying that someone's sexual orientation is their own business. We never gave a damn about Brock's orientation, or yours, or that Polish guy's on the staff [Wlady]. At the *American Spectator* we'd be just as happy all to be considered homosexuals, except for the Polish guy."

As far as I knew, there were only two sour notes, and they stick out in my memory because they seemed to be exceptions. In a piece about a conservative conference in the *Washington Post*, the reporter juxtaposed a scene in which I was besieged with autograph seekers with the comments of an anti-gay psychologist named Paul Cameron, who also attended the conference. Cameron was quoted as saying of me, "I'd say shame on him. Maybe there are 1,500 people here and three of them are child molesters. As long as they don't try to push it, you know, get up and say 'I've tried it with 8-year-old girls and it's good,' it's not really my problem." I'd never heard of Cameron, so his remarks didn't mean much to me, but another discordant note was struck closer to home.

In February 1994, a month or so after the Kurtz article appeared, I attended the annual *American Spectator* dinner, where, for the first time, I was a featured speaker. Also for the first time, I showed up accompanied by another man as I took my seat at one of the head tables with Jeane Kirkpatrick, Charles Murray, and Michael Joyce. With me was Andrew, who happened to be in town from California and was eager to see me in my element. Though Andrew and I were just friends, my dinner mates surely thought he was a male date, which is just the way I wanted it. In what for me was a critical test of whether I could thrive in the movement as a gay man, when I approached the podium in the Four Seasons ballroom, I got an extended standing ovation from the conservative notables in the audience—members of Congress, ex–GOP cabinet members, officials of the Republican National Committee, and the like. Out in the audience, Elliott Abrams, President Reagan's contra point man, was sitting next to someone who, unbeknownst to Abrams, was a good friend of mine. A few days after the dinner I heard that as Abrams sat on his hands, he told my friend how dismayed he was that conservatives would give an open homosexual a rousing reception.

I ignored such warning signs, simply denying to myself that they represented anything but a few individual cases of bigotry and intolerance. In coming out, I knew I had done the right thing; as the first self-validating experience of my adult life, it would ultimately help me to chart an independent path and break from the movement's grip. But since I had come out mostly for the wrong reasons, and I had executed it in a disingenuous way, any personal or political awakening that might have resulted from the experience was blocked by my ambition. On the contrary, rather than seeing that as an openly gay man I was on the wrong side of the culture war, I felt a sense of relief that my public and private lives could become one. I even felt emboldened. Because I was accepted, because the *Spectator* stood behind me, because I no longer felt any fear of having my personal life hamper my ascent in the movement, I thought I was home free. I calculated, moreover, to exploit my sexual orientation to further my career on the right. Overnight, I became the only openly gay conservative in the country. I prepared myself to use my presence in the movement to help the movement deflect legitimate criticism that it was antigay. I also knew that my odd status could be used to attract even more attention to my journalistic exploits.

Only after I left the conservative movement was I able to begin to confront the real attitude toward homosexuality in the upper echelons of the right. For some, I'm sure, the antigay rhetoric and homophobia were mere political posturing, designed to inflame the prejudices and win the votes of the conservative base far outside the Washington Beltway. Bob Tyrrell, for example, seemed genuinely without personal prejudice against anyone, and I don't think he ever held my homosexuality against me. Bob's cruel references to "Rock Hudson's disease" were simply a way of pandering to the Limbaugh audience.

Others, I became convinced, were willing to accommodate me, to make an exception to their fervent antigay convictions only in my case, because I was doing so much to forward their political agenda. In Troopergate's wake, Norman Podhoretz had been the first to compliment me as a right-wing Bob Woodward; apparently, my "buggering" could be overlooked. Bill Kristol, who had placed an encouraging post-outing telephone call to me, would soon be a featured speaker at a conference of right-wing academics who promoted the quack notion that homosexuality could be "cured" like a disease.

Then there was the case of David Horowitz, the neoconservative fire-brand whose publication had rushed out a piece when I came out of the closet, using the occasion to proclaim the conservatives' tolerance toward homosexuality. Soon thereafter, Horowitz uttered a hurtful antigay slur to an editor friend of mine whom Horowitz didn't know was gay. At the time, I shrugged it off, unwilling or unable to face the truth about my friends and supporters. Not until such epithets were hurled at me would I realize that I had been on a fool's errand in trying to carve out a place for myself as an openly gay icon in the conservative movement. Only then did I begin to see that by allowing myself to be used as a kind of gay right-wing poster boy, I had been complicit in the bigoted politics and rank hypocrisy of the conservatives.

CHAPTER NINE

"A WOMAN NAMED PAULA"

I was working at home on Valentine's Day 1994, six weeks after the Troopergate ruckus, when I took a call from a very jittery Wlady at the *Spectator*, who wanted to know whether I had heard that a woman was coming forward at a press conference across town, at the Conservative Political Action Committee, to say that she was the Paula from my Troopergate article, and that she was going to claim that Bill Clinton had sexually harassed her. Though I had no idea what Wlady was talking about, suddenly I was as jumpy as he was. I grabbed a copy of "His Cheatin' Heart" off a bookshelf and rifled the pages. Paula who?

As it happened, I had appeared at CPAC at the Omni Shoreham Hotel earlier that day for a panel on media coverage of Clinton's presidency, but I hadn't heard a peep about Paula. I did hear Clinton denounced as "an enemy of the people—the most anti-gun president in the history of the United States." I heard Clinton's election compared to "an alien invasion." I saw Bill Bennett, Bob Dole, Texas Senator Phil Gramm, and lots of "Impeach Hillary" bumper stickers and buttons, but not a hint of Paula. I had been surprised, though, when I ran into Cliff Jackson and troopers Larry Patterson and Roger Perry at CPAC. The trio approached me warily. We had not spoken since my story was published, owing to their understandable hard feelings about the strong-arm tactics I had used to force the piece out. Cliff told me they were at the conference to announce the establishment of a Troopergate Whistleblowers Fund, complete with an 800 telephone number, from which they eventually reaped some $40,000. Though the troopers held on to their state jobs despite their fears of retaliation from the "Clinton machine" in Arkansas, they were happy to grab whatever extra cash they could. In this appreciative crowd of activists from around the country, they were showered with $1,000 checks from an organization linked to Oliver North, and Newt Gingrich saluted their patriotism.

I soon learned that the Paula in question was a woman named Paula Jones, whose appearance at CPAC, the most partisan venue imaginable, was being stage-managed by none other than Cliff Jackson. According to Jones, she had been visiting her family in Arkansas at Christmas when a friend, Debra Ballentine, read her the passage in my article referring to "a woman named Paula." Jones realized she was the Paula being written about, but she didn't like what she was hearing, for when trooper Danny Ferguson told the story to me, he made it sound as though Paula had had consensual sex with Clinton in his hotel room. As she was leaving the room, Ferguson quoted her as remarking to him that she was willing to be Clinton's "regular girl-friend." Jones's version of the story was quite different: Clinton had made an unwelcome sexual advance on her; she rebuffed the overture and left the room feeling humiliated. She maintained, furthermore, that she never made the "regular girlfriend" comment to Ferguson. Jackson distributed to reporters two affidavits from friends of Jones, including Ballentine, in an attempt to establish contemporaneous corroboration of Jones's version of the story.

The Jones press conference at CPAC bombed. Jones and her Little Rock lawyer, Danny Traylor, were coy with the press about the details of the inappropriate sexual behavior Clinton allegedly had engaged in. After several rounds of vague answers from the Jones camp about what had actually happened between Clinton and her, Reed Irvine, the head of a right-wing media watchdog group called Accuracy in Media funded by Richard Mellon Scaife, stood up and asked Jones if the sex act Clinton had asked her to perform was something she could have performed remaining clothed. At that point, the assembled reporters groaned, closed their notebooks, and called it a day, concluding they had witnessed another Arkansas burlesque show. Initially, the Jones charges rated barely a mention in the press. The *New York Times* ran a small item deep inside the paper, and the *Washington Post* published a cheeky "Style" section piece on the CPAC conference that dismissed Jones as an "eruption, yet again, of Mount Bimbo." In spite of

Troopergate—and for some, no doubt, because of it—reporters were still reluctant to wade into the muddy waters of sex stories.

Most reporters, that is. At the *Washington Post*, investigative reporter Michael Isikoff was looking seriously into Paula Jones's claims. At CPAC, Isikoff had persuaded Cliff Jackson to grant him exclusive access to Jones. Cliff envisioned using the credible *Post*, just as he had used the *Los Angeles Times* in Troopergate, to legitimize the Jones story. Isikoff was a dogged investigator who had become a reporter in the mid-1970s, inspired by Bob Woodward and Carl Bernstein's role in toppling Richard Nixon. A short, unkempt character in smudgy glasses and Dockers, Isikoff seemed to have no politics. He was out for the damaging story no matter whose ox was being gored. Isikoff was working the Clinton sex beat before I was. In July 1992, he reported on efforts by the Clinton campaign to knock down stories of the candidate's alleged womanizing. It was a mark of how the journalism culture had changed since Watergate that Isikoff, essentially a sex investigator for a major newsweekly, would emerge as an award-winning Woodward of the 1990s.

Now, Isikoff was hot on the Jones trail. According to his memoir, *Uncovering Clinton*, Isikoff won approval to pursue the Jones story in part because *Post* editors were influenced by the Arkansas troopers' caricature of Clinton as a lecherous man-boy. The preoccupation with sexual scandal was moving beyond the president's enemies into the mainstream institutions of journalism. When he completed his reporting on the Jones case, Isikoff was permitted by *Post* editors to probe into Clinton's personal life further, ostensibly to establish patterns of inappropriate behavior. "One of the country's preeminent newspapers was in effect launching an open-ended investigation into the president's sex life," according to Isikoff. By Isikoff's own account, the fruits of his search beyond Jones were meager. He found no other credible evidence of sexual harassment in Clinton's past, and for that reason, his story was held by the paper's managing editor, casting it into limbo. Word of the story inevitably spread into Washington's gossip mills and became the talk of the town for weeks. Just as I had helped force the hand of *Los Angeles Times* editors by mentioning their pending story in my Troopergate article, the right wing got wind of the stalled Isikoff story and mounted a public campaign to pressure the *Post* to run it. A front-page story in the *Washington Times* announced, "*Post* Sex Story about Clinton Gets Spiked." Reed Irvine took out ads in the *New York Times* and the *Post* itself imploring the paper to publish the Jones story.

Encouraged by Isikoff's interest in her story, Jones moved toward filing a sexual harassment suit against Clinton. Initially, Jones had asked Clinton for a statement acknowledging that they had met in the hotel room and that, contrary to the implication of the *Spectator* account, she hadn't done any-thing wrong; Clinton declined the request. Of course, as the author of the piece, I was more than a little curious about why Jones had asked Clinton to undo the damage that Ferguson and I allegedly had done to her reputa-tion. Under normal circumstances, the person making an allegedly libelous statement, and the person publishing it, would be on the hook. Years later, Jones said in an appearance on *Larry King Live* that she had called me at the *Spectator* seeking a retraction; but if she did, she never reached me, she didn't leave a message, and she never had a lawyer contact the magazine on her behalf. Jones and her advisers obviously had bigger fish to fry.

As Jones deliberated her course of action, I was tipped off to ongoing dis-cussions within the Jones camp about suing the *Spectator* for libel. The case might have been difficult, since Jones came forward and identified herself as the Paula in my article in front of dozens of reporters at CPAC; I had not identified her fully. Yet the main reason I wasn't sued was that a conniving cadre of right-wing lawyers and operatives was secretly calling the shots in the Jones case to forward its own political agenda of undermining the Clinton presidency, which meant leaving me out of it. A trio of Clinton opponents from Troopergate—Cliff Jackson, Peter Smith, and former Bush administration official Richard Porter—put Jones's Arkansas lawyer, Danny Traylor, in touch with the Landmark Legal Foundation, a right-wing public interest law firm generously funded by Richard Mellon Scaife, who was also the main benefactor of the *Spectator*, where all the trouble began. Of all peo-ple, Rush Limbaugh sat on the legal foundation's board of advisers.

Landmark's Washington office was run by Mark Levin, a former chief of staff to Edwin Meese. Heavyset, bald, and looking two decades older than he was, Levin spearheaded Landmark's strategy of filing a barrage of lawsuits and ethics complaints to harass the Clinton administration, a marked shift from its prior concerns with substantive issues like tort reform and property rights. As a high-profile Clinton enemy, Landmark avoided stepping into the Jones case publicly, so as not to taint it. Landmark, however, was active behind the scenes. With his face twisted into its persistent unpleasant contortion, Levin told me that he and Landmark's president, Jerry Jones, who was a close friend of *Spectator* board member David Henderson, had signaled to Traylor to lay off the *Spectator* if he wanted conservative movement support for the case. Soon thereafter, Scaife made a cash contribution to the Jones case of $50,000 through an entity called the Fund for a Living American Government. Had these conservatives not intervened in the way they did, Jones might have sued the *Spectator*, rather than the president, and though I might have been in the dock, the catastrophic political consequences of her lawsuit might have been avoided.

Through my lawyer friend Ann Coulter, I saw a deeper level of partisan scheming and political manipulation in the Jones case, which Coulter herself later described as "a small, intricately knit right-wing conspiracy." The day after my Troopergate story appeared in the *Spectator*, I flew to New York City to flog it on a popular drive-time radio show hosted by Bob Grant, a fire-breathing right-winger known for referring to African Americans on the air as "savages." After the broadcast, I arranged to have celebratory drinks with Coulter, whom I'd known through conservative legal circles, and who made no secret of her hatred for the Clintons. Raised in a wealthy conservative Republican family in Connecticut, Ann had come out of the same militant right-wing campus culture as the rest of us—she founded the *Cornell Review*, a *Dartmouth Review* knockoff, as an undergraduate, and then chartered the Federalist Society chapter at the University of Michigan Law School. Unlike Ricky and Larry's generation of conservatives, who were steeped in conservative ideology and seemed to deeply believe the stuff, Ann and I reflected the bumper-sticker conservatism of the younger set. Thinking back on my relationship with Ann now, it's dismaying to realize how a certain kind of politics can corrupt every aspect of your life. As with my later relationship with Laura

Ingraham, Ann and I never had a serious conversation about politics, or any-thing else. Instead, we smoked, drank to excess—Ann seemed to live on noth-ing but chardonnay and cigarettes—and vented our anger and cruelty by hurling all manner of epithets at liberals and the disadvantaged among us. We both eschewed subtlety. To Ann, my "nutty/slutty" line was a stroke of genius. Our only disagreement was over abortion: Ann called me a "baby-killer."

In the thrall of extremist politics, Ann moved to Washington after the Republican takeover of Congress later in 1994 to work for Federalist founder Spencer Abraham in the Senate. She soon grew bored with life on the Hill and moved on to become a television pundit, where she crafted a niche for herself as a "poster girl for the militia crowd," as *New York* magazine put it. In her television appearances, Ann regularly labeled Clinton as "crazy," "like a se-rial killer," "creepier and slimier than Kennedy," "a horny hick," and "white trash." "I think it is a rational question for Americans to ask whether their pres-ident is insane," she declared. "I just want to get rid of him." To Ann, Hillary Clinton was a "prostitute." In a CNN segment on the dragging death of James Byrd, an African American man, in Texas, Ann fumed, "There is a constitu-tional right to hate." She eventually left her job as a commentator on MSNBC after telling a disabled Vietnam vet in a debate, "People like you caused us to lose the war." I never did figure out what Ann was really mad at.

A leggy, rail-thin blond who was as renowned for her skimpy skirts as she was for her tart tongue, Ann later resurfaced with a best-selling book urging Clinton's impeachment for telling a sex lie, though Ann herself hardly seemed well positioned to take up a moral brief against the Clintons. According to the *New York Observer,* she carried on a relationship with Bob Guccione Jr., scion of a fortune made in publishing pornography, while he was fending off a sexual harassment lawsuit. Defending George W. Bush against allegations of cocaine abuse in an appearance on the cable show *Rivera Live,* she seemed to condone lying to FBI background investigators to cover up illicit use of drugs by Republican friends nominated to Justice Department posts: "In fact, it becomes a kind of joke that, you know, your friends you saw doing drugs constantly all the way through college were never, you know, not stoned. You always tell the FBI, 'No, never even saw them smoke pot.'" And though she had dated Jewish neocon John Podhoretz, a virulent anti-Semitism that I indulged her in for far too long punctuated Ann's private conversations. That she wanted to leave her New York law firm "to get away from all these Jews" was one of her gentler remarks.

Ann had asked a close friend of hers to join us for drinks, a young partner at the high-powered New York law firm of Wachtel, Lipton, Rosen & Katz, George T. Conway III. I had met Conway, a graduate of Harvard University and Yale Law School and former law clerk to Federalist Society patron Ralph Winter on the Second Circuit Court of Appeals, a couple of times before, at dinners with Ann in New York. Conway was a year younger than me, short, plump, with the insistent manner of a successful litigator. Conway made his million-dollar-a-year salary defending tobacco companies. Even more so than the rest of us, Conway was an instinctive right-winger, or "wing-nut," in Ann's phraseology. Like Ann, Conway usually referred to Clinton as a "scumbag," or worse.

We met Conway at his office, treading lightly through the plush corridors and closing Conway's door behind us, as we knew that the pugnacious Bernard Nussbaum, Clinton's former White House counsel, was a senior partner in the firm. As it happened, Conway had the small TV set on his credenza tuned to the ABC Evening News, which was airing a report on the fallout from Troopergate. When the correspondent told the story of Clinton receiving oral sex in a parked car—and the words "oral sex" flashed on the screen—Conway leapt up from his chair triumphantly, with his fist raised high above his head. I got a kick out of the report, too, but Conway's prurience made me wonder why he seemed more excited about my story than I was. I knew Conway was a lonely workaholic whose clumsy attempts at dating right-wing babes like Coulter always seemed to fall flat. For the next few years, Conway—one of the best and brightest of the young conservatives—spoke to me about little but Clinton's rumored sexual habits, and the supposed size and shape of his genitalia. On some level, Conway's hatred of Clinton seemed attributable to raw jealousy. As events unfolded in the coming years, this one disgruntled New York lawyer almost single-handedly brought down the president. (In 2001, Conway got his wish, marrying blond right-wing pundit Kelly Ann Fitzpatrick.)

Shortly after the Jones suit was filed in May 1994, Conway volunteered his services to Gil Davis and Joe Cammarata, two Virginia Republican lawyers who had taken over the case from Danny Traylor and were widely seen as in over their heads. The assignment was a doubly odd one for Gil Davis, a failed politician and head of the Christian Action Network, a Virginia-based religious right group dedicated to promoting "traditional morality and family values." In Virginia political circles, the enormously round, jolly lawyer was notorious for his womanizing. We hung out together at a reception one evening at the Georgetown Four Seasons Hotel, where Davis was a font of virtually nonstop sexual banter. "Look at those tits on her!" he drooled. As another woman passed our table, Davis barked out, "You'd look good lying in bed next to me."

Though pro bono work is supposed to be cleared by the partnership of a law firm, George Conway concealed his work for Gil Davis from his Wachtel colleagues. Conway, Coulter, and a third conservative lawyer, Jerome Marcus, a Federalist Society member in a Philadelphia law firm who was working on the case incognito as well, referred to themselves as the "elves." Marcus, who once wrote in the *Washington Times* that Clinton's presidency was a "cancer" on the country, had joined the group at the behest of Richard Porter, the former Bushie and Peter Smith's Troopergate adviser. With Coulter involved at the margins, Conway and Marcus secretly ran legal strategy and churned out the major briefs in the Jones case, including the one that produced the landmark 9–0 Supreme Court decision in June 1997 that sitting presidents could be subject to civil lawsuits while in office. Conway brought Federalist legal heavyweights Robert Bork and Ted Olson into the case to conduct a moot court with Gil Davis before his Supreme Court argument.

The involvement of such high-powered lawyers from the Federalist Society was striking evidence of how radicalized the conservative movement had become since the 1980s. The society had been known for holding that executive privilege was sacrosanct, the idea of suing a president while he was in office on a private civil matter was unconstitutional, and impeachment was a threat to an independent presidency no matter who was in office. To shield President Reagan and President George H. W. Bush from criminal prosecution in the Iran-contra affair, Federalist lawyers like Bork, Olson, and C. Boyden Gray had framed their defense of the Reagan-Bush administration as a defense of a strong presidency and broad executive branch prerogatives. Prior to Clinton's election, the Federalists had trashed Anita Hill and criticized recent sexual harassment law as overly broad in allowing plaintiffs to conduct fishing expeditions into the personal lives of defendants. Now, in the Jones case, they were all for hamstringing a sitting president with civil lawsuits; soon, they would win a motion to introduce information on Clinton's consensual sex life into the case that the trial judge would rule had no legal bearing on the harassment claim.

Having won a Supreme Court victory, the team of Davis and Cammarata pushed Jones to settle the case. This would have been a wise move for Jones, because she had no evidence that she had been harassed, and the judge eventually ruled that she had no case. (Some years later, Jones would throw away whatever credibility she had by posing nude for *Penthouse.*) But other advisers around Jones—her then husband, Steve, her media adviser and antiabortion activist Susan Carpenter Macmillan, and the three elves— wanted to keep the case going for political reasons. When various settlement offers were rejected by Jones, Davis and Cammarata quit the case and were replaced by lawyers working with the right-wing Rutherford Institute, which had been founded with the support of Christian Right reconstructionist R. J. Rushdoony, who was an early board member.* Rutherford, which received funds from Richard Mellon Scaife, teamed up with a law firm in Dallas by the name of Rider, Campbell, Fisher & Pyke, one of whose principals, Don Campbell, was known in Texas for working to reinstate the state's sodomy law after it had been found unconstitutional in the courts.

Though Davis and Cammarata were out of the picture, George Conway told me that he increased his covert influence over the case through the Dallas law firm. I kept in touch with Conway as the Jones case wound its way through the courts, and in one memorable telephone conversation, I asked Conway straight out if, from his insider perspective, he believed Jones

---

*The Reverend R. J. Rushdoony believed that civil law should be replaced by Biblical law "to suppress, control, and/or eliminate the ungodly." He advocated the death penalty for abortion, adultery, sodomy, and incest as well as for blasphemers and "propagators of false doctrines." Rushdoony was also a Holocaust denier.

was telling the truth. As if the answer were self-evident, he scoffed and said no: "This is about proving Troopergate." Conway went on to explain that the Jones team was planning to grill Clinton under oath about his consensual sex life, and hopefully catch him lying about it—a deliberate perjury trap. If the trap didn't ensnare Clinton, they could still use the deposition process as an open-ended invitation to explore every Clinton sex rumor ever voiced and embarrass the president by leaking the details to the press. For the right, it was a no-lose situation. No matter the outcome, the Jones case would detract from Clinton's agenda and drain his political and financial resources. As the case proceeded, Conway would personally write the motion that allowed evidence of Clinton's consensual involvement with other women into the Jones case—a fishing expedition that would turn up Clinton's consensual affair with White House intern Monica Lewinsky.

Like George Conway, I also had trouble believing Jones's story of sexual harassment. I tended to believe the version of events told to me by Danny Ferguson, which implied that if anything had gone on between Clinton and Jones, it had been consensual. After my experiences with the Arkansas troopers, I also had doubts about Jones's motivations. Reading the Michael Isikoff piece in the *Washington Post*, which finally ran as Jones prepared to file one of the very few civil lawsuits ever against a sitting president, I had a sense of déjà vu: Jones and her lawyer had signed a contract with unusual provisions for the sale of book and movie rights, and within a few days, Jones's sister Charlotte charged that before Jones filed suit, Jones had told her: "Whichever way it goes, it smells money." While conceding no second thoughts about his work, even Isikoff seemed to realize that by their nature all such he said/she said sex stories are impossible to document because there are no records and no eyewitnesses. "We couldn't prove it," he later wrote of the Jones allegation. "In fact, the charge was, by its very nature, unprovable."

Despite my private doubts about Jones's veracity, I shamelessly played to the conservative party line, supporting her case and eagerly seeking to claim credit for unearthing it. The Isikoff piece in the *Post* had been filled with salacious details: In the hotel room, Clinton had allegedly fondled himself and asked Jones to "kiss it." Jones also claimed she could identify a "distinguishing characteristic" in Clinton's genital area, though Clinton's doctors later confirmed that no such thing existed. Evidently, in just a few months' time, for all of the justified condemnation heaped on Troopergate by its critics in the press, the story nonetheless had done its job of turning a newly tabloidized mainstream press against Clinton, and I felt responsible for engineering the shift. I puffed up my achievement, strutting around Washington with an "I Believe Paula" button on my lapel. And I placed on my home answering machine a message saying, "I'm out trying to bring down the president."

I was sporting the button one warm spring night at the Silbermans' as we met for one of our frequent dinnertime brainstorming sessions. With its possibility of tying Clinton in legal knots, the Jones case had electrified Ricky and Larry, as it had much of conservative Washington. Never mind that these two conservative stalwarts had spent their careers fighting against overly broad interpretations of the sexual harassment laws, criticizing the feminist movement for politicizing relations between the sexes, and defending strong executive branch powers. Those principles were consumed in the blazing partisan fires. Though she had warned against publishing Troopergate, now that a legal claim had sprung out of it, Ricky was delirious at the prospect of using a tenuous sexual harassment charge to humiliate Clinton. Hillary Clinton's presentation of an award to Anita Hill at a convention of the American Bar Association in 1992 had stuck in Ricky's craw. Talk about an eye for an eye!

The right-wing machine was gearing up, right there in the Silbermans' kitchen. Ricky recently had left her post at the Equal Employment Opportunity Commission and founded an antifeminist group, the Independent Women's Forum, which was an outgrowth of the ad hoc Women for Judge Thomas. The purpose of IWF, as Ricky explained it, was to "challenge radical feminists" in "the propaganda wars," by signing up women to spout the orthodox conservative antifeminist viewpoint on the op-ed pages and television talk shows where political controversies were hashed out. With its glossy magazines and attractive spokespeople, IWF

provided a smart, hip contrast to the 1950s-feeling, midwestern antifemi-
nism of Phyllis Schlafly, yet the agenda was the same. The members of IWF
opposed pay equity and affirmative action for women, and fought legislative protections for victims of domestic violence and sexual harassment—
despite Ricky's interest in the Jones case. In making their arguments, they
highlighted statistics showing violence committed *by* women; blamed
women themselves for the fact that they often were paid less than men;
and published spurious data on male/female biological differences.

Naturally, I suggested to Ricky that she seek start-up funds from Scaife,
whose millions washed through just about every conservative organization
and publication in town. I also said she should approach Elizabeth Lurie,
who had cut a check to underwrite my Anita Hill research at the *Spectator.*
Scaife ponied up, and Lurie became chairman of Ricky's organization. Lynne
Cheney, the chairman of the National Endowment for the Humanities
under President Bush and wife of Dick Cheney, Wendy Gramm, another
Bush administration appointee and wife of the Texas senator, and Reagan-
era civil rights official Linda Chavez joined various IWF boards.

With Scaife's backing, Ricky was ready to put her fledgling group at the
service of the anti-Clinton jihad, and as one of its first moves, she wanted
IWF to file a friend of the court brief in the Paula Jones case, supporting
Jones's contention that her case should go forward even while Clinton was
president. And Ricky had a particular lawyer in mind to draft the brief:
Kenneth Starr. I certainly knew the name. Starr, a Federalist Society stalwart,
had been a D.C. Circuit Court judge in the Reagan years and solicitor general in the Bush administration, and he was often mentioned as a possible
Republican Supreme Court nominee. Ricky told me she planned to approach
Starr, now a lawyer in private practice representing big tobacco and other
corporate interests at the firm of Kirkland & Ellis, to draft the IWF brief supporting Jones. (Reacting to Clinton's proposals for cigarette tax increases, and
more federal regulation of nicotine, tobacco companies had shifted their sizable political contributions overwhelmingly to the GOP column.)

While Starr's voting record on the appellate court was as conservative as
Robert Bork's, and despite the fact that he was a pro-life fundamentalist
Christian, Judge Starr, as he wished to be called even though he was no

longer on the bench, was widely seen as a moderate conservative and an independent jurist. Favorably described by Georgetown doyenne Sally Quinn in the *Washington Post* as a member in good standing of the Washington establishment, Starr was the ideal front man for the job Ricky had in mind. Larry Silberman, who had served with Starr on the D.C. Circuit Court, agreed. In conversations with me, Silberman, who once threatened to punch a fellow judge in the nose in a dispute over an affirmative action case, told me that he and other top members of the right-wing legal establishment regarded Starr as a weak, unprincipled opportunist who was more interested in advancing his own ambitions than in conservative ideology. He was also considered naïve and politically clumsy. Starr's concern for burnishing his reputation and his desire to ascend to the Supreme Court, Larry said, made him susceptible to pressure from the liberal political establishment and the liberal Washington press corps. Of course, if Larry's view was correct, Starr was also susceptible to pressure from his patrons in the conservative movement, who mistrusted him and could make or break his career. Starr's actions showed that he was, in fact, easily manipulated by the right wing into situations that would hurt his own long-term goal of winning a Supreme Court seat. In the Jones case, Starr tried to have it both ways, doing the conservatives' bidding, but under a veil of secrecy. He declined to file the brief for IWF, but the $500-an-hour corporate lawyer donated his time in several surreptitious telephone conferences with the Jones lawyers throughout the spring of 1994.

A few months later, Starr would suddenly be designated as the point man in a strategy by the Republican establishment, looking toward the November 1994 elections, to use political scandal to destabilize the Clinton presidency. Though the Clintons were still reviled as avatars of big-government liberalism, in 1993, after gays in the military, health care, and a Clinton tax increase on the wealthiest Americans, the conservatives discovered the limits of ideological warfare. In a coordinated and sustained fashion, the Republican right would now work to show that the Clintons were criminally minded. Allegations of financial corruption that had been used by the right to create "Bill" and "Hillary" during the 1992 campaign would be forced into evidentiary proceedings as the Clintons and their associates were prosecuted by a corps of Federalist Society lawyers under Starr's direction. Starr should have known that heading up the polarizing Clinton investigation would essentially end his career, as those who appointed him may well have appreciated, but he apparently didn't understand.

At the root of this effort was, once again, Richard Mellon Scaife and his millions. When the buoyant Bill Clinton came to office, a frustrated, embittered, and conspiracy-prone Scaife redirected his money away from promoting conservative ideas and toward proving that the Clintons were leaders of a criminal syndicate. Scaife's delusions had the effect of reorienting the entire conservative movement, which Scaife largely underwrote, to that end. Among other heinous deeds, the billionaire believed that Vincent Foster, the deputy White House counsel and close friend of Hillary Clinton who committed suicide in July 1993, was murdered by the Clintons to cover up their crimes in Whitewater, a failed real estate deal the Clintons had invested in back in the late 1970s. In a rare interview Scaife granted to *George* magazine in 1999—after two congressional probes, two separate independent counsel criminal investigations, and Scaife's own investigative projects all turned up no evidence that Foster's death was anything but a suicide—Scaife still saw the Foster case as "the Rosetta stone to the Clinton administration . . . Once you solve that one mystery, you'll know everything that's gone on or went on—I think there's been a massive cover-up about what Bill Clinton's administration has been doing, and what he was doing when he was governor of Arkansas. . . . Listen, [Clinton] can order people done away with at his will. He's got the entire federal government behind him. . . . God, there must be 60 people [associated with Clinton] who have died mysteriously."

After Foster's death, the right exploited the tragedy to suggest a nefarious but illusory conspiracy involving Whitewater, a story that had lain dormant since it was first told in the *New York Times* in March 1992. The *Times* piece suggested that the Clintons had engaged in several conflicts of interest in their dealings with their Whitewater business partner, a crooked Arkansas savings-and-loan operator named James McDougal. Nothing came of the *Times* story, because there was no wrongdoing to find. Eighteen months later, and three months after Foster died, in October 1993 the press reported that the Clintons had been named as possible witnesses in a criminal probe of McDougal's bank by the Federal Resolution Trust Corporation, which polices S&Ls nationwide. In December, the *Washington Times* published an insinuating report linking Foster's death to Whitewater that turned out to be wrong. The *Washington Times* report made the paper the very same week that Troopergate was unleashed by the *Spectator*, creating a media frenzy in the legitimate press. Reacting to two bogus news stories from the right wing, editors at major publications and networks dispatched battalions of reporters to Arkansas to investigate the Clintons' past. The editors instructed reporters to focus on something, anything, so long as it wasn't the sex scandal. They wanted a clean follow-the-money story to supplant a dirty one, and Whitewater fit the bill. The right wing now had an unwitting partner in its destabilization effort.

Led by Bob Dole, Republican leaders, who had always opposed the independent counsel statute passed after Watergate as an unconstitutional violation of the separation of powers doctrine, would now call for a special investigation of a Democratic president, stalling his legislative progress in 1994, particularly on health care reform, and sowing the seeds of a Republican takeover of the House. As rehashed Whitewater stories blanketed the press, Republicans clamored for an independent inquiry into Whitewater and the Foster death. At the time, there was no independent counsel law on the books, leading Clinton to ask Attorney General Janet Reno to appoint a special counsel. In mid-January 1994, she named a respected Republican lawyer from New York named Robert Fiske.

Fiske was a reviled figure in the conservative movement, dating back to the days when he sat on an American Bar Association review panel that gave Robert Bork a low rating and damaged his confirmation prospects in the Senate. When Bush attorney general Richard Thornburgh sought to nominate Fiske as his top deputy, conservatives, led by the Scaife-backed Washington Legal Foundation, which had Federalists Ted Olson and Ken Starr on its board, shot Fiske down and saw to it that archconservative William Barr filled the slot instead. When special counsel Fiske issued a definitive report finding that Foster had committed suicide and that the death was not related to Whitewater, the right wing saw its chances of implicating the Clintons in criminal wrongdoing evaporate. Led by the *Wall Street Journal* editorial page, *New York Times* columnist William Safire, and the Scaife-backed Accuracy in Media organization, the right mounted a public attack on the integrity of the Fiske investigation and conservatives brayed for his dismissal.

When Congress reauthorized the independent counsel law in the summer of 1994, the conservatives made their move. Independent counsels are named by a panel of three appeals court judges controlled by the chief justice of the U.S. Supreme Court, William Rehnquist. Rehnquist, a Republican activist from Arizona, was appointed to the high court by Richard Nixon and elevated to chief justice by President Reagan. As a law clerk, Rehnquist had written a memorandum in 1952 favoring state-supported segregation, and during elections in Arizona in the 1960s he worked in a Republican Party effort to harass minority voters at the polls. During his Senate confirmation hearings, Rehnquist's critics charged that he committed perjury in denying his past views and actions under questioning from senators.

Though the post usually went to more senior judges, in 1992 Rehnquist named D.C. Circuit Court judge David Sentelle to head the panel that appoints independent counsels. A Reagan appointee who had named his daughter Reagan after the president, and a protégé of North Carolina Republican Senators Jesse Helms and Lauch Faircloth, a vocal Fiske critic, Sentelle was a hard-line right-winger. In a 1991 review of Robert Bork's *The Tempting of America* in the Federalist-sponsored *Harvard Journal of Law and Public Policy*, Sentelle accused "leftist heretics" of attempting to turn the United States into a "collectivist, egalitarian, materialistic, race-conscious, hypersecular, and socially permissive state." Quoting from the Book of Ecclesiastes, Sentelle wrote, "Finally, in *The Tempting of America*, 'that which was written was upright, even words of truth.'"

Rather than reappoint Fiske under the reauthorized independent counsel statute to finish the Whitewater investigation, Sentelle's panel fired Fiske and named Starr. Conservative insiders like the Silbermans and Sentelle knew that Starr, though he would pass muster as independent to the outside world, would prove to be a reliable anti-Clinton partisan. In later Senate testimony, Sentelle conceded that he had actively sought a political opponent of

Clinton's to head up the Whitewater inquiry, a maneuver that helped create the fog of scandal that enveloped the Clinton presidency for the next six years. In conversations about Sentelle, who sat with Silberman on the circuit court, Larry suggested to me that he sometimes deployed Sentelle, whom Larry said he considered to be a dim bulb, as a stalking horse for his own machinations. Sentelle had provided Silberman with a crucial second vote in the overturning of the Iran-contra conviction of Oliver North by a vote of two to one. The unsigned opinion was issued per curiam, or by the court, which obscured Silberman's fingerprints. Had the Republican senators, and perhaps even Chief Justice Rehnquist, used Sentelle in the same fashion?

CHAPTER TEN

THE ARKANSAS PROJECT

As the Paula Jones case moved forward, the *American Spectator* capitalized on its notoriety as the leading anti-Clinton publication in the country. Circulation had soared from 30,000 to 150,000 after my Anita Hill article, and in the early months of 1994 following Troopergate, it doubled again to more than 300,000—three times the circulation of the *New Republic* and twice that of *National Review*—giving it the largest circulation of any opinion magazine in the country. Forgoing any role it had played as an intellectual force in conservatism, the *Spectator* launched the Arkansas Project, a multimillion-dollar dirty tricks operation against the Clintons. Everyone at the magazine, along with hordes of other movement operatives, started playing investigative reporter.

My first brush with the Arkansas Project was auspicious, occasioning my first and only private meeting with the reclusive Richard Mellon Scaife. The white-haired, red-faced billionaire was in town to attend the annual dinner of the *American Spectator*, where he was always introduced as the one man who was responsible for keeping it going. He had given the magazine close to $6 million since 1970. Scaife typically stood to acknowledge his ovation with a stiff wave, but he never spoke.

At lunch at the Four Seasons Hotel in Georgetown, Scaife and his top aide Dan McMichael asked me to undertake an investigation of former Arkansas senator William J. Fulbright, one of the early mentors of Bill Clinton, who had interned in Fulbright's office in the late 1960s. Well into his seventies and looking like a gargoyle, McMichael professed an interest in national security and intelligence matters and seemed stuck in the Cold War period. Years earlier, he had written a novel about a Soviet takeover of the

United States. He told me he believed that Fulbright, an outspoken opponent of the Vietnam War who had been smeared by right-wingers in Arkansas as a tool of the Communists, had been an agent of the Soviet KGB and had recruited Clinton as a Soviet spy.

Though McMichael's suspicions about Clinton's ties to Moscow echoed the false charges made by GOP operatives in the '92 campaign, he had no evidence to support the story he wanted me to write. I scarcely could believe my ears when he suggested that I secure a meeting under false pretenses with Fulbright, then in his nineties and in poor health, and lure him into incriminating himself. Scaife said little during the lunch. But after McMichael spoke, Bob Tyrrell, who was also present, enthusiastically chimed in, promising that I would get right on the story. As I was in no position to contradict my boss, I humored everyone at the lunch table, toyed with my food, and planned to quietly drop the assignment later on.

As he showed at lunch, Scaife was a mysterious figure, even to the recipients of his largesse. Most of Scaife's grant making was done through McMichael and Richard Larry, a former marine with a hard-right ideology who had worked for Scaife for more than thirty years. On a Chesapeake Bay boat trip in mid-1993, four men—Larry, Tyrrell, longtime *Spectator* board member David Henderson, and Washington lawyer Stephen Boynton—held the initial discussions that led to the Arkansas Project, which for several years remained a tight secret within the magazine. A retired public relations executive with skin as thick as an old leather briefcase, Henderson had forged close relations with Richard Larry when he worked on the Scaife-funded libel suit filed by General William Westmoreland, also a *Spectator* board member, against CBS News in the early 1980s. Westmoreland, a general in the Vietnam War who blamed the Democrats in Congress and the media for the American pullout and the subsequent Communist takeover of South Vietnam, was charged by CBS with deceiving his superiors in Washington about the direness of the situation on the ground. The suit, which the general settled in return for a statement from CBS that his patriotism had not been challenged, became a cause célèbre on the right as evidence of liberal media bias. Since then, Bob had regarded Henderson as his "Scaife connection," the guy who kept the money flowing into the magazine's coffers, so Bob was predisposed to go along with just about anything Henderson wanted.

Not coincidentally, as the foursome set sail off Maryland's Eastern Shore, a Byzantine political scandal was unfolding in Arkansas, where the disgraced political figure and con man David Hale was facing a federal indictment for embezzling more than $2 million in federally backed small-business loans. Word was circulating through the right wing in Washington that as part of his plea negotiations, Hale would offer to implicate President Clinton in pressuring him to make an illegal $300,000 loan to Clinton Whitewater partner Jim McDougal's wife, Susan McDougal—the never-substantiated allegation that would become the core of independent counsel Starr's Whitewater probe. Around the same time that they were meeting with Dick Larry and Bob Tyrrell about the project's financing, Henderson, who had been an acquaintance of Hale's for years, and Stephen Boynton were meeting with Hale in Arkansas to discuss his legal troubles.

At its inception, then, the Arkansas Project was a means of providing covert support for Hale to implicate Clinton in a crime. Boynton's role in the project was more curious than Henderson's. A moon-faced Washington lawyer who represented fur-trapping and hunting trade associations in fighting environmental protection of endangered species, as far as I knew Boynton had gotten involved simply because he was a fishing and hunting buddy of Henderson's and Larry's. From documents that were mistakenly left in a photocopying machine at the *Spectator*, I pieced together Boynton's role as a conduit between the *Spectator* and the Arkansas Project. Large checks, up to $50,000 a month, were being cut by the *Spectator* to Boynton, who then disbursed the funds to keep the project running. Though Boynton did no legal work for the *Spectator* that I am aware of, the funds were listed on the *Spectator* documents as "legal fees." It looked to me like no one but Henderson and Boynton and possibly Larry knew where all the money was going.

I wasn't the only one at the magazine who suspected that at least some of the money was being funneled to Hale. I never met Hale, but throughout 1994 and 1995, Henderson told me that he and Boynton were spending significant amounts of time in hidden locations throughout Arkansas with Hale,

who by then had won a plea arrangement with Starr in exchange for testimony against Clinton and was a federal witness under the protection of Starr's
agents. Hale was a frequent source for articles in the *Spectator*, by a writer
named James Ring Adams. Adams told me that he was deeply troubled when
he heard Boynton, who controlled the project's books and disbursements,
speak of "getting checks to Mrs. Hale." According to a later report in the
Washington Post, Dick Larry had approached two other conservative foundations that were not involved in journalism about taking on the Arkansas
Project, but they were turned down. Tyrrell, however, agreed to house the
project at the *Spectator*; the journalistic activities of the project, therefore,
seemed to be little more than a convenient cover for Scaife's covert support
of Hale.

I had gotten a taste of the seamy, vengeful side of anti-Clintonism, and the
self-interested motives of many of Clinton's accusers, in my experience with
the Arkansas troopers, and I would see all that and more in several trips to
Arkansas in 1994 and 1995 under the auspices of the Arkansas Project, sometimes to check out tips about the Clintons' past generated by Henderson and
Boynton, and sometimes to check on my own leads. The anti-Clinton scandal machine became quite a profitable business for right-wing publishers,
pundits, and radio talk show hosts, and we at the *Spectator* were pioneers. In
the three years that the $2.5 million Arkansas Project ran, Henderson paid
himself $477,000 and Boynton made $577,000. Of course, my own greed
motivated me to play along with these Keystone Kops, who knew nothing
about journalism. Yet I took down their preposterous accusations that the
Clintons were involved in everything from sex orgies to drug-running to
murder as if they were legitimate, and did what I could to check them out.
This was part of my job at the *Spectator*, and I was being paid handsomely
for it. All of us at the *Spectator* were in it together at one level or another,
scamming Scaife.

On the ground in Arkansas, I soon learned that the Arkansas Project had
several odd features, including a ramshackle ranch house in West Little Rock,
which Henderson and Boynton referred to as "the safe house," where they

often met with David Hale. The house was rented from a man named Parker Dozhier, a friend of Stephen Boynton's who was hired as the project's "eyes and ears" in Arkansas. A rough-edged fur trapper in his mid-fifties who ran a bait-and-tackle shop on Lake Catherine in Hot Springs, Dozhier seemed an unlikely informant. His main preoccupation was fighting the Arkansas Game and Fish Commission's regulations; the dusty little bait shop also was littered with gun magazines like *Soldier of Fortune* and assorted right-wing militia literature. One hot summer night in mid-1994, Dozhier took me out by the lake and tried to teach me to shoot a semiautomatic pistol so that I could defend myself in the wilds of Arkansas. Other than knowing Boynton, Dozhier's credential for the *Spectator* job appeared to be his rabid hatred of Bill Clinton, the same sort of vein-popping rage I had seen in Cliff Jackson, only cruder and with a rather large dose of hypocrisy thrown in. At our first meeting, Dozhier bragged through his broken teeth of what he claimed was his own illicit affair with Gennifer Flowers. "I bedded Gennifer just like Billy," he growled.

Hanging out at Dozhier's bait shop provided me with a bird's-eye view of the underbelly of Arkansas's political culture, a hotbed of conspiracy and lunacy. I was beginning to understand that making up stories about one's political enemies—the more lascivious and bizarre the better—was something of a political tradition in the state. Clinton had been dogged with apocryphal stories since he first ran for public office in 1974, when he was widely said to have been the longhaired, bearded mystery protester who displayed an anti-Nixon poster during the president's 1969 visit to Fayetteville for an Arkansas football game, even though Clinton was in England when the incident occurred. When Clinton became president, this sort of storytelling was exported out of the state by political foes of the president, some of whom deluded themselves into thinking that the malicious stories were true; others didn't care if they were true or not, so long as they could be floated to injure Clinton.

Many mornings, Dozhier sent a fax into the *Spectator*'s office with the latest anti-Clinton gossip, gleaned from his telephone conversations with buddies around the state, people like Cliff Jackson, David Hale, and, most frequently, the former state supreme court justice Jim Johnson, the granddaddy of Arkansas Clinton-haters. Justice Jim, as he was known, hated Clinton, whose first few jobs in politics were in campaigns opposing Johnson, for Clinton's progressive record on race relations. In other words, the culture war being prosecuted by conservative leaders in Washington had an analogue in Clinton's home state.

A former state director of the White Citizens Council of Arkansas, as a state senator Johnson had called for the resistance of desegregation orders for the Arkansas schools by citing the precedent of the Confederate challenge to federal law. He ran failed races for governor and senator in the mid-1960s, declaring integration to be a worse crime than rape or murder, calling his critics "nigger lovers," and spreading false stories that an opponent committed sodomy with black men. Thirty years later, this tradition of sexual McCarthyism was still alive and well in Parker Dozhier's bait shop, and I wasn't the only visitor who soaked it all up. Micah Morrison, who had been hired by the conservative *Wall Street Journal* editorial page to write about Clinton scandals, was a guest of Dozhier's, and Dozhier bragged that even journalist Michael Kelly, when he was working on a Clinton profile for the *New York Times Magazine*, had stopped by. (Kelly would later become one of the most savage Clinton critics in the mainstream press.)

I also learned how, for all their seeming eccentricity on the right-wing fringe, the Arkansas Project gang—whether angry, greedy, or, as it sometimes seemed to me even then, emotionally disturbed—was able to move the debate in Washington. The project had a direct pipeline to Republican aides on Capitol Hill who were investigating the Whitewater affair and thus driving coverage of it in the press. Foremost among these aides was a man named David Bossie, whom I had known when he worked for Floyd Brown's anti-Clinton operation, Citizens United. Floyd Brown, a rabble-rousing former operative for Senator Bob Dole who specialized in smearing liberal political figures, had orchestrated the Bush campaign's Willie Horton attack on Michael Dukakis and the Bush administration's assault on Democratic senators who opposed Clarence Thomas. In the 1992 campaign, Brown began publishing a newsletter called *ClintonWatch* that warned against Clinton's "radical socialist agenda." In one missive, Brown wrote, "Bill Clinton's America sees no difference between families of 'homosexual lovers,' and the traditional, monogamous, faithful family. In addition, Mr. Clinton has completely surrendered to the pro-abortion feminists who dominate the Democratic Party." Brown's organization also set up a 900 number so callers could hear Gennifer Flowers's doctored tapes of her telephone conversations with Clinton for a fee. In the wake of my trooper story, Brown began to issue special "Fornigate" reports on Clinton.

David Bossie, who, like Grover Norquist and Ralph Reed, had been a former College Republicans activist, served as Brown's point man on Whitewater, where he was stunningly effective marketing Whitewater stories to major media. He also investigated Clinton's personal life, in one case harassing the family of a deceased woman who had been a law student of Clinton's when he taught at the University of Arkansas in the 1970s. Bossie was chasing a rumor that the woman, who was eight months pregnant at her death, had committed suicide while carrying Clinton's baby. The woman's distraught family was able to persuade Bossie to go away; the rumor was groundless. When Clinton was elected, Bossie, who had developed close ties both to Newt Gingrich and to GOP Congressman Dan Burton of Indiana, the leader of the anti-Clinton investigations in the House, landed a series of powerful posts as a Republican Congressional investigator. Bossie was in regular contact with Arkansas Project figures like Justice Jim Johnson and Parker Dozhier; he also ferried David Hale around Washington in 1993 as Hale shopped around his unverified Whitewater accusations against Clinton. In 1998 Bossie, under pressure, would resign his post with Burton after it was discovered that he had overseen the editing of tapes of former Clinton Justice official Webster Hubbell's jailhouse conversations while he was serving a sentence for tax evasion in a way that appeared to implicate Hillary Clinton in a criminal cover-up in Whitewater. The Burton committee had taken out portions of the conversations demonstrating that Hillary Clinton wasn't involved at all. The misleading tapes were released by Bossie to the press, which trumpeted the false allegations widely.

Bossie was a gruff, beefy young man who seemed ill at ease in the Capitol Hill uniform of oxford shirts and red ties. A lonely guy who seemed to have nothing in his life but trashing the Clintons, he lived in a suburban firehouse where he was a volunteer. My contacts with Bossie showed me that it was

not only in Arkansas, but also in Washington, where my Republican comrades knew no bounds in pursuing Clinton. An unremitting viciousness had
gripped the lot of them. While working as a Whitewater adviser to the far-
right senator Lauch Faircloth of North Carolina, Bossie schemed to win control of the investigation from a fellow Republican investigator. One
morning, Bossie called me at home and asked me if I could help him find
the information he needed to blackmail his nemesis, who was trying to run
the inquiry with a degree of professionalism and fairness, into being tougher
on the Clintons.

I knew this fellow fairly well as both a source and a friendly acquaintance. I had first met him at dinners hosted by his close friend Ann Coulter
in New York in the early 1990s. Like Coulter, he was another member of
the cabal of Federalist lawyers who had embraced me after the Anita Hill
destruction job. At the Coulter dinners, which were attended only by other
trusted members of the movement like George Conway, he spoke openly
of a problem he had in his past. He said he had been implicated in a sex
scandal in his undergraduate days that resulted in disciplinary action
against him.

The committee staffer aspired to move up in the movement, hoping
someday to be appointed to a Senate confirmable post, and he lived in fear
that his past would come back to haunt him. With Coulter's help, I led discussions on how he could cover up his past in anticipation of his being
asked about it under oath. We ran an assessment of who knew of his exact
role and whether any of them might rat him out. Coulter and I then suggested various weasel words by which he could minimize his role if it ever
came out.

Yet when Bossie called looking for the details of the damaging incident,
I quickly obliged, calling Coulter for help. When I told Coulter what
Bossie wanted and why he wanted it, Coulter immediately spat out the
specifics of the event and the time it had occurred, and told me that the
scandal had been covered by the student newspaper, which kept a morgue
file. I called Bossie back, and he soon reported to me that he had located
the relevant articles. Though I had always enjoyed the company of the

committee staffer, and considered him a friend, in that moment with Bossie, he was expendable to the aims of the movement. His close friend Coulter betrayed him just as I had.

After hanging up with Bossie and reflecting on the swift chain of events, I could see that he was engaged in blackmail. I could see that Coulter had sold out her friend. I don't think I ever spoke to Bossie again, despite his possible usefulness to me as a source. And my relationship with Coulter was irreparably hurt. But I was able to block out my complicity in the incident.

Through Justice Jim and Parker Dozhier, the *Spectator* came to hire a private investigator named Rex Armistead, who was paid $350,000 to work with Arkansas Project reporters. Armistead was a former chief investigator for the Mississippi Highway Patrol now in business as a private detective. As a Mississippi state police officer, Armistead had been a leader of white resistance to the civil rights movement, and as a private investigator, he had been linked to a covert sting operation to falsely implicate a Democratic candidate for Mississippi governor as a homosexual. In the fall of 1994, with the hotly contested congressional elections only weeks away, Bob Tyrrell took me to Miami to meet with Armistead. A man of about sixty, tall, burly, and packing heat, Armistead had us to his bleak suite at a hotel near the airport to brief us on the death of Vincent Foster, which he claimed was an assassination ordered by the Clintons. As I listened to Armistead talk in menacing tones about missing fingerprints on Foster's gun, and how no bullet was ever found, I could see that the *Spectator* was pouring money down a rat hole.

Armistead's "leads" had been gleaned from the work of a reporter named Christopher Ruddy, who had written a series of dubious investigative articles on Foster's death for a Pittsburgh newspaper, the *Tribune-Review*, which was owned by Scaife. In this circular fashion, disinformation emanated from one Scaife-paid source to another. Like me, and dozens of other conservatives aspiring to get into the Clinton investigations racket, Ruddy, wearing a trench coat and a pencil-thin mustache, fancied himself a skilled gumshoe, though he seemed more like Inspector Clouseau.

Scaife hired Ruddy after he left Rupert Murdoch's *New York Post* where he had reported on the Foster case. Of course, as O. J. Simpson's lawyers could attest, there are anomalies at every death scene, which Ruddy used to suggest foul play when there was never any remotely credible evidence of it. Despite—or was it because of?—the fact that a *60 Minutes* investigation showed Ruddy to be a fraud who made up evidence, he became a cult hero on the right, publishing a book, brought out by Free Press, in which he detailed his theories about Foster's death. This was the sort of crackpot stuff that Ruddy found an eager audience for on the right: "I declare to you that America may face a greater crisis now under Clinton than it did during the bloody civil war under Lincoln," Ruddy wrote in a piece of direct mail promoting his work. "That's why I tremble for the future of our country. . . . This man and his wife have so abused the power and trust of their office that they threaten our way of life. . . . Bill and Hillary are ten times worse than Nixon ever thought of being. Consider what a Nixon confidant, who frequently spoke to Nixon during his presidency and until his death, confided in me why Clinton won't resign or be removed from office. He told me there are just too many dead bodies linked to Clinton."

Ruddy's revelations reverberated through the right wing, giving the erroneous impression that there was more than one source for it all. Ruddy's work was publicized through yet another Scaife-funded entity called the Western Journalism Center, which placed full-page ads in the *Washington Times* reprinting his articles from the *Tribune-Review* so that they would be seen by movement operatives in the capital. Soon enough, Pat Robertson's *700 Club* dedicated a broadcast to the question "Suicide or Murder?" And in February 1994, Martin Anderson, the respected former senior economics aide to President Reagan at the right-wing Hoover Institution at Stanford University, wrote an op-ed in the *Washington Times* calling the "murder of a senior White House adviser monstrous to contemplate." (By now, Wesley Pruden, an Arkansan whose father was connected, along with Justice Jim Johnson, to the White Citizens Council of Arkansas, edited the *Times*.)

When Ruddy claimed that Foster had met his death in a "hideaway apartment" in suburban Virginia owned by Hillary Rodham Clinton, the false story was reprinted by James Davidson, president of the Scaife-backed

National Taxpayers Union, in one of his newsletters. Davidson, author of the book *The Story of a One-Term President*, which forecast a "bloodbath in U.S. stocks and bonds" under Clinton, wrote that the Foster death was an "extra-judicial execution" and a sign of "incipient fascism." Next, David Smick, a former aide to Jack Kemp, noted the rumor's circulation on Capitol Hill in his investment newsletter. Rush Limbaugh cited the Smick report on his radio show and stated, "The Vince Foster suicide was not a suicide," causing the stock market to plunge. Though in an appearance on ABC, Limbaugh claimed, "Never have I suggested that this [Foster's death] was murder," Roger Ailes, the hardball political strategist for the Bush campaign in 1988, who went on to be a Limbaugh producer before being named to run Rupert Murdoch's Fox News Channel, appeared on the Don Imus radio show to promote Limbaugh's reports of a "suicide cover-up, possibly murder." Ailes stated, "The guy who's been doing an excellent job for the *New York Post* [Ruddy] . . . for the first time on the Rush Limbaugh show said that . . . he did not believe it was suicide. . . . Now, I don't have any evidence . . . These people are very good at hiding or destroying evidence."

The Foster case caused dissension within the *Spectator*. After sitting through the Armistead briefing, dutifully taking notes, I returned to Washington, where I warned Wlady that if the *Spectator* indulged the Foster conspiratorialists, the magazine's credibility would be damaged. In voicing opposition to the Arkansas Project with the utmost conviction, and a good deal of indignation, I was not yet questioning the goal of the anti-Clinton enterprise, but rather trying to shield it from charlatans like Rex Armistead and Chris Ruddy. If I was going to be a paid assassin, I wanted to hit my targets. Within the limits of my own mind-set then, I had written Troopergate with a concern for factual accuracy, and, though it was inadvertent, my reporting had prompted Paula Jones to sue the president for sexual harassment. I now had a stake in the *Spectator*'s reputation, a franchise to protect. These morons threatened to screw everything up.

Wlady agreed with me. In one internal memo on the progress of the Arkansas Project in 1997, Wlady wrote, "There always seemed to be lots of hush-hush and heavy breathing, but it never amounted to anything concrete enough for a story." Bob was adamant in ordering up an article, not necessarily because he found Armistead more impressive than I had, but because the Foster case was a special obsession of Scaife's, and when Scaife said jump, Bob asked how high. When I declined to write the piece, Bob turned to British journalist Ambrose Evans-Pritchard, who had reported from Central America in the 1980s for the *Economist* and the *Daily Telegraph* in London. When Clinton won the presidency, Ambrose was named Washington bureau chief of the *Sunday Telegraph* of London, which is owned by conservative Canadian-born media mogul Conrad Black. Ambrose, whose work in the British press was frequently cited in conservative U.S. media outlets like the *New York Post* and broadcast widely on U.S. talk radio, described himself as a "Tory hooligan" engaged in "insurgent warfare" against the Clintons.

Soon after Foster's death, Ambrose began traveling to Arkansas to look into the Clintons' past on what he called an "anthropological expedition." Of all the "Clinton crazies" I would meet—the term was one that Ambrose and many others openly embraced—Ambrose was the least cynical of the bunch, and perhaps the craziest. He seemed to truly credit the seamy gossip that I now knew anyone could hear if they poked around Arkansas for a few days. Ambrose had no capacity to judge the credibility of sources; to him, the word of a drug-addled ex-con was as good as anybody else's, or perhaps better. I began to think that Ambrose had spent too much time in Nicaragua, a Third World dictatorship where truth was more easily gleaned from the streets than from the government or its agents. He distrusted anyone—right, left, it didn't matter—who was tied into the American political system, which he viewed as thoroughly corrupt. Ambrose's work would condition the movement to believe that Arkansas was a mirror image of Sandinista Nicaragua, a corrupt, backward, one-party state.

One night Bob and I visited Ambrose at his home in the Maryland suburbs to hear about his latest scoop. This one involved Clinton's alleged abuse of the penal system in Arkansas, where Ambrose said he compelled prison wardens to make inmates available to him for his sexual gratification. When we arrived at the house, a sparsely furnished suburban rambler, Ambrose drew the shades and asked if we had been followed. The CIA, he was sure, had tapped his phones, and he believed his house was under surveillance by the Clintons' "death squads." A few minutes into the conversation, it was apparent to me that poor Ambrose had lost his grip on reality.

I'm not sure what Bob was thinking—perhaps he was trying to pump up *Spectator* circulation, perhaps he simply wanted to please his paymaster Scaife—but soon thereafter Ambrose was assigned to write an article on Foster's murder for the magazine, in which he embraced the notion of a grand conspiracy by the U.S. government to cover up the truth about Foster's death. The smoking gun, he claimed, was the case of Patrick Knowlton, a passerby who had been in Fort Marcy Park on the day that Foster's dead body was discovered. Though Foster had driven a gray Honda, Knowlton remembered seeing a brown Honda parked near the death scene. Ambrose took Knowlton's memory and trumpeted it as proof that Foster had not driven himself to the park where his body was found. Knowlton turned out to be a self-discrediting witness: Before he was to appear before a Washington grand jury investigating the Foster death, he made the accusation that he was being harassed by a team of thirty FBI agents, who were tailing him through the streets of Washington to intimidate him so that he wouldn't testify. As Ambrose told the story in his book *The Secret Life of Bill Clinton: The Unreported Stories*, which was decked out with extensive footnotes and elaborate "documentation," Ambrose patrolled the streets of Foggy Bottom, the Washington neighborhood where Knowlton lived, armed with an umbrella, to "protect" Knowlton from the "street fascism" of the FBI. (Among Ambrose's admirers was conservative columnist Robert Novak, who gave his book a rave review.)

Wlady and I, and publisher Ron Burr, opposed the Evans-Pritchard article, "The Death That Won't Die," yet Bob was determined to force it into the magazine over everyone's objections. Ron, who confided that he had been able to manage Bob's erratic and at times abusive behavior for years while shielding the magazine from any damage, could see that the piece was so shoddy it had to be stopped. While Wlady retreated behind his closed office door, Ron encouraged me to sound out board members and other *Spectator* advisers for help.

My first call was to Ted Olson, who, beginning in 1994, had close ties to the *Spectator* and was also a friend of mine. Ted, who served in the Reagan

Justice Department and then became President Reagan's private lawyer at the prestigious firm of Gibson, Dunn & Crutcher, where he served as managing partner, had always seemed the model of a sober, careful lawyer with impeccable judgment. To be sure, he fought hard for the conservative agenda. He was involved in the Jones case as one of the appellate super-lawyers George Conway had asked to conduct the moot court for the Jones lawyers before their Supreme Court appearance. But surely, I thought, a stickler for the facts like Ted would know better than to publish Ambrose. At dinner meetings where the Arkansas Project matters were discussed, Ted, whose firm was paid from Arkansas Project funds, gave reasonable advice about what criminal laws or ethics violations might be implicated in our anti-Clinton investigations. In addition, I knew that Ted, the chairman of the Washington chapter of the Federalist Society, was one of Ken Starr's best friends and former law partners. Starr's conservative deputies had been quite critical in private conversations with me of the right-wingers who were promoting Foster conspiracy theories. They were wasting a lot of time and money trying to disprove them, as Robert Fiske had already done.

After I faxed the piece to his law office, Ted, an affable man in his late fifties with thick white-blond hair and aviator-style glasses, told me bluntly, in a tone of voice that I had never heard him use before, that while he believed, as Starr apparently did, that Foster had committed suicide, raising questions about the death was a way of turning up the heat on the administration until another scandal was shaken loose, which was the *Spectator*'s mission. The statement stunned me. Though I was all for harassing the administration, I was not ready to accept the reality that the *Spectator* was a propaganda organ. And I found Ted's advice that such trash ought to be published inconceivable for a blue-chip lawyer who represented major media conglomerates like the *Los Angeles Times*. This telephone call with Olson essentially ended my relationship with him.

I also had thought that Ted, of all people, would have been sensitive to the way Washington's permanent culture of investigation had allowed people to be tarred with unproven allegations. Not only had he represented former President Reagan in the Iran-contra affair, but Ted also had been the target of a costly four-year independent counsel investigation when he was a senior Justice Department official back in the mid-1980s. As the probe commenced, Ted stood accused of lying to Congress about the administration's anti-environmental policies. While concluding that Ted's testimony was "literally true" and bringing no criminal charges against him, the independent counsel report described Ted's testimony as "disingenuous and misleading." In the meantime, Ted brought suit to challenge the constitutionality of the independent counsel statute, which was upheld by the Supreme Court in *Morrison v. Olson*. Apparently, Ted drew a different lesson from the experience than I had thought he might have.

Like many conservatives of the age, Ted seemed more interested in partisan revenge than principle. My conversation with him crystallized so much of what was beginning to upset me about the Republican right in Washington. I had no doubt that countless conservatives outside the Beltway were people of decent will, and strong convictions, people who lived the values they preached, and probably believed the worthless reports they were reading in places like the *Spectator.* So, too, did eccentrics like Scaife and Evans-Pritchard. Yet the people I knew at the highest levels in Washington, the Ted Olsons of the world, understood that the Clintons, while they certainly weren't free of compromise, cronyism, and even an occasional whiff of sleaze, were no different from many other successful politicians at the top of a sleazy business. Canny lawyers, the Clintons played things too close to the line, and gave their critics too much ammunition, but they were not murderous thugs or felons or even ethical or moral abominations, and no one in Olson's set of canny conservative lawyers really thought they were. The problem for the Clintons was that they were successful—and far from perfect—*Democrats.* The Republican insiders, exaggerating every real flaw and exploiting every cockamamy angle they could find, were after one thing only: power for themselves and for the right-wing social and economic interests they represented.

Olson's connection to the *Spectator* and its Arkansas Project exemplified a curious but disturbingly widespread phenomenon of the Clinton wars: Here was a figure at the pinnacle of the Republican establishment, who had the respect of bar colleagues on both sides of the aisle, yet who also led a kind of double life as a consigliere to the Clinton-hating extreme right. No one outside the movement knew who Ted really was. I was so disappointed in Ted that I brought the matter up with his close friends, the Silbermans. Ricky told me she attributed Ted's uncharacteristic "recklessness" to the malign influence of his new young girlfriend, Barbara Bracher, a hotheaded lawyer working as an anti-Clinton investigator on a key House committee. Barbara Bracher had attended college in her native Houston before going to Hollywood, where she worked as an actor's assistant, en route to law school in New York. According to Ricky, Barbara arrived in Washington for an internship in the Bush administration's Office of Legal Counsel in 1989 with no special GOP political ties or conservative affiliations. Barbara, a voluble, shapely blond with fine features, had been married once before; she met her future beau, the twice-married Ted Olson, who was many years her senior, at a legal conference during her time in Washington. She returned to the city when she graduated from law school and soon moved to the head of the class within the conservative movement, in part on the strength of her budding relationship with Ted. During the Thomas confirmation hearing, she volunteered her services to the lawyers working for Senator Strom Thurmond in their effort to discredit Anita Hill and other witnesses. After stints in private practice and in the U.S. Attorney's office as a federal prosecutor, Ted helped her secure a post on Capitol Hill, where she tried to show her right-wing colleagues that she could be more flamboyantly extreme than them—the behavior of an insecure wannabe that I recognized well. Barbara also may have been overcompensating for a lack of talent, for in the years to come, when she became a source of mine on the Hill, she was frequently unable to explain basic facts of the cases on which she worked.

I understood Ricky's reservations about Barbara, whom Ted later married, after spending some time with her and an obstreperous band of her fellow GOP investigators from Capitol Hill. One night in the winter of 1995, as the scandal over the firing of workers in the White House travel office reached a crescendo on the Hill, I received a late night telephone call from one of Olson's colleagues on a House investigative committee, Barbara Comstock. Around the committee, the two Barbaras were known as "the Barbarellas," a reference to the 1968 movie starring Jane Fonda as a space-age vixen whose cosmic adventures take her to bizarre planets via rocket ship. Late-night calls from Barbara Comstock were not unusual. She often telephoned with the latest tidbit she had dug up in the thousands and thousands of pages of administration records she pored through frantically, as if she were looking for a winning lottery ticket she had somehow mislaid. A plain woman with tousled reddish brown hair, she once dropped by my house to watch the *rerun* of a dreadfully dull Whitewater hearing she had sat through all day. Comstock sat on the edge of her chair shaking, and screaming over and over again, "Liars!" As Comstock's leads failed to pan out and she was unable to catch anyone in a lie, the Republican aide confided that the Clinton scandals were driving her to distraction, to the unfortunate point that she was ignoring the needs of her own family. A very smart lawyer by training and the main breadwinner for her charismatic, happy-go-lucky husband and kids, Comstock remarked that maybe she couldn't get Hillary's sins off her brain "because Hillary reminds me of me. I am Hillary." In this admission a vivid illustration of a much wider "Hillary" phenomenon can be seen. Comstock knew nothing about Hillary Clinton. Comstock's "Hillary" was imaginary, a construction composed entirely of the negative points in her own life.

Comstock invited me to go along on an expedition to the Washington home of senior White House aide David Watkins, the central figure in the travel scandal Olson and Comstock were probing. A short time later, Republican lawyers Comstock, Olson, and other congressional investigators, including David Bossie, and Whitewater investigator Christopher Bartomolucci, pulled up outside my house in an SUV. Though I wasn't sure what the group hoped to accomplish—they were visibly frustrated with their inability so far to incriminate Watkins—I went along for the ride. Olson explained that Congressman Sonny Bono had cleared us into the private, gated community where both Bono and Watkins lived, in the northwest section of Georgetown. When we arrived at our destination, Olson giddily leapt from the truck, trespassed onto Watkins's property, and hopped down a steep cliff that abutted his home. Barbara peered into Watkins's windows, where she observed him . . . watching television. No crime there.

As it turned out, Ted Olson had been a poor choice if I was looking for someone to rescue our sinking ship. Though I didn't know all the details at the time, at a meeting with Arkansas Project representatives in his

Washington law office in early 1994, Olson had agreed to provide legal representation to the anti-Clinton witness David Hale. Hale ran up $140,000
in legal fees with Olson, whose firm later wrote off the debt. According to
a later report in the *Los Angeles Times*, Arkansas Project records suggested
that the *Spectator* had paid some of Hale's bills. Moreover, Ted was the secret
author of a series the *Spectator* began running in the front of the magazine,
under the byline of a fictitious law firm called Solitary, Nasty, Brutish &
Short. In what amounted to a smear campaign by a member of the bar to
tar innocent people, the series accused the Clintons and their "cronies" of
violating various criminal laws and skewered Attorney General Janet Reno
for failing to investigate Foster's "mysterious death." In one article, Olson tal-
lied unsubstantiated reports against the Clintons and concluded that Bill
Clinton might face 178 years in jail and that Hillary Clinton had a "total
potential criminal liability" of 47 years behind bars. "Comparing Clinton to
Nixon," Ted wrote in one of his anonymous missives, "may underestimate
the scope of the administration's problems . . . [when] the appropriate
comparison for Bill Clinton may well turn out to be Don Corleone."

Another chunk of Arkansas Project cash was spent trying to prove that
Clinton, as governor of Arkansas, allowed the CIA to run guns and drugs
through Arkansas's Mena airstrip as part of its Nicaraguan contra resupply
efforts. In some variations of the story, Clinton was said to have been cut in
on a share of the profits from the cocaine smuggling and even to have
become a coke addict himself. Though cocaine apparently did come into
Mena in the early 1980s through a notorious drug smuggler named Barry
Seal, who later became a government informant, there was no proof of CIA
complicity in Seal's operation, much less knowledge of it by Bill Clinton.
Two federal grand juries investigated the goings-on at Mena in the 1980s
without returning indictments.

No one at the *Spectator* took the Mena stories seriously, if only because
as conservatives we were unwilling to accept the notion that Ronald Reagan,
Oliver North, and the CIA were complicit in a cocaine smuggling ring.
When the Mena allegations first surfaced in the *Nation* in the 1980s, con-

servatives were quick to throw cold water on them. Bob Tyrrell, however, had no regard for intellectual consistency. Following the worldwide attention Troopergate garnered, Bob decided he would get into the anti-Clinton reporting game as well, and Mena became his lodestar. Wlady told me Bob was jealous of the attention Troopergate had brought me. Also, I suppose, after the Evans-Pritchard fiasco, Bob began to feel pressure to nail Clinton, to show that the millions Scaife was pouring into the Arkansas Project were not being frittered away. Bob was a talented memoirist, whose books *The Liberal Crack-Up* in the late 1970s and *The Conservative Crack-Up* in the early 1990s were politically prescient, beautifully written, and highly entertaining. The trouble was that he had never done an investigative article and had contempt for the fact-gathering techniques of journalists. Bob didn't care about getting things right; he wanted to make a splash. Like Ambrose's, Bob's was another career ruined by a fixation on ruining the Clintons.

Bob's Mena fetish grew out of a piece published in the *Spectator* in the spring of 1994 by writer Danny Wattenberg called "Love and Death in Arkansas." Wattenberg had interviewed yet another Arkansas trooper, L. D. Brown, who decided to get in on the action in the wake of the publicity that surrounded Troopergate, to tell even more graphic tales of Clinton's alleged sexual escapades. Better-educated, more charming, more clever—and, as it turned out, more imaginative—than the troopers I had interviewed, L. D. claimed to have set up "more than 100" sexual liaisons for Clinton while serving on his security detail—for less than two years!—in the mid-1980s. L. D. also told Wattenberg that married troopers such as himself had used their positions on the governor's detail to procure women for themselves, providing Danny's story with an even tawdrier backdrop than mine. When the troopers talked about "Bill," it turned out they were talking about themselves.

After the Wattenberg piece appeared, Bob struck up his own relationship with Brown, flying him to D.C. and wining and dining him on Scaife's dime. Brown's visits often included a private dinner at Bob's home, just outside the Beltway in a well-manicured Republican suburb of Virginia. I usually was summoned to join Bob and L. D., often David Henderson, and occasionally the Olsons, for dinner. Bob's house was newly built, on a sizable piece of property at the far end of a cul-de-sac. Though part of the house looked like a done-up English gentleman's club, other rooms were dull and spartan, and I surmised that Bob's wife had left him before the interiors were finished. A gregarious woman of what I took to be Caribbean descent served a bland Irish meal—or was it supposed to be English?—of undressed salad, meat, and boiled potatoes. Alcohol flowed freely as Bob held court, playing the part of raconteur and wit as he told stories of cavorting through Rome or London with this or that notable European writer or intellectual—Italian writer Luigi Barzini, Sir Peregrine Worsthorne, Kenneth Minogue, and the like. As Bob imbibed, the pitch of his voice got increasingly high and shrill, and the subject inevitably turned to darkest Arkansas.

As Bob fished for revelations, L. D., an accomplished storyteller with all the brazenness of a professional con man, was only too happy to supply them. Bob didn't seem fazed by L. D.'s prior assurances to Wattenberg, under tenacious grilling, that he had told him everything he knew about the Clintons of any conceivable news value. In no time at all, L. D. had sold Bob on a convoluted tale designed to implicate Clinton in drug running at Mena. According to L. D., who was a former narcotics officer, while he worked on Clinton's security detail, he also moonlighted as a CIA contract employee, with Clinton's encouragement. While working for the CIA, L. D. claimed that he had helped Barry Seal move M-16 rifles into Central America for the contras and smuggle into Mena several duffel bags filled with cocaine. Clinton had knowledge of Seal's illicit activities, L. D. alleged, and he also claimed to know of a CIA plot to assassinate Clinton because Clinton could implicate the agency in wrongdoing.

But L. D. couldn't document that he was ever a CIA employee, and his "evidence" of Clinton's knowledge of drug running at Mena consisted of innocuous comments allegedly made by Clinton that L. D. presented as incriminating. For example, L. D. described the following ambiguous scene on returning from one of his supposed trips with Seal: "Clinton asks me, 'Well, are you having fun yet?' I said, 'Yeah, but this is some scary stuff.' He said, 'Oh, you can handle it' and pats me on the back. He knew before I even said anything. He knew."

Bob wrote up his interviews with L. D. and submitted the manuscript to

Wlady for publication. Especially when it came to the Clintons, Wlady's own journalistic standards were weak, but the piece wasn't publishable by any standard. Even if L. D. were taken at his word, Bob hadn't been able to construct a comprehensible narrative out of the tale, much less undertake the most elementary steps to corroborate it. The story made no sense; when I read it, I thought Bob had dropped acid before sitting down at the computer.

Bob's insistence that the Mena piece run sparked an editorial crisis. The deputy managing editor, Christopher Caldwell, who was married to Bob Novak's daughter Zelda, quit rather than edit the piece and quickly found another job in the movement at the *Weekly Standard*. Wlady—who had been told by Bob that all corroborating sources for the piece were dead—made it known that he, too, was calling around town trying to find another job. Also around this time, Danny Wattenberg decamped, after Bob refused to take him off the Clinton scandal beat and allow him to write on other subjects. One experience with L. D. had been enough to retire Danny.

Late one night, Bob ordered me to the office to help edit the article. Bob could be irrational and belligerent when he was hitting the Scotch, as he surely was that night, and I always dealt with Bob in classic enabling behavior. I tried to avoid conflict and hoped that the terrible moments would pass before any real harm was done. And, frankly, I didn't have the courage of Chris or Danny; I wanted to protect my job at the magazine, a lucrative gig the likes of which I would probably never see again. This time, my strategy of humoring Bob failed disastrously.

When I arrived at the magazine, I found John Corry, the former *New York Times* correspondent who wrote a monthly column of media criticism for the *Spectator*, slumped over a desk, chain-smoking, already at work on the article. I could see why my services were needed. A distinguished reporter and cultural critic who had left the *Times* for what he said were political reasons, Corry arrived in Washington down on his luck, and wound up at the *Spectator*. He didn't know the first thing about Arkansas, couldn't operate a computer, and certainly couldn't make heads or tails of Bob's manuscript. He looked like a broken man. Sad it was, that John's career had come to this, ordered to put in print an investigative news article that he and I both knew had no merit. Like Wlady, who had trouble finding another job and had a family at home to support, we had made our peace with the devil. We did the best we could with it, set it in type, and went out and got drunk.

The next day, I felt sick, and not only because I had a nasty hangover. Worried about my complicity in the Mena travesty, I decided to get to the bottom of a rumor that had been swirling through the magazine during the course of Bob's courtship of L. D. Brown. L. D., it was whispered, was being paid money to talk to Bob. If this were true, and I had helped put Bob's article into print over Wlady's and also Ron Burr's objections, the whole magazine could go up in flames, and I would be partly to blame. But in a departure from my usual way of handling Bob, I called him into my *Spectator* office, closed the door, and asked him point blank if L. D. was getting money from the *Spectator* or the Arkansas Project. When Bob told me no, he shot me a look like a kid caught with his hand in a cookie jar. At the time, I had no information to the contrary and I figured as long as Bob had denied paying off L. D., my ass was covered. Of course, my fears were baseless, since journalistic ethics meant little to the right wing. I later found out that L. D. had received about $15,000 cash in compensation and expenses from Arkansas Project funds.

The publication of Bob's Mena article, "The Arkansas Drug Shuttle," destroyed whatever credibility the magazine had, even in our own eyes. Some months later, CNN authoritatively debunked the piece, showing that Barry Seal had spent the day that L. D. claimed to be flying with Seal to Central America in Baton Rouge, Louisiana, making a documentary film of his life as a government informant. For all his cleverness, L. D. had made a fatal mistake that Larry Patterson and Roger Perry avoided: He supplied Bob with specific dates and times that could be checked. The article was a fantasia.

CHAPTER ELEVEN

THE BEST AND THE RIGHTIST

The crowd was cheering so loudly I thought the windows of my town house would blow out. It was November 4, 1994, and CNN had just announced the defeat of liberal icon Mario Cuomo in his bid to be reelected governor of New York. Cuomo kayoed, by a nobody named Pataki! The Election Night party, cohosted by soon-to-be conservative pundit Laura Ingraham, a former Supreme Court clerk to Clarence Thomas, was planned in my living room just one day before the vote, as a historic Republican victory was in sight. We didn't really think it would happen, this delicious humiliation of the Clintons, but on the chance that it somehow might, it would have been a terrible night not to have a party. My town house—some friends called it the house that Anita Hill built—seemed the logical place to convene.

I had a tent pitched in the courtyard, a big white tent, and more than two hundred people, a garrulous mob wearing "Newt" caps and waving cigars, streamed in. Not the marquee politicians—the man of the hour, the new Speaker of the House, Newt Gingrich, was home in Marietta, Georgia—but the federal judges, Capitol Hill aides, Federalist Society lawyers, talking heads, writers, and editors who made the city tick: the Silbermans, the Olsons, Bob Bork Jr. and his wife, Republican lawyers Boyden Gray, Richard Leon, Paul Capuccio, and Michael Carvin, and columnists Mona Charen, Paul Gigot, and Michael Barone. We learned before CNN flashed the news that the Republicans had taken the House for the first time in fifty years in a phone call from a top GOP aide monitoring the vote in the Capitol. The whoop that went up, a guttural whoop, not a whoop of joy, or hope, but of revenge and retribution, caused a neighbor to come by and complain. That was Georgetown for you, filled with Dems. Screw 'em, I thought, this was our night.

Though most of us had come to Washington and cut our political teeth during the Reagan revolution, Gingrich, with his ideological fanaticism and brutal political style, was really the dominant figure in our lives. We had worked our tails off to make tonight happen, to foment our own revolution, and we were getting pretty sloshed in celebration of our feat. Although we were advancing the rightest of right-wing agendas for the country, in private our values weren't in sync with the Bible Belt fundamentalism that dictated official party ideology. As the evening wound down, I escorted one prominent conservative magazine columnist out the front door after he pushed me onto a bed, into a pile of coats, and tried to stick his tongue down my throat.

When the cigar smoke cleared the next morning, the scope of the GOP victory began to sink in. Republicans gained fifty-two seats in the House, the largest midterm gain posted by either party in fifty years. The first two years of Clinton's administration had provoked the Republican base to rally in opposition. Clinton's attempt to allow gays to serve openly in the military, his plans for universal health care, his 1993 tax hike, and a ban on assault weapons as part of a crime bill energized the key antigovernment constituencies of the Republican Party, including Ralph Reed's religious conservatives, small businessmen, Grover Norquist's antitax activists, and gun owners. In an attempt to present a unified agenda and nationalize the election, Newt Gingrich designed a Contract with America, the first high-level effort to galvanize the party around a set of issues since the collapse of the Reagan anti-Communist coalition, and the party's loss of identity during the presidency of George Bush. In signing the contract, Republican candidates committed themselves to a balanced budget, term limits to end entrenched incumbency, a line-item veto, and sweeping welfare and regulatory reform. The ambitious agenda was honed specifically with the 20 million voters who bolted both major parties and backed Ross Perot's independent bid for the presidency in 1992 in mind. Gingrich adviser Frank Luntz, a doughy, red-haired pollster who had worked for Pat Buchanan's insurgent campaign in 1992, convened focus groups to test the specific language of the contract to maximize its appeal to these swing voters.

Conspicuously absent from the contract was any mention of the social issues that had been highlighted so prominently by people like Pat Buchanan, Rush Limbaugh, and Newt Gingrich himself. Planks on abortion and school prayer were left on the cutting-room floor. According to Ralph Reed in his book *Active Faith*, the Christian Coalition, in negotiations with party leaders, accepted Gingrich's argument that including the social issues would allow the media and the Democrats to tag the contract as a radical right-wing document. The coalition agreed to pour money into the Republican effort to take back the House with an unspoken understanding that if Gingrich became Speaker, they would be repaid for their efforts. The Republican stealth strategy was consistent with a plan Ralph Reed had outlined in 1993, in an article in the Heritage Foundation's *Policy Review*, to mainstream the Christian Coalition and neutralize the efforts of its opponents to paint it as socially intolerant. "The pro-family movement's political rhetoric has often been policy thin and value-laden, leaving many voters tuned out," Reed had written. "The pro-family movement must speak to concerns of average voters in areas of taxes, crime, government, waste, health care, and financial security." Had there been any question about Newt's true commitments, a little-noted speech he delivered at the Heritage Foundation a few weeks before the November election provided ample clarification. "I do have a vision of an America in which a belief in the Creator is once again at the center of defining being an American," Gingrich declared. "That is a radically different vision of America than the secular, anti-religious view of the left."

Laudable though the effort to inspire voters to coalesce around conservative issues was, the election was being fought on a second front, in an unprecedented campaign of personal vilification of the Clintons. As Dan Balz and Ronald Brownstein reported in their book *Storming the Gates: Protest Politics and the Republican Revival*, while Newt and the GOP leadership promoted the contract, the Republican National Committee's statewide ads and direct-mail fund-raising campaigns were "red meat . . . one hundred percent anti-Clinton." Among the RNC's messages, the pair reported, was this statement: "In Bill Clinton's eyes, if you worked hard and succeeded—you're the enemy." The Clintons were attacked in GOP ads for

supporting "far-out social concepts of diversity, multiculturalism, and political correctness."

Meanwhile, outraged Republican demonstrators burned Hillary Clinton
in effigy, protesting her plans to reform health care, and Rush Limbaugh discussed on the air reports filed by Ambrose Evans-Pritchard in the *Sunday
Telegraph* charging Clinton with cocaine use. Some journalists investigating
Whitewater, Limbaugh claimed, "have died." During the congressional
debate on the assault weapons ban in August 1994, Representative Dick
Armey remarked pointedly of Clinton, "Your president is just not important
to us." Senator Jesse Helms warned that Clinton might be shot if he visited
a military base in North Carolina. At a meeting with corporate lobbyists
before the election, Gingrich described Clinton as "the enemy of normal
Americans," and vowed to shut down the Clinton presidency by launching
a series of ethics investigations once the GOP took power. Nationwide polls
taken before the election showed that one in five Americans, conditioned
by this barrage of propaganda, said they "hated" Clinton.

Exit polling and postelection analysis found that the Republicans had ridden waves of anti-Washington, anti-Clinton sentiment to power. Beyond
that, there was little consensus on a direction for the country, but the
Gingrich revolutionaries read the election results as a sweeping mandate for
radical conservatism, slashing government spending, eliminating federal
departments, and enacting huge tax cuts, even though the Contract with
America, the rallying point for the Gingrich Revolution, was found by poll-
sters to have moved few voters into the GOP column. On the contrary, polls
showed the Democrats had been able to stave off even greater losses by
campaigning *against* the contract and the specter of Gingrichism, which suggested that the Republicans would have difficulty turning victory into a governing majority. Still, the mood in the conservative movement remained
heady. Gingrich protégé Grover Norquist sent out an invitation to a postelection party at his Capitol Hill home. Quoting from the movie *Conan the
Barbarian*, it said: "To crush enemies, see them driven before you, and hear
the lamentations of their women."

From my vantage point, the revolution moved into what conservative policy wonk Jim Pinkerton called the "sumptuous imperial phase." My most
vivid memories of the period are of glamorous socializing of a kind unknown
to Washington's rumpled right-wing environs. An article in *National Review*
noted "the alarming discovery that conservatives may be having fun," and to
make her point, writer Jennifer Grossman described an "intimate supper" at
my home, where over a catered feast of three-pepper soup and pecan-
encrusted snapper, guests took turns doing dramatic readings from Gennifer
Flowers's steamy memoir, *Passion and Betrayal.* In one of my favorite quotes
from the book, Flowers wrote, "Laughter was always a big part of our relationship, so we had fun creating names for our private parts as well. I called
mine 'Precious,' and his penis was 'Willard.'" *National Review* quoted me as
an expert on the new conservative nightlife: "Losers don't have good parties.
Part of what energizes the Washington social scene is being in power."

My social circle widened considerably. The group swept to prominence
in the Gingrich era was a new breed entirely: attractive, media savvy, and
committed to conservatism largely as a marketing technique, not a philosophy. I got on much better with this flashy crowd than I had with the gray-
visaged, embittered true believers, with their defeatist air of the perennially
excluded, I had met in prior years. Having come out of the closet, seemingly
with no repercussions, and reveling in my notoriety, I also felt freer, more
confident, and able to lighten up; "Can someone get Brock to lighten up?"
had been a long-running joke of Bob Tyrrell's in response to my somber
manner. After eight years in D.C., I reached out beyond the *Spectator* circle
and the friends of Clarence Thomas to forge even closer relations with top
conservatives.

The leading social light in the new GOP power structure in Washington
was Arianna Huffington, whose husband, multimillionaire ex-congressman
Michael Huffington, had narrowly lost a bid to unseat California Senator
Dianne Feinstein in November 1994. The indefatigable Huffington, whose
failure to comply with the laws governing household help probably cost her
husband the election, returned to Washington determined to reinvent herself as the godmother of the Gingrich Revolution. Since her debut as the
first woman member of the Cambridge Union student debating society, the

witty, articulate Greek-born beauty had set out, with brio, to conquer her world. In the 1970s, she took London by storm, writing a famous antifeminist manifesto at the height of the women's movement, and carrying on a high-profile affair with the British intellectual Bernard Levin. Moving on to New York in the Reagan years, she hosted the likes of Brooke Astor and Barbara Walters at glittering dinner parties, dated real estate mogul Mort Zuckerman, and found an intellectual home at Buckley's *National Review*.

Relocating to Los Angeles, Arianna became a devotee of Shirley MacLaine's New Age mysticism, joined a cult under the direction of a man who claimed to be the Messiah, and was linked romantically with Governor Jerry Brown, a left-wing populist. She met Michael Huffington, a Republican heir to a Houston oil fortune, at a party at the San Francisco home of Ann Getty in 1985. In a few months they were married and on their way to a first tour in Washington, where Michael had gotten an appointment in the Reagan Pentagon. In the early 1990s, suddenly flush with cash after the sale of his father's business, Michael enrolled in a GOPAC training session and bankrolled his own congressional bid from Santa Barbara, where he and Arianna settled in a $5 million Italianate villa overlooking the Pacific. With Arianna honing the campaign's conservative message and even standing in for Michael in candidate debates, Huffington confounded political experts and won the seat. The only discernible theme through it all was Arianna's boundless ambition. "The Sir Edmund Hillary of social climbers," as *Los Angeles* magazine put it.

Arianna drew the attention of Newt Gingrich during Michael's first congressional term, when she published a book called *The Fourth Instinct*, in which she argued that the welfare state should be replaced by reviving the concept of tithing, or charitable giving. Arianna was right that the conservatives had no antipoverty agenda, and her concern for the poor seemed genuine. Indeed, unlike most conservatives I knew, Arianna had a strong social conscience, even though her solution of ending government entitlements in one fell swoop was itself impracticable and socially irresponsible. A deft student of the use of rhetoric in politics, Newt soon made Arianna a fellow of his Center for Effective Compassion, and she became part of Newt's unofficial brain trust. Meanwhile, urged on by Senator Phil Gramm, the head of the Republican Senatorial Campaign Committee, Huffington was in Congress for a matter of months before declaring against Feinstein. Huffington spent an unprecedented $30 million of his fortune on the race, much of it on television advertising designed to show him as a family man devoted to conservative values, complete with the endorsement of William Bennett. Only after losing the race and divorcing Arianna in 1997 did Michael reveal in a magazine interview with me that he had entered the marriage, eleven years before, with Arianna's full knowledge of his sexual interest in men.* The conservative fun couple of the Gingrich era were not what they seemed.

I was drawn to Arianna's larger-than-life persona and her social connections, and I stood in awe of her ambition, her energy, and her prodigious talent for self-promotion—half the time I wanted to *be* Arianna. She was fabulous company as I assumed the role of cocktail party walker on the many occasions when Michael made himself unavailable. In a moment of high camp, each of us dressed to the nines with heavily lacquered hair, we waltzed arm in arm into the American Enterprise Institute's annual black-tie Francis Boyer lecture and dinner, otherwise known as the conservative prom, shortly after I came out of the closet. Arianna introduced me to publisher Mort Zuckerman, celebrity interviewer Barbara Walters, and GOP socialite Georgette Mosbacher.

Though I never quite trusted Arianna, I regarded Michael as a closer friend. Though he was woefully miscast as a politician—during our first dinner, shortly after his defeat in the Senate race, I recall that he wasn't quite sure who legendary newsman David Brinkley was—Michael was not an empty suit, as he was portrayed in most of his press clippings. On subjects ranging from art to philosophy to religion, he was quite erudite and insightful, and he had the capacity for a rich spiritual life. In retrospect, I can see that I bonded with Michael—who stood almost seven feet tall and yet still appeared slight, with his orange hair, ghostly pallor, sticklike limbs, and weak blue eyes—because he was lost, numbed emotionally, and alienated from his true self. His platform as a Republican politician was inherited from his con-

---

*Michael approached me to write the piece in July 1999, after divorcing Arianna. It was published by *Esquire* in December 1999.

servative father, Roy, a Texas oil tycoon, and refined by Arianna. And, as was apparent to me from his inquisitiveness about the gay world in our conversations, he was grappling painfully with his hidden sexual desires while doing the work of the Republican right.

With Michael searching his soul after his loss at the polls, Arianna set out to establish a salon, bringing together intellectuals, politicians, and activists, in the grand tradition of such Washington hostesses as Evangeline Bruce, Pamela Harriman, and Sally Quinn. In Washington, the Huffingtons lived in a cavernous but architecturally unexceptional $4 million mansion in the Wesley Heights section of town, off Embassy Row, which Arianna had decorated as a gilt-encrusted Italian palazzo. Ostensibly, these "critical mass" dinners were organized around the constructive purpose of narrowing differences between liberals and conservatives by identifying middle-ground solutions, beyond partisan labels, to social problems. A dinner on the subject of abortion, for example, focused on adoption and crisis-pregnancy centers as alternatives. Huffington taped the events, which became fodder for a fledgling op-ed column she began to write in her new role as political provocateur. Yet Huffington's columnar voice betrayed few signs of the intellectual subtlety or postpartisan themes of her dinners. Rather, the columns were glib and gimmicky, designed to tap into the revolution's anti-Clinton zeitgeist. For example, she described Clinton as having "the vision of a mole and the conviction of his latest political consultant," and once asked, "If Hillary is indicted, can Al Gore become First Lady?"

Though she was extraordinarily focused and clever, Huffington, who had been forced to settle a plagiarism claim out of court arising from the publication of her biography of Pablo Picasso, became infamous in conservative circles not only for taping her dinner parties, but also for taking copious notes at social gatherings and recycling bits and pieces of the collected wisdom into her writing. Much of the real work was done with the assistance of a slew of ghostwriters, joke writers, and researchers, working sweatshop hours out of a warren of offices in her Washington mansion, all underwritten by Michael. Soon enough, though, Arianna was syndicated nationally, signed a half-million-dollar contract for a satirical political book, and— though her voice coach, hired from the film *Forrest Gump*, never muted her accent—became a popular talking head. By 1996, she would cohost Comedy Central's coverage of the national political conventions in her nightgown, from a queen-sized bed shared with comedian Al Franken. In Huffington's hands, the Gingrich Revolution became farce.

If Arianna's pronouncements in such venues lacked substance and purpose, she was still a fierce infighter within Gingrich's inner circle. As the courtiers around Newt began pointing fingers to explain his failures, Arianna launched a vicious personal attack on Joe Gaylord, whom she blamed for blocking access to the Speaker. In early 1997, Arianna, who was described by her husband's Senate campaign strategist Ed Rollins as "the most ruthless and ambitious person I've met in thirty years in politics," encouraged me to write an exposé on Gaylord, whom she claimed "was betraying the revolution" by cutting off Newt from anyone Gaylord could not control. "We have to get Gaylord" became a favorite refrain, sung in her Zsa Zsa Gabor accent.

Arianna, whom Michael told me often hired private investigators to collect dirt on her foes, sent me her "file" on Gaylord in the hope that I would write a piece about him. It contained an account of a staff meeting at the Republican National Convention where Gaylord, who was trying to reinforce his message that politics is war, distributed "tiny toy soldiers to pump up the troops." According to Arianna's file, at the meeting, Gaylord stepped in front of an African American staffer and said, "And here is our affirmative action." Arianna also tried to get me to out Gaylord, who she told me was a homosexual, even as she peppered our mutual friends about whether I thought that her husband was gay. When I declined to pursue the matter, she took up the subject herself in a column for the Capitol Hill newspaper *Roll Call:* " 'There will be no freelancing' is one of Gaylord's driving principles. And to ensure that he knows everything that goes on when Gingrich is out of sight, he has an intimate friend, Barry Hutchison, always traveling with the Speaker," Huffington wrote in a reference clearly intended for those in the know. "Hutchison—who is listed in Federal Election Commission reports as Hutchison Consulting—seems to have as his primary responsibility covering Gaylord's base."

Few on the right had the political and social connections, not to mention the money, to match Arianna. One who came close was Gay Gaines, an aging, blond-maned Palm Beach socialite who held the reins of Gingrich's political action committee, GOPAC, as chairman. Gaines hosted Gingrich and Rush Limbaugh and William Bennett at poolside retreats in Palm Beach, a testament to her bravery, if nothing else. Gaines also gave frequent small dinners in her lavish New York penthouse-style town house in the Kalorama section of Washington, where the business of the revolution was conducted behind heavy satin draperies.

Soon after the new Congress was sworn in, Gaines put together a dinner party to introduce me and another conservative journalist, John Fund of the *Wall Street Journal* editorial page, to three members of the new GOP majority: Congressmen Bob Barr of Georgia, Ernest Istook of Oklahoma, and Tim Hutchinson of Arkansas. They were a striking departure from the Republican congressmen, even the conservative ones, I had known before. Southern, closely identified with the Christian Right, leading sponsors of pro-life, pro-gun, and antigay legislation, and rabidly anti-Clinton, the three men were archetypes of the Gingrich Revolution brought to power by an electorate one-quarter of which was white evangelical Christians. In the new Congress, nine of ten GOP leaders hailed from southern or western states, where the religious right controlled local party factions and Rush Rooms abounded. Having thrown bombs from the sidelines for years, I was so impressed by my access to power, and by their implied acceptance of me, that I never asked myself what it meant to be an openly gay man breaking bread and plotting political strategy with this menacing trio, who literally seemed to me like cavemen.

While the Republicans now controlled Congress for the first time since I had been in Washington, I was struck that virtually no conservative policy initiatives were mentioned during the evening's discussion. There was no Contract with America, just a Contract on Clinton. Republicans were laying all of their emphasis on opposing one man. As Newt had promised before the election, these congressmen were devoted to using the congressional investigative apparatus now at their disposal to hammer away at the Clinton scandals. The stories generated by the *Spectator*'s Arkansas Project—

from Troopergate, to Whitewater, to Travelgate, to Mena, to the morbid speculation about Foster's death—would be front and center in the new Congress. At least half of the twenty committees controlled by the Republicans launched investigations of the Clinton administration and the Democratic Party. Ginni Thomas, the wife of the Supreme Court justice and a senior aide to Dick Armey, who listened closely to the dictates of Limbaugh at noon on the radio, issued a secret memo to committee chairmen seeking information on "waste, fraud, and abuse" and "dishonesty or ethical lapses" in the Clinton administration. Several sets of hearings, costing millions of dollars, were held on Whitewater alone. Republicans opened two inquiries into the mysterious doings at Mena.

At the Gaines dinner, the air was thick with blind fury against the president, and his alleged sexual escapades were topic A. Bob Barr, the Georgia Republican who gave a keynote speech to a white-rights group that preaches against integration and who sat on the House Judiciary Committee, had a messy personal life of his own. Though as a leading member of the pro-life caucus in the House Barr had stated that he would do "anything in his power" to stop a family member from having an abortion, even in the case of rape, the second of his three wives, Gail, said in an affidavit that Barr had raised no objections when she had the procedure done, and in fact drove her to the hospital and paid for it. In a deposition in their divorce, Barr swore that he opposed the abortion. "Any statement that he expressed his opposition to the abortion is simply not true," Gail said. While Barr has made defense of the "family unit" a centerpiece of his political career, Gail also charged Barr with committing adultery, noting that he married his third wife within a month of their divorce. In the divorce proceeding, Barr refused to answer a question about whether he had been faithful to Gail. At dinner, Barr asked me what I thought about bringing the Arkansas state troopers before the Republican-led Judiciary Committee to testify about Clinton's philandering.

The presence of Hutchinson, a Baptist minister who would be elected to the Senate in 1996 and replaced in the House by his brother Asa, who with Barr was one of the Republican floor managers in the GOP-led impeachment of Clinton, was a symbol of how the Arkansas Clinton-haters now had been joined, in toxic combination, to the Gingrich wing of the GOP. Hutchinson suggested I chase down a rumor about a waitress in a rural Arkansas town who supposedly once had a fling with Clinton. Shortly after voting to impeach Clinton in the Lewinsky scandal, Hutchinson divorced his wife and married an aide.

My dinner mate John Fund of the *Journal*'s editorial page was a close political associate of Gingrich, and similarly hypocritical. Though he took positions aligned with those of the Christian Right, Fund had not discouraged a young ex-girlfriend—the daughter of another Fund ex-girlfriend—from seeking an abortion he offered to pay for. "I respect life, but I also make judgments and I have different variations on that theme," Fund told the young woman, according to a transcript of a telephone conversation she released to a reporter. Despite the illusion created by his *Journal* credentials, Fund, a ghostwriter of Rush Limbaugh's book *The Way Things Ought to Be*, was more activist than journalist. Carrying with him an ever-expanding girth, the peripatetic Fund shuttled constantly between *Journal* headquarters in New York and Gingrich's chambers on Capitol Hill, where he offered political advice, an arrangement unlikely to be countenanced on editorial pages like those of the *New York Times* or the *Washington Post*. But we weren't like other journalists, even other opinion journalists; for the Gaines dinner, no ground rules were set, because no ground rules were necessary among comrades. In no way did we view ourselves as independent actors, a reflection of the movement mind-set I had been inculcated in since my earliest days at the *Washington Times*. Our publications functioned as adjuncts to the conservative movement; we were coconspirators in the anti-Clinton jihad.

The invitation to the *Journal*'s Fund was a telling sign of the new congressmen's priorities, for nowhere was the trend toward attack journalism more striking than on the editorial pages of that august newspaper, once known primarily for its advocacy of anti-Communism and supply-side economics. *Journal* editorial page editor Robert Bartley, who had once said that in the United States "there aren't any poor people, just a few hermits or something like that," was the author of *The Seven Fat Years*, in which he argued that tax cuts for the rich and major corporations in the Reagan years had brought about a tremendous economic boom, despite the conclusions of even Republican economists that the Reagan combination of tax cuts and deficit spending had wrecked the economy. Ideologically, the editorial boards of newspapers like the *Journal*, Conrad Black's *Sunday Telegraph*, and Murdoch's *New York Post* had an interest in opposing any tax increases or new regulations on business proposed by the Clinton administration. Then there was Bartley's more personal interest in Clinton.

Under Bartley's leadership, the editorial page appeared to have concluded that Clinton was corrupt even before he took office. Intrigued by the Bank of Credit and Commerce International, or BCCI, scandal, Bartley considered BCCI to be "a pack of Arab crooks . . . at the center of a vast international criminal network that was in many ways more powerful than individual governments." According to Bartley's conspiracy theory, Little Rock banker Jackson Stephens, whom Bartley took to be a loyal Clinton patron, had "played a central role" in bringing BCCI to America. In a letter to the *Journal*, Stephens convincingly rebutted Bartley's charge about his ties to BCCI, which Stephens called "reckless and irresponsible." Bartley also was wrong that Stephens was a reliable Clinton backer. Stephens had supported Clinton in some elections, and Clinton's opponents in others, depending on Stephens's interests at the time.

I met the taciturn, reclusive Bartley, who had the beady eyes of someone who never saw daylight, when he summoned me to New York some time after the Troopergate story was published. In a meeting in his office and then over lunch atop the World Trade Center, he said virtually nothing for the longest stretches of time as he gazed into a goblet of red wine. Occasionally, he looked up, squinted, and made a cryptic reference to "the Clinton scandals," which he suggested as the subject for my next book. I wasn't sure if I was at lunch, or in a séance.

The *Journal* considered Clinton "an accidental president," elected with only 43 percent of the vote. The page's campaign against what it considered to be an illegitimate administration began almost immediately, with exaggerated claims and baseless insinuations of corruption and law breaking against high-level White House aides, including White House deputy counsel Vincent Foster. In the weeks leading up to his suicide, the *Journal* published a taunting editorial series entitled "Who Is Vincent Foster?"

Apparently traumatized by the *Journal's* assault on his work as the admin-istration's ethics counsel, Foster mentioned "WSJ editors [who] lie without consequence" in his suicide note. Shortly after Foster's death, the *Journal* sought to deflect attention from its role in the tragedy by implying that Foster had been murdered. "Those who knew him consider him an unlikely suicide. We're told he had no history of depression," the *Journal* confidently and wrongly declared. The page also expressed a "debt of gratitude" for the reporting of Foster conspiratorialist Christopher Ruddy. "Until the Foster death is seriously studied, a Banquo's ghost will stalk . . . the Clinton admin-istration," one editorial warned, in a self-fulfilling prophecy.

Bartley considered Whitewater to be a metaphor for Clinton's character, and he eventually published four volumes of books compiling the *Journal's* editorials on the subject. Chafing under the balanced news coverage of the paper, Bartley invented what he called "the reported editorial" to generate his own spin on the news. Filled with guilt by association, the pieces con-tained suggestive lines such as this one accompanying a lead editorial on Whitewater: "The facts recounted above contain no 'smoking gun' but they surely arouse suspicion." Although they invariably missed their target, the editorials were quite influential in the upper reaches of Republican politics. The *Journal's* lonely but sustained attack on the ethics of Robert Fiske, the widely respected first Whitewater special counsel—"Fiske: Too Much Baggage," "The Fiske Cover-Up," and the like—undoubtedly impressed the panel of conservative justices who replaced Fiske with Starr. As Whitewater flamed out, the *Journal* reached farther afield. "Mysterious Mena" was a Bartley favorite. "Reporters now trolling Arkansas are pulling up many sto-ries that may have only fleeting relation to Whitewater or the Clintons, but are worth telling simply for their baroque charm," the *Journal* said in one editorial. After Bob Tyrrell published his fallacious Mena piece, the *Journal* duly followed up with an editorial headlined "Investigate Mena."

The *Journal* even entertained crackpot conspiracy theories linking the Clintons to a number of "unexplained deaths." It published the 800 num-ber for ordering the fabricated *Clinton Chronicles* video, accompanied by the disclaimer ". . . we decline in the name of responsibility to print what we've heard." In yet another example of how the *Journal* backed into such fringe terrain, one editorial explained: "Pondering the string of violent coincidences, we felt some duty to share with readers one factor that colors our thinking about the Arkansas connections. In particular, with drugs comes violence, and also money laundering. And laying aside any thought of the President's involvement, there is a story here worth our attention and yours." *Journal* editorialist Micah Morrison wrote a series of pieces on the deaths of two Arkansas teenagers who had been run over by a train; in the fevered imaginations of the right, Clinton "death squads" murdered the teens to cover up the supposed drug-running conspiracy at Mena. While the only established connection between Clinton and the deaths was that he was the governor of the state when they occurred and had appointed the medical examiner who ruled them an accident, a full-page editorial graphic titled "Obstruction and Abuse: A Pattern," laying out such Clinton scandals as Whitewater, Paula Jones, and Travelgate, included a box called "Train Deaths." In disbelief, the *Arkansas Democrat-Gazette*, a Republican newspaper, ridiculed Morrison as "half Karl Marx, half Jules Verne" and "a space age visitor."

More than anyone, of course, it was the *Journal*'s hero Newt Gingrich who led the GOP to the point where it could only be seen as petty and vindictive, standing for nothing, and slowly poisoning the political system with such ravings. Documents that later surfaced showed that shortly after taking power, senior aides to Gingrich drafted a plan to attack the ethics of the Clinton administration. Notes of a meeting of the Gingrich high command made by political consultant Joe Gaylord included tactical maneuvers such as "indict the Clinton administration," "change the battlefield to one where Democrats are on the defensive," "bring back to life Dem ethical problems," and "show why Gingrich is different than the dirty Democrats of the past." The hypocrisy involved in this plan was spectacular, for the assault on the Clintons was undertaken partly to block an investigation by the House Ethics Committee of Gingrich's own ethical improprieties, which found that Newt had violated tax laws in using tax-exempt foundations for political activities and had misled the committee in sworn testimony, and fined him $300,000. One Gaylord action item included: "Get the Clinton administration under special prosecutor problems and have the Clinton administration get the House Dems to back down."

The seriousness with which Gingrich's own advisers took the ethics charges was reflected in an e-mail message Arianna Huffington provided me as part of her Gaylord file. "Newt's current Ethics Committee situation invites a follow-up to your column about the sinister influence Joe Gaylord exerts on Newt," Gingrich adviser James E. Higgins wrote Huffington in late 1996. Referring to a trio of aides to Richard Nixon who were indicted and convicted in the Watergate scandal, Higgins asserted, "Gaylord is Newt's Haldeman, Ehrlichman, and Colson all rolled into one. He encourages Newt's dark side—in this case, denial that there was any real problem with the Ethics Committee."

As the new Congress opened, Newt was the most powerful figure in town. So it was something of a coup when Gingrich accepted an invitation from the *Spectator* to appear as its featured guest at the Saturday Evening Club, the monthly dinner meeting where top conservative editors and pundits convened to plot strategy and compare notes. Prior to the dinner, I had been warned by Arianna Huffington that Newt considered conservative journalists who strayed from the reservation to be traitors. Like many conservatives, Newt believed that since the press was waging war on the Republican Congress, conservatives in the media had a duty to buck up their own side. Huffington had complained to me of a personal note she had received from Newt, after she penned a mildly critical column, in which he upbraided her for taking a position that was "strategically counterproductive" for the revolution. At the Saturday Evening Club, Newt began his remarks by flying into a red-faced, table-pounding rage at columnist Bob Novak, who had criticized Gingrich in a column as insufficiently hard-line in his handling of legislation to eliminate racial preferences.

More astonishing still was the direction the dinner table conversation took once Gingrich got his temper under control. With his ever-present aide Joe Gaylord standing at the rear of the room, taking it all in, one could almost see Gingrich's wheels turn as he grew fascinated with a presentation by Ambrose Evans-Pritchard about Vincent Foster's murder. As even many

conservatives around the table stared at their plates and moved their silver-
ware around in embarrassment, Ambrose prattled on about phantom witnesses, stray footprints, and safe houses. Though special counsel Fiske had
ruled the Foster death a suicide, Gingrich soon announced that there was
sufficient doubt about the circumstances of Foster's death to warrant yet
another GOP-led congressional inquiry. As a mark of how effective disin-
formers like Ambrose and Christopher Ruddy were in drawing the leadership of the Republican Party into their web of conspiracy-mongering, the
leader of the House inquiry, GOP Representative Dan Burton, became preoccupied with the notion that the position of the dead man's bullet wounds
showed they could not have been self-inflicted. To test the theory, Burton,
who publicly referred to Clinton as "a scumbag," reenacted the Foster death
by firing a .38 caliber revolver into a watermelon.

If such private dinners were a recognition of the place at the table my generation of conservatives had won in the November election, a much more
public sign of our arrival on the political stage of the mid-1990s was also in
the works. In February 1995, the *New York Times Magazine* ran a cover story
headlined "Look Who's the 'Opinion Elite' Now." The tag line read: "They're
young, brainy, and ambitious—an adversarial band of conservatives winning
the war against liberalism and having a grand old time." I appeared on the
cover along with Adam Bellow, the Free Press editor; Lisa Schifferen, a former speechwriter for Dan Quayle, who had penned the attack on Murphy
Brown; James Golden, a young African American producer for Rush
Limbaugh; and, clad in a tight leopard-print miniskirt, Laura Ingraham. The
"counter-intelligentsia" that right-wing financier William Simon had incu-
bated in the 1980s had come into its own.

The author of the article, a timid, bespectacled intellectual from New
York named James Atlas, knew little, if anything, about this strange "new
establishment" he had been assigned to profile. As if he were embarking on
a study of a primitive tribal society, Atlas telephoned me as he began his
research to ask if I would arrange a dinner in Washington where he could
meet a couple of dozen young conservative writers. A few weeks later, we

gathered at my house for a catered champagne reception, then went off to dinner at Citronelle, a tony restaurant imported to Georgetown from Los Angeles, where we talked politics with Atlas over Chilean sea bass and chardonnay. I made myself believe I was happy to become the Gingrich Revolution's openly gay dancing bear.

For an outsider, Atlas did a masterful job of capturing the values and viewpoints of the people who had helped define the cultural landscape that made Gingrich's electoral triumph possible. He captured the way we spoke, dividing the world in two—"your side," "our side," "your people," "our people." Uncertainty, doubt, factual inquiry, reason, all of these, Atlas concluded, were "anathema to this crowd." Atlas noted that for a group of writers and thinkers who talked a lot about "ideas," we were oddly bereft of any actual ideas. Some of us—like Bill Kristol, whose faxes to Republican leaders had helped sink the Clinton health care bill—were strategists; others of us were essentially publicists. Together, we practiced a brand of attack politics that required no alternative vision to Clintonism. As an example of our Limbaugh-style political advocacy, Atlas pointed to a bumper sticker I had purposely planted on a table in my foyer: "President Gore—Don't Pardon Hillary." In describing us as an "elite," Atlas meant to convey that a rich, East Coast Republican establishment financed us—one obnoxiously frank *Journal* editor, David Brooks, was quoted as saying that he "liked the idea of bankers running the world." Atlas also found that the culture of the conservative elite—Ivy League educated, and open, so far as he could tell, to professional women, Jews, and gays—looked a lot more like the liberal elite than the fundamentalist heartland whose values we fronted for. Such contradictions didn't trouble us. One Jewish neoconservative remarked to Atlas, "Deep down, I believe that a little anti-Semitism is good for the Jews—it reminds us who we are."

The Atlas article made us hot, hot, hot. I was listed in the *National Journal* as one of "The Best and the Rightist," profiled in the *Philadelphia Inquirer* as one of "The Brash Conservatives," and photographed with Laura Ingraham in a campy *Fortune* magazine feature on the sartorial tastes of young conservatives—pinstripes, French cuffs, and good cigars for the boys. And for the girls, well, that iconic leopard miniskirt, we often joked, launched Laura

Ingraham's career. (For this, I can take some credit, or blame, as the case may be. Before she became a television personality, I often teased Laura, a bit of a tomboy who never bothered fixing her limp hair or wearing makeup, that she didn't know how to put herself together as a woman. True to form, for the New York photo shoot, Laura had shown up in a frumpy, Lane Bryant–type peach polyester suit, at least two sizes too big. She had brought the leopard-print skirt along, which a friend had left behind in her closet, and which I often dared her to wear, as a gag. I told her either she was wearing the skirt or I was.)

Though she was not yet a writer or television personality, and though at the time I had known her for only a few months, I invited the slender, blond associate at a downtown Washington law firm to the Atlas dinner because she could light up a room with her forceful personality and raucous humor. My intention was to show Atlas that conservatives were confident and fun loving, not the four-eyed geeks he might have imagined. As was her way, Laura won a coveted spot on the *Times* cover not on the basis of any accomplishment, but by transfixing Atlas with over-the-top tales of her adventures in the mid-1980s on assignment for the *Dartmouth Review* in support of El Salvador's right-wing military regime—she was "murdering nuns," as she flippantly put it. When I introduced Laura to Atlas, her one desire in life was to leave her law firm and get herself on television as a political pundit, despite the fact that she was the only person I knew who didn't appear to own a book or regularly read a newspaper. Though the *Dartmouth Review* was her sole experience in journalism, through sheer force of will Laura became the prototype for a legion of brassy, blond, not terribly well-informed pundits whom television producers, lacking a stable of conservative voices in a moment when conservatism had suddenly become chic, booked to interpret the Gingrich Revolution for their audiences. The blond pundits were pleased, but they did the revolution no good.

Though Gingrich, Limbaugh, and the *Spectator* already had substituted name-calling for reasoned conservative discourse, Ingraham and a merry band of imitators would bring Limbaugh meanness to millions of American television viewers, stigmatizing Gingrichism as ignorant and inane. Laura also was a symbol of the trouble Newt's revolution would have in establishing a broad-based appeal to women; she frequently attacked feminism for making women unhappy and resentful, while betraying those same qualities in her commentary. Laura's stock-in-trade was the politically incorrect sound bite. Showing up at one interview in a full-length fox coat, she mocked the "squealing baby foxes, which were cute when they were alive." In an op-ed, she questioned actor Harrison Ford's "manliness" after he appeared on the cover of *People* magazine wearing an earring. And the subjugation of women, she claimed, could be alleviated if more women became gun owners. "Some of us," Ingraham once remarked, "are proud to be meanies."

In 1999, Laura would publish *The Hillary Trap: Looking for Power in All the Wrong Places*. After signing the mid–six figure contract, she quietly struck a deal with the talented *New Republic* writer Ruth Shalit to essentially draft the book for her. When Shalit wisely backed out, Laura was left with a lame manuscript whose sole purpose was to hold the Clintons' marriage up to moral scrutiny and ridicule. "Certainly, she [Hillary] is not a good role model for women," Laura announced. "Her personal life has turned into a bizarre, sad relationship where both husband and wife depend in desperate and unhealthy ways on each other at different times in their lives." A more transparent case of projection I have rarely seen.

Yet of all of the conservatives I had met since coming to Washington, I grew closest to Laura. For several months after we met in November 1994, we were inseparable companions. Laura drew me out of my shell; she helped me to relax and enjoy myself among the conservatives. She was a much more prodigious networker than I was, and she was also a wicked gossip, befriending the likes of Rush Limbaugh and George Will, then repeating their often creepy confidences to me. Though I was now out of the closet, my socializing was still strictly confined to the conservative political orbit, and I had no romantic life. The more ensconced I became in the conservative firmament, the more I felt that it would be easier for the conservatives to accept a nonpracticing homosexual. In many ways, Laura took the place of a mate. We were out on the town virtually every night together, cohosted several parties and dinners at my home, and vacationed in southern California with the Huffingtons. We shared lots of laughs. Despite her public persona as a voice of Gingrichism, I also saw in Laura a glimmer of humanity, softness, and vulnerability, buried beneath all of the role-playing. In candid moments, she confided she didn't believe much of what she was saying on the airwaves. Channeling into our politics our emotional problems (in Laura's case, the pain of a difficult childhood, and her tortured relations with men, whether married or not), we were both trapped in devices of our own making.

I hadn't known of Laura's antigay past at Dartmouth, where, along with her then-boyfriend Dinesh D'Souza, she had participated in the infamous outing of gay students, who were branded "sodomites," until I cringed as I read about her *Dartmouth Review* exploits in a 1995 profile in *Vanity Fair.* To make matters worse, I was quoted in the piece saying that Laura was unreservedly accepting of homosexuality, which in my presence she always had seemed to be. On more than one occasion, I had taken her barhopping along the gay strip in Washington, where she seemed to have a blast. Inevitably, though, as we drowned ourselves in more and more alcohol, the evening would take a ghastly turn. One night, after downing several cocktails and snorting an unidentifiable white powder an acquaintance had given me—which turned out to be the cat tranquilizer Ketamine—I was sick in the bathroom for several hours trying to get my bearings as Laura, in a drunken stupor, crawled through the packed two-story dance club on her hands and knees looking for me. Her purse had been locked in my car trunk, causing her to call a friend in the wee hours of the morning to rescue her. In the meantime, she had managed to leave me a series of violent messages, threatening to "break every window in my house" if I didn't return the keys immediately.

Among all of her friends, Laura had asked only me, and a former classmate from Dartmouth named Debbie Stone, to speak on her behalf to *Vanity Fair,* but in the end, I was the only one quoted. When I asked Laura's friend Debbie, a conservative political gadfly who had been involved in promoting a book by Floyd Brown called *Slick Willie* during the '92 campaign, why she backed out, she said she wasn't about to cover up for Laura: "What am I supposed to do? Talk about how she pulled a gun on a boyfriend after he broke up with her?" No wonder I was the only one who talked—I started to think that I didn't know Laura all that well after all.

After reading the article, I was chagrined and felt used but never confronted Laura about it, though Congressman Barney Frank, the openly gay Democrat from Massachusetts, did. At a black-tie gala at the Washington Building Museum, Frank and his companion spotted Laura and me milling through the crowd. Frank approached us and proceeded to denounce Laura's history of gay bashing. I remained mute during the harangue, because I agreed with everything Frank was saying. He then turned to me and snapped, "And if you want to front her, that's fine." I was speechless, red-faced and humiliated. Of course, Frank was right, but I didn't have the courage or self-regard to do anything about it. Blithely, I continued to revel in the gossip-page glitz and heartless sarcasm of my right-wing fag hags—the Ariannas, the Lauras, and the Ann Coulters. At this point in life, this transparently empty right-wing circle was all I had.

CHAPTER TWELVE

STRANGE LIES

While my friends were drinking to celebrate, I was drinking to forget. As I made the rounds of Republican victory celebrations and tended to my press notices, I was simultaneously struggling with a piece of unfinished business that for me turned the Gingrich Revolution into a hollow victory virtually overnight.

The publication of Jane Mayer and Jill Abramson's book *Strange Justice* a few weeks before the November 1994 elections was the final battle in the war over the Clarence Thomas–Anita Hill case. Though the case had receded from the headlines, the book was hotly anticipated by partisans on both sides of the historic cataclysm as the answer to *The Real Anita Hill*. Now, we would see the fruits of Mayer and Abramson's three years of research—whether they had any goods. My own reputation, which had been sullied by the two authors in the *New Yorker*, to say nothing of Clarence Thomas's, and that of the political cause he represented, hung in the balance.

My telephone rang shortly after dawn on the morning that *Strange Justice* was excerpted across the front page of the second section of the *Wall Street Journal*, where Mayer and Abramson then worked as reporters. (Only the *Journal*'s editorial pages, not the news department, leaned to the right.) I had examined the excerpt carefully before answering the phone that October morning. While interest in pornography is no scandal in itself, Thomas's history with pornography was central to Hill's charge of sexual harassment. Through interviews with the owner and patrons of a Washington video rental store that stocked X-rated films, the authors corroborated Hill's story by revealing that Thomas was an avid consumer of the type of pornography Hill described in her testimony. They also produced a new witness who attested to Thomas's obsessive interest in porn during the years that he supervised Hill. Yet so far as I was concerned, the case was already settled. Since we had the truth on our side, new facts to the contrary had to be lies, part of the relentless campaign by the left to strip Thomas of his legitimacy as a justice and advance the liberal agenda.

When I lifted the handset off the console, Ricky Silberman was on the other end of the line. The vice chairman of the Equal Employment Opportunity Commission under Thomas and a close friend of his, Silberman had been one of my most trusted sources, going back to the time I first paid her a visit while researching my *Spectator* article three years before. Ricky's confident testament to Thomas's character, her absolute certainty that Thomas was incapable of doing anything like what Hill accused him of, had shaped my early thinking about the case. Her husband, Larry, who sat with Thomas on the D.C. Circuit Court of Appeals, had fortified these impressions. I would have expected Ricky, of all people, to share my opinion that Mayer and Abramson hadn't put a dent in Thomas's armor. If belief in Thomas's innocence was a leap of faith for me, for Ricky it was a matter of experience. She knew him, I didn't. "Have you read it?" Ricky roared into the phone, referring to the *Journal* excerpt. "He did it, didn't he?"

"He did it, didn't he?" The words burned through my being with the force of a blowtorch. Surely the excerpt, sensational though it was, could not have shaken the stalwart Ricky. What was going on? Was this the same woman who had assured me that Hill's charges were impossible? Who had marched on the Senate chambers as founder of Women for Judge Thomas? Who had testified under oath to his impeccable character? Did Ricky know something I didn't? Stunned, I couldn't find it within myself to confront her—though I wanted to say, "What the hell are you talking about, 'He did it?'" Instead, I anxiously sought to calm her down and persuade her that the excerpt was no cause for alarm; it was a predictable left-wing hit job. In an odd reversal of roles, I was trying to talk one of my key sources into her own position. As I worked to convince Ricky, I was trying to convince myself, too, trying to hold on to the convictions that I thought we had shared.

Ricky's primal reaction stood in the way. It spoke volumes: Even

Thomas's closest friends didn't believe him, maybe never had. In the face of this knowledge, how could I maintain my position as a true believer in the Thomas cause? Was my book a Big Lie? I felt used by Ricky, on whom I had relied to tell me the unvarnished truth.

Yet as if our telephone conversation had never occurred, as though we were in denial about a dark family secret, Ricky and I sprang into action to discredit the Mayer and Abramson book. At mid-morning, we met at the Capitol Hill offices of Paul Weyrich's Free Congress Foundation, the most powerful right-wing lobby behind the Thomas nomination. Weyrich's operation was housed in a modern complex, including an impressive television studio, that took up much of a city block near the northeast side of the Capitol. Ricky was joined by Barbara Ledeen, a neo-conservative operative who was the executive director of the Independent Women's Forum, the antifeminist group Ricky had formed, in part with Scaife money, from Women for Judge Thomas. Ledeen was married to Michael Ledeen, a shadowy intriguer who was involved in Iranian arms deals during the Iran-contra scandal. Referring to herself as an "ex-hippie," she displayed the same zealousness of 1960s left-wing extremism, now from the other side. Like many neocons I knew, Barbara had remained in the same emotional state of all-out war for the past thirty years. If only for the hell of it, Barbara was boiling mad.

I was angrier and more disappointed with Ricky than with Mayer and Abramson. I could hardly see straight. Yet I was able to displace my rage. Like the Hiss-Chambers case, the Thomas-Hill case lent itself to endless hairsplitting over the true meaning of obscure factoids. I knew the ins and outs of the case better than anyone on our side, and I knew how to twist and turn them to our advantage. I had done this previously, in my book, in the service of a sincerely held belief. Now, I wasn't sure why I was doing it. I was just doing it. As Barbara Ledeen took notes on a legal pad, I played the role I was expected to play. Donning my defense lawyer hat, I dissected the Mayer and Abramson excerpt, methodically turning back each new damaging allegation they raised and patching up the sizable holes they had shot in Thomas's defense.

The three of us then collaborated on a radio script for Rush Limbaugh's show at noon. Many on the right believed that Mayer and Abramson had published their book just before the election to boost the prospects of the Democrats, in a replay of 1992's "Anita Hill effect." We would use Rush to crush Mayer and Abramson, defend Justice Thomas, and protect Republican prospects in the impending election that would bring Newt Gingrich to power. We faxed off the script. Tuning in to his show, I listened as Limbaugh read from the fax virtually verbatim. The war was on! Hearing Rush blast those feminazis gave me a jolt of adrenaline. I was back on message. Forget that hysterical Ricky Silberman, I told myself. I'd show her, too, by going out and proving that Mayer and Abramson were frauds and liars. Consumed by a kind of mania, as if my entire worldview and indeed my self-conception depended on the outcome, I was now on a mission to sink *Strange Justice.*

Working harder than I ever had, I set about re-reporting the book for a review for the *Spectator.* By the time I finished, I must have covered the 360-page book in several hundred yellow Post-it notes. I did find a few factual errors of the type that all nonfiction contains, and patches of the reporting relied on arguable interpretations of events. That was not enough for me. With my faith in Thomas's innocence now shaken—and with it, my faith in the entire political enterprise of the right—I felt it necessary to eviscerate every piece of evidence, every allegation, every question that the authors raised in making their case. This was the only hope of regaining my ideological and personal bearings.

My work on the *Spectator* review inevitably caused me to reinterview sources I had relied on in writing my book. One of them was Armstrong Williams, who had been on Thomas's Equal Employment Opportunity Commission staff at the time Anita Hill also worked for him in the early 1980s. A decade later, Williams, a short, lithe, stylishly dressed man with a militant demeanor, was a prominent African American conservative in his own right, hosting a popular radio show (on which I had promoted *The Real Anita Hill*) and a television program on Paul Weyrich's National Empowerment Television network. He also wrote a column for the *Washington Times.* Williams drew attention for an interview he conducted on Weyrich's network with Senator Trent Lott, in which Lott compared gays to alcoholics and kleptomaniacs.

In my book, I relied heavily on Williams's recollections to discredit the testimony of Hill and of another ex-employee of Thomas's, Angela Wright, who also claimed that Thomas had behaved inappropriately toward her. Williams had supplied me with a particularly evocative anecdote that I used to show Thomas—in contrast to Anita Hill's portrait—as prudish in sexual matters. According to Williams, Thomas had once compelled him to dispose of a copy of *Playboy* Williams had been toting, telling his aide the magazine was "trash." I had interviewed Williams in his Dupont Circle office and on the telephone several times, and we had kept in touch since the book's publication, though we hadn't spoken at any length since I had come out as gay in the *Washington Post* eight months before. Williams invited me to discuss *Strange Justice* over dinner at a Tex-Mex place on the Hill, then asked me back to his apartment for a drink.

Sitting on an overstuffed sofa not far from me, Williams had something else besides *Strange Justice* on his mind. As he began to pepper me with graphic questions about whether I was dominant or submissive in bed, I shuffled uncomfortably in my seat, looked away, and tried to change the subject. Williams, who was unmarried, countered with increasingly lewd banter until I quickly brought the conversation to a close, thanked him for his time, got up, and walked out. Was Williams baiting me like an antigay bigot? Was he coming on to me? I had no way of knowing for sure, but either way, I had to conclude that he had been a poor character witness for Clarence Thomas.* Coming so soon on the heels of the Ricky Silberman incident, I grew agitated as I glimpsed some uncomfortable truths about who these conservatives really were, and what they really represented. *"He did it, didn't he?"* My world was falling in.

Whether I was following the ugly dictates of partisan politics, the personal vanity and careerism of a professional writer in a literary cat fight, or the ability I had to wind myself up for battle while cutting my emotions dead, I reacted by denying what was happening, and taking things up another notch. I defended my position, my work, my cause, with more vigor

---

*Some years later, Williams was sued for sexual harassment by his producer and former trainer, who charged that Williams repeatedly kissed him on the mouth and grabbed his buttocks and genitals on business trips. The suit was settled out of court.

and more ingenuity than before. When that proved inadequate, I quite consciously became what my critics believed I was all along: a witting cog in the Republican sleaze machine.

The biggest problem raised by the *Strange Justice* authors for the Thomas camp was the testimony of yet another woman, Kaye Savage, who had not been heard from during the first round of hearings. Savage made the claim, billboarded by the authors as a prized piece of evidence missed by the Senate committee, that she had seen *Playboy* pinups papered along the walls of Thomas's apartment in the early 1980s, when she and Thomas had been friends and Anita Hill was working for Thomas. Though the presence of *Playboy* centerfolds in Thomas's bachelor apartment did not in itself prove misconduct toward Hill, I felt compelled to smash the highly publicized anecdote anyway. Appearing on the ABC newsmagazine *Turning Point* in connection with the publication of *Strange Justice*, Savage spoke of having seen *one* pinup from *Playboy* in Thomas's kitchen. She didn't mention the rest of the apartment being plastered with pinups, as she had described it to Mayer and Abramson. I seized on this apparent discrepancy, and prepared to confront Savage about it, hoping to discredit her account.

Shortly after the *Turning Point* broadcast, I reported for work at mid-morning to the *Spectator*, where I was hard at work on my review. I called Mark Paoletta at his Washington law office and discussed the Savage matter with him. Mark had been helping me on all other aspects of the review, and we developed a plan for dealing with Savage. I needed to find out quickly who she was and what negative information might exist about her before confronting her and trying to force her into backing off the story she had told the *Strange Justice* authors. I was intent on doing to Savage what had been done to Anita Hill and Angela Wright during the Thomas hearings. Mark said he would call Clarence Thomas and see what he could find out. I was thrilled. This was the first time I would have access to Thomas, whom I had met for the first time at a christening of one of Mark's children at Mark's home just the prior month.

Within an hour or so that morning, Mark phoned me back. He said he had posed my question about how to discredit Savage to Thomas, who knew I was at work on a review of the Mayer and Abramson book. Mark told me that

Thomas had, in fact, some derogatory information on his former friend Savage; he passed it along to Mark so that Mark could give it to me. Quoting Thomas directly, Mark told me of unverified, embarrassing personal information about Savage that Thomas claimed had been raised against her in a sealed court record of a divorce and child custody battle more than a decade ago. Thomas also told Mark where Savage worked after Mark related that I was eager to hunt her down as soon as possible. Surely skirting the bounds of judicial propriety to intimidate and smear yet another witness against him, Thomas was playing dirty, and so was I.

I hung up the phone with Mark, called Savage, and immediately got through. I identified myself, told Savage I was investigating her statements against Thomas, and told her I knew of something bad in her past. Pushed and prodded by me, she seemed to hedge on her quotations in *Strange Justice*. Though this was not unusual behavior for a skittish source who has supplied a reporter with sensitive material and is suddenly thrust into the headlines, I moved in for the kill, pressuring her to meet with me, and she nervously agreed.

I was now determined to take advantage of the uncertainty and fear Savage had shown on the telephone by getting Savage to retract her statements in *Strange Justice*. As we sat in the bar of the Marriott Hotel in downtown Washington, I grilled Savage, a mild-mannered, middle-aged African American civil servant, with the menacing threat of personal exposure hanging in the background. I then told her that she could either cooperate with me and give me what I needed to discredit *Strange Justice*, or I would have to discredit her as a witness by disclosing whatever personal information I had about her, just as I had blackened the reputations of all the other women who had come forward with damaging information about Thomas. In the face of this threat, Savage refused to recant her accusations. I continued to press for anything I could get her to say to blunt the impact of her accusation. We agreed that Savage would give me a written statement in which she would say the *Strange Justice* authors had distorted and sensationalized her quotes. When I got back to my office at the *Spectator*, Savage faxed me a statement, but it was too weak to be of any use: the *Strange Justice* account would still stand. I called Savage at her office and insisted on some changes that would allow me to cast at least some doubt on the way Mayer and Abramson had quoted her. After a struggle on the phone in which I renewed my threats, Savage made some handwritten changes to the document and faxed it to me again. I ran through the creaky hallways of the *Spectator* brandishing the statement triumphantly. I knew Savage had given me enough to work with so that I could use the statement in my review to make it appear as though she had recanted the story, when in fact she had not.

While one could argue that as a journalist I was entitled to ask Savage about the personal information covertly passed along by Thomas in order to assess her credibility as a source for Mayer and Abramson, I was dishonest in using the material to strong-arm Savage, an unsteady and vulnerable woman, into saying what I wanted her to say. Threatening a woman who had come forward to talk to two journalists in the context of a sexual harassment case was the conduct of a scorched-earth defense attorney, not a journalist, even one with a political agenda. Up to this point in my career, even when I fell short, I had always believed I was pursuing accurate information. Now, I let go of my own standards. I wanted Savage's allegation to go away, truth be damned.

I next set out to blow away the Mayer and Abramson story that Thomas had been a frequent customer of an X-rated video store near Dupont Circle, called Graffiti, where in the early 1980s he was alleged to have rented X-rated videos of the type that Hill claimed he had discussed with her in graphic terms. In the hearings, Thomas had pointedly refused to answer questions about his personal use of pornography, other than to categorically deny that he had ever talked about porn with Hill. The Graffiti story was another theretofore unknown piece of evidence for Hill's case, and it was a powerful counterpoint to the prudish image of Thomas presented by supporters like Armstrong Williams and repeated by me in *The Real Anita Hill*. Now that Mark had opened up a channel directly to Thomas, I asked him to find out for me whether Thomas had owned the video equipment needed to view movies at home in the early 1980s. Such equipment was not then as commonly used as it was in the mid-1990s, and I figured if I could assert in the review that Thomas had no way of watching the movies, the matter would be settled definitively.

Mark came back with a straightforward answer: Thomas not only had the video equipment in his apartment, but he also habitually rented pornographic movies from Graffiti during the years that Anita Hill worked for him, just as Mayer and Abramson reported. Here was the proof that Senate investigators and reporters had been searching for during the hearings. Mark, of course, was still a true believer in Thomas's innocence. He couldn't see the porn rentals as at all significant. To Mark, Hill was still a liar despite suggestions to the contrary. But I had some distance from Thomas and I was troubled by the damaging report. It made Hill's entire story much more plausible. I can still remember exactly where I was sitting when Mark let me in on what had to have been one of the most closely guarded secrets within the Thomas camp, a secret, no doubt, that had been kept for three years among Thomas's most trusted advisers. I was in Laguna Beach, visiting Andrew for Thanksgiving, sitting on a blue linen sofa in his library. When I hung up the phone, I was shaken, and mentioned the conversation to Andrew. Because Mark and I had not established ground rules for our conversations, I was free to publish the information. But I was a loyal henchman and was never tempted to do anything but keep it to myself.

In the heat of the moment, I then mounted a cover-up to protect Thomas. As I drafted the lengthy review on deadline back in Washington, I met Mark and Lee Liberman, the Federalist Society founder who had orchestrated Thomas's appointment as Boyden Gray's deputy in the Bush White House. We convened at Mark's small but charming cottage in the Virginia suburbs, which was filled with the joyful sounds of two adorable young children, and two frisky Siberian huskies. In a team effort, Mark and Lee also had been combing through the book looking for ways to undermine it while salvaging Thomas's reputation. We were all hyped up for battle. A brilliant lawyer and former clerk to Antonin Scalia, Lee was the ideological commissar of the operation. This was no time to be thinking for myself. Lee had a few typewritten notes that I snatched from her hands and plugged into my draft.

As I sat in Mark's cozy blue-and-white living room, I had a flashback to a conversation I once had with Lee while I was researching *The Real Anita Hill*. In an awkward aside, Lee told me to "stay away" from the subject of Thomas and porn. I hadn't paid the warning any heed at the time, but now

I understood what Lee must have been telling me. The Bush White House must have known all along about Thomas's vulnerability on the subject and done a good job of covering it up. Lee must have been giving me a comradely heads-up not to go out on a limb to defend Thomas on allegations she knew could be proven true.

Now that I had the damning report, I could have done what Lee originally suggested, avoiding the subject of Thomas and pornography altogether, and letting the Graffiti allegation stand. I had plenty of other material to work with for my review. But I wouldn't let it go. I remained in a dependent condition; I had to win one more for the movement, and I crossed a line I had never crossed before. I shredded Mayer and Abramson's porn story as full of misquotation and unreliable secondhand sourcing. There was no evidence, I concluded in the *Spectator*, "that Thomas had rented even one pornographic video, let alone that he was a 'habitual' consumer of pornography." When I wrote those words, I knew they were false. I put a lie in print.

The publication of my *Spectator* review, under the Orwellian headline "Strange Lies," set in motion another literary and political contretemps between Mayer and Abramson and me. The authors, I charged, had perpetrated "one of the most outrageous journalistic hoaxes in recent memory." The controversy was covered in several major newspapers, and a slew of conservative commentators and editorial pages cited my review in denouncing the book as a sham. The conservative counterattack spilled onto the airwaves, where conservative writer Fred Barnes, appearing on CNN, called the review "devastating." The review also helped vindicate Thomas in some high-level liberal circles. I was told by Judge Silberman that Supreme Court Justice Stephen Breyer, a Clinton appointee, had let it be known around the court that the review settled the case for him in Thomas's favor.

Writing in Mayer and Abramson's defense was *Times* columnist Frank Rich, who interviewed a lawyer consulted by Kaye Savage after my intimidating encounter with her. In a column headlined "Brock's Strange Journalism," Rich wrote, "This time Mr. Brock's partisan desperation has led him to a tactic that is beyond the pale of even tabloid journalism and that would make any citizen think twice before talking freely again to any journalist: He tried to bully a source in *Strange Justice*, a onetime Hill and Thomas associate named Kaye Savage, to get her to sign a statement denying her own contribution to the book." As he had in his column accusing me of misogyny, Rich once again stung me by exposing the truth about my work. And once again, I moved swiftly to try to spin my way out of an embarrassing and humiliating situation with cleverly worded denials. My coauthor in this denial was not Adam Bellow, but Mark Paoletta and another top Federalist Society legal gun, Michael Carvin, a battle-scarred veteran of the Reagan Justice Department. I was so chagrined and angry at Rich for exposing my scheme in print that I felt I needed to make a dramatic move, suing him for libel for accusing me of blackmail. Mark was all whipped up as well, and he took me to a meeting in Carvin's office, where we went over the facts of what had transpired, though I don't think we told Carvin that I had gotten the Savage smear story from Thomas. Carvin soon talked me down from initiating any legal action: He could see that I was actually quite vulnerable to the charge Rich had made and pointed out that Savage could do far more damage to my reputation in litigation than Rich had already done. The three of us agreed that I would write a letter to the *Times*, which they helped me draft, denying that I had done anything dishonest—one lie piled on top of another.

Mark and I had fallen into the habit of exchanging Christmas gifts. After the review appeared, I told Mark all I wanted for Christmas was a signed photograph of Clarence Thomas, who had surely read my review and seen how I lied for him on the porn issue and tried to discredit Savage's truthful account. The photo arrived, Thomas in his black judicial robes, with the inscription "To David, With admiration and affection, Clarence."

I had weathered the storms over *The Real Anita Hill*, Troopergate, and even over my own sexuality, keeping myself and my mission intact. But the storm over the *Strange Justice* review was one I could not weather. Gone was the confidence I had in the moral stature of the pro-Thomas camp and the broader political movement that backed him. I was being forced to give up the hubristic illusion that defending Clarence Thomas and all he stood for was right and good; it had all been just another power game in the service of a hard-right ideology that I never shared. Worst of all, I had seen myself as a truth-teller; after reviewing *Strange Justice*, I knew I was a liar and a fraud in a dubious cause. My foundations were irrevocably shaken. I could see that my reportorial method in *The Real Anita Hill* was shoddy, not only in the sources I had trusted, but in the obvious fact that I had missed significant evidence that showed that Hill's testimony was more truthful than Thomas's flat denials after all. My version of the Thomas-Hill controversy was wrong, my belief in it as truth was a delusion. Perhaps the errors of *The Real Anita Hill* could be attributed to journalistic carelessness, ideological bias, and my mis-directed quest for acceptance from a political movement. In the review of *Strange Justice*, however, to protect myself and my tribe from the truth and consequences of our own hypocrisy, smears, falsehoods, and cover-ups, I con-sciously and actively chose an unethical path. I continued to malign Anita Hill and her liberal supporters as liars. I trashed the professional reputations of two journalists for reporting something I knew was correct. I coerced an unsteady source, I knowingly published a lie, and I falsified the historical record.

I had begun my career by suppressing my liberal social values to get ahead in the conservative movement; I then abandoned the conservative traditions of restraint and civility for Gingrichian ends-justify-the-means radicalism. As a closeted gay man, I did the work of the right-wing lawyers of the Federalist Society, the Christian Coalition, and the worst bigots from Arkansas—racist, homophobic Clinton-haters. Through it all—the destructive partisanship, the careerism, the personal aggrandizement—in my mind I managed to rationalize each of my actions and hold on to the idea that I wasn't like the Ruddys, the Scaifes, the Falwells, the Tyrrells, the Funds—I was better than they were. Whatever else I may have been, I wasn't a liar. But I was no better than the Arkansas Project brigade after all. The strange lies were mine. All the attacks, the hateful rhetoric, the dark alliances and strange conspiracies, an eye for an eye, nuts and sluts, defending Pinochet, throwing grenades, carpet-bombing the White House, Bob Bork, Bob Tyrrell, Bob Dornan, Bob Bartley, Bob Barr—it all led right here: I lost my soul.

CHAPTER THIRTEEN

THE SEDUCTION OF HILLARY RODHAM

Three months after publishing my attack on *Strange Justice*, I entered into discussions with my agents about a second book. I had created a market niche as a right-wing gumshoe, and with the Republicans in power in Congress and the Clintons on the ropes politically, now seemed a good time to cash in. For years in Washington, I leapt out of bed in the morning, seeking the thrill of battle, propelled forward by my mission to defeat the left. Now, I was having trouble getting out of bed and facing myself each morning as I languished in a fog of ideological confusion and personal angst. The push to sell another book came as much from my agents and my publisher as it did from me. The only thing that got me past the negotiations was how easily I glided through.

We all agreed that Hillary Rodham Clinton was an irresistible target for my next attack book. Like Anita Hill, Hillary was an icon of the feminist movement, and at this point she had been the subject of only a couple of instant books providing the kind of puff treatment usually seen in Hollywood fan magazines. Yet the right had cast Hillary as the central villain in the Whitewater criminal investigation, and her controversial initiative for universal health care was credited with bringing Republican voters to the polls in droves in the 1994 elections. Among my audience, she was easily the most reviled figure on the national scene, even more so than her husband. To *New York Times* columnist William Safire, Hillary was a "congenital liar"; to Bob Tyrrell she was "Hillary Milhous Clinton." In a column in which he argued "maybe we've been too tough on President Clinton," *Washington Times* editor Wesley Pruden wrote, "He did Gennifer Flowers and Paula Jones, all right, but the devil in Miss Hillary made him do that, too. . . . Maybe Hillary's long-suffering husband deserves not censure but a night out." Critics compared Hillary to Leona Helmsley, Ma Barker, Eva Braun, and Minister Louis Farrakhan. Right-wing radio talk show host G. Gordon Liddy charged, "I think the woman's been getting away with everything short of murder. . . . It's just amazing to me that this woman is, to date, not yet under indictment." Newt Gingrich's mother revealed in a television interview with CBS's Connie Chung that her son referred to Hillary as a "bitch." An exposé on Hillary was sure to be a hit.

Fresh from negotiating a $4.3-million book deal for the new House Speaker, my agents put the bounty on Hillary's head at a $1 million advance, and offered the book on an exclusive basis to the Free Press, which had been sold by Macmillan to Simon & Schuster. Though I wrote no proposal, everyone understood that I was to follow the lucrative formula of the Anita Hill book, producing a scathing indictment that would play to the same political prejudices, personal resentments, and even misogynistic impulses of my market. I was to construct for the right a book-length "Hillary," timed to coincide with the 1996 presidential election. I attended only one short meeting with the publisher of Simon & Schuster, Jack Romanos, who asked me only one question before okaying the $1 million. Did I think Hillary Clinton was a lesbian? Romanos wanted to know. With a smirk, I assured him that if she were, I was just the man to find out.

As I sat on a leather sofa in Romanos's expansive Sixth Avenue office, I could see through my own role-playing. Was this smirking asshole really me? A few days later, my agents called with news that the deal had been inked. My emotions swung wildly: Elated by the money, depressed about having to forage through the trash again.

The act of doing something evil in the review of *Strange Justice* was bringing on guilty convulsions, creating a crisis of conscience that I didn't understand. All I knew was that my zeal, my partisan loyalties, my allegiance to the conservative movement, my hatred of and desire to destroy the left—it was all slipping away. As I tried to soldier on, more and more reality began to sink in: The Foster and Mena travesties at the *Spectator;* Paula Jones's own lawyers admitting to me that the case was a cynical effort to "get" Clinton by people who didn't believe her; the blackmail scheme of David Bossie;

and disturbing new revelations that the Arkansas troopers were making paid appearances in which they supported wild claims that Foster had been murdered. I got off to a sluggish start, wasting months in a drunken funk. I eventually settled down to work for one reason alone: I wanted the million bucks.

By mid-1995, I had staffed up with a small brigade of researchers to get the job done. Washington and Arkansas were full of Hillary-haters, and by the time I was done, I felt as though I had talked to every one. I checked out every conceivable lead, and a lot of inconceivable ones, too. I spent days on the phone with Republican investigators on the Hill, everyone from the Barbarellas to Bossie, who gave me everything in their quiver. Olson and Comstock were especially intent on proving that Hillary had lied about her role in the firing of the White House travel office workers. Back in the spring of 1994, I had done a *Spectator* piece on Travelgate, framing the investigation for the Republicans around Hillary's role in it, illustrated on the cover with Hillary astride a broomstick. But testimony that the two Barbaras had elicited in their subsequent investigation showed, to everyone but them, that nothing nefarious had gone on. I tracked down a former Clinton White House worker fired by Hillary, who turned over computer disks he had taken from the White House showing every entrant into the Clintons' personal residence for several months, most of whom I also tried to grill. I spent weeks chasing down a rumor that had started at a Georgetown cocktail party that Hillary had demanded from Bill a power-sharing arrangement in government in exchange for her defense of him in the *60 Minutes* interview about his relationship with Gennifer Flowers in the '92 campaign. When I finally found the source, the story was not anything he was in a position to know, just a surmise. I drove to Heber Springs to quiz the staff at a mountain resort outside Little Rock, where the Rose firm kept a cabin, the rumored rendezvous point, according to the troopers, for Hillary and Vincent Foster. No one had seen them there together. I dined at a fancy Italian restaurant with Senator Alfonse D'Amato, who was heading up the Whitewater inquiry, but *he* was looking for information from *me*. The

Republican state auditor of Arkansas promised me a list of Hillary's lesbian lovers, but the list never materialized. I flew to Florida to interview Hillary's first secretary at the Rose firm in the 1970s. All she could tell me was that Hillary didn't tweeze her eyebrows in those days: They grew together, in the shape of a caterpillar.

I had higher hopes when I arrived in Little Rock for an appointment with Sheffield Nelson, perhaps the most vengeful Clinton enemy in the state. I had scheduled a meeting at his downtown Little Rock law office to intro- duce myself and ask if he had any fresh leads to pass on for my book. Nelson, who had made millions as head of the Arkansas-Louisiana Gas Company, was a commanding presence with a rich, bellowing voice. In the hard-fought 1990 race for governor, Nelson, a former Democrat who switched parties to run against Clinton, had been enmeshed in the same sort of shady financial scandals that he persisted in peddling about Clinton even now, years after Nelson lost the race. Stung by his defeat at Clinton's hands, in 1992 Nelson operatives secretly arranged for the *Star* tabloid to approach Gennifer Flowers about her alleged affair with Clinton, and he also helped *New York Times* reporter Jeff Gerth get the first interview with James McDougal, Clinton's partner in the Whitewater land deal.

I wasn't in Nelson's office ten minutes before he reached into the drawer of his enormous oak desk and fished out a letter written in 1992 by a man named Philip Yoakum. Yoakum, Nelson explained, was a friend of a woman, Juanita Broaddrick, who claimed that Bill Clinton raped her seventeen years ago when he was attorney general of Arkansas. The letter purported to be a summary of a confession the woman had made to Yoakum and Nelson dur- ing an interview she gave them in 1992. Yoakum's Fayetteville address was listed on the letterhead. Given the gravity of the accusation, Nelson seemed awfully casual about it. When I asked if he believed the story, Nelson looked at me with snake-eyes and said he wasn't sure what to make of it, but that it was worth looking into.

On my next trip to Arkansas, I took my main research assistant, Becky Borders, along to help me confront the sensitive subject. Becky was a politi- cal conservative and anti-Clintonite whose trips to Arkansas were something of an epiphany for her as well. A harried, zaftig mother of two whose husband worked on Capitol Hill for an archconservative member of Congress, Becky had done some of her own freelance work for the *Spectator* and was beginning to conclude that either Bob and the other Arkansas Project types were hallucinating or we were. Every time she got her meaty hands around a supposedly solid Clinton scandal, Becky clicked on her built-in bullshit detector and it turned to sand.

On the way to Fayetteville, a college town in the northwest part of the state, we stopped in Little Rock, where we had dinner with a former state legislator, Tommy Mitchum, an Arkansas Project informant, and his buddy, Trooper L. D. Brown. That night at the Macaroni Grill, Mitchum was brimming with ribald sexual gossip about various political figures in the state. After dinner, at a jazz bar in the yuppie Heights section of the city, Mitchum leaned over and asked Becky if she had ever heard about "the rape tape." As Mitchum told the story, Sheffield Nelson had a tape of a woman claiming that Clinton had raped her. A rape tape! I was frothing at the mouth about the possibility—I ran to the bathroom to scribble down notes of our conversation—but I wondered why Nelson hadn't mentioned a tape to me. When I settled down, I realized that the rape story wasn't the exclusive I thought it was, for if Mitchum knew of it, the tale probably had been told and retold around Arkansas for years, and nothing had ever come of it.

Becky and I arrived unannounced at Phil Yoakum's house in Fayetteville. A gnomic man in his late forties with thinning red hair and a pasty complexion, Yoakum came to the door and appeared startled when I handed him my *American Spectator* card, told him I had visited Sheffield in Little Rock, and brandished a copy of his letter to Broaddrick. "This is like Mike Wallace showing up in your living room," I said with a dramatic flourish. "You better sit down and tell me everything." Joined by his lugubrious wife, who wore black hosiery with the toes cut out, Yoakum took a seat on a dingy sofa, the arms covered in tattered hand towels, and began to tell his story.

In the early 1980s, Yoakum had been in the nursing home business, as was Juanita Broaddrick. Yoakum, Broaddrick, and a nurse who worked for Broaddrick named Norma Rogers all became friends. Rogers mentioned to Yoakum that Broaddrick once had a bad experience with Clinton. According to Yoakum, when he asked Broaddrick about it, Broaddrick told him the following story: It all started on a Clinton campaign swing through Van Buren in 1978, when the gubernatorial candidate stopped at Broaddrick's nursing home, caught her eye, and told her if she were ever in Little Rock, she should look him up. A short time later, Broaddrick and Rogers attended a nursing home convention in Little Rock. Broaddrick called Clinton, and the two arranged to meet in the coffee shop of her hotel, the Camelot, on the Arkansas River. On arriving, Clinton said there were too many people around for them to really talk and suggested they have coffee in her room. Once in the room, Clinton forced himself on Broaddrick, biting her lip in the process. When Rogers returned to the room, she found Broaddrick crying, nursing a bruised lip.

Over the years, Yoakum moved on to a series of failed businesses and lost touch with Broaddrick. When Clinton declared for the presidency in 1991, Yoakum contacted Sheffield Nelson, now cochairman of the Arkansas Republican Party, and related the story to him. Yoakum then called Broaddrick, who at first said she didn't want to talk about it; eventually, he was able to convince her to meet with him and Nelson in Van Buren. According to Yoakum, he and Nelson showed up wired for the surreptitious taping of his friend, an alleged rape victim, and teased the story from her.

I had every incentive to believe the rape story, just as I had believed the troopers. It was just the sort of sensational allegation that would incite my audience, especially in the midst of the 1996 campaign season. But there were chinks in the story, chinks that I was now training myself to look for; after several reporting trips to the state, I was on to the Clinton-haters' modus operandi. So, I wondered, why hadn't Nelson released the tape in 1992 when, if the allegation was true, it might have stopped Clinton cold? Yoakum's explanation was that Broaddrick had decided not to go public, but I failed to see why that would have stopped a treacherous enemy like Nelson, who had stage-managed both the Gennifer Flowers and Whitewater stories in 1992, from scheming to expose the story anyway. I was also troubled by the Yoakums' paranoia, which I had come to associate with Clinton crazies like Ambrose Evans-Pritchard. Though they offered no details, the Yoakums claimed their lives had been threatened in 1992 as Phil worked on Juanita to get her to go public. "Is this story worth his life?" Yoakum's wife asked me plaintively at one point. After a silence, I answered sarcastically, "Wellll." At this juncture, Yoakum informed us that his teenage son was hovering in the backyard, watching us through a window off the living room, with a shotgun trained on us. Becky and I got the hell out of there.

During this period, I was still in daily contact with Mark Paoletta, who on the one hand served as a painful reminder of what I had done in the *Strange Justice* review, and on the other continued to perform the same function for me that he always had, that of lawyer and facilitator for my journalistic thuggery. True to form, he advised me on how to overcome Yoakum's intransigence and force the Broaddrick story into print. Mark reasoned that since I already had Yoakum on the record, I was free to publish his secondhand account with no further corroboration. He had a deal in mind for Yoakum—I would protect Yoakum and his family from exposure in exchange for the tape—and was busy drawing up an agreement for Yoakum's signature to that effect.

When I met Yoakum for coffee at my hotel a few mornings later, Yoakum demanded payment for the tape and for his help in locating Norma Rogers. He wanted a cut of my book deal. When I told him paying sources was out of the question, he said he didn't have the tape after all and suggested the rape story might not be true. For one thing, he said, Sheffield never believed it. And neither did Dave Broaddrick, who had been Juanita's boyfriend in 1978 and later married her. Now I understood the import of a curious line in Yoakum's 1992 letter to Juanita: Yoakum had written to Juanita that she should come forward and charge Clinton with rape to prove to her husband, Dave Broaddrick, her "innocence in the matter." When I first read that line, I was suspicious. To me, it suggested that Dave Broaddrick had suspected Juanita of having consensual sex with Clinton and that Juanita came up with the rape claim later to get herself out of trouble with her boyfriend.

Becky and I drove to Van Buren to check the story out for ourselves. Hoping to confront Broaddrick, Becky, the kind of woman who would stick a beer in her purse on the way to Little League practice, charged into the nursing home Broaddrick owned, wired for sound, and learned that Friday was her day off. We pulled over to a pay phone and called Broaddrick's home, but when a woman answered, I foolishly hung up. We jumped in the car, sped to Broaddrick's farm on the outskirts of town, and knocked on the door. No answer. Sure that she was hiding inside, we circled the house and waited for a while. Identifying myself as an *American Spectator* reporter working on a book, I wrote Broaddrick a note saying that I was in town looking into a story about a personal incident involving her and Bill Clinton. I left my hotel number in Fayetteville. She never called, and no one answered the phone at the Broaddrick residence for several days thereafter.

When I returned to Washington, I telephoned Sheffield Nelson. What the hell was this about a tape? I demanded. Nelson claimed he had turned it over to a private detective he had hired in 1992 to conduct yet another privately funded anti-Clinton dirt-digging operation. As it happened, the investigator, a Republican operative from Arkansas, was now doing opposition research at the National Republican Senatorial Campaign Committee in Washington. Marty Rile, a sweaty, corpulent man Becky and I code-named Fat Boy, agreed to meet with me. There was more than one tape, Rile told me, as my heart pounded yet again. There was a Nelson tape and a tape Rile himself had made of Broaddrick during his investigation. Both were stored in the basement of his parents' home in Hot Springs, Arkansas. When I asked if there was some way I could get them, Fat Boy said it wasn't worth the trouble: He had discovered that the rape story had problems, too. "It's not what she says it is," Rile told me.

In her deposition in the Paula Jones case, Broaddrick told the Jones lawyers under oath: "I do not have any information to offer regarding a non-consensual or unwelcome sexual advance by Mr. Clinton." Broaddrick later changed her sworn testimony to the Jones lawyers and charged Clinton with rape in a series of interviews in 1999. Following the pattern of the Clinton scandals, the *Wall Street Journal* editorial page ran the story first; perhaps not coincidentally, the *Washington Post* published its own story the next day. The right wing then mounted a pressure campaign on NBC News to air an interview Lisa Myers had taped with Broaddrick, which the network eventually broadcast in March 1999.

For all I know, had I gotten an on-the-record interview with Broaddrick in 1995, I might well have included the story in my book. By the lax standards of *The Real Anita Hill* and Troopergate, however, there were any number of ways to tuck the rape story into the book even *without* Broaddrick, just as Mark Paoletta had urged me to do. Sheffield Nelson and Phil Yoakum could not allege rape firsthand, but they were on the record with a saucy tale that I ordinarily would not have passed up. Surely they were as credible as the anonymous assailants of Anita Hill, or the troopers. I drafted a section about the rape allegation. Something was changing inside me. I was gaining a semblance of judgment and balance as I learned to question the veracity and motives of those who were peddling what I wanted to hear. I was beginning to reject the scurrilous right-wing campaign against the Clintons. I had too many doubts about the story to try to float it for political or commercial gain. No one who knew anything about it seemed to believe it. I threw it in the junk pile.*

Back in Washington, one of the original purveyors of the Whitewater scandal, former Bush White House counsel C. Boyden Gray, invited me to lunch. In the fall of 1992, Gray had tried to engineer an "October Surprise"—an election-eve dirty trick—to save the election for Bush by trying to get federal investigative agencies, including the Justice Department, then under the direction of William Barr, to look into a criminal referral on Clinton Whitewater partner James McDougal's savings and loan that mentioned the Clintons as possible witnesses to a check-kiting scheme. The referral had been rejected by the Republican U.S. Attorney in Little Rock for lack of persuasive evidence. Though the FBI in Washington, prodded by Barr's inquiries, ordered local agents to review the rejected referral again for action three weeks before the election, the FBI's Little Rock office affirmed its opinion that there was no factual basis to suggest criminal activity by any of the people named as potential witnesses.

By 1995, the Resolution Trust Corporation had completed its investigation of McDougal's finances and concluded by fully exonerating the Clintons of any wrongdoing in the myriad of allegations that had come to be known simply as Whitewater. Yet the Starr investigation and the right-

---

*I later learned that the Juanita Broaddrick story also had been pursued and rejected by Bill Rempel of the *Los Angeles Times* and David Maraniss of the *Washington Post*. Broaddrick came forward years later in an interview with NBC News.

wing legal establishment in Washington would not let go. At lunch at the exclusive Metropolitan Club in downtown Washington, a lurking, baleful Gray urged on me the conclusion that Foster's "suspicious" death—whether a suicide or not—was linked to skeletons in the Clintons' financial closet. "No one at that level in government has committed suicide since James Forrestal [the treasury secretary under Franklin Roosevelt]," Gray murmured. Gray said there was evidence being amassed by Starr's investigators that had not yet come to light that would surely cause the Clintons grave political problems in the coming election and deliver victory to Bob Dole. All I had to do was get it, he implored me.

Two of Starr's Washington deputies—Brett Kavanaugh and Alex Azar—were social friends of mine through Federalist circles. I had avoided trading on those relationships because I knew that leaking confidential investigative matters to the press was potentially illegal. Dropping Gray's name, I told the two I was interested in knowing anything I could learn, especially about Hillary, that was not yet in the public domain. Azar responded quickly, telling me to contact Starr's top deputy in Little Rock, Hick Ewing. Azar, whom I met through his close friend Laura Ingraham, gave me a telephone number that Ewing answered directly so that no one else would know of our contacts. When I called Ewing, everything seemed to have been prearranged: I was to meet him at a Mexican restaurant in a strip shopping mall in West Little Rock.

Ken Starr had been chosen for his post for several reasons, but prosecutorial experience was not one of them. Because Starr had none, the prosecutors on his staff wielded disproportionate influence on the investigation, none more so than Hick Ewing. Ewing, a former Reagan-appointed federal prosecutor from Tennessee, where he had brought several high-profile public corruption cases, approached his job presuming the guilt of his targets, though his results in court were mixed. Ewing's wife was prominent in the antiabortion movement, and his political base in the state was among activists of the Christian Right. His prosecutorial activities, he maintained, were guided by God's will. After a long conversation in which Ewing speculated that Hillary had had an illicit affair with Vincent Foster, Ewing told me that he had drafted an indictment of the first lady, charging her with perjury and obstruction of justice. Hillary, he maintained, had lied to investigators about how she had come to represent her Whitewater partner McDougal at the Rose firm, what type of work she had performed for him, and how she was compensated for her services. What Ewing didn't tell me was that the draft indictment was not pending: He had circulated it to other lawyers in Starr's office, and he had been unable to persuade them to present it to the grand jury. Ewing was trying to plant a false story on me that Hillary was facing criminal indictment.

I was determined to try to think for myself. For the first time as a writer, I felt capable of analyzing facts with a degree of impartiality. I began to relish the complexity of my subject. I realized I had never known what journalism was. I had been trained as an unthinking attack dog. Working my way to my own independent conclusions, to a mixed view of Hillary, motivated by a desire not to accuse or condemn but to explain, I felt as if I was emerging from a giant vat of gelatin and could finally breathe in air. I could see and feel—and write—as I never could before. I was skeptical of what Ewing was telling me.

I returned to Washington from Little Rock and decided to investigate Ewing's charges for myself. I repaired to the bedroom on the top floor of my town house, piled high with reams of Hillary's billing records, the Resolution Trust Corporation report, and volumes of congressional testimony on Whitewater. I had the same problem with Ewing's theories on Whitewater as I had had with the Olson-Comstock accusations in Travelgate: When I examined the underlying record, I found that rather than implicating Hillary along the lines suggested by the Republicans, it exculpated her. As I drafted sections on these scandals, I had no choice but to write the truth. I may have convinced an audience of their plausibility; I was no longer able to convince myself. I never mentioned Ewing's indictment scheme, because I could see that Hillary wasn't a crook after all.

My first book had been a surprise best-seller, and judging by the million-dollar advance, the Hillary book was expected to be a blockbuster. I knew what it would take to enlist conservative media types like Rush Limbaugh and drive the Anita Hill audience into the bookstores, and I was well aware that the only Clinton books that sold in large volume were anti-Clinton books that, wittingly or not, told the right wing exactly what it wanted to hear about the Clintons. Without having seen the manuscript, my publisher's marketing department was already circulating a "tip sheet" to booksellers comparing my book to Kitty Kelley's gossipy slam on Nancy Reagan that brought in more than three hundred thousand orders. I still had a book to write. I was at the pinnacle of right-wing journalism. Professionally, politically, personally—to me there really had never been a difference—my whole future was riding on this book.

I saw a train wreck in the making. I knew I had the ability to twist the book into a hit piece that conservatives would buy in droves. Both Barbara Olson and Reagan and Bush speechwriter Peggy Noonan subsequently wrote anti-Hillary books while doing far less research and reporting than I had. These authors simply skewed the available facts and evidence, tossed in an assortment of gossip and innuendo and fantasy, and put a wicked spin on it all.

According to Olson, in her book *Hell to Pay: The Unfolding Story of Hillary Rodham Clinton*, Hillary was "angry, bitter, obsessive, and even dangerous." Hillary, Olson wrote, had "gone to the brink of criminality to amass wealth and power." Olson claimed that she had "come to know Hillary as she is," but Olson did not know Hillary. Many of the negative attributes she gave Hillary I had seen in Olson herself. Noonan's book, *The Case Against Hillary Clinton*, was not a case at all, but rather a catalog of personal resentments against a "highly credentialed rube," a "mere operator," a "person who never ponders what is right," a "squat and grasping woman." Page after page is littered with admittedly imaginary dialogue and demeaning fictional scenes designed to show Hillary as a "pathological narcissist" who "appears to be disturbed." Both books were major best-sellers, promoted on the right-wing media circuit, and bought in bulk by Hillary-hating conservatives. I could have written a book like either of these in my sleep, twisting the Hillary gossip I had collected into salacious tidbits that would have pleased both my readers and my benefactors, but I no longer shared the agenda of those authors.

After almost two years of research and writing, retracing every step of Hillary's life, doing more than one hundred interviews, and collecting virtually every piece of paper that had Hillary's name on it going back twenty years, I had something balanced to say about Hillary. Neither saintly nor evil, Hillary was a rare combination of passionate idealist and gutsy streetfighter. I was able to put myself in my subject's shoes, to judge her by the standards of the real world, not impossible ideals, to sympathize with the trials and tribulations she faced, and even to see a kind of beauty as a good soul tried to assert itself in difficult choices. I pulled no punches in describing when and why I thought Hillary had gone awry, but I also tried to capture and appreciate what her supporters saw in her—a steadfast commitment to public service, and a deep desire to affirm the good and the virtuous in politics all too rarely seen in her generation of politicians.

Friends knew I was wrestling with a dilemma—I was often depressed and losing weight rapidly—but since they were all in the movement, I felt I couldn't tell any of them what was really going on. Propelled by the good, pulled back by the bad, I was stuck on a damn seesaw. *Be fair. Slime her.* At times, I wanted nothing more than to fall back into my comfortable Clinton-bashing role, appease my audience, earn out my advance, and hold my world together. I sat over my computer keyboard literally tearing the hair out of my head, and I broke out in a bad case of acne rosacea, the first skin problem I had suffered in twenty years.

I had confidence in my work, and I didn't want to throw in the towel. At stake was my independence: I was turning on my own side, with no other political movement to back me up, and no fan club waiting in the wings. Publishing the book was a critical test of whether I believed in myself, whether I would begin to conquer my demons or succumb to them. In the end, I could not falsify or toss aside my book. I knew the book would please no one but myself and, for once, that was enough. In finding Hillary Clinton's humanity, I was beginning to find my own.

I then braced my editor, Adam Bellow, for what was coming. Erwin Glikes had died in 1994, and Adam was now the top dog at Free Press. I told Adam that I intended to submit a manuscript that found no basis to allege criminal wrongdoing or cover-up by Hillary Clinton. Adam took the news surprisingly well. Another publisher might have found a way to cancel the book, which was contractually late. Though I had never promised a written proposal to produce a Hillary-bashing book, my manuscript certainly was not the one the publisher thought it had bought. Still, Adam said he wanted to publish it.

Adam believed that the book would have no trouble finding a receptive conservative audience, so long as Hillary's liberal ideology was unmasked. Inevitably—and even perfunctorily—I was still writing as a right-wing critic of Hillary's ideas, and some parts of the book, especially my overheated discussion of her youthful political activities, was a parody of a right-winger's view of what the left is really like. Adam went to work on the manuscript, torquing up the rhetoric in an attempt to placate conservative readers. Adam compared Hillary's rise to power to a Maoist "long march" and called Bill Clinton "an old-fashioned Southern misogynist." The book would be titled *The Seduction of Hillary Rodham*, using Hillary's maiden name to suggest a theme of initial innocence that was betrayed, at key moments, by a blind commitment to advancing her liberal ideology. Of course, the seduction theme was an easy one for me to spin out, because I was describing what had happened to me.

Mark Paoletta, who was reading the book in draft, knew more about my personal life than anyone in the movement, since I had turned to him to draft my will shortly after I began working on the Hillary book and he had also helped me out of an embarrassing personal jam. During the months of drunken carousing before I settled down to work on the book, I crashed my Mercedes into another car while attempting to park it near my house. Very drunk and scared, I raced my car across Washington's Key Bridge to my office at the *Spectator* in Virginia and parked it in the magazine's underground garage. I stumbled back to Georgetown on foot. I called Mark at home and told him what had happened. He suggested that I move my car to the lowest floor in the garage, backing it in to hide the dent, leave it there for ten days or so, then whisk it to a nearby auto body shop for repairs. I followed his advice, and from that day forward wondered if Mark was capable of holding the incident over me as a way of keeping me in line ideologically. I was compromised.

Mark was growing increasingly frantic as he read the book, pressuring me to reverse course and still bitter that I had abandoned the Juanita Broaddrick story. Mark kept me on the phone until the wee hours of the morning, trying to talk me out of my conclusions about Whitewater. I wouldn't budge, but Mark and I had been through so much together that he retained something of a hold over me, even though, or perhaps because, I no longer trusted him.

As I finished up the book, Mark and I had a crazed tug-of-war over the one piece of dirt I had gotten a source to give me on the record. A man named Ivan Duda, who said he was a private investigator in Little Rock, told me that Hillary had retained his services to spy on her husband and report back to her on his womanizing. I had serious doubts about including his account in the book because Duda had no evidence to back up his claims, he had a shady past, and he appeared to harbor a grudge against Bill Clinton. Mark told me the book would be an utter failure with the right wing if I didn't "give them something." I was able to get the Duda anecdote past a very careful libel review, so I left it in, betraying my better instincts one last time.

As I prepared to submit a draft of the manuscript in June 1996, my agent, Lynn Chu, flew to Washington to have a look. Like many conservatives, even from her aerie in New York City, Lynn had become transfixed by the Clinton scandals, so much so that she herself had written a contorted, accusatory essay for *Commentary* on the Whitewater affair. As Lynn began reading the book, I thought I was going to need smelling salts to revive her. Failing to talk me out of my conclusions, which I had labored over carefully for months, Lynn returned to New York in a huff and essentially washed her hands of the book. A month later, I ran into my agents Lynn and Glen at a birthday bash for Arianna Huffington in an enormous suite at the Waldorf-Astoria in New York. Spying me from the corner of an eye, Glen, a tall, wiry fellow with blazing blue eyes, lunged through the well-heeled crowd at the buffet table and spat, "How can you defend that bitch?" Conservatives—even my own literary agents—didn't want a book from me at all. They wanted red meat.

CHAPTER FOURTEEN

THE GARY ALDRICH AFFAIR

Glen Hartley's hyperthyroidism was not the only forewarning I had of how the conservatives would react to *Seduction*. While I was researching the book, a Republican source of mine on Capitol Hill had put me in touch with an ex–FBI agent by the name of Gary Aldrich, who had recently left his posting in the Clinton White House. Expecting a treasure trove of hot stuff for my book, I telephoned Aldrich in the summer of 1995, and we agreed to meet for lunch near my office at the *Spectator* in Arlington.

A stout man in his fifties with reddish blond hair, thick five-and-dime plastic glasses, and a permanent sourpuss, Aldrich had begun his career with the FBI as J. Edgar Hoover's mail clerk. He had been posted to the White House in 1990, midway through the Bush term, and stayed on under the Clintons, processing background checks for White House employees. Though he represented himself as a White House insider, the Deep Throat of the Clinton era, Aldrich seemed to know less about the backgrounds of its key figures than I did. Over lunch, he repeated the same trivial West Wing gossip that I had heard many times before, though with his furtive glances and dark intonations, Aldrich told it all with a bone-chilling malice that I had rarely witnessed in Washington.

Still, I wondered whether Aldrich was holding back the dirt I really wanted, so I invited him to lunch a second time, and a third, to a wretched little "French" café near the office that Aldrich favored, floating every wild rumor I had ever heard about either of the Clintons to see if Aldrich might bite. For years now, Washington's political culture had become like that of Arkansas, awash in bizarre sexual gossip about the Clintons: Bill with virtually every woman he had ever met, in every conceivable circumstance;

Hillary with other men; Hillary with women; Hillary with everyone but Bill. With his best poker face on, Aldrich took it all in and said little.

He showed no flicker of recognition, either, when I began to tell him a detailed but admittedly improbable story that I had heard about Clinton slipping out of the White House for late-night trysts. Supposedly, Clinton hid under a blanket as he was ferried to the downtown Marriott Hotel in the backseat of a sedan driven by his trusted counselor, Bruce Lindsey. As these things often went, I had heard the tale from a Republican investigator on the Hill, who had heard it from a friend who was in town visiting for the weekend, who had a friend who worked at the Marriott. When I asked Aldrich if it would have been possible for Clinton to slip his Secret Service detail to visit the Marriott, Aldrich told me no—the first and only firm answer I had gotten out of him. Given his law enforcement credentials, I took Aldrich's word as definitive, and soon forgot about the Marriott story.

I didn't hear from Aldrich again for several months, until late one evening in the winter of 1996, when he telephoned me at home and told me that he was working on a book of his own about the Clinton White House. When he asked me if I had a "proprietary interest" in the Marriott story, I told him I had not been able to verify it, but he was welcome to it if he could pin it down. I assumed Aldrich's book was a pipe dream, since in my estimation he had neither the skills nor the goods to pull it off. I didn't give the conversation a second thought and went back to work on *Seduction*.

As it turned out, Aldrich was busy churning out a book, which was published by Regnery, a right-wing publishing house, in July 1996. *Unlimited Access* was a product of the culture war the right had been waging against the Clintons since 1992—a dyspeptic, rumor-filled attack on the climate of liberal permissiveness the author claimed the Clintons brought with them to the White House. Aldrich's animosity toward the Clintons was fueled by a clash of manners between the starched-shirt Republicanism of the Bush years, which Aldrich idolized, and the culture of the Clinton crowd, which Aldrich described as "Berkeley, California, with an Appalachian twist." As Aldrich explained it to Rush Limbaugh in an interview in Limbaugh's newsletter, "It was also about the counterculture. I came face to face with the people I used to investigate in the 1960s. I didn't know it at first; it took me a while to understand that. But then finally I did: it was drugs, sex, and rock 'n roll aged about twenty years."

Aldrich described the Clintonites as "broad-shouldered, pants-wearing women and pear-shaped, bowling pin men." In the Clinton White House, Aldrich had seen "jeans, T-shirts and sweatshirts, men wearing earrings and ponytails," and "one young lady dressed entirely in black, black pants, black t-shirt, black shoes, even black lipstick." Another female staffer wore a "very short skirt . . . [and] kept ostentatiously crossing and uncrossing her legs." The book featured such steamy "revelations" as lesbian sex in the White House basement showers, widespread drug use by top Clinton associates, and presidential sex and alcoholism. Hillary Clinton particularly aroused Aldrich's ire. Hillary "runs the entire government," issued an order that no one in the White House be allowed to look directly at her, preferred lesbian to "straight" appointees, hated the traditional family, and selected porno-graphic ornaments for the White House Christmas tree, all according to Aldrich.

Regnery Publishing had been founded fifty years ago by Henry Regnery Sr., and was known for having brought out a long line of distinguished conser-vative classics, including Russell Kirk's *The Conservative Mind*, William F. Buckley Jr.'s *God and Man at Yale*, Whittaker Chambers's *Witness*, and Barry Goldwater's *Conscience of a Conservative*. Regnery's son Alfred succeeded him at the helm. Al Regnery had served in the Reagan Justice Department, where he informally headed an antipornography campaign on behalf of Attorney General Meese. Regnery abruptly resigned from the administra-tion shortly before the press reported that a stash of hard-core pornography had been found in Regnery's home during a police investigation of a claim made by Regnery's wife that she had been sexually assaulted by an intruder.

Al Regnery returned to the family business. In the early '90s, Tom Phillips, a short, oily newsletter publisher and a top-one-hundred donor to the Republican National Committee, purchased the sleepy but respectable intel-lectual press. Phillips and Regnery turned the house into a strictly partisan operation, hawking their wares through the Phillips-owned Conservative

Book Club and buying up as authors such conservative politicians and activists as Pat Buchanan, Dick Armey, Steve Forbes, RNC chairman Haley Barbour, Dinesh D'Souza, David Horowitz, and National Rifle Association president Wayne LaPierre. Regnery also began to publish a series of faux Clinton investigation books. These included, among at least a dozen titles, Bob Tyrrell's *Boy Clinton*—which was so poorly done it had been canceled by Free Press—in which Bob retold L. D. Brown's phony drug-running tales; Ambrose Evans-Pritchard's *The Secret Life of Bill Clinton: The Unreported Stories;* Ann Coulter's *High Crimes and Misdemeanors;* and Barbara Olson's *Hell to Pay: The Unfolding Story of Hillary Rodham Clinton.* More than half of Regnery's Clinton titles became best-sellers, with none selling more than *Unlimited Access,* which may have topped five hundred thousand copies.

Regnery put on a full-court press for *Unlimited Access,* hiring veteran conservative publicists Greg Mueller, a former spokesman for Pat Buchanan, and Craig Shirley, whose clients included the NRA, the American Conservative Union, Paula Jones, and the *American Spectator,* to manage the promotional campaign. On the day of publication, Mueller saw to it that its most sensational revelation—the Marriott story—was plastered across the front page of the *Washington Times.* What jolted me that June morning as I sipped my coffee and read my copy of the *Times* was Aldrich's description of his source on the Marriott story: "a highly educated, well-trained, experienced investigator who is conducting his own investigation into the Clintons." Although I wasn't really any of those things, I had a nauseous feeling that I was in the middle of another comedy of errors: While I thought I had been interviewing Aldrich, *he* had been interviewing *me.*

A few hours later, I received a call from *Newsweek's* Michael Isikoff, who was writing a piece on the election year furor incited by the Marriott allegation. Isikoff and I had a complicated relationship. While I was researching *Seduction,* he had passed on to me a handful of Clinton sex stories that he was not able to get past his editors in the hope that I would follow them up. I chose not to. Now we were collaborating on knocking down a Clinton sex story. In an interview earlier that morning, Aldrich had told Isikoff that his source for the Marriott story was a journalist. Coincidentally, Isikoff and I had had lunch a few weeks before; we learned that we had both pursued

Aldrich as a source, and we had both concluded that he was pretty much worthless. So Isikoff knew I knew Aldrich, and acting on a hunch, he asked me if I was possibly the journalist who told Aldrich the Marriott story. When I said I thought I was, Isikoff asked if I was willing to go on the record. Uhhh . . . yes, I was. I spoke to Isikoff from my gut. I had firsthand knowledge of a smear being broadcast nationwide, and I felt I had a responsibility to tell what I knew.

After hanging up with Isikoff, I decided I had better get in touch with Aldrich to make certain that I *was* his source. I reached Aldrich at the office of my friend from the Paula Jones case, Mark Levin, head of the Washington office of the Landmark Legal Foundation. I knew that Levin had been helping Aldrich secure legal representation from another right-wing group, the Scaife-funded, Atlanta-based Southeastern Legal Foundation, which had close ties to Speaker Gingrich.* When Aldrich came on the line, I asked him if I was the source of the Marriott story, and when he told me I was, I protested that I couldn't be the source because, as I had explained to him some months before, I had never been able to verify it. I had no firsthand or even secondhand knowledge of the story; it was repeated to me thirdhand. "Well, why can't you be the source," an enraged Aldrich asked me. "Because you're a journalist?" So far as I knew, there *was* no story, I said for the final time. I then told Aldrich I had given Isikoff an interview disavowing it. "What are you doing to me?" Aldrich wailed.

Almost as soon as I got off the phone with Aldrich, word leaked out in movement circles that I was publicly challenging the accuracy of *Unlimited Access*. I received a flurry of phone calls from prominent Republicans that weekend warning me to stay quiet. A fuming Mark Levin, in his typical

---

*Southeastern, which took on Aldrich as a client, was headed by a man named Michael Glavin, yet another in a long line of Clinton detractors who lived in a glass house. Glavin later resigned his position after being charged for a second time with public indecency during a sexual overture to a male park ranger in Georgia. Glavin pleaded no contest to the first charge and served six months' probation and paid a fine. He has denied the second charge.

high-pitched squeal, told me, "If he goes down, we all go down." Levin said I should have stonewalled Isikoff, and he urged me to leave town to avoid further press coverage. Judge Silberman also defended the book, which he hadn't read, citing Aldrich's FBI credentials, and he advised me to halt my criticism. I also spoke with conservative writer Lisa Schifferen, who told me flatly that the false stories in *Unlimited Access* notwithstanding, it should be supported because it was hurting Clinton. John Fund of the *Wall Street Journal* editorial page, which was promoting the Aldrich book, was smoother, suggesting that we "coordinate" our message before appearing in televised interviews together. With the exception of George Will, who eviscerated Aldrich on David Brinkley's ABC Sunday morning talk show after speaking with me earlier in the day, the conservatives, hoping to damage Clinton in an election year, were closing ranks behind *Unlimited Access*, whether it was accurate or not. At the *Washington Times*, my alma mater, "Prudenizing" editors went so far as to delete from their reporters' stories any references to my statements challenging *Unlimited Access*. Rush Limbaugh told Aldrich, "Well, you're doing the Lord's work . . . we're glad you were born in America."

Though perhaps I should have known better given the paper's track record on the Clinton scandals, John Fund and the *Wall Street Journal* disappointed me most. A few weeks before the book was published, Fund had arranged for Aldrich to gain credibility by appearing on the op-ed page of the *Journal*, where he was identified only as "an investigative writer." When Aldrich's book appeared, the *Journal* immediately ran an excerpt, even though, I learned from a source directly involved in the controversy, the editors had found a significant factual error in the piece while preparing it for publication. Rather than holding the shaky article and examining the entire book more thoroughly, the editors excised the material they knew to be false, and rushed the balance of the article out to its two million readers. The *Journal* stuck by Aldrich even after Aldrich himself was pressed to admit that the Marriott story was "hypothetical" and "not quite solid." As Aldrich promoted his book and other media organizations exposed it as largely fictional, the defiant *Journal* ran a graphic of a campaign button emblazoned "I Believe Gary Aldrich." (After the flap died down, Al Regnery telephoned me to concede that there had been significant factual problems with the Aldrich book.)

The Aldrich affair was another step forward for me, though I paid a price. Since coming out of the closet almost three years before, I had barely felt a ripple of antigay prejudice from my right-wing friends. So long as I was on the team, my anti-Clinton credentials must have checked any latent bigotry about my personal life, for at the very moment I broke ranks, my sexuality was used to discredit me. To take the sting out of my criticism of their client Aldrich, his publicists maintained that I was denouncing the book because I was a homosexual. They quietly put out word that what really troubled me about *Unlimited Access* was not its inaccuracy, but its antigay themes. At the time I spoke to Isikoff, of course, I had seen only the *Times* story, not the book itself; I hadn't yet known of Aldrich's pathetic claim that Hillary Clinton had adopted a hiring policy that favored "tough, minority and lesbian women" and "weak, minority and gay men." Soon enough, a leading conservative columnist called, seeking a response to the charge that the "gay thing" had turned me against Aldrich. I hung up the phone, more furious and humiliated than I had ever been.

The antigay offensive instantly shattered the false reality I was living in. Apparently, I had been kidding myself all along; I had never won the acceptance that I had sacrificed so much of myself to win. Several months later, still wounded by the whole thing, I discussed the gay-baiting incident with my friend David Keene, who over the years had been a close adviser to Senator Bob Dole and also headed the American Conservative Union, an umbrella group for a range of public policy interests that also employed Craig Shirley as a publicist. A soft-spoken man in tortoiseshell glasses, Keene had the world-weary manner of a longtime Washington insider who had seen it all and didn't take his politics so personally. Even after my apostasy in the Aldrich case, and later over Hillary Clinton, he was still quite willing to help me in any way he could. Over breakfast at the Willard Hotel across the street from the White House, Keene was surprised to hear from me that I had no idea how negative the private reaction among conservatives had been to my coming out as gay in the *Washington Post* in 1994. He suggested matter-of-factly that all would have been well with the conservatives had I just kept my sexuality a secret. I had been headed for a fall for some time as the only openly gay person in the country identified with the conservative movement, Keene gently told me; it was only a question of when. I had been living in a house of cards.

My criticism of *Unlimited Access* gave the conservatives an opening for the blackballing and excommunication that would intensify once *Seduction*, which was completed just before the Aldrich story broke, arrived in bookstores a few weeks hence. As Aldrich wrote in a poison-pen letter to me, in which he intimated that his law enforcement pals were lying in the weeds waiting to harass and discredit me: "From what I hear, there is deep, deep disgust and hatred for what you did to me." Of course, he was right. I soon learned I had been passed over as an invited speaker at the Conservative Political Action Committee's annual meeting, which draws political activists from around the country to the capital to hear the likes of Newt Gingrich, William Bennett, Jack Kemp, Phyllis Schlafly, and Oliver North, and, in the past, me, even as an openly gay man. One friend who attended the CPAC planning session told me that when my name was considered for a panel on the Clinton presidency, I was denounced as a turncoat. When I found out that my replacement on the panel was Gary Aldrich, I didn't know whether to laugh or cry. How could they lionize Gary Aldrich the way they had lionized me?

But that was just the point, I later came to see. Insofar as the conservative movement was concerned, there really was no difference between Aldrich's work and mine. They hadn't cheered *The Real Anita Hill* and Troopergate because they thought the works were journalistically solid, but because they were politically useful. In fact, at a dinner party some time later, Ricky Silberman expressed pretty much exactly those sentiments to Mark Paoletta. The conservatives sided with Aldrich because he was doing their bidding, and they turned on me because I suddenly wasn't. The biggest slap in the face came from my own employer, the place I still considered home, the *Spectator.* When I learned that the magazine planned to fete Aldrich at a Saturday Evening Club dinner, I decided to boycott the event. Sitting among my colleagues and friends, Aldrich denounced me as "Judas."

The more I reflected on the Aldrich affair in the months to come, the more troubling it was. I had been wrong to think that the movement had accepted me as a gay man; my belief that my team had more integrity than the other team was a delusion also. Moreover, I could see that the problem with the conservatives went well beyond their defense of Aldrich's lies. By promoting a mean-spirited diatribe filled with every conceivable cultural prejudice from the Stone Age, the conservatives were revealing who they really were.

Though I didn't yet have the self-awareness to recognize it, the conservatives were right about my work, and me. I really was just a more sophisticated version of Gary Aldrich. We were doppelgängers. *Unlimited Access* tapped into the same hateful vein, the same devious desire to upend the Clinton presidency, that Troopergate did. Aldrich and his supporters were sticking by a lie for the cause, just as I was doing in the Clarence Thomas case. At bottom, I was tormented by the Aldrich affair, and so driven to denounce him, out of self-disgust.

CHAPTER FIFTEEN

BREAKING RANKS

In late summer 1996, I was a guest at the glittery wedding of Barbara Bracher and Ted Olson. Gathered under a white tent in the leafy Virginia suburbs for the joining of Washington's premier conservative power couple was the entire anti-Clinton establishment, everyone from *Wall Street Journal* editorial page editor Robert Bartley to Clarence Thomas to Kenneth Starr. At the reception, C. Boyden Gray grimly joked that since it looked like Starr was not going to find the silver bullet, it was up to me to derail Clinton's reelection with the forthcoming publication of *Seduction*. I smiled wanly and stared into space.

I understood Boyden's frustration. Following the Republican takeover of Congress in 1995, Clinton had adopted a policy of "triangulation"— occupying a middle position between the Gingrich revolutionaries on the right, and the Congressional Democratic leadership on the left. He signed a balanced budget, and turned historic deficits into surpluses, co-opting the Republican Wall Street constituency. In his 1996 State of the Union address, Clinton declared that "the age of big government is over." A few months later, he ended welfare as a federal entitlement. Though it was a truism in Republican circles after 1994 that Clinton could not possibly be reelected, he appeared headed for an easy victory over Republican nominee Bob Dole.

Things had not gone so well on the Republican side of the aisle. In some ways, the Republicans were victims of their own success, having nudged Clinton to the center, but it was Clinton, rather than the Republicans, who reaped the political credit for popular initiatives like the balanced budget and welfare reform. The Republicans enacted needed reforms of Congress, such as stripping the dictatorial powers of committee chairmen by ending proxy voting, and requiring that Congress be governed by the same laws as every-one else, but the big-ticket items from the Contract with America, such as term limits and a constitutional amendment requiring a balanced budget, failed to pass. Voters were not ready to abolish the departments of commerce or education; Republican attacks on the school lunch program and public broadcasting also proved too extreme for the political moment. And the Republican tax cut was then seen as unnecessary in economic good times, especially if revenue reductions meant cuts in Medicare or Social Security.

In the fall of 1995, the Republicans forced the shutting down of the federal government in a budget showdown with Clinton. Particularly given the timing, coming some months after an antigovernment terrorist had bombed a federal building in Oklahoma City, the move was a fiasco of the first order. Their reliance on government programs that cut across political lines, like retirement benefits, turned vast portions of the electorate against the Republican-led Congress, all but ending the Gingrich Revolution in less than a year. To voters, the Republicans seemed to have no program, no convictions, no vision for the country after liberalism was reined in. By successfully triangulating, Clinton left the Republicans clinging to a cluster of unpopular right-wing social issues. The only other thing holding the GOP together was its dead-end anti-Clinton investigations and a common loathing of the Clintons—which persisted, and even grew more intense, as Clinton adopted the most appealing parts of their agenda.

What was left of the conservative intelligentsia during this period seemed more out of touch, intolerant, and dangerous than did the Republican leadership in Washington. Riven by disagreements on everything from affirmative action to immigration to foreign policy, the ex–Cold Warriors pushed their culture war themes to their logical extreme. Writing in *Commentary*, Norman Podhoretz vented his antigay obsessions, lamenting the fact that the culture no longer regarded homosexuality as a "perversion or even a mental illness," and warning of a new wave of young boys being "encouraged and seduced" into homosexuality because "feminism" had made "young girls more formidably intimidating." Bill Kristol, who once tried to broker a moderate compromise in the GOP between pro-life and pro-choice Republicans, now laid down a much harder line in the *Weekly Standard*, a new conservative magazine published by Rupert Murdoch: "But the truth is that abortion is today the bloody crossroads of American politics. It is where judicial liberation (from the Constitution), sexual liberation (from traditional mores), and women's liberation (from natural distinctions) come together." One leading book from the Free Press, *The Bell Curve*, by Charles Murray and Richard Herrnstein, argued that blacks were genetically inferior, while another, *The End of Racism*, by Dinesh D'Souza—who confessed to having a "slightly malevolent cast of mind"—argued that blacks were culturally inferior. In *Slouching Towards Gomorrah*, Judge Robert Bork called for the "rise of an energetic, optimistic, politically sophisticated religious conservatism." Having formerly represented himself as a "strict constructionist," Bork revealed himself to be unqualified to sit on any court with his call for a constitutional amendment that would permit Congress to overrule any federal court decision with which it disagreed.

The madness of the moment was perhaps best captured by the conservative journal *First Things*, which published a symposium entitled "The End of Democracy? The Judicial Usurpation of Politics." Contributors pilloried recent liberal court decisions on abortion, gay rights, and assisted suicide and concluded that the American "regime"—its entire system of government— had become "morally illegitimate." With the endorsement of Bork and a number of influential movement intellectuals, the magazine's editor, a Lutheran turned Catholic theologian named Richard John Neuhaus, compared the United States to Nazi Germany, and suggested that the time had come when "conscientious citizens" might properly engage in seditious activities "ranging from noncompliance, to resistance, to civil disobedience, to morally justified revolution." In sanctioning the use of force against the "regime," these conservatives made the parallel between the outer fringes of 1960s-style radicalism and the radicalism of the Gingrich era explicit and complete.

As *Seduction* hit the stores in October 1996, a few weeks before the election, William Safire in the *New York Times* and the *Wall Street Journal* editorial page were predicting Hillary Clinton's imminent indictment for obstruction of justice—the very line that Starr prosecutor Hick Ewing had failed to get me to publish in my book. The *American Spectator* was accusing Hillary Clinton of engaging in "an obstruction of justice at the highest level since Watergate." And Bob Tyrrell, while dispatching David Henderson, the head of the Arkansas Project, to deal with Tyrrell's son's drug abuse problems, was claiming to have unearthed evidence that Clinton used drugs heavily and "may have been treated for a drug overdose." Clearly, there would be no pleasing these people with a rational book on the First Lady.

On the day the book was published, I opened the *Washington Times*, where I once had worked, to find a story splashed across the front page headlined "Sainthood from a Hillary Critic." The infuriated tone of the article and the lead quotes announced to the leadership of the conservative movement, which regarded the *Times* as the Bible, that the book was a whitewash, written to please my liberal critics. Publisher Alfred Regnery observed, "The people he's trying to please hate him." Tagging me as an "apologist" for the First Lady, the *Times* piece ensured from day one that the book would not get a hearing on the right.

In the Murdoch-owned *New York Post*, the neoconservative critic Hilton Kramer argued that I was soft on Hillary because my psyche could not endure another round of attacks from the left after *The Real Anita Hill* and Troopergate. "It is always a bad sign in a tough-minded journalist when he begins to exhibit symptoms of wanting to be liked. But this seems to have been the impulse that had overtaken the writing of *The Seduction of Hillary Rodham*," Kramer wrote. "The book closes with a hearts and flowers image of 'Hillary in her role as successful mother.' It isn't the only moment when the reader needs a strong stomach to get through it." In a sardonic review in the *Weekly Standard* titled "Brock Loves Hillary," which even Wlady told me he found homophobic, Midge Decter seemed to imply that what goes on in a marriage between a man and a woman was beyond my comprehension. Decter instructed me to return to "my proper calling, the unearthing of dark secrets."

Along with these reviews came outright disinvitations to appear on the conservative media outlets that had promoted my earlier work, including G. Gordon Liddy's and Oliver North's popular radio talk shows. After years in the movement, I thought I had earned the right to a forum, even if now a skeptical one, to make my case. Yet Bay Buchanan, Pat's sister and the cohost of CNBC's *Equal Time,* told me flatly that only if I had taken "the right perspective" on Hillary would the conservatives have been willing to host me. At one of Grover Norquist's Wednesday Group strategy sessions, with seventy leading conservative activists in attendance, many of them close associates of mine over the years, I was nominated in absentia for the Kevin Phillips Award, so named for a Republican who makes a living "helping the other team."* The *American Spectator* ran an excerpt from the book on Hillary's health care debacle, and Bob and Wlady, either out of personal loyalty or respect for my prior work, I'm not sure which, seemed to stand behind me. Yet Richard Mellon Scaife wanted me fired. (Scaife was understandably upset, for in an arrangement that had the sanction of my employers, some Arkansas Project funds ended up paying the salaries of some of the *Spectator* researchers who worked on *Seduction.*)

Perhaps to buck up my spirits, Bob invited me to accompany him to a November 1996 election night party being held by William F. Buckley and his socialite wife, Pat, at their maisonette apartment on the Upper East Side of Manhattan. Bob generously put me up at the New York Athletic Club on Central Park South, and before heading over to the Buckleys', he took me to meet the author Tom Wolfe for cocktails at Wolfe's Upper East Side apartment. In the 1960s, Wolfe had been an originator of first-person, participatory New Journalism, a literary style he appropriated in a series of critically acclaimed and commercially successful novels that emphasized conservative cultural themes such as *The Right Stuff* and *Bonfire of the Vanities.* He also sat on the *Spectator*'s board of editorial advisers. Walking off the elevator into Wolfe's Art Deco style apartment, with its gleaming Biedermeier antiques, was like stepping into the pages of one of those pretentious, aesthetically sterile *Architectural Digest* spreads.

Wolfe greeted us in his trademark white wool three-piece suit and pastel-colored shirt and tie. A fan of my Troopergate piece, Wolfe inevi-

---

*Phillips, a Republican political strategist and author who first gained notoriety by explaining how the GOP could become a majority party by making cultural appeals in the conservative South, angered the right wing in later years by criticizing orthodox Republican economics.

tably brought up the subject of the just published *Seduction*. Referencing Midge Decter's review in the *Weekly Standard*, Wolfe told me not to despair. "Those people"—by which he meant the Jewish neocon *Commentary* circle—"have never appreciated my work either. They're congenitally negative." Wolfe's comment was cold comfort.

Given the trends in the election returns favoring Bill Clinton, the Buckleys' party turned out to be a somber, sparsely attended affair. I don't think I laid eyes on Bill all evening—perhaps the languid eminence had already retired—but when Bob and I arrived at the grand first-floor apartment that seemed to me to sit on an entire quarter city block, I recognized a mummified Pat Buckley, drink in hand, wandering through a wide entry hall as if she had no idea where she was. I had met Bill through an appearance I had made on his PBS show *Firing Line*, but never Pat. As Bob darted off to greet his friend Taki Theodoracopulos, Pat fixed an icy stare on me. Not knowing what else to do, I introduced myself, and she said she knew exactly who I was: She had seen a review of *Seduction* in the Sunday *New York Times* a few weeks before, by the respected journalist James Stewart, who had written that I tried to "achieve justice for my subject in the broadest sense." In a manner that suggested she was three sheets to the wind, Pat declaimed, "Well, you screwed that up!"

Back in Washington, for several weeks I hardly heard a word of encouragement or support or even concern from anyone I had known in the movement. One exception was Mary Matalin, the Republican political adviser turned talk show host. Mary had read and liked the book. From what she had gleaned over the years from her husband, Clinton insider James Carville, the book rang true, she told me. She made a point of inviting me on her nationally syndicated radio show to discuss it.

The right-wing dissing of the book might well have been predicted, for in publishing it, I was willfully defeating the expectations of my market and purposely thumbing my nose at the Clinton crazies. After all, I had gone much further than I really had to, taking several of Hillary's conservative critics to task by name, and pointedly exposing the fallacies of their arguments. And in the epilogue, I denounced the politics of hate and mindless Clinton-bashing that had deformed the modern conservative movement.

Not surprisingly, considering the size of the advance, the enormous print run, and the sudden lack of audience, *Seduction* was a commercial disaster, selling less than half the number of copies of *The Real Anita Hill*. (In the book publishing industry, authors keep their advances regardless of how a book performs. The advance represents a guess by the publisher about how the book will sell, and if it underperforms, the publisher eats the loss. The disappointing sales of *Seduction* would undoubtedly impinge on the size of any advance for a future book, I knew, but writing another book was the farthest thing from my mind. So, with two-thirds of the advance for *Seduction* due on the date of publication in October, financially speaking, I had a soft landing.)

On the Friday night of the week my book came out, I was planning to attend a party at the Olsons' to celebrate the end of the first session of Congress under Republican control in more than four decades. The crowd the Olsons were expecting was essentially the same cast of characters— Republican lawyers, Capitol Hill aides, and conservative writers—whom I had often entertained in my own home. Barbara Olson's cohost was Ginni Thomas. On the day when the *Washington Times* blasted my book, I retrieved from my car phone a voice mail message from Barbara, and I almost drove off the road. "Given what's happened, I don't think you'd be comfortable at the party," she deadpanned. Though Clarence Thomas went to the party and vigorously defended me, I was no longer welcome in my own circle. Despite Adam Bellow's optimism, I never expected the conservatives to praise *Seduction* or to rush out and buy it. What I didn't anticipate was the personal dissing. I never thought I would lose friends over what I did or didn't write. Naively, I guess I was still expecting some level of acceptance on the right for what to me was a transparently honest act.

In Washington, the professional and the social overlap to an extraordinary extent. A handful of my closer conservative friends did stick by me. Michael and Arianna Huffington, for instance, were kind enough to throw a small party to celebrate the book's publication. Ricky and Larry Silberman came, and Laura Ingraham, and Bob and Wlady from the *Spectator,* and Mark Paoletta and Lee Liberman, and Arnaud and Alexandra de Borchgrave. As was her way at such events, Arianna filled out the room by tacking on several other hangers-on from her Rolodex whom I did not know well, and had tried to avoid over the years, such as the priggish neocon writers David Frum of the *Weekly Standard* and his wife, Danielle Crittenden, who edited the Independent Women's Forum newsletter. The scene was funereal as we sucked on our baby lamb chops and looked at our shoes, a far cry from the champagne-popping toasts to *The Real Anita Hill*. No one seemed happy to be there, nor was I.

Soon enough, excommunication became a two-way street. Since my relationships were based on little else but partisan politics, there was little to sustain them once I deviated from the party line. I lost many party invitations; others I turned down, including a huge fete hosted by Boyden Gray at his Georgetown mansion in honor of Rush Limbaugh. I reluctantly accepted Laura Ingraham's invitation to watch Bill Clinton's State of the Union address in January 1997 with her and her friends at her town house in Woodley Park. As I arrived at the house, which was decked out in an oversized southwestern motif more appropriate for a bachelor's mountain hideaway, the network cameras were coming on. When I saw one of Ken Starr's deputies, Brett Kavanaugh, who was sitting across from me, mouth the word "bitch" when the camera panned to Hillary, I excused myself and sat in the darkened pine-scented dining room alone, smoking. I started again soon after *Seduction* was published because I didn't know what else to do.

As for Arianna, we parted ways over the direction she was taking in her syndicated column. After a poor start, Arianna turned out some solid columns as a deft critic of the Gingrich Revolution and seemed to resist succumbing to the Clinton scandal mania that infected the ranks of the conservative pundits. Yet at a Christmas luncheon I attended at her spacious Brentwood home in 1997, where she had moved with her two young daughters as part of the divorce settlement with Michael, taking the gaudy interiors with her from Washington and tacking them up in the California sunshine, Arianna was curiously preoccupied by a story that had been reported in *Insight* magazine, charging that the Clinton administration was "selling" burial plots at Arlington National Cemetery to fat-cat donors.

Based on anonymous sources, the story quickly spread from the radio—
G. Gordon Liddy accused the administration of "defiling the sacred dead of
the country"—to Capitol Hill, where indignant Republican congressmen
demanded an inquiry. The story had all the earmarks of the obvious hoax it
turned out to be, and at lunch that day I practically begged Arianna to let it
go. The anti-Clinton mania—I began to think of it literally as a disease—had
seeped into her brain cells, too. She mounted a furious campaign to get the
body of former Clinton ambassador Larry Lawrence dug up from Arlington
National Cemetery after Republicans discovered he'd exaggerated his military record. In the event, Arianna got sued for libel for asserting that
Lawrence had been inappropriately interred at Arlington because his
widow, Sheila, had been having an affair with Clinton.

At least in part, I attributed the anti-Clintonism of both Laura and
Arianna to the new influence on our circle of Internet gossip Matt Drudge,
who, I was surprised to see, was also present at Huffington's Christmas
lunch. I suppose by now I should have grown accustomed to Arianna's
style of entertaining, in which she used every opportunity, even Christmas,
to network. As Arianna's ancient Greek mother roamed barefoot through
the oddball crowd proffering a platter of stuffed grape leaves, Drudge
swept in, accompanied by Julia Phillips, the ex–movie executive who
had written the tell-all book *You'll Never Eat Lunch in This Town Again*.
Though Phillips was obviously drunk at the time, Arianna continued refill-
ing her tumbler with champagne as she pumped her for Hollywood dirt.

I had first met Drudge six months before, in June 1997, when Laura, who
had struck up an e-mail relationship with him, suggested we cohost a
Washington dinner party for Drudge. Though his one-man website was
widely read by political and media insiders, back then Drudge was toiling in
anonymity from a small apartment in downtown Hollywood. Since I had
done no entertaining since *Seduction* came out—I had no one to entertain!—
I went along with Laura's suggestion that we assemble a few journalists and
politicos to meet and take a measure of the man behind the *Drudge Report*.
By design, or, I suppose, by necessity, the group was more eclectic than any
I had ever drawn together: among others, Andrew Sullivan, Ruth Shalit, and
Jeffrey Rosen from the *New Republic;* Bill Press from CNN's *Crossfire;*

Howard Fineman from *Newsweek;* Tucker Carlson from the *Weekly Standard;* James Warren of the *Chicago Tribune,* who appeared to be one of Laura's suitors; journalist Elizabeth Drew; Republican Congressman Mark Foley; and Michael Huffington.

Drudge was a self-created, self-trained, and self-edited phenomenon of the Internet age. He had gotten his start e-mailing tips picked up about ongoing film projects and confidential box office numbers, often literally out of trash cans, at the CBS Studios, where he worked as a gift shop cashier. As his e-mail list mushroomed, he set up a website, which provided links to newspapers, magazines, and popular columns, and expanded his coverage to include politics, specializing in anti-Clinton gossip. Though he skillfully exploited the fact that he worked from the West Coast, often being the first to report news that would appear in the morning papers on the East Coast by combing their websites the evening before, many of his exclusive scoops, such as reports that Hillary Clinton would be indicted, or that Commerce Secretary Ron Brown, who had died in a plane crash, might have been murdered, proved notoriously unreliable. His most sensational stories involved outing the sex life of President Clinton. Predictably, the right wing embraced Drudge as the newest frontier in the propaganda wars, and in the next few years, he would host a talk show on Rupert Murdoch's Fox News Channel, sell a book through the Conservative Book Club, and appear as an honored speaker before organizations of the Christian Right.

A mischievous imp, Drudge often was clad in an ill-fitting seersucker suit and straw fedora, in a seedy imitation of his idol Walter Winchell, who had invented the modern gossip column. He delighted in challenging and tweaking the media elites, a quality I had always admired. He had an unerring talent for giving his readers what they wanted, and a nebbishy, beguiling personal charm. His politics were right wing—he often expressed support for Pat Buchanan—though no serious thought seemed to have gone into his convictions. His Clinton bashing appeared designed merely to drive attention to his site. A loner, he seemed to be looking in the wrong place for attention. In all of these ways, I identified with Drudge, all the more so during an amusing interlude in which I learned that Drudge and I had even more in common than I thought.

After the June Washington dinner at my house, Drudge stayed in touch. We made arrangements to have dinner again when I was visiting Los Angeles in late July to celebrate my thirty-fifth birthday. Drudge picked me up at a friend's house in the Hollywood Hills in his red Geo Metro, arriving with an impressive bouquet of yellow roses. Jesus, I thought, Drudge thinks we're going on a date. After dinner at the famed West Hollywood restaurant Dan Tana's, he suggested we go barhopping along the gay strip on Santa Monica Boulevard, which Drudge navigated like a pro. At a bar called Rage, I accepted his invitation to dance, but I was much more interested in checking out two guys who were dancing nearby. When the couple disappeared, I asked Drudge if he had seen where the pair had gone. "Yeah," Drudge quacked, "I saw what was going on there, and I stepped on one of their feet really hard to get rid of them." The gesture was sweet, in a way, but also scary, and I quickly called it a night. (Six months hence, I received the following e-mail message from Drudge, under the subject heading "XXX." Drudge wrote: "Laura [Ingraham] spreading stuff about you and me being fuck buddies. I should only be so lucky.")*

My talks with Drudge focused on how he was being manipulated by the right, on what *not* to do with his career. During this period, I had similar conversations with Huffington and with Ingraham, who was now doing commentary on the CBS Evening News on Sundays, in an attempt to persuade her to modulate her extremist rhetoric. I thought both Drudge and Ingraham, neither of whom had ever worked as journalists, might learn something from my war stories. We talked about Troopergate, Gary Aldrich, and Hillary Clinton. Needless to say, my concerns made no impression on them. Arianna, Laura, Drudge—sadly, they were all lost causes. They needed to enroll in Clintons Anonymous.

Back in Washington, I was in a political no-man's-land, just me and my smokes. For several weeks after *Seduction* came out, I did little but sit alone

---

*Drudge later denied a report that he was gay in the 1999 book *Dish: The Inside Story of the World of Gossip* by Jeannette Walls.

in my house in Georgetown, the scene of so many raucous right-wing dinner parties, thinking and reflecting and smoking like a chimney. It felt amazingly good to have acted freely, I was stronger for having endured the controversy, and I had no regrets about the editorial decisions I had made. Aside from the conservatives, on the whole, reviewers had found *Seduction* to be fair, well balanced, and accurate—"more perspective and calm than usually given elsewhere," as the *Los Angeles Times* put it. I was proud of the book. Still, for a while, I was perplexed and hurt by what had happened to me. Though I had anticipated some stormy moments in my career, I hadn't been ready to blow up my world and sacrifice the only self-identity I had. I was sorely disappointed in the conservatives; and, in what was admittedly something of a rerun of the emotional cycles of my young adulthood, I blamed them for using me and tossing me aside. With a tone that was far too self-righteous and emotionally overwrought, I went public with my raw criticisms and bruised feelings.

Some weeks before *The Seduction of Hillary Rodham* was published, I received an invitation to participate in a panel discussion on the Clintons at an annual conservative retreat held over New Year's weekend. Buoyed by the Republican takeover of Congress back in 1995, Laura Ingraham and I dreamed up the idea of having an alternative event to the Democrats' Renaissance Weekend, an annual policy retreat and networking fest in Hilton Head, South Carolina, which the Clintons had done much to popularize in liberal circles. What began as a typical mocking conversation between Laura and me over drinks in my living room soon became a conservative institution, bankrolled with right-wing money, covered in the national media, and attracting the Republican congressional leadership. Judge Silberman had coined the fitting name Dark Ages for our counterweekend. Hunkered down writing the Hillary Clinton book, I had skipped the first Dark Ages Weekend in Miami in 1996, and I debated skipping the second, knowing that I would feel like a skunk at a garden party. My connection to cofounder Laura, which I had not yet severed, ensured that my invitation was not withdrawn. When I saw the lineup for the panel, perhaps the most hostile setting one could have devised for me, I couldn't resist the challenge of walking into the belly of the beast.

Navigating my way through the lobby of Arizona's luxurious Biltmore Hotel in Phoenix was nightmarish, since it was the first time since the Hillary book came out that I came nose to nose with my conservative critics. As I gazed into the crowd, I had to make an instant assessment: Which ones were, or most likely were not, speaking to me anymore? As they gazed back at me, these people who had made my career, who had cheered me on and defended me and fought by my side for so long, what were they thinking? Because I barely had a drop of alcohol and was under immense stress in the final several months of the Hillary project, I had lost about twenty pounds since the booze-soaked days of my Gingrich house parties. According to Laura, the rumor du jour was that I was suffering from AIDS-related dementia. How else to explain my soft spot for Hillary?

A thick cloud of bitterness hung over the conference. In November, Clinton became the first Democratic president since Franklin Roosevelt to win reelection, and the Gingrich Republicans, unable to address the social and economic conditions of the country, had failed to build up their congressional majority. Conservatism was adrift, bereft of ideas, as never before. Yet influential conservative commentators like William Bennett argued that the Republican candidate, Senator Bob Dole, had lost because he failed to mount a forceful attack on Clinton's ethics. Thus after most of the attendees spent the morning on a shooting range firing antique guns, courtesy of the National Rifle Association, the panel on "the Clinton scandals," rather than any forum on the future policy direction of the Republican Party, drew a full house.

It is hard to describe, but the Republican right, with religious-like faith and fervor, continued to maintain that the Clinton scandals represented a wide pattern of vague criminality by the first couple, and therefore that it was only a matter of time until the truth would be revealed, the Clinton administration would be brought down, and the world would be set right again. They seemed to believe this, or at least they asserted it, all the more intensely the more they failed to prove any of it, and they went around the bend as the promised indictments never came. Appearing on the dais with me were John Fund, Barbara Olson, and G. Gordon Liddy. I licked my chops as I listened to the presentations of my copanelists, culminating with Liddy's loopy theories about Vincent Foster's murder, delivered in his familiar nasal sarcasm. From the podium, Liddy bragged that he used photos of the Clintons for target practice on a shooting range. When my turn came, I blasted the conservative movement for undermining its own cause by making dishonest and unjust claims against the Clintons. Specifically citing Fund and Liddy, I concluded, "Injecting hatred and phony charges into our politics is a pretty bad thing, no matter who is targeted."

For the most part, the audience listened politely, if unenthusiastically, but my talk did resonate with at least one conservative in the room. As I left the podium, my old *Washington Times* boss John Podhoretz approached me breathlessly, congratulated me on the presentation, and asked if he could publish my remarks as an essay in the *Weekly Standard*, which John now edited. Gratified, if shocked, that there was a constituency for my message on the right, I told him I would be more than happy to comply. Perhaps, I thought, the intellectual neoconservatives, who stood apart from the Clinton crazies, might help the Republicans get back on track. Because I didn't really know how else to think of myself, I wrote the *Weekly Standard* article as a nominal conservative. Yet I knew I was an outsider.

Shortly after returning from the conference, I received a call from an editor at *Esquire* magazine, Mark Warren, who said he was interested in speaking to me about doing some freelance political profiles. Over drinks at the Mayflower Hotel in downtown Washington, before we turned to discussing whatever article ideas Mark had for me, I told him of the reaction in the conservative movement to *Seduction*, and of the personal toll it had taken on me. With his sonorous voice and his editor's eye for a compelling narrative, Mark convinced me to write up the account as my first piece for *Esquire*, which the magazine published in June 1997 under the headline "Confessions of a Right-Wing Hit Man." In the article, I told the story of "my fall from grace in Washington," recounting the public attacks and private slights that I had suffered at the hands of the conservatives. I then disassociated myself from the conservative movement, and resigned for good the niche I had created, declaring melodramatically, "David Brock the road warrior of the right is dead."

Publicly quitting the conservative "team" drew an important line of demarcation for me personally, ratifying in print all of the interior growth I had experienced in the prior two years. As far as it went, the article contained a lot of truth—about the psychology and politics of hate, about the stifling intellectual intolerance and the stamping out of dissent in the ranks common to many political sects, and about the elusive nature of friendship in Washington. Yet I unintentionally left out a major aspect of the story, which gave it a self-serving and even misleading slant, creating a wrong impression of my victimhood to the movement and even of my martyrdom to honest journalism. The article fell short in telling the truth about myself, about my role in the events described, and about my own flawed work. Only a few months had passed since the publication of *Seduction*, not enough time to allow me to see my own actions for what they were and to take responsibility for them. That process was a contemplative one, it would have to come from within; no editor, no one, could direct me to do it. I was just too blocked by my instincts for self-preservation, and by my narcissism, to see myself as I really had been, and too weak to face the humiliation of public self-revelation.

I reflexively stood by the accuracy of both *The Real Anita Hill* and Troopergate. During the editing process, I did instinctively signal my discomfort with the Anita Hill book in a conversation with Mark. It was hardly a signal, actually; it was little more than a hesitant inflection in my voice, a verbal flinch that prompted Mark to say that I ought not write anything that could cause my critics to dismiss my first book as "a work of political immaturity." Though Mark's description fit *The Real Anita Hill* well—indeed, it was far too kind—I accepted Mark's understandable concern for my authorial reputation. I put my inchoate misgivings about my work back in cold storage, and took the easy way out. Confessing to my past journalistic sins would have disturbed the story line in which I naturally wanted to portray myself as I had long seen but misrepresented myself—as a person of high integrity, a truth teller always, a good guy, suddenly and unfairly excommunicated by a disreputable political movement. This point of view was driven home by a gimmicky full-page photo, in which I posed tied to a tree, buried up to my waist in kindling wood, in a representation of a sainted heretic being burned at the stake—"Saint Joan in jeans," as Hilton Kramer memorably described it. Yet I was no martyr.

Though when I wrote the *Esquire* piece I saw myself as an aggrieved party, I was no victim, either. As more time passed and I gained more perspective, I could see that the way in which the conservatives behaved toward me was warranted. The conservatives correctly labeled me as the author of a sympathetic Hillary biography. And so, as they did in the Aldrich case, the conservatives behaved as movements or cults do—they killed my subversive book, denounced me personally, and treated me as the heretic that I was. Tellingly, my heresy was not yet a rejection of conservatism, but of Clinton-hating, the conservatives' only remaining creed.

The conservatives also were right in their suspicion that my decisions to come out of the closet, and to break ranks over the Arkansas Project, and Gary Aldrich, and Hillary Clinton, were not isolated events, but rather difficult and uneven steps on a path of self-discovery. I had a deep, though still mostly unconscious, desire to be cast out of a movement in which I never belonged. The conservatives saw that through my actions, I had broken with them first. In boycotting my book and kicking me away, they hadn't done anything that I hadn't invited them to do. I *was* a turncoat, and they treated me accordingly. The issue the conservatives misunderstood was one of causality. I did not contrive to somehow "change" myself, stage a defection from the movement, impress people who hated me, and execute a senseless scheme to reinvent what was by my lights a wildly successful career on the right. Rather, it happened the other way around: After consciously lying and covering up and bullying a source in the review of *Strange Justice*, as my descent into conservatism reached its nadir, writing the Hillary book changed me and helped me find my character.

Some of the estrangements pained me, but I learned that Washington is above all else a political town. I knew that Mark Paoletta, for example, was having trouble defending his relationship with me to his Republican colleagues on Capitol Hill, where his job was to investigate the Clinton White House, and we gradually drifted apart. Mark had a brood of children at home to support and a promising career ahead of him. Who could blame him? One of the last times I saw him was at a small Sunday night dinner at Lee Liberman's split-level home in suburban Virginia, well after my *Esquire* defection. I had never spoken with Mark or Lee about the *Strange Justice* fiasco, for which I held myself solely responsible. The evening seemed uncomfortable for everyone, and I found myself wondering why Lee had made the effort. Was it to see how far I would go in revealing state secrets? To check my sanity? Or did Lee really care on a human level about what I was going through?

In any case, the vast majority of the friendships I lost weren't friendships at all. I lived in a mutual use society. The conservatives used me. What I wasn't yet ready to admit in *Esquire* was that I used them, too. When we could not or would not be of use to one another any longer, the relationships dissolved. I now know that this parting of the ways wasn't nearly as much their fault as it was mine. People could only understand me as I understood myself—as a right-wing hit man. They couldn't know me, they couldn't be my friends, they couldn't love me, because I didn't know or love myself. By the same token, I didn't really know what friendship was, nor was I ready to give it.

I could see these realities and let go of my hard feelings only through several more months of arduous self-examination. I had to pass through the all-too-familiar phase of feeling rejected and rejecting back. Frankly, I had to resist the fallacy of my first instinct, which was to adopt an "us versus them" mentality in reverse and seek vengeance on the conservatives for spurning me. Instead I worked to find a separate sense of self and move on with my life.

With the exception of Andrew, who had been a constant, reassuring presence, and the ever faithful Becky Borders, who remained so, I was literally starting over. With the exception of a couple of other friends who were not involved in politics, almost everyone else in my life—people from different walks of life, gay and straight, of varying political persuasions—was new. Although the early months of 1997 were sometimes dark and lonely, I began to learn a lesson of life: As long as I am true to myself, I can handle being alone. Happily, in what was really no time at all, I was blessed to have more than a dozen new friends, genuine friends who were not interested in what I could do for them, or vice versa.

Shortly after *Seduction* was published, I leased a pied-à-terre on the top floor of a four-story walk-up in the West Village of New York City to escape the Washington doldrums, and I used it as a base to meet new people who had fewer preconceptions about me. I went on the first real vacation I had taken in years, to the Caribbean island of Mustique, with friends from New York. I took the now-divorced Michael Huffington on a tour of the gay nightlife in London. I began working out with weights for the first time, and I found acupuncture therapy to be a godsend. I learned to dress without imitating someone else's sense of style. Learning the ropes of maintaining healthy dating relationships at age thirty-five was more challenging, but in time I have managed to do that, too. These experiences were a powerful antidote to the tangle of misplaced emotions, self-loathing, and rigid isolation that had shaped my past frame of mind, and therefore my early writing career. Life outside the conservative bubble held the promise of liberation.

Through most of 1997, as I began to metamorphose, I remained nominally employed at the *American Spectator*, appearing at the office irregularly and rarely writing. Though I went out of my way to exempt *Spectator* editor Bob Tyrrell from criticism in *Esquire* because I wanted to hang on to my salary, the situation at the *Spectator* grew more tense anyway. A problem that appeared with the publication of *Seduction*, and grew with my speech at Dark Ages, now metastasized. By attacking the right-wing scandal machinery, I was directly attacking the *Spectator*'s raison d'être. To make matters worse, some conservatives came forward and agreed with the thrust of my *Esquire* piece. "There is a type of thinking on the right that if you don't agree with everything, you're a traitor to the movement," Bill Kristol told the *Washington Post*. Other commentators condemned the piece as a disgraceful publicity stunt, including Brent Bozell, the chairman of an influential right-wing media watchdog group, the Media Research Center, who wrote in the *Washington Times*, "Brock has become a whiny, ungrateful embarrassment to the conservative movement—and to the *American Spectator*." In an on-line column in *Slate*, conservative writer Tucker Carlson slammed me as an opportunist who was "more marketable than ever" after breaking ranks. I suppose Tucker was trying to make me feel better when he told me in a subsequent conversation that his wife had chided him for attacking me, since she knew that he agreed with everything I had written in *Esquire.* "I do agree with you," Tucker told me, "but I told her it was a few hundred bucks for a few minutes' work."

The private reactions were more noxious still. I learned through Ricky Silberman that Judge Silberman considered my criticism of fellow colleagues and ex-friends in *Esquire* an act of supreme disloyalty, and my relationship with the couple ended soon thereafter. They simply stopped telephoning, and so did I. Walking around my Georgetown neighborhood, I would occasionally see my old surrogate parents, averting my glances and cutting me dead. I shuddered during these difficult moments until I learned through another gay friend of the Silbermans, who approached me at a social event, that the Silbermans attributed my breaking ranks to emotional problems inherent in my homosexuality. Apparently, I was "acting out," just like the "lesbian" Anita Hill had.

Wlady telephoned to tell me that Barbara Ledeen, director of the antifeminist Independent Women's Forum, whose husband, Iran-contra figure Michael Ledeen, I had criticized, not in the *Esquire* piece, but in the follow-up discussion on-line with Tucker Carlson, had threatened hyperbolically to "firebomb" my house. Such feelings of betrayal were understandable. The article was a betrayal. It was not a betrayal of friendship, though I had once considered the Silbermans and the Ledeens to be friends. It was a betrayal of the only thing that had forged our bond: the conservative movement.

A couple of weeks after the article appeared, Bob summoned me to dinner at the Jockey Club to chastise me. Bob brought Grover Norquist along as his enforcer of omerta, the Mafia's code of silence. "There are ways of dealing with these things privately, by calling people on the telephone, rather than airing them publicly," Norquist warned me darkly. What I couldn't laugh off was my predicament at the *Spectator.* Now that I refused to take dictation from the movement, what kind of work could I possibly do at the magazine? Not much, as I soon found out.

Unsure if I could craft a piece that I would be comfortable writing, and that my editors would be comfortable publishing, I didn't write much in 1997. In September, I filed a profile of conservative Utah Senator Orrin

Hatch, who had come under attack by the keepers of conservative dogma as a squish. I argued that Hatch's belief that the government had a role in maintaining a social safety net for those most in need was not incompatible with conservative values, and that his willingness to work with Democrats to solve social ills was preferable to Newt Gingrich's survival-of-the-fittest politics. I lauded Hatch for his work on the Ryan White legislation funding research for AIDS, and for his efforts to reach across the aisle to the Democrats to pass a children's health insurance bill. In my years at the *Spectator*, I had never once had a piece held. When I inquired about the holdup, an irritated Wlady told me that I seemed to be "defending socialism." The writing was on the wall. My attempt to introduce anything but liberal-bashing pieces into the magazine would fail.

The Hatch debacle was not the only ominous sign of my imminent demise at the magazine. The month of September also saw internal tumult at the *Spectator* surrounding the Arkansas Project, the anti-Clinton dirt-digging operation. For some time, *Spectator* publisher Ron Burr had been concerned that, since the project's focus was not primarily journalistic but rather to provide covert support to Starr Whitewater witness David Hale, the magazine might be running afoul of tax laws governing nonprofits that prohibit partisan political activities, meaning that the *Spectator* could lose its tax-exempt status. He was also concerned about the issue of "personal inurement," given that project heads David Henderson, who was also a *Spectator* director, and Stephen Boynton were paying themselves hundreds of thousands of dollars, and the magazine was picking up many of Bob Tyrrell's personal expenses. When Ron asked Tyrrell for authorization to bring in an independent accounting firm to conduct a forensic audit to find out how the $2.4 million in Scaife funds was being spent, Tyrrell and Ted Olson went ballistic.

Henderson, Scaife's man on the board, had been instrumental in Olson's joining the board. To head off the Burr audit, Tyrrell and Olson maneuvered to put Henderson into a formal management job at the magazine. At a *Spectator* board meeting in May 1997 at the Waldorf-Astoria in New York, Olson seconded the motion to give Henderson the job. According to Burr, problems with the Arkansas Project were discussed at this meeting, but the discussion was not reflected in board minutes because one director moved to strike any references to it. Things came to a head in early July, at a meeting in Ted Olson's Washington law office, when Tyrrell walked in and stated that Richard Larry of the Scaife Foundation had charged Burr with misallocating Arkansas Project funds.

Feeling as if he were being set up, Burr presented his demands for an independent audit. In early October, Burr was fired at a hastily called meeting of the board on a Sunday evening at Tyrrell's home. Though he was a member of the board, Burr was not informed of the meeting and thus could not defend himself against whatever accusations were being leveled against him. A few days later, Burr called me and told me he had learned that Olson had run the rump board meeting and engineered his firing. Burr, who had worked for the magazine since its founding thirty years before, was told by Tyrrell to negotiate his severance with Olson. Burr was then told he would get no severance unless he agreed in writing never again to discuss *Spectator* business or the Arkansas Project.

Why Olson, who had assiduously courted Bob since going on the board some months back—"infantilizing him" in Wlady's words—worked to cover up the Arkansas Project remains a subject of speculation. I believe his main motivation was to protect Starr's witness, Hale, from being tainted by his close association with the Scaife-backed project. Recruited by Henderson to be Hale's lawyer, Olson had provided Hale with about $140,000 in free services. Testimony by Hale was central to Starr's office winning fraud convictions in 1996 against James and Susan McDougal, who had been partners of the Clintons in the failed Whitewater investment. At the time of the Arkansas Project cover-up, Starr was still trying to prove Hale's allegations against Clinton and that Clinton had lied under oath about his dealings with Hale. Whatever Ted's personal motives may have been, several changes were made within the *Spectator* organization to install Olson loyalists and protect the Arkansas Project from exposure. Olson himself was elected to replace Burr on the board as secretary-treasurer. Terry Eastland, a close friend of Olson's and Starr's, was brought in as publisher. P. J. O'Rourke, a close friend of Burr's who had just written an op-ed in the *New York Times* warning the right of the futility of Clinton-bashing, quit the editorial advisory board. Columnist Bob Novak joined the foundation board, as did none other than newlywed Barbara Olson. The *Spectator* soon commenced a review of the project, not an audit, and refused to disclose the results.

Following the rump board meeting, unsolicited word was sent to me, through a conservative acquaintance of mine who was a close associate of Olson's at Gibson, Dunn & Crutcher, that my position was not in jeopardy. Olson *was* calling the shots. "You're okay," I was told by Olson's emissary, but Burr, who had shown courage and integrity in taking on the Arkansas Project, thought otherwise. A few days after his firing, Burr telephoned me at home with the admonition "You're next." Burr explained that Scaife had wanted me fired since the Hillary book came out and implied that he, Burr, had protected my job for the past year.

At the annual *Spectator* dinner in November, I was seated far from my usual place at one of the head tables. Most of the guests stared at me as if they had seen a ghost, and I suppose in a way they had. The next afternoon, my research assistant called me at home and told me that he had heard that I had been removed from the magazine's payroll. A day later, Bob telephoned to say that I had been dismissed not for anything I had or had not written, but for financial reasons. When I asked if anyone else had been affected by the cutbacks, Bob said no. I told him I understood and hung up. What I understood was that the magazine couldn't afford to pay me if I wasn't writing the kinds of pieces that kept up circulation, a reasonable enough position. In the four years since my Troopergate article appeared, circulation had fallen from a high of more than three hundred thousand to less than half that, and a defense of Orrin Hatch's social conscience wasn't going to put the magazine in the black. Though I thought that Bob had handled my firing in a graceless fashion, the firing itself came as no great shock or disappointment. Bob was right to fire me. And I needed that kick in the ass to get off the Scaife teat.

That evening, Wlady called me at home. He had stood by me through thick and thin—even coming close to fisticuffs with a wild-eyed David Horowitz at the Dark Ages weekend as he tried to defend *Seduction* against charges of treason—and he didn't want to let go. He stumbled, and fumbled, and mumbled before telling me he would be happy to consider publishing me on a freelance basis. We were both a bit choked up. I thanked him for the warm offer, but told him not to expect any submissions. We never spoke again.

The days of six-figure salaries and seven-figure book contracts were gone once I split from the movement. When I could commit to an idea, no easy task in a period when I was in many ways a clean slate, I found other magazines in the journalistic mainstream willing to publish me, despite my checkered journalistic past. The experience was an eye-opening one. I'll never forget the panic that came over me when I received the first call from a fact checker at *New York* magazine, asking me to submit my notes for a story. In twelve years of right-wing journalism, my work had never been fact-checked.

Yet solving whatever professional difficulties that might have arisen from my firing did not make me feel any better. I could not overcome an uneasiness that had set in six months before, after I published "Confessions." As I waited for the *Esquire* article to hit the newsstands, I had a vague expectation that going public with my experiences would have a cathartic effect on me. My life would change. I would feel better. This was a nice thought, but of course it didn't work out that way because my conscience was standing in the way. I still didn't know what the trouble was, why I didn't feel like writing, or finding a new job, or putting together a new book proposal. Somehow, trading on my notoriety and switching journalistic gears didn't seem like the right course. I was stuck.

Things started to come into focus in the closing weeks of 1997, when I picked up a copy of a book Anita Hill had recently published about her experiences testifying against Clarence Thomas in the Senate, *Speaking Truth to Power.* I checked the index for my name, and sure enough there were half a dozen references to various allegations I had published against her in *The Real Anita Hill.* As I read the passages where Hill referenced my allegations, I was again struck hard by the realization that I no longer believed in my own book, and for the first time, I began to contemplate the personal consequences for Anita Hill of having been the subject of a well-publicized, best-selling book that attacked her, wrongly, as a liar. I made this woman's life a living hell. I flipped to the beginning of the book, intending to read it straight through, but I couldn't get past the opening pages describing her childhood in rural Oklahoma. Learning about Anita Hill, the human being behind the political target, was just too painful.

Around this time, I was booked to appear as a commentator on the debut of sports personality Keith Olbermann's new political talk show on MSNBC. My copanelists were Christopher Hitchens, a provocative left-wing writer for the *Nation*, and Naomi Wolf, a prominent young feminist and best-selling author. I had never met Wolf before, but I did have a little bit of history with Hitchens, who eyed me warily as I entered the greenroom, where guests wait before a show begins. When I first came to Washington in the mid-1980s, Hitchens, a British expatriate who considered himself a man of the left, was a frequent target of vitriol from right-wingers, particularly the neocons. Midge Decter's Committee for the Free World's newsletter took to deriding him as "Hitchy-poo." When Clinton came on the national scene, Hitchens became a principled critic, from a leftist perspective, of Clinton's New Democrat policies on welfare reform and crime. In later years, however, he drew far more notice—writing a best-selling anti-Clinton diatribe and winning a berth on the second-tier cable talk shows—as perhaps the lustiest booster, outside the right wing, of the salacious and unsubstantiated Paula Jones and Juanita Broaddrick stories. In his book *No One Left to Lie To: The Values of the Worst Family*, Hitchens set himself up as moral arbiter, seeking to show how "Clinton's private vileness meshes exactly with his brutal and opportunistic public style." As he began to make appearances at such right-wing gatherings as the Dark Ages Weekend, now run under the auspices of David Horowitz's Center for Popular Culture, a scornful Hitchens took to referring to Clinton as "a real serious crook, a rapist, a war criminal, a perjurer, a thief . . . not just sleazy or cheap or shifty, but a monster." In other words, as the Clinton era drew to a close, Hitchens and I had arrived at pretty much opposite places.

It hadn't always been so. Shortly after Troopergate was published back in 1994, Hitchens invited me to a celebratory dinner at a French café, La Fourchette, near his apartment on the edge of Kalorama. I barely knew Hitchens, but I accepted because I was fascinated with the way rabid Clinton-hating, even then, was successfully penetrating far beyond the right-wing precincts I normally traveled in. The obvious reasons for the phenomenon—ratings and book sales—didn't seem to be enough to explain the intensity of the feelings.

Prior to his bilious anti-Clinton appearances on television, Hitchens had been known primarily for a book, *The Missionary Position,* in which he sought to expose Mother Teresa as a fraud. He was a terrific hater, which if nothing else made him an amusing dinner mate, at least at the beginning of the evening. A misshapen, unkempt, and seemingly unshowered man of about forty, Hitchens was also a notorious drinker, and this night was no exception. Though I could slam them down too, never in my life had I seen such self-destructive imbibing. As the drinking continued at his condominium in a fancy doorman building nearby, where I met his attractive wife, Carol Blue, Hitchens's voyeurism about Clinton became marked by a rapaciousness that struck even me, the author of the trooper piece, as annoyingly unpleasant. Slowly but surely, Hitchens transmogrified into such a slobbery, abusive, miserable shambles of a man that for years thereafter I avoided him. Thus I never discovered what demons inside Hitchens accounted for his Clinton-hating, but I was convinced that whatever it was, it had nothing whatsoever to do with the Clintons, who were nothing more than a Rorschach test for him. (To top it off, Hitchens was a deadbeat. He stuck me with the La Fourchette check, which I charged to the Arkansas Project. Hitchens later wrote for the *Spectator* as the magazine's "saloon" correspondent.)

After the MSNBC show, which was done live from studios in New Jersey, Hitchens slithered off, but Wolf and I began to chat amiably and agreed to share a car back into Manhattan. Wolf, a stunning woman, was curious about me. She volunteered that she had "hated" my Anita Hill book—and I recalled her withering criticism of it for using "trumped-up evidence" in her book *Fire with Fire.* She also had read *Seduction,* which she said had impressed her with its scholarship and fair-mindedness. How on earth, Wolf asked me in her mellifluous voice, could I have taken the opposite approach in my first book? In the year since the publication of *Seduction,* no one had put that question to me, and I had done a good job of avoiding thinking about it. By now, our car had reached Wolf's hotel, and, not wanting to end the conversation, I suggested we have a drink in the hotel bar.

We ordered a couple of margaritas, and before they arrived, I began, in a halting voice, to spill out the truth to Wolf. I believed *The Real Anita Hill* was an accurate and truthful book when I wrote it, I told her. Yet in the years since, I continued with tears welling up in my eyes, I learned things from the Thomas camp that shook my confidence, not only in the book's validity, but also in my association with the conservative movement. The things I learned about Thomas and his supporters I had hidden from everyone, even my new set of friends, I said, but I couldn't wish them away. Nor could I forget my own disgraceful actions, which were causing me, I realized as I vocalized all this to another person, a virtual stranger, for the first time ever, incredible discomfort. Though I hadn't known she was a friend of Hill's, Wolf told me that if I ever wanted to communicate my feelings to Hill, she could see to it that a confidential letter would reach Hill's hands. I said nothing, but I left our conversation with a powerful sense of relief, if not emancipation or peace. I had made a huge deal of publishing my vaunted "confessions," but I could see that I hadn't yet confessed to anything.

As I had done for several years, within a few weeks I left Washington for Laguna Beach, to spend Christmas with Andrew. With the Naomi Wolf conversation ringing in my ears, I was reminded that it had been in Andrew's house two Christmases before that I received the information from Mark Paoletta about Clarence Thomas's habitual use of pornography. Every time I looked at the navy blue linen sofa where I took that call from Mark, I was sucked into a downward emotional spiral.

To Andrew, living a world away from Washington on the beach, the chaos and collapse in my life following *Seduction*, and the guilt and shame and depression that still afflicted me after "Confessions," were impossible to fathom. I couldn't explain myself to him, my best friend, and he couldn't console me. And I was too ashamed and too scared that I would never be able to expiate the wrongs I had committed to bare my soul to my new friends. I was alone, consumed by my tortured thoughts of hopelessness and worthlessness. My mind turned several times over the holidays to slipping away from it all. I saw myself get up from the navy blue sofa, walk into the garage that was attached to the back of the house, close the door, climb into Andrew's black Range Rover, rev the engine, and breathe in deeply. Maybe David Brock the road warrior of the right literally should be dead.

CHAPTER SIXTEEN

MONICA, SIDNEY, AND ME

At my last Saturday Evening Club dinner with the *American Spectator* crew, in October 1997, just days before my firing and three months before the world knew the name Monica Lewinsky, I caught a glimpse of the future. The featured guest was the dour Congressman Bob Barr, who had come to enlist our support for a resolution to open an impeachment inquiry against President Clinton. Four months before, in June 1997, Barr had sent a letter to the chairman of the House Judiciary Committee charging Clinton with unspecified "systematic abuse of office," and urging that impeachment proceedings begin. Conservative activist Floyd Brown of Citizens United and former Reagan attorney general and Federalist Society lawyer Edwin Meese, now an official of the Heritage Foundation, joined Barr at the press conference where he released the letter to the media. In the intervening months, the idea had gone nowhere.

During a dinner of poached salmon and crème brûlée, the assembled editors and writers chewed over the question of whether impeachment was a worthwhile political strategy. When one editor objected that the thin substantive grounds for impeachment in the Barr resolution came nowhere near the "high crimes and misdemeanors" standard for removing a president set forth in the Constitution, John Fund didn't miss a beat, responding that impeachment was a matter "not of law, but of political will" by Clinton's opponents. Listening to these influential Republican conservatives contemplate trampling the Constitution for partisan ends, to gain power they couldn't win in an election, almost physically repulsed me.

Though it attracted little attention outside of our circle, the idea of impeaching the president had been gaining momentum for almost a year before Clinton became enmeshed in the scandal over his sexual relationship with White House intern Monica Lewinsky. After Clinton was resoundingly reelected in 1996, the political right, true to form, refused to recognize the legitimacy of the election. And even as it became clear to all but the most deluded anti-Clinton partisans that the Starr investigation had found no prosecutable crime in Whitewater or any of the other constantly shifting accusations in the Clinton scandals, the right wing pressured the Republican Congress to remove Clinton from office. In the January 1997 newsletter of Citizens for Honest Government, the group that had produced the *Clinton Chronicles* video, former Republican congressman William Dannemeyer published a piece titled "Why Congress Must Impeach Bill Clinton." Dannemeyer wrote: "I for one believe that both Bill and Hillary Clinton know where, when, why and by whom Foster was killed, and it was no suicide . . ."

In October 1997, the *Wall Street Journal* editorial page published a long op-ed by Mark Helprin, a neoconservative polemicist and former speechwriter for failed presidential candidate Dole, headlined simply "Impeach." Labeling Clinton "the most corrupt, fraudulent, and dishonest president we have ever known," Helprin asserted, with no evidence, that Clinton had "purloined FBI files, used the IRS to intimidate opponents, plotted to cage government business, met with drug dealers, arms traders, and mobsters, raised illegal campaign money, sold influence and shook down the Chinese." Helprin concluded: "The task is to address the question of President William J. Clinton's fitness for office in light of the many crimes, petty and otherwise, that surround, imbue and color his tenure. The president must be made subject to the law." A week later, *Journal* columnist Paul Gigot spun out a theory for why Clinton's reelection had been fraudulent. Gigot argued that Clinton had stolen the 1996 election by taking advantage of a loophole in the campaign finance laws that allowed the Democratic National Committee to pay for ads that benefited his reelection (the Republicans also had done this). "In this age of media politics, breaking campaign laws to run tens of millions of dollars in TV spots is the moral and practical equivalent of stuffing ballot boxes . . . We know the election was lost even before Mr. Dole had entered the first Republican primary," Gigot wrote. Simultaneously, the impeachment movement sprang off the rarefied pages of the *Journal* and into the streets of Washington, where Pat Matrisciana, who had produced the anti-Clinton videos, Randall Terry of Operation Rescue, and radio talk show host and future GOP presidential candidate Alan Keyes appeared at a "Take Back America" demonstration near the steps of the U.S. Capitol that turned into a pro-impeachment rally.

Also in October 1997, Regnery Publishing brought out a book by Bob Tyrrell, *The Impeachment of William Jefferson Clinton*. According to the dust jacket, the book was a "masterful work of 'future history' that propels you into the center of the most heated political debate of the century. It shows how Clinton could be impeached in an astonishingly realistic scenario that will leave you wondering not if it will ever happen but when." Tyrrell, who cowrote the book with Anonymous, whose identity was widely thought within the *Spectator* offices to be Ted Olson, envisioned impeachment hearings in 1998, presided over by Representative Henry Hyde of Illinois, prompted by a report to Congress on Whitewater by Ken Starr. Though the book was billed as a "work of imagination," Tyrrell seemed serious in arguing that if the Republican Congress convened impeachment hearings, the public "will come to see impeachment move from the realm of the plausible, to that of the reasonable, and on to the necessary." Tyrrell's book came with a foreword by Bob Barr, who wrote, "This powerfully persuasive volume should be required reading for every citizen of this country who cares about the integrity of our political process." Though Tyrrell's book was fictionalized, the Saturday Evening Club proceedings showed that he and Barr in fact were conspiring to make impeachment a political reality. In a review of Tyrrell's fictional book in the December 1997 issue of the *Spectator,* Robert Bork took things a step further, arguing that Tyrrell's "evidence" was "enough to make the Nixon administration seem merely, almost mildly, errant by comparison." The cover article depicted a towering, glowering Bork, clad in black judicial robes, pointing a crooked finger at a diminutive Bill Clinton. The former judge's sanctioning of the pre-Lewinsky impeachment movement revealed a frame of mind in the right wing that was willing to employ extra-constitutional means to achieve, essentially, a coup d'état in the country.

The next month, in January 1998, Clinton was deposed in the Paula Jones sexual harassment case, where he was grilled about his relationship with Lewinsky. Though the judge later agreed that the Lewinsky affair was irrelevant to the Jones case, Clinton's efforts to conceal it during his deposition led independent counsel Starr to widen his Whitewater investigation to include possible perjury and obstruction of justice by the president. Republicans spent the following year consumed by the goal of impeaching Clinton for his actions, while advocating no program for the country going into the midterm elections. While he was conducting his own illicit affair with a congressional aide, Newt Gingrich vowed to say the word "Monica" in every speech. The impeachment debate recalled nothing so much as a yearlong 1992 GOP Houston convention, a neoreligious crusade in which the conservative movement tied the impeachment explicitly to its social agenda. In a fund-raising letter from his Liberty Alliance, the Reverend Jerry Falwell declared that if Clinton was not removed from office, "the Clintons, the radical homosexuals, anti-family feminists, Godless atheists and the liberal media will have won." Referring to Starr, the *Wall Street Journal* editorial page asked, "Who better to bring Bill Clinton to justice than a hymn-singing son of a fundamentalist minister?"

Though they claimed that they wanted to remove Clinton for lying and covering up, not for committing adultery, the Republicans' rhetoric told a different story. Originally, only the extreme right had signed on to the stratagem of making Clinton's private life a political issue. Now, in a sign of how the party had succumbed to the Sunbelt moralism of its base, the entire Republican leadership exploited the cultural fault line in the country over sexual matters and the constellation of 1960s values. In the *Washington Post*, Robert Bork said that the Starr effort was useful to "kill off the lax moral spirit of the Sixties." "It would be an enormous emetic—culturally, politically, and morally—for us to have an impeachment," said Richard John Neuhaus, the editor of the magazine *First Things*, which already had sanctioned armed insurrection by the right wing against the American "regime." Representative Chris Cannon, a Republican member of the House Judiciary

Committee, explained: "The first thing [Clinton] did was create a debate about homosexuality, by talking about homosexuals in the military." Then Clinton "hired Jocelyn Elders as his surgeon general [who resigned from the administration after publicly discussing masturbation]. The whole point was to have an advocate for weird alternative lifestyles. The administration has had a policy goal of public discussion of weird sex."

Precisely because the scandal revolved around conflicting views of sexual mores, social traditionalists of a more intellectual bent, who had shown little interest in Whitewater or the other Clinton scandals, joined forces with the Clinton crazies. The usually careful, bow-tied George Will, who had once compared Gingrich to Joe McCarthy, now did a fair imitation of McCarthy himself, quoting the discredited Arkansas state troopers, "primarily as to an aesthetic judgment about the Clintons' vulgarity." (That Will had his own well-publicized marital problems did not seem to temper his moral condemnation.) Midge Decter, the mother of "Tiffany Midgeson," praised Ken Starr's "manliness." *National Review*, which had held itself above the fray of Clinton-bashing through most of the decade, suddenly celebrated Lucianne Goldberg—the literary agent who had engineered the scandal by persuading Lewinsky's friend Linda Tripp to secretly record their telephone conversations—and even hired her insipid son, Jonah, as a columnist. William Kristol, who had preached the need to engage Clinton on the battleground of ideas, warned me against printing Troopergate, and published my Dark Ages speech, also flew off the rails. His *Weekly Standard* referred to Clinton as "the man from grope," published false rumors about Clinton's "love child," and engaged in speculation as to whether the president might be sterile. (*Weekly Standard* editor Fred Barnes had once remarked that putting heinous caricatures of the Clintons on the cover was the only way the *Standard* could sell magazines.)

Several writers in the *Weekly Standard* laid out the ideological underpinnings of impeachment. John J. DiIulio Jr. suggested that impeachment was a way of eradicating "creeping paganism," which he defined as "the growing currency of seductive ethical doctrines that consult only our convenience and invite us to abandon or kill the unborn and the infirm elderly; the refusal of a majority of religious leaders to declare absolutely wrong any form of consensual sex between adults (adults only for now); misogynistic rap lyrics sung with feeling by tattooed and body-pierced kids from all zip-codes." In a *Commentary* symposium, Bill Kristol stated, "Just as the right to abortion is the one right that can never be abridged; just as homosexuality is the one practice that can never be criticized; so consensual sexual behavior is the one realm of human activity about which any sort of public moral judgment is illegitimate." Echoing Kristol, David Frum of the *Weekly Standard*, who described Clintonism as a "disease," wrote, "What's at stake in the Lewinsky scandal is not the right to privacy, but the central dogma of the baby boomers: the belief that sex, so long as it's consensual, ought never to be subject to moral scrutiny at all."

Conservative leaders framed the debate on impeachment as an apocalyptic cultural referendum, and then condemned the public for disagreeing with them. Polls showing that clear majorities approved of Clinton's performance as president and opposed impeachment were taken as evidence that the public itself was morally lacking. Republican Senator Bob Smith of New Hampshire said, "My wife likes to say they must be polling people coming out of Hooters on Saturday night." Writing in the *Weekly Standard*, David Gelertner concluded, "Americans regard presidential adultery as no big deal because they regard adultery as no big deal. In modern America, adultery is a moral misdemeanor at the outside; usually it's more like a parking ticket. . . . Fifty years ago, things were different. Americans on the whole found adultery revolting." Morality czar William Bennett wrote a book, *The Death of Outrage*, accusing the public of "making a deal with the devil. . . . It's a lesson in corruption." The greater challenge, Bennett said, was not removing Clinton, but eradicating "decadence" and "moral rot" in the country.

Bennett himself knew from decadence. While he was not a hypocrite in the manner that so many other conservatives I knew were—by all accounts, he is a faithful husband and devoted father—the hulking Bennett got very rich in the virtue industry while doing little but bloviating. After leaving government service in 1993, Bennett joined with Jack Kemp and Jeane Kirkpatrick to establish a group called Empower America, largely underwritten by Wall Street investment banker and *Spectator* patron Theodore Forstmann. The plan was to set up a shadow opposition government. In late

1993, however, Bennett published his tome *The Book of Virtues*, designed to instill character in young people by exposing them to classical literary texts, the book became an immediate best-seller, and Bennett became a one-man empire. As Empower America foundered from lack of direction, Bennett took well over $300,000 from its coffers from 1993 to 1995 while cashing in on the paid-lecture circuit and turning *The Book of Virtues* into a multi-million-dollar series. Bennett hired researchers to unearth the classic works that were republished in the Virtues series, and he employed a ghostwriter to craft prose that was mostly published under Bennett's name alone. As he emerged as perhaps the foremost Republican advocate of impeachment in 1998, he continued to hold a chair at the Heritage Foundation, endowed by Richard Mellon Scaife, for which Bennett appeared to do no work; and he sat on the board of one of Scaife's trusts, the Sarah M. Scaife Foundation, during the time that Scaife was underwriting the Arkansas Project. Bennett's only self-confessed vices were eating red meat, drinking martinis, and casino gambling, yet other of the virtues that Bennett preached, hard work and humility among them, clearly eluded him.

As in Robert Bork's Supreme Court nomination battle more than a decade before, the conservatives never for a moment considered whether *they* might have been out of touch with the mainstream American values that they always had claimed to represent. Rather, they saw themselves as beleaguered victims of a malevolent political force—tricky lawyers, liberal pundits, and an all-powerful Clinton spin machine. They alone were defenders of "the rule of law." Representative Henry Hyde, the chairman of the House Judiciary Committee, who had once defended the illicit actions of Oliver North on the grounds of a "higher moral good," bellowed: "Have you been to Auschwitz? Do you see what happens when the *rule of law* doesn't prevail?" They said it over and over again; they said it on CNN's *Larry King Live*, on CNBC's *Rivera Live*, on MSNBC's *Hardball*, on the network Sunday shows, they said it until they were blue in the face—an army of operatives, all quietly connected to the anti-Clinton campaign, posing as commentators: Ann Coulter, Barbara Olson, Robert Bork, Mark Levin, Mark Braden, William Bennett, John Fund, and on and on and on. The unpopularity of their cause seemed to affirm its divinity. Clinton was compared to the devil, the impeachment leaders to Jesus Christ. Henry Hyde said on ABC: "Look, if Jesus Christ had taken a poll, he would have never preached the Gospel."

Though the conservatives had reason to be disappointed when their culture war appeals fell flat, the public's views on the scandal were more nuanced than the conservatives let on. Polls showed that most Americans, while perhaps more skeptical of those seeking to push their personal moral judgments into the political realm than they were of Clinton, *did* morally disapprove of Clinton's affair with an intern in the White House. Majorities also believed that Clinton had given misleading and evasive testimony under oath in the Jones civil deposition, which he later admitted. Yet the public also concluded that this was a private offense, not a public one against the state, and therefore did not justify removal from office under the constitutional standard of "high crimes and misdemeanors." The danger to the Constitution, the public seemed to be saying in siding with Clinton, was posed by the Republican leadership's push for a party-line impeachment, on insufficient grounds, against the wishes of the vast majority of Americans.

When the Lewinsky scandal broke, I found myself out of sync with the political and journalistic establishment in Washington. My phone rang off the hook with interview requests, as reporters and TV producers, many of whom were now drawn into the morass of scandal just as I opted out, expected me to jump at the chance to proclaim that my disputed trooper story had been vindicated by the Lewinsky revelations. Clinton was a lying sex fiend after all! I remember one particular call along these lines from Lisa Myers of NBC News, who had dogged the Clintons for years from her beat on Capitol Hill, and later aired the Juanita Broaddrick rape allegation. I was doing no interviews, I told Myers. But wasn't I feeling vindicated? she wanted to know. Not exactly, I said. In the five years since Troopergate, I began to explain, no evidence had emerged to connect Clinton's personal life with his performance as president. Well, the husky-voiced Myers pressed on obtrusively, as if she hadn't heard a word I said, Clinton had been lying about so much for so long, wasn't it great that he finally got caught? I clicked off.

Conversations like these left me frustrated, for what exactly had Clinton been lying about for so long, other than adultery? Insofar as I was concerned, Clinton merely had been caught being a human being. Because of my history with the *Spectator*, I had a very different view of the Lewinsky scandal than did much of the press corps, which, if Myers was any indication, was pretty well convinced on day one of Clinton's criminal culpability. The Washington press knew little of the decade-long dirty war to bring about Clinton's ruination, but flashing back to 1993, when I had first heard Cliff Jackson, the handler of the Arkansas troopers, say that if the truth could be told about Clinton, he would be impeached, I knew that the right wing long had been plotting to nullify the results of the presidential election—and to use the media to do it. As Myers's comments underscored, by early 1998, the Arkansas Clinton-haters, the relentless teams of Republican investigators, and the Big Lie machine of conservative cable pundits and radio talk show hosts had succeeded in creating a widespread impression of corrupt wrongdoing by Clinton while never proving it. When a sex scandal finally hit after years of smears, the Republican establishment and a good deal of the regular media already were primed to pile on in a way that was out of proportion to what Clinton, disappointing and dishonest as he was in the Lewinsky matter, had actually done.

Observers rightly said that Clinton had given his enemies the rope to hang him. Yet I knew that the story wasn't so simple. I knew that the Jones case, if it had ever had any merit at all, had been hijacked by operatives working covertly to manipulate the courts for political ends. One of the secret legal strategists for Paula Jones had told me years earlier that the purpose of the sexual harassment suit was to probe Clinton's consensual sex life through the deposition process, and then to question Clinton under oath about it. In other words, the Jones case had become a vehicle to create a crime where one may not have otherwise existed. And the Jones team had done just what Jones lawyer George Conway had said it would do, seeking women with sexual ties to Bill Clinton, turning up Lewinsky, and forcing the story, as it had so many others, into the media bloodstream, this time by leaking it to Matt Drudge. (I was privy to Conway's e-mail traffic to Drudge through Laura Ingraham, who had hooked the two up, and was copied on some of them. Conway had been a Drudge tipster long before Lewinsky surfaced. In one e-mail from Conway to Drudge, Conway claimed that Clinton suffered Peyronie's disease, which causes curvature of the penis. Drudge posted the canard.)

To me, the two star players in the Lewinsky saga, Linda Tripp and Lucianne Goldberg, were familiar types. Tripp and Goldberg first came into contact when Tripp tried to secure Goldberg's representation for a tell-all book Tripp planned to write about the Clinton White House, where she had worked as a secretary. Like Gary Aldrich, with whom she maintained a friendship, Tripp was a hostile holdover from the Bush administration, an angry troublemaker who was offended by the Clintons' politics and personal style and wanted them out of office. Tripp would instigate the revenge of the Bushies. While she identified herself as a political conservative, Tripp's animosity toward the Clintonites seemed to be personal as well. What irritated her about the Clinton White House, she once said, was George Stephanopoulos's "dirty hair." Tripp seemed tailor-made for a media age in which such petty grievances could mushroom into a massive political scandal.

Tripp's book was tentatively titled *Behind Closed Doors: What I Saw Inside the Clinton White House,* and featured chapter titles like "Mrs. President" and "The President's Women." After moving from her job in the White House to one in the Pentagon, Tripp met and befriended one of those women, former intern Lewinsky; at Goldberg's suggestion, Tripp began secretly recording their telephone conversations, in which Lewinsky described her relationship with the president. According to Gary Aldrich's publisher, Alfred Regnery, who was approached by his friend Goldberg about the project, Tripp wanted half a million dollars for it. In an interview about Clinton scandal books, Goldberg observed, "It's much more fun to read about, oh, was Vince Foster murdered? Or, oh, is the First Lady going to be indicted?"

The deal died, but Goldberg stayed on the case, ultimately getting the news about Lewinsky to the Jones camp, setting in motion the perjury trap. Goldberg, who referred to herself as an "agent provocateur," was once a paid undercover operative for Richard Nixon, infiltrating the 1972 presidential campaign of George McGovern. Anthony Lukas, author of *Nightmare: The Underside of the Nixon Years*, quoted Goldberg as saying: "They were looking for really dirty stuff. Who was sleeping with whom, what the Secret Service men were doing with the stewardesses, who was smoking pot on the plane—that sort of thing." According to the *New Yorker*, Goldberg had harbored a hatred for Democrats since Nixon's forced resignation, but she was also in it for fun and profit. Herself the author of a novel called *Madame Cleo's Girls* about the lives of high-class prostitutes, Goldberg told the *New Yorker*, "I did it because it's fucking fascinating. I love dish. I live for dish."

For me, the Lewinsky scandal and the impeachment drive, with its hidden political agendas and financial motives and even talk of "killing" the president by those who fomented it, was the defining moment, the point of no return, that exposed the truth about everything I had been involved in for the past decade. Though the realization may have been long overdue, it was my Kronshtadt. One had only to hear Ann Coulter, author of *High Crimes and Misdemeanors*, entertain the question of whether "to impeach or assassinate"; or watch Bob Barr declare "a civil war"; or see the *Weekly Standard* explicitly tie the impeachment cause to the GOP's bigotry against gays and its drive to make abortion illegal; or read of the deranged claim of Lucianne Goldberg in the *New York Press* that Clinton had "finger-fucked Chelsea [his daughter]," to know that it was all making a kind of horrible sense. There were the blond pundits, several of whom were far from being above reproach themselves, taking moral offense at adultery. There was the closeted pro-impeachment Republican congressman, who had pursued me drunkenly through a black-tie Washington dinner offering a flower he had plucked from a bud vase, condemning Clinton for demeaning his office. There was Judge Silberman, my Troopergate adviser, striking down the executive privilege claims Clinton made in the Starr investigation rather than recusing himself. There was Ricky Silberman, hosting an Independent Women's Forum conference on the Lewinsky scandal called "The Law, the Spin, the Moral Consequences." The chutzpah! Not one Republican voice

was raised against any of these outrages. Only Clinton could be held responsible for his moral turpitude and for the lies he told to hide it; but the sentiments and intentions and hypocrisies of his Republican opponents struck me
as the far greater travesty.

As for the Starr investigation, I knew Ken Starr only peripherally through
conservative circles. When I had seen him at the Olsons' 1996 wedding in
McLean, a few months before my Hillary Clinton book was due in the bookstores, Starr, apparently under the widespread misimpression that my book
would be damaging to the First Lady, took me aside and furtively remarked
that we ought to be careful not to have our photo taken together. More
recently I had seen him at a book party celebrating the publication of
America in Black and White, by neoconservative historians Abigail and
Stephan Thernstrom, who were close friends of the Silbermans. In the *New
York Times*, Nicholas Lemann wrote that the Thernstrom book was "financed
by congeries of conservative foundations . . . and aims to bring down affirmative action and most other policies whose stated goal is to give special
help to African-Americans." For most of the evening, Starr stood in a corner,
deeply engrossed in conversation with one of his closeted gay aides, whom
I knew socially. When I walked in, the aide signaled to me through a facial
expression that he did not wish me, his openly gay friend, to acknowledge
him in Starr's presence. I knew that two of Starr's deputies hailed from the
same kick-ass Third Generation that I did, and I knew that Starr's chief
Little Rock deputy, Hick Ewing, was as much a Clinton-hater as I had ever
known. I watched as Starr continued to do paid legal work for tobacco companies while investigating Clinton. I saw him consider resigning to take a
post at a law school funded by Richard Mellon Scaife. I was surprised—and
voiced public criticism—when Starr turned his investigation to presidential
sex long before Lewinsky came along, interviewing none other than the
Arkansas troopers and even setting up a Trooper Project. "I was left with the
impression that they wanted to show he was a womanizer. . . . All they
wanted to talk about was women," said one trooper of the Starr agents. Still,
up to the time that Starr reached far afield from his original mission by
aggressively moving to take over the Jones case—a case that was so weak on
the factual merits that it would soon be dismissed on summary judgment

by the presiding judge—I tried to reserve judgment. Now, it seemed plain, Starr had decided to bring to bear the full prosecutorial force of the government to what had been an utterly failed crusade to humiliate and destroy the president and overturn an election. The Republican leadership's agenda and Starr's were joined.

With all of my experiences in more than a dozen years in Washington coming to a head in the looming cultural and political war over the Lewinsky scandal, and with network news commentators predicting Clinton's imminent resignation or impeachment, I found myself unable to retire from the swirl of events. I decided to disclose what I knew about the anti-Clinton plot while it was politically relevant. What I had seen, and what I had participated in, was wrong; I wanted to do what I could to redeem myself, inform the public, and hopefully move events onto a more just course.

In opposing Clinton's impeachment, I was not, as it might seem, reflexively switching sides from right to left. In one respect, I was recovering the classically liberal political values that, in reaction to the PC left, I had identified as "conservative" fifteen years ago in Berkeley—respect for the Constitution, skepticism about government power, defense of privacy and individual liberty, pluralist discourse, civility, and restraint. In the real world of Washington politics that I saw up close in the following decade, the conservative movement stood more often than not for precisely the opposite of all of these salutary values. And I quickly surrendered most of them myself on the way up the right-wing ladder.

To be sure, members of the Christian Right and the neocon culture warriors had every reason to voice their own view of politics, held by many with deep conviction and even patriotic fervor, but those views were not mine, and I could no longer front for them. In terms of social tolerance, civil liberties, fairness, choice, and civil rights—in my heart, I always was a social liberal, even as I betrayed myself by defending Bork, Thomas, and Gingrich and set off the first flare in the Clinton wars. Only as I gave up my cherished place in the movement, which allowed me to confront the false right-wing ideology of exclusion, intolerance, prejudice, and hate that I had advanced so blindly, did I find my conscience and principles underneath. Now I was free to follow them.

The years of shallow reaction, ersatz beliefs, empty careerism, misdirected desires for validation, and drift were receding behind me. I had no partisan or professional interest in the fate of Bill Clinton, about whom I still felt a bit queasy, as did most of the country. I had no allegiance to a political platform, I was a member of no party or movement, and I was on no one's team. I was following only the facts of my personal experience, and my interior convictions. While it was only human to have gotten some satisfaction out of what amounted to ratting out the conservatives, the truth is that a year and a half after publishing *Seduction*, I was spending most of my time in New York trying to live in the present and rebuild my life. I felt that if someday I could find a way of reckoning with my past misdeeds, I had a chance of living along a better path. I was so relieved to feel morally and psychologically unburdened by membership in the movement that by this point I harbored no personal ill will, nor held any grudge, against the conservatives. I didn't hate the right or anyone in it. Nor had I ever been a genuine Clinton-hater, whether in the ideological, cultural, or personal sense. More than anything else, maybe that's why at the end of the day I could not sit back and watch the Republican right try to win political power by abusing prosecutorial power, distorting the meaning of the Constitution, and inciting a moral panic in the country. As I saw it, the impeachment had little to do with Clinton or his presidency per se. To me, the issue was that if the Republican right was successful in abusing our political and legal system, they could misuse their power to destroy any American for any reason.

Through yet another unlikely twist of fate, Sidney Blumenthal became my interlocutor. I knew Blumenthal only through his writings, and by reputation, as a journalist and author with a committed liberal viewpoint. When I came to Washington in the mid-1980s, Blumenthal worked at the *New Republic*, and then at the *Washington Post*, where he chronicled the rise of the conservative movement of the Reagan years with a critical edge. In the early 1990s, Blumenthal became an avid journalistic booster of the Clintons. When Clinton won office, Blumenthal joined the Washington staff of the *New Yorker*, where he penned several admiring, some said fawning, pieces about the new administration. As the Starr Whitewater inquiry heated up, and the mainstream press began to devote serious attention to it, Blumenthal fell out of favor at the *New Yorker* when he refused to give the scandal any credence and was replaced by Clinton-basher Michael Kelly. Sidney viewed Whitewater as a phony political scandal ginned up by the right wing—a conclusion, at least with respect to Hillary Clinton, that I, too, had reached on my own while researching *Seduction*. In mid-1997, Sidney joined the Clinton White House staff. The joke around town was that he was owed back pay. (Yet perhaps the *New Yorker* owed Sidney back pay: Former *New Yorker* editor Tina Brown later told me that Sidney had been right, and Kelly wrong, about the Whitewater scandal.)

A tall, meticulous man in his early fifties in wire-rimmed glasses, Sidney managed to make the typical Washington uniform of navy blue suit, white shirt, and red tie look slightly stylish through good tailoring. He spoke omnisciently, in a tinny voice. He also prided himself on being a tough guy who hailed from the rough-and-tumble streets of Chicago politics. As I flew home to D.C. from my dinner date with Matt Drudge in Los Angeles in August 1997, Drudge was posting on his site an exclusive item, citing unnamed Republican sources, falsely claiming that newly appointed White House aide Sidney Blumenthal had a history of spousal abuse. Though Blumenthal's telephone number was listed in directory information, the incendiary item contained no comment from Blumenthal, or from the White House. Apparently, Drudge had not bothered to test his information. The next day, Blumenthal denied the charge, hired a libel lawyer, and Drudge issued a retraction. Unsatisfied, Blumenthal and his wife, Jacqueline, filed suit.

With his publication of this attack on Blumenthal, I now considered Drudge, along with Gary Aldrich, to be an emblem of the most reprehensible aspects of anti-Clintonism. When I was called for comment on the Blumenthal controversy by *Washington Post* media writer Howard Kurtz, I criticized Drudge and told an anecdote about my first encounter with him. Several months back, Drudge had posted a wrong, though harmless, item about me, saying I planned to leave Washington for New York permanently. Drudge had made no effort to contact me to verify the story before posting it. When I met Drudge at my home, I offered him my telephone number so that in the future he could check facts about me before publication. "Why would I want to do that?" Drudge giggled.

Blumenthal, no doubt, saw my criticism of Drudge in the *Post*. Meanwhile, as a well-connected media insider, he had learned of the dinner Laura and I had hosted for Drudge in June. Looking for information that might support his lawsuit, Blumenthal called me the day the Kurtz piece appeared and suggested that we meet for lunch. I rarely eat lunch, so we agreed to meet for dinner at a popular nouveau American restaurant called Tahoga, near my home in Georgetown. We took a table in the front room, and the conversation reminded me of a Socratic dialogue as we carefully assessed each other. We were certainly an odd couple—Sidney, once the foremost journalistic advocate of the Clintons, and me, once one of their foremost detractors. We shared some common ground, however, for we had both been blackballed, in our separate worlds, when we concluded that there was no criminal wrongdoing in the Whitewater or other scandals. And, from opposite ends, we were both interested in the subject of the Clinton scandals and the Republican right, though Sidney, who had written a book on the conservative movement in the mid-1980s called *The Rise of the Counter-Establishment*, had a jaundiced view of the right wing that I didn't always share. Once, in a later discussion about my personal odyssey, Sidney recommended that I speak to a historian of Nazi Germany who had written an account of how doctors in the Nazi regime rationalized their actions. Gee, I thought, it hadn't been quite *that* bad.

The Blumenthals were clearly aggrieved parties, so I was happy to share with Sidney anything I knew about Drudge and his modus operandi that might be pertinent to the libel case. Sidney seemed to think that the wife-beating rumor might have been passed on to Drudge at my dinner party; I doubted this was the case, but I gave him the guest list. Though one always must be careful in quoting Drudge, because one never knows whether or not he's telling the truth, I told Sidney that shortly after the Blumenthal item appeared, Drudge had told me that Richard Carlson, a prominent Republican and ambassador during the first Bush administration, was one of his sources. When Drudge revealed this, I recalled a conversation I had once had with Carlson, who was a social acquaintance of mine and a sometime *Spectator* writer. Carlson had fed me gossipy tips about Clinton's supposed womanizing and made the trifling assertion that Diane Blair, a friend of Hillary's who served on a board with Carlson, was a loose woman because she showed up to board meetings braless. Some months later, at the Huffington Christmas lunch, Drudge suggested that John Fund of the *Wall Street Journal* was another source of the false story. Soon after the Blumenthal item appeared, Tucker Carlson, Richard Carlson's son, canceled a drinks date with me because he said he was on deadline writing a piece for the *Weekly Standard* identifying Fund as Drudge's source. The piece never ran. I also told Sidney what I knew of the right-wingers who had rallied to Drudge's defense in the libel case, among them *Spectator* patron Scaife, who funded the Center for Popular Culture in Los Angeles, headed by David Horowitz. The Matt Drudge Information Center and Defense Fund was run through the Center for Popular Culture's anti–affirmative action Individual Rights Foundation, and Horowitz served as a trustee of the Drudge fund. (In 2001, Blumenthal, who was spending his savings to fight Drudge, who was subsidized by the right, dropped the suit.)

Sidney and I continued to talk periodically throughout the fall and winter of 1997, always by telephone, since I was often in New York. Having been singed in my relations with the conservatives, at the beginning of our relationship I had no expectation of friendship or loyalty from Sidney. On the contrary, I regarded him with a fair amount of suspicion, and even trepidation. I was quite conscious of what I saw as his possible agenda with me, instrumentalizing a high-profile defector from the conservative camp. Though I came to see that Sidney's agenda and values were nothing like those of Judge Silberman, I thought Sidney, with his surpassing intellect and his fervent devotion to the Clintons, had the capacity to end up being a younger left-wing version of the judge. I was acutely aware that another Svengali was the last thing I needed in my life.

Nonetheless, though I had not provided Sidney with exclusive information about Drudge—in the coming weeks I would give out the same information, on the record, to several reporters who were covering the Blumenthal-Drudge lawsuit—Sidney came to regard me as his informant

in the right wing. And I regarded him as my informant in the inner sanc-
tum of the Clinton White House. Because Sidney was a confidant of
both Clintons, he offered me the kind of perspective that no journalist,
especially one like me who had observed and written about the Clintons
for years from the outside, could resist. Our conversations continued as
Sidney was dragooned into the impeachment inquiry himself, becoming
one of only three witnesses called to give deposition testimony in the
Senate trial. Though it was never clear to me who was the reporter and
who was the source, we each learned quite a bit by comparing notes from
our different, though in some ways overlapping, experiences. Sidney's
voice mail messages sometimes simply said, "I have information." The
reporter in me was intrigued by it all.

During the week in January 1998 that the Lewinsky story broke on the
Drudge Report and then in the *Washington Post*, I received a call from Sidney,
who often came on the line and said only, "Hey, anything?" By this he meant
had I heard anything in the Washington gossip mills worth repeating. As I
was now out of the political loop, I usually disappointed him. On this day,
I had heard nothing new, but I did have a lot on my mind. In this conversation and others that were to follow, I outlined what I knew about the plot
by the Jones lawyers to set a perjury trap for Clinton. There was much more
to the saga than the *Post* headlines suggested. As I spilled my guts, one of us,
I believe it was Sidney, used the word "conspiracy" to describe the set of facts
I laid out.

I wanted nothing in return from Sidney. I never told another soul about
the contents of our conversations. As when I spontaneously blew the whis-
tle on Gary Aldrich in my conversation with Michael Isikoff, and again when
I blurted out the truth about *The Real Anita Hill* to Naomi Wolf, this
unpremeditated purging was its own reward.

In the coming days, I decided to tell Sidney everything I knew that could
help the Clinton White House defend itself against the effort to drive the
president from office. I told Sidney all about billionaire Richard Mellon
Scaife, who had funneled more than $2 million through the *Spectator* to dig
up and publicize damaging information on the Clintons, which at this point
was a closely guarded secret within the magazine. The Arkansas Project's

directors, David Henderson and Stephen Boynton, had a close association with, and a possible financial pipeline to, David Hale, the star witness against the president in the Whitewater inquiry. When questions were raised about the project internally, *Spectator* board member Ted Olson, Ken Starr's best friend and David Hale's lawyer, acted swiftly to fire Ron Burr and shut down the independent audit Burr had sought. Troopergate, I revealed, had been instigated behind the scenes by Peter Smith, a major financier of Speaker Gingrich's GOPAC. Smith also turned out to be the one who first put Lucianne Goldberg in touch with the Jones team; she let them know about Linda Tripp's tapes. I also knew that Starr had been approached by the Independent Women's Forum to draft a brief in the Jones case; Starr failed to disclose his subsequent secret contacts with the Jones lawyers when he sought jurisdiction over the Jones case from the Justice Department.

Perhaps most significantly, I told Sidney that one of Peter Smith's advisers on the trooper project was former Bush administration lawyer Richard Porter, who worked in the Chicago office of Ken Starr's law firm. At Smith's suggestion, Porter, who later was forced to identify himself as the "switch-board operator" of the entire Lewinsky scandal, had worked in the shadows to recruit key members of the covert Jones legal team and then tipped off those lawyers to Lewinsky. I revealed the identities of the so-called elves, lawyers George Conway, Jerome Marcus, and Ann Coulter, whose existence was unknown outside the Jones camp. I identified Paul Rosenzweig, a lawyer I knew who worked on Starr's staff, as a likely point of contact, and possible collusion, between the Jones elves and Starr. According to a later account in the *New York Times*, Marcus and Conway *did* tell Rosenzweig about Lewinsky at a secret dinner in Philadelphia, a fact that Starr would fail to disclose in his later report to Congress on Lewinsky. I knew that James Moody, the lawyer for Linda Tripp, was a close friend of Conway and Coulter. Coulter had told me that the Tripp tapes had been played at her Washington apartment over the holidays, before Clinton's Jones deposition. I also knew that Moody had done work for the Scaife-funded Landmark Legal Foundation, which played a role in orchestrating the Jones litigation. In addition, I noted, most of the lawyers involved on the anti-Clinton side of the Lewinsky scandal, including Ken Starr, were members of the Scaife-funded Federalist Society, the vast legal network of the Reagan and Bush administrations.

Among other things, Sidney's job was developing communications strategies at the White House, so he seemed well positioned to make sure that the information got where it needed to go. Exactly what he did with the download, I didn't ask, but I assumed he passed it on to Clinton's lawyers, to other political advisers in the White House, to the Democratic National Committee (which, I discovered months later, produced talking points that contained some of the material I had given to Blumenthal), and to the press. The information helped the White House pull back the curtain and reveal the machinery behind the Lewinsky scandal. It enabled the Clinton defense team to identify the opposing players and connect the political and financial dots among them more swiftly than they otherwise would have. And in an odd— one might even say surreal—historical footnote, given Sidney's proximity to the First Lady, it may have been the germ of the first line of defense: that Clinton was targeted, as Hillary Clinton soon charged on the *Today* show, by a "vast right-wing conspiracy." (Years later, Sidney told me that immediately after our phone conversation on the day the Lewinsky story broke, he "went straight to Hillary.")

The press scoffed at Hillary's claim, as did even some of Sidney's White House colleagues, who took to calling him "G. K.," for "grassy knoll," poking fun at his conspiracy theorizing. I might have quibbled with the word "vast," but otherwise I knew it was no exaggeration. There was, as Hillary said, "another story waiting to be written" about the subterranean origins of the scandal. The press was not very interested in pursuing it, at least not in the opening months of the unfolding scandal. For one thing, the story of the right-wing conspiracy was far less sensational than the story of the president and the intern. Another obstacle, it seemed to me, was that the press was too literal-minded about the notion of a political conspiracy: Did the existence of a conspiracy mean that any and every lapse Clinton made in office was attributable to his enemies? Then there was the unfortunate fact that Hillary and Sidney, both of whom were apparently lied to by Clinton about his relationship with Lewinsky, were using the notion of "conspiracy" to defend their belief that the right wing had invented the Lewinsky scandal, as it had so many others. Since I was by no means a Clinton loyalist, despite his public denial, I believed from the moment I heard the story that Clinton likely had dallied with Lewinsky, besmirching himself and his office. Yet I also knew that there *had* been a conspiracy, in this sense: Clinton's private transgression with Lewinsky became a matter of public knowledge, and placed Clinton in political and legal jeopardy, only through the dedicated machinations of his foes, who sought to use it for seditious purposes.

Having filled in Sidney, I also spoke openly and on the record to any reporter who called. Foremost among them was Joe Conason, a friend of Blumenthal's and a liberal columnist for the *New York Observer*, who was writing a book, with coauthor Gene Lyons of the *Arkansas Democrat-Gazette*, titled *The Hunting of the President: The Ten-Year Campaign to Destroy Bill and Hillary Clinton*. Joe had called me the prior October, in 1997, before the Lewinsky scandal came to light, seeking background on Troopergate and the *Spectator*'s editorial operations for his book. I remembered that Joe had written a column in 1996, during the controversy between Aldrich and me, in which Joe facetiously characterized it as a lovers' quarrel between two right-wing homosexuals. For this reason, I hesitated to meet with Joe, but considering my own journalistic excesses, I decided not to hold the column against him. As I later explained to Joe, I decided to help him with his book because of a series of columns he had written in 1995 about Hillary Clinton's role in Whitewater. While I was researching the subject for *Seduction*, Joe's interpretation of the material seemed more accurate than any I had read.

We met at Bistro Lepic, a country French restaurant on the edge of Georgetown. Joe, who looked the part of a former writer for the *Village Voice* in his mid-forties, with thick salt-and-pepper hair and a leather bomber jacket, had invited his younger girlfriend, Elizabeth Wagley, a Laura Linney type, to stop by for dessert. Apparently Elizabeth, who worked in New York for an international humanitarian relief agency, had never known any conservative ideologues, and she was quite curious to quiz me about my alien philosophy. I sheepishly explained that if she had wanted to chat with someone who would defend the conservative movement, she was about two years too late. As we became friends in the coming months, Joe and Elizabeth taught me more than I taught them. Through my relationship with the pair, I was able to see for the first time that there were kind and generous human beings on "the other team."

When the Lewinsky story surfaced, the material I supplied Joe for his book became more than a matter of historical interest. Taking my tips, he developed several other sources and published a series of columns blowing the lid off the *Spectator*'s Arkansas Project. He was also the first reporter to reveal the secret role of the right-wing elves in politicizing the Jones case. I talked with several reporters from Salon.com, an Internet publication, who were pursuing similar story lines. Through their own sources, Salon documented how the *Spectator* had spent hundreds of thousands of dollars in Scaife funds on shady private investigators and turned up allegations that Arkansas Project funds did go to the care and feeding of Starr Whitewater witness David Hale, just as I had surmised. The Salon stories prompted a Justice Department investigation of the Arkansas Project that saw Scaife himself brought before a grand jury to testify. At issue in the investigation was the question of whether, in its extensive dealings with David Hale, the Arkansas Project had tampered with a federal witness. The investigation concluded that the Arkansas Project figures, while they were collaborating with Hale, had not tried to get Hale to testify falsely against Clinton. The project did everything it could to support Hale and his claims, which was not found to be illegal. Unfortunately, the results of the Justice investigation were announced in a press release from Starr's office and the report itself has never been fully released. However, it is known that two of Starr's agents were referred to Justice for disciplinary action in light of what the Arkansas Project probe uncovered. Documents later released by the Senate in the controversy over Ted Olson's nomination as solicitor general showed that Starr deputy Hick Ewing met with a paid Arkansas Project private detective named Tom Golden to discuss an "indictment of Hillary Clinton."

Soon enough, several other independent news organizations verified and filled out the spectacular scope of the anti-Clinton campaign. The Associated Press reported extensively on the Arkansas Project, as did the *Washington*

Post. The *New York Times* wrote major articles on the role of the Federalist Society elves in the Paula Jones case.* Later, two books published about the impeachment—*Uncovering Clinton,* by Michael Isikoff, and *A Vast Conspiracy,* by Jeffrey Toobin—documented in more detail the connections and activities I had laid out for Sidney when the scandal first broke. In describing the events behind the impeachment, both reporters saw fit to use the word "conspiracy."

My final step involved accounting for my own role in the anti-Clinton campaign. I spoke with no one but my editor Mark Warren at *Esquire* as I began drafting an open letter to Clinton apologizing for writing the unreliable Troopergate story as part of a plan to wreck his presidency. This was the second installment of my confessions, only this time, with a sense of contrition, I would begin to confess my own mistakes. The letter was conceived in a conversation with Mark, from my Greenwich Village apartment, on the day that Clinton, in an unprecedented media circus, was hauled in front of the Jones lawyers to testify under oath—before anyone knew the name Monica Lewinsky, before Clinton got into a political and legal jam. I told Mark, whom I jokingly accused of acting as a therapist or priest as well as an editor, that I thought the Supreme Court had been wrong to allow a president to be sued in a civil case while he was in office. Through my conversations with the elves, I had learned how the legal process was being abused by these partisan foes. And I had been reminded of my own cheerless role in it all for the prior two weeks, as the Jones lawyers sought to subpoena my notes from the trooper article. They were looking for names of women Clinton had supposedly had sex with, potential leads for their fishing expedition. Apparently thinking that I shared their agenda, before the subpoena was issued, the lawyers first asked me to hand over the notes voluntarily. I essentially told them to go to hell. A

---

*The stories were coauthored by Jill Abramson, who had left the *Journal* for the *Times.* As she researched the story, we met for coffee. Though I was as forthcoming as I could be about the Arkansas Project and the Jones case, I was relieved that the subject of Anita Hill was not broached. I would not then have been ready to deliver to Jill the apology I owed her.

few nights later, I was served with a subpoena at my home in Washington, which I was able to resist on First Amendment grounds. Whatever role I had played in bringing the Jones case to light, I was not proud of it.

Predictably, when it was published in the April 1998 issue of *Esquire*, the letter to Clinton prompted a vituperative reaction from my former colleagues on the right, who were understandably furious that I had given aid and comfort to the enemy in the midst of a political war. The attacks sounded familiar themes—I was in it only for fame and fortune—though how I was advancing my career by admitting I had been a political operative, more than a journalist, and that the biggest story of my career was no good, escaped me.

Shortly after the apology was published, my old boss from *Insight*, Tod Lindberg, now the editor of the *Washington Times* editorial page, invited me to lunch. I had done some editorial writing for Tod some years back, and we had kept in touch sporadically in the years since I left the *Times*. Tod was another of those exceptions in my world of Washington conservatives who could see beyond the partisan politics of the moment, and as I broke ranks, we maintained a warm, respectful relationship. Tod had asked me to meet him at Galileo, an expensive Italian restaurant in downtown Washington, to tell me that he had not participated in the trashing of my reputation, much of it done anonymously in the right-wing press, that followed the publication of my letter. For instance, Tod's best friend John Podhoretz, now an editor at the *New York Post*, had published a column apologizing to America for offering me my first job and labeling me a financially desperate "disgrace." "No one can figure out why you did it," Tod finally said, breaking an interminably pregnant silence on the subject. "I've been telling them that maybe you believe it."

Such conservative criticism was predictable by now, with the exception of one curve ball. When the letter hit newsstands, false rumors began to circulate through the right wing that I had apologized to Clinton because I was having an affair with Hillary Clinton's former press secretary, Neel Lattimore. I was stunned. Washington really had gone mad. The rumor was put in circulation by the *New York Post*'s Page Six gossip column under the suggestive headline "Just Friends?" The *Weekly Standard* stoked it further, reporting suggestively, "Brock denies, however, that his new acquaintance with Lattimore is in any way responsible for his newly solicitous attitude toward the Clintons." The rumor was soon spread all over the country by talk radio.

Coincidentally, at the end of a week of food fights on the cable news channels over my letter to Clinton, Washington lawyer Bob Bennett, who represented Clinton in the Paula Jones lawsuit, held a press conference to release depositions from the Arkansas state troopers to bolster Clinton's defense in the case, which had not yet been thrown out. Like his brother Bill, Bob Bennett was a big, blustery Brooklynite who cut a high-profile figure on the Washington stage as a pricey criminal defense lawyer for the political class. Unlike Bill, whose sense of things seemed to be crimped by his moral pomposity, Bob hadn't lost his humor as he became a power player. In one of those only-in-Washington moments, I had rubbed elbows with Bob Bennett at the White House Correspondents' Dinner, an annual ritual of the city's political elite, four years before, soon after Paula Jones had filed her lawsuit against the president. Trying to avoid a confrontation as we literally bumped into each other in a crowded hallway of the Washington Hilton, I stared down at Bennett's fat feet, stuffed into formal black pumps. "I'm going to *ruin* your career," I heard him growl. When I looked up, stunned by Bennett's ferocity, the president's lawyer put his arm around me, introduced me to his wife, and thanked me for generating the legal fees he said were putting his children through college.

The timing of Bennett's press conference was dumb luck on my part, or perhaps it was providence. I hadn't known that the troopers had even given testimony in the Jones case. As I watched Bennett, live on CNN, I finally understood what he had meant a few years back about ruining my career. Though Larry Patterson and Roger Perry for the most part stood by their stories, two of the other troopers I had relied on for verification of several allegations seriously undercut the credibility of the entire trooper article once they were put under oath. Danny Ferguson testified that he had no firsthand knowledge that Clinton had had extramarital affairs, and he swore that many of the stories told by Patterson and Perry were exaggerated or not true at all. Though I reported in Troopergate that Clinton had called Ferguson in an attempt to shut down the story, Ferguson testified that was wrong. Ferguson had called the president to let him know that the other troopers were talking to the press. Contrary to my reporting, Ferguson also testified that Clinton never offered him or another trooper a federal job. Trooper Ronnie Anderson conceded that he had corroborated Patterson's and Perry's interviews with me even though he had no firsthand knowledge of the information. Anderson swore, "From what I heard the other troopers say and from [what] I . . . read in the *American Spectator*, the stories that were provided were nothing more than old fish tales with little if any basis in fact." Bennett also produced a deposition from the troopers' former supervisor, Buddy Young, who testified that the men had used their positions on Clinton's security detail to pimp, not for Clinton, but for one another.

In releasing the depositions to the press, Bennett was good enough to note that I had apologized for the trooper piece earlier in the week. When Bennett was finished, Susan Carpenter Macmillan, the attractive, blond-maned conservative activist who served as a spokesperson for Paula Jones, appeared live on MSNBC to rebut him. Questioned about my apology, a defensive Carpenter Macmillan sought to discredit me by claiming, falsely, that Lattimore and I were lovers, living together in my Washington town house. In a fitting final act to a long-running drama, I now knew what it was like to be the object of a right-wing smear.

When my friend Neel, who happened to be watching MSNBC, called me with the news, I did a double take. Here was another conservative, using a homophobic appeal to her right-wing patrons and grassroots supporters, whom I knew to be privately friendly to gays, at least while they were on the team. A few years back, I had dinner with Carpenter Macmillan in a trendy West Hollywood restaurant. An archetypal denizen of Los Angeles, she arrived in a Mercedes convertible, swept in with a fur on her shoulders, and gave me a glamour wave as she approached the table. We had a jolly time. At the end of dinner, Carpenter Macmillan promised to fix me up with a gay fellow she knew in Washington who worked for, of all people, Paul Weyrich.

I had not known Neel Lattimore, a loquacious, chain-smoking North Carolinian in his late thirties, and a master of the bon mot, when he was serving as Hillary Clinton's press secretary and I was writing *Seduction*. A few months after the book came out and Neel was leaving the White House, we were introduced by a mutual friend, and the three of us went to a house party together in Dupont Circle. Neel and I hit it off. We quickly became the best of friends. Though the introduction ostensibly was made because of our professional connection to Hillary Clinton, our friendship, as it developed, had nothing to do with politics; we rarely spoke of the Clintons (more his idea than mine), nor did we take more than a passing interest in each other's work lives. The idea that Neel somehow induced me to write the letter to Clinton was nonsense. No one but Mark Warren had any idea I had written the letter until it hit the newsstands.

Yet my critics saw fit to drag Neel, who now worked for a major Washington consulting firm, into the mud. The campaign of hate had come full circle and was hurting my friend. I had told Arianna Huffington and Laura Ingraham, among others, that Neel and I were friends, and they may have drawn the wrong conclusion from it that he and I were romantically involved. Another possible peddler of the rumor was a freelance writer named Norah Vincent. For reasons that I still can't fathom, Vincent, who had been an editor at the Free Press during *Seduction*, took an intense personal dislike to me. On assignment for the *New York Press*, Vincent called me with a mixed-up tale about Lattimore and me. When I told her that what she had heard was false, she declined to publish it. The charge didn't especially bother me—I long ago had acknowledged my own homosexuality, and false charges were simply par for the course by now—except for its impact on Neel, an innocent bystander who had never had a reason to reveal his sexual orientation publicly. Hearing it discussed on television, he later told the *New Yorker*, was an "out of body experience. You want to breathe but you can't think about how to bring air back into your lungs again. . . . It's like watching a storm destroy your house when you're not in it." As I prepared for an appearance on NBC's Sunday show *Meet the Press*, I talked with Neel about whether and how to address the issue of our relationship. Neel agreed that if given the opportunity, I should simply tell the truth—we were friends, not lovers—rather than sidestep the controversy to protect him from further exposure.

Tim Russert, the show's moderator, had a reputation as the toughest inter-viewer in the Sunday morning talk show lineup. When I arrived at the NBC studios before 8 A.M. that Sunday, Russert popped his head into the green-room, which was littered with coffee and Danish and filled with the day's other guests, including Dan Quayle. Russert asked me to have a word with him in the hallway outside, where he told me that the Brock-Lattimore rumor had turned the town upside down. Displaying a sensitivity that surprised me, Russert said he would leave it up to me whether I wanted to address it on the air. I readily agreed to do so, and with that airing the controversy was laid to rest.

Yet as I walked onto the freezing cold *Meet the Press* set, which can feel like facing a firing squad even under the best of circumstances, I was sud-denly struck with fear over something I had done just before the Lewinsky scandal broke, before I ever had cause to talk to Sidney about the Jones case or apologize to Clinton for Troopergate. Shortly after speaking with Naomi Wolf in late 1997, when I arrived back in Washington after that terrible Christmas in Laguna Beach, I found myself at my desk in front of my com-puter; the first thing I found myself doing, with no forethought, was tapping out a letter to Anita Hill. I don't know exactly what I said—my nerves were so jangled I didn't keep a copy—but as I recall the letter, I told Hill, respect-fully and remorsefully, that I had second thoughts about what I had written about her in *The Real Anita Hill* and offered to meet with her to discuss it. I dropped the letter in the mail to Naomi Wolf. My intention then was to reach closure, a private reconciliation, with Hill.

Just as the letter to Clinton was going to press some ten weeks later, Anita Hill called me at home, responding to my letter. The call went to voice-mail. Before I could make contact with Hill in return, I was engulfed in the Clinton apology controversy. The consequences of apologizing simultaneously for my two best-known pieces of work were just too terrifying to fathom. I could not get up the nerve to return Hill's call.

Now I was worried: What if the indefatigable Russert somehow knew about the letter to Hill? Following a week of nationwide publicity over my apology to Clinton, what if Hill had decided to release the letter? Although by now I had deep reservations about my first book, I had not reread it in years, and I wasn't ready yet to be cross-examined about it, possibly even to retract and disown it, on national television. Russert, it turned out, knew nothing about the letter—as far as I know Hill has kept it private to this day—but he did quiz me about my prior writings on the Hill-Thomas case. I noted that in a television appearance promoting *Seduction* a few years back I had apologized to Hill for my use of invective in the *American Spectator* article (the "nutty/slutty" line), but I did not let on to harboring any doubts about *The Real Anita Hill*. That would take more time, more guts, and more heartache to sort out. I never did call Hill back.

As I returned home from *Meet the Press*, my spirit felt higher than it ever had before. Whatever effect, if any, my conversations with Sidney and the letter to Clinton may have had on the public's understanding of the impeachment, I knew I had done the right thing in coming clean. This, despite the fact that many in the Washington press corps—with their justifiable questions about my credibility, given my past writings—greeted the apology with skepticism and even derision. In a reference to the letter to Clinton, *New York Times* columnist Maureen Dowd, a reliable bellwether of Beltway buzz, had asked: "What is that green goo coming out of David Brock's mouth?" When I arrived at my door in Georgetown after *Meet the Press*, I found an open bottle of champagne on my doorstep, overflowing with a slimy green substance. I lifted the bottle delicately, took it inside, looked around the house to make sure that I was safe, and warily opened the soggy note that was attached. "Loyalty, alas, is a two-way proposition. For all I know the bottle is filled with green goo." The note was from Wlady. The bottle of champagne was one that I had given my boss at Christmas a year and a half ago. This spooky adolescent prank was a fitting epitaph to my career at the *Spectator.*

In the fall of 1998, as the Starr Report made its way to Capitol Hill, brimming with obscene sexual details of Clinton's private life but falling short of proving perjury or obstruction of justice, I attended for the first time the annual black-tie dinner of the Human Rights Campaign, a bipartisan lobby for gay and lesbian civil rights. As I listened to the program—a graceful poem by Maya Angelou, and a heartfelt speech by Vice President Al Gore—

I thought back to where I was exactly four years before on that very night, across town at the Washington Hilton, sharing the stage with right-wing luminaries as I touted the troopers' obscene descriptions of Clinton's private life at the Christian Coalition's annual Road to Victory conference. I was happy, finally, to be in the right place, both morally and emotionally, just another face in the crowd, at a table surrounded by friends who didn't want me to say or be anything but myself.

The Gingrich era in American politics seemed to end on November 3, 1998. In the off-year, midterm elections, which Republicans made a test of impeachment by spending heavily on ads on the Lewinsky scandal in the closing days of the race, Democrats picked up an unprecedented five House seats. The public rejected the Republican right's sanctimonious public moralizing, poisonous scandal politics, and empty rhetoric about "character." In the coming days, Gingrich, who symbolized how extreme the GOP leadership had become, would be forced to resign as Speaker. The sexual witch-hunt directed against the president boomeranged against its leaders. Several Republicans, including Gingrich's short-lived successor, Representative Bob Livingston, as well as Representatives Henry Hyde and Dan Burton, were forced to admit to adulterous affairs, and, in Burton's case, also to having fathered an out-of-wedlock child.* (Newt's illicit affair surfaced in the press several months later.) Though a lame-duck Gingrich Congress impeached Clinton on a party-line vote, the Republican-controlled Senate rejected the charges and acquitted him. In the recriminations that followed, New Right leader Paul Weyrich declared that the culture war had "probably been lost," and implored conservatives to withdraw from politics altogether, and "drop out of this culture." Bill Kristol concluded that "the founders were right to have a certain distrust of democracy." And the Reverend James Dobson, a leader of the Christian Right, declared, "Our people no longer recognize the nature of evil." The firewall around the president put the nails in the coffin of the Gingrich Revolution and kept the ayatollahs at bay.

---

*Salon further reported allegations of sexual harassment against Burton. "According to several sources, Burton has also maintained sexual relationships with women on his congressional and campaign payrolls," Salon reported.

On election night, my house in Georgetown was dark. I had no trouble with the neighbors as I had had four years before, boisterously celebrating the Republican takeover of Congress. In Washington, where careers are built on fierce partisan loyalties, I had none. I was content to spend the evening alone with a nice bottle of wine, watching the returns roll in. If I was alone inside the Beltway, voters across the country were registering the same sentiments toward the GOP from afar that I felt having participated in the events of the '90s myself. The divisive, hypocritical, and undemocratic GOP, at least under its leadership then, simply did not merit support. The conservative movement, in its pathological quest to expose and unseat Clinton, had succeeded only in exposing itself and unseating its own unworthy leadership. As McCarthyism had set back the anti-Communist cause, the radical conservatives had betrayed whatever of value could be found in conservative philosophy. No, I was not one of them, I was not a conservative. And I was free to tell the tale.

I let out my own quiet whoop.

EPILOGUE

In the fall of 2000, I registered to vote as an Independent. What was remarkable was that I registered to vote at all. As a student, I had voted for Jimmy Carter in 1980 and then for Ronald Reagan in 1984. Since coming to Washington in 1986, in the next dozen years that I worked so zealously as a movement conservative, I never once took the time to vote. I told myself that I didn't have the time to bother, that as a resident of the overwhelmingly Democratic District of Columbia, my vote would not count, or even that journalists should not vote to protect their impartiality—an absurdity in my case. The truth is that these were merely avoidance strategies. I didn't vote because the act of voting, the truest and purest expression of one's political values as a citizen, would have forced me to confront the political lie that I was living. While doing everything I could to advance the right-wing agenda, in the privacy of the voting booth, just me and my conscience, I don't think I ever could have pulled the lever for the party of all those Bobs—Bork, Tyrrell, Dornan, Bartley, Barr.

It was a short walk to the Georgetown elementary school that served as the polling place for my neighborhood. I fumbled with the unfamiliar punch card ballot, but the choice was easy. I voted for Al Gore because I came to realize in writing this book that what set the Democratic ticket apart from the Republican one was that the Republicans, in all of the manifestations I had seen, from Reagan to Bush to Gingrich to Bush again, pursued a politics of self-interest that too often aligned them against the public good. When my social conscience was stirred as I read Bobby Kennedy's speeches in high school, I had been on the right track after all.

As George Bush took office, I wondered if everything I had seen on the right in the '90s was just a prelude for what was about to happen. As Bush's government was assembled, with Clarence Thomas's wife Ginni handling the flow of résumés from the Heritage Foundation over to the White House personnel office, many of the key players made up a rogues' gallery from my past. As I scanned a column in the *Washington Post* each morning where the new Bush appointees' names were announced, it was glaringly apparent that this is what the Clinton wars had been about all along. The Federalist Society of right-wing lawyers who had been at the heart of the anti-Clinton conspiracy turned out to be a virtual Bush government in exile; the new administration's policies of tax cuts for the wealthy, slashing environmental protections, and rolling back civil rights bore the Society's stamp, as did many of Bush's nominees to the federal bench.

Ted Olson was named solicitor general of the United States and possibly was being groomed for the high court himself. Larry Thompson, the adviser and witness for Clarence Thomas during his nomination fight, was picked as deputy attorney general. Federalist founder Spencer Abraham became energy secretary. Lee Liberman was named his general counsel. Tim Flanigan, who helped direct me to the leak of Angela Wright's FBI file, was named deputy White House counsel, where he vetted judicial nominees. Brett Kavanaugh, from Ken Starr's office, and Christopher Bartolomucci, who had gone on the wild ride to David Watkins's house, worked for Flanigan. Barbara Comstock—"I am Hillary"—had become chief of research for the Republican National Committee. Impeachment culture warriors John DiIulio and David Frum served on the senior White House staff. David Horowitz emerged as an influential Bush consigliere. With his portrait of Lenin and his boa constrictor, Grover Norquist presided over conservative movement strategy sessions on the Bush tax plan and for the bitter battle over Christian rightist and Pat Robertson ally John Ashcroft's nomination as attorney general. Ashcroft, who had been among the shrillest voices for impeachment, came under fire for ties to a neo-Confederate magazine and for blocking Senate confirmation of a Clinton appointee who was openly gay. Ashcroft fit no one's notion of unity or inclusiveness. Norquist appeared at a bipartisan Republican unity breakfast on the day of Bush's inauguration, took the podium, and declared, "The lefties, the takers, the coercive utopians . . . They are not stupid, they are evil. EVIL."

Ashcroft was sworn in by Clarence Thomas, who paid back the conservative allies to whom he was beholden by providing a fifth vote in *Gore v. Bush*. Thomas, who gave the Francis Boyer Lecture at the American Enterprise Institute's conservative prom just after the inauguration in early 2001, denigrated the importance of civility and moderation in politics, bemoaned the "culture of death," a code phrase for abortion rights and euthanasia, and lustily observed that the country was in the midst of "not a civil war, but a culture war." In the GOP, the more things seemed to change, the more they remained the same.

During the Bush inaugural festivities, about four hundred conservatives gathered at a Washington hotel for "The Funeral: A Conservative Celebration of the Death of the Clinton Administration." The Reverend Jerry Falwell gave the invocation. The Bobs—Bork, Tyrrell, Barr—were in attendance. "I love this group," Bush's ill-fated labor secretary nominee Linda Chavez declared. The *American Spectator*'s Wlady Plesczynski summarized the proceedings in a column: "Two large convention-size screens flashed images from Clinton's greatest TV hits. Sometimes he appeared to be behind bars or testifying, but always there was an appropriate caption or warning, such as 'Here Lies (Over & Over) The Clinton Administration (1993–2001)' or 'This testimony may be explicit and inappropriate for some viewers.' . . . It included such unforgettable moments as . . . Clinton on his campaign plane in 1992 sliding his hand inside the thigh of the stewardess he'd sat next to. 'Man, I never saw that,' someone at the table behind me exclaimed."

The only face missing from the crowd was that of Richard Mellon Scaife, who, in a fit of pique, had cut off the financial pipeline to the right-wing monthly where the anti-Clinton conspiracy had begun. Unlike the other institutions of the conservative movement that seemed to move seamlessly into the Bush era, the *Spectator* had fallen on hard times, with circulation plunging and editorial budgets slashed. Scaife's move had forced Bob to sell the magazine at a fire sale price to right-wing economist George Gilder, who inexplicably made it into a politically irrelevant forum on high-technology policy. Ironically, old man Scaife had pulled the plug after reading a review of Christopher Ruddy's book on the death of Vincent Foster in the magazine, in which John Corry cast doubt on the theory that Foster had been murdered. In the end, the *Spectator* was destroyed by the same manic passions it had provoked.

As I broke ranks with the conservatives in 1997 and 1998, relations with my father somehow became even easier than during the thaw of the early '90s, when I was making a name for myself as a conservative writer. In the spring of 1998, Mom and Dad came to visit me in Washington for the first time ever, for the Cherry Blossom festival. I noticed that they had seemed to grow markedly closer as they reached their late sixties and had begun to travel through Europe together; or perhaps I was just appreciating for the first time something that had been there all along. Of course, Dad and I continued to joust, though playfully now. I had a good laugh when I learned that after I published my letter apologizing to Clinton, he had sent a letter to Ken Starr apologizing for the apology. And he had a good laugh when I wrote a few columns in 1999 for the *New York Observer* when my friend Joe Conason took a leave of absence to finish his book. "Just tell me you're not becoming a liberal," Dad said, in a manner that suggested it didn't really matter. I understood from his inflection, and from other chats that we had just begun to have about our lives on our drives to and from the Dallas airport, that whatever I was, I was okay by him. I didn't need a surrogate father or love and acceptance from a political movement after all. I guess we both had mellowed considerably as I matured and found my bearings and started thinking for myself. And maybe he somehow sensed that he was dying.

It was a Friday evening in mid-June 1999 that I got the call from my sister, Regina. I was at Andrew's loft apartment in New York City, where he had moved from California in 1998, planning a thirtieth birthday party for

Joe's girlfriend, Elizabeth. The doctors had told Mom that Dad had a couple of days left to live, and he had been given last rites. Just a few months before, he had been diagnosed with liver and pancreatic cancer.

I arrived in Dallas on Saturday morning and drove straight to the hospital, where I had visited Dad for several days the month before—and where, I will forever be thankful, we had had one last private conversation in which we made our peace with the past as best we could under the difficult circumstances. When I got to the hospital, Dad was still alive, taking morphine intravenously, eyes half-closed, unable to talk. The nurses said he could probably still hear. Mom was there, and Regina, and my mom's brother, and my dad's sister. I said good-bye about 8 P.M., grabbed some dinner, and checked into the Melrose Hotel in Dallas. I then went out and nursed a beer at J.R.'s, a gay bar near the hotel. I sat on a bar stool composing my father's eulogy in my head, realizing how little I really knew about him.

When I arrived back in my room shortly before midnight, I drew the heavy drapes across an enormous set of windows in my room, closing them tightly. I only mention this because for me, it was a highly unusual ritual. I always sleep with shades or drapes wide open, so that I can wake up naturally with the sunrise, rather than be jolted out of sleep by an alarm. I was asleep for maybe a couple of hours, when I became conscious of a bright, white beaming ray of light that seemed to have come through the drapes and hover at the foot of my bed. I calmly raised my head slightly off the pillows and felt a warm, reassuring, peaceful presence. I knew Dad had died. I fell easily back to sleep.

At 8 A.M., I was awakened by a ringing telephone. I had asked the front desk for an 8 A.M. wake-up call, but I knew it was my mother. Dad had died that morning, at 1:26 A.M.

At my father's wake, I learned that since I came out in 1994, he had an ongoing dialogue with his sister Marge, trying to come to terms with my homosexuality in a surprisingly positive and human way. I regretted that we had not shared those conversations together. I tried to make that regret into a gift. After a dozen years of estrangement, more or less, as I was absorbed in my career and channeled my emotional life into partisan politics, I made a commitment to myself to be a better son to my mother, a better brother to my sister, and a presence in the lives of her four fantastic young children. Mom was happy to have me around more, but she needed no more coaching from me at the ballot box. She volunteered that a few years back she had stopped voting for her Texas congressman, Dick Armey, after he referred to Congressman Barney Frank as "Barney Fag." She even seemed prepared to let go of her penchant for discretion and evading certain truths, and to take this book in stride. Shortly before it went to press, she cracked: "Just tell it like it is. Joan Crawford's daughter did it to her, and Nancy Reagan's did it to her."

As for me, I had turned thirty-nine, and I didn't have much of a game plan for the rest of my life beyond publishing this book. The impact of my father's death was such that I took the probing of my prior political commitments and ethical failings to a deeper level. I wondered whether the lessons I learned during my time in the right wing might be applied more broadly to the dangers of all political zealotry, whether of the right or the left. I despaired as to whether our politics might ever return to a point where civility and good faith might be assured on both sides. I now knew that the need for meaning and for a connection with something larger than myself could not be met simply through politics or journalism. I was able to forge a loving relationship with a fellow named James, who has helped me see that self-discovery is a daily process, and that whatever my future commitments may turn out to be, they must be grounded in compassion.

I was struck by this thought more than once as I worked on this book. Laura Ingraham lost her mother to cancer shortly before I lost my father. Though our old bond was gone, I had a long talk with Laura on the telephone in which I offered whatever support I could, in what I knew was an extremely trying moment. Then I bumped into Ricky Silberman in the Georgetown Safeway. Rather than look away as she typically did, this time Ricky turned to greet me and told me she was on her first outing since being treated for breast cancer. I told Ricky that I wished her well, but the moment was jarring for us both, and I wasn't sure she heard me. Perhaps I should have said more, all of the water under the bridge notwithstanding, for at the end of the day, people are people. Then came the terrible news that Barbara Olson had died in the September 2001 terrorist attack on the Pentagon, a tragedy beyond words.

I tried to navigate these human concerns as best I could in telling this story. But as I sought to hold accountable for their hypocrisies those who sought the destruction of others for partisan ends, I can't say unreservedly that I succeeded. For I have been around politicos convinced of the virtue of their own cause long enough now to know that the most likely result of whatever I wrote would be another round of rage and retribution by those who will undoubtedly think they have not been treated with equanimity. All I can say is that, having rid myself of any rage or desire for retribution, I am personally at peace that the inherent moral tensions in this work were resolved, *mutatis mutandis*, to achieve an admittedly imperfect proximity of justice.

And since I planned to stay in Washington for a while, I took Harry Truman's advice and adopted an amazing dog.